# ESSENTIALS OF CANADIAN LAW

# THE LAW OF SENTENCING

160201

## ALLAN MANSON

Faculty of Law
Queen's University

IRWIN LAW

A Quicklaw Company

THE LAW OF SENTENCING
© Allan Manson, 2001

Published in 2001 by
Irwin Law
Suite 930, Box 235
One First Canadian Place
Toronto, Ontario
M5X 1C8

ISBN: 1-55221-029-4


Canadian Cataloguing in Publication Data

Manson, Allan
  Law of sentencing

(Essentials of Canadian law)
ISBN 1-55221-029-4

1. Sentences (Criminal procedure) – Canada.  I. Title.  II. Series.

KE9355.M36 2000        345.71'0772        C00-931744-9
KF9685.M36 2000


Printed and bound in Canada.

1   2   3   4   5        05   04   03   02   01

# SUMMARY
# TABLE OF CONTENTS

# DETAILED
# TABLE OF CONTENTS

CHAPTER 11:
## PREVENTIVE DETENTION    *314*

# FOREWORD

Sentencing was largely ignored by scholars and judges until the late 1980s or early 1990s. Few jurists examined the tenets underlying sentencing and most contented themselves with those principles enunciated in *R. v. Morrissette*[1] and *R. v. Gardiner*.[2] The subject was considered more an 'art' than a science. Beginning in 1914, commissions of inquiry were held at least once in each decade of the 20th century to consider sentencing and the effectiveness of imprisonment. Yet despite the fact that these inquiries consistently advocated restraint, recommending that imprisonment be used as a last resort, and that all aspects of sentencing be reassessed, imprisonment was, and remains, the punishment of choice in this country. The call for a re-examination of the principles underlying sentencing fell largely on deaf ears.

It was not until the introduction of Bill C-91 and the subsequent filing of Bill C-41 in Parliament that serious consideration of the approach to sentencing began in Canada. Law faculties and academics largely ignored the subject prior to that time. In 1993, Professor Hélène Dumont of the Université de Montréal wrote the first text in French on punishment and sentencing.[3] Some law schools began to teach sentencing and academics began to write about various aspects of the topic including victims' rights, parole, probation, and sentencing. However, not until the publication of this volume have we had a comprehensive text in English that discusses the rationale for sentencing and the principles and rules that shape and determine the ultimate sentence.

Allan Manson is perhaps the most insightful scholar now writing in Canada on the law of sentencing. He has set out a comprehensive and readable examination of punishment and sentencing, including a discussion of the justifications for punishment from both an historical and

---

1   (1970) 1 C.C.C. (2d) 307
2   [1982] 2 S.C.R. 368
3   Hélène Dumont, *Pénologie, Le droit canadien relatif aux peines et aux sentences* (Montréal: Les Éditions Thémis, 1993)

current perspective, as well as an analysis of the substantive principles of sentencing. But he has done much more than that. He has considered each topic in a manner that is relevant to a wide audience. His stated purpose was to write a book that would be useful not only to practitioners but also to law students. In my opinion he has succeeded in achieving that difficult objective. There is sufficient historical and theoretical background to help students understand the principles that govern the determination of a sentence. The book will also assist the experienced practitioner in preparing a cogent submission on sentencing.

The first three chapters of the book deal with a brief history of punishment and sentencing and with the justification for punishment. This is followed by a chapter-by-chapter consideration of the principles and rules of sentencing and the effect of mitigating and aggravating factors. The discussion of sentencing hearings will be of particular importance to practitioners and especially useful in the context of restorative justice and conditional sentences of imprisonment. This is an aspect of sentencing too often overlooked by counsel when making submissions to the court on behalf of their clients, particularly when seeking to have sentences served in the community.

Professor Manson has covered the subject in a comprehensive manner and has also provided the reader with further readings and material at the end of each chapter. This useful information will assist both students in their understanding of the subject matter and practitioners in better representing their clients.

I congratulate Professor Manson for such a thoughtful and complete work.

Hon. William J. Vancise, Saskatchewan Court of Appeal

# ACKNOWLEDGMENTS

Over the years that I worked in this area, I have been lucky to have collaborated with various skilled lawyers and academics, too numerous to mention individually, whose experience and insights have substantially influenced my attitudes about sentencing issues. Also, it is not possible to write about sentencing law without recognizing the contributions of earlier texts and their authors: Clayton Ruby, Paul Nadin-Davis and, in the United Kingdom, Nigel Walker and Nicola Padfield. While working specifically on this book, I have enjoyed the advice and opinions of a small number of colleagues and friends: Tony Doob, Patrick Healy, Julian Roberts, Gary Trotter and Elizabeth Thomas. I want to thank the SSHRC for funding some of my research on historical issues and in Yukon communities. Irwin Law, and in particular, Bill Kaplan, Jeff Miller and Jo Roberts, have been especially encouraging and helpful.

# CHAPTER 1

# INTRODUCTION

Most people who read newspapers, listen to the radio, and watch television have some understanding of what sentencing is all about. For many reasons, it is one aspect of our social existence that receives a lot of attention. However, in order for us to develop a detailed and critical understanding of this process as it is carried out in hundreds of courts across Canada every day, sentencing needs to be put into context. First, it needs to be understood as an essential element of the criminal justice process. To paraphrase Sir James Fitzjames Stephen,[1] sentencing is to the criminal justice system what dinner is to the restaurant: everything leads up to it. It's what everyone remembers, but it is part of a larger process. Second, it needs to be placed into historical perspective. Different forms of punishment have historical roots linking them to the cultural and political environments from which they have derived. Identifying these roots explains the longevity of some of the more usual forms of punishment — it also explains the process of change. Looking from an historical perspective at the sequence of legislative action discloses not only the antecedents of various rules that may still apply but also the source of the language still contained in the *Criminal Code*. Third, sentencing needs to be understood as the pragmatic aspect of an ongoing philosophical and political debate about

---

1    The actual quotation from an 1863 magazine article, as repeated by Dickson J., in
     *R. v. Gardiner* (1983), 30 C.R. (3d) 289 (S.C.C.) at 329–30, is: ". . . the sentence is
     the gist of the proceeding. It is to the trial what the bullet is to the powder."

1

punishment, sanctions, and relations between citizens and the state. While contemporary practice may not reflect the dynamics of the contemporary debate, it is certainly influenced by it. Over time, these influences can be observed. Again, understanding the debate helps explain the sources and dimensions of change.

This book is intended for two audiences: practitioners and law students. It is intended to provide a summary of the legal principles and rules that shape the current process of sentencing. Lawyers will appreciate the way the process works and will want to know about particular issues of current applicability. Students will come to the subject with little practical experience. While these two groups may have different expectations, the structure of the book should serve both sets of needs. It is based on the pattern that I have used for over two decades in the various courses on sentencing and imprisonment that I have taught. It begins by placing sentencing in context, by providing both the historical and philosophical background of the current process. The book then moves to the decision-making methodology, especially the relevant principles and rules that the judiciary apply when sentencing offenders. Next is a discussion of the structure and procedure of the sentencing hearing. This is followed by a detailed account of all available sentencing options, beginning with the least intrusive and moving up the ladder to imprisonment. Separate attention is paid to the specific issues of sentencing in homicide cases and preventive detention. Lastly comes the subject of sentencing appeals and the role of the appellate courts. I have found that this order provides the necessary sequence of ideas and material. Chapters 1 and 2 (history and philosophy) may seem superfluous or turgid for those with an intimate involvement in sentencing who are looking for more practical material. On the other hand, they provide background which, I believe, is essential for an integrated understanding of sentencing in Canada today.

## A. THE SCOPE OF THE CRIMINAL LAW

All organized communities need a normative structure which includes a set of rules intended to protect the things considered most valuable to the community and its survival. Throughout history, these rule sets have all been accompanied by some mechanism of enforcement. The modern generation of these rules are known usually as penal codes or criminal codes. Some codes deal with substance, including general statements about responsibility, incapacity, justifications, and excuses. Other jurisdictions have codified models which detail procedures from

investigation and arrest all the way through to the structure of adjudicative and penal regimes. By comparison, some other codes may appear
skeletal. But all modern codes have two common characteristics: they
contain descriptions of offences and statements of prescribed punishments. Crime and punishment — this is the stuff of criminal law.

While some criminal law pronouncements may have a moral tone,
the domain of the criminal law within a social structure is not congruent with conceptions of morality. It is an instrumental regime that
derives from the political character of the jurisdiction. Its role has been
aptly described by Turner:

> In fact, criminal offences are basically the creation of the criminal
> policy adopted from time to time by those sections of the community
> who are powerful or astute enough to safeguard their own security
> and comfort by causing the sovereign power in the state to repress
> conduct which they feel may endanger their position.[2]

This explains the variability of criminal law over time and the political
nature of its changes. It also encompasses the basic components of
criminal law: policy, state power, and repression. Conspicuously absent
is any reference to moral legitimacy or justification.

If the articulation of the criminal law expresses what a community
chooses to protect, the enforcement of the criminal law provides the
state with an instrument for pursuing that goal. First, it requires a process for determining when a violation has occurred: this is the guilt and
responsibility stage. Then, there is the question of responding to the
proven violation. In modern terms, the formal response is usually
called the sentence. Consequently, sentencing is the process by which
an appropriate response is determined and imposed.

## B. PUNISHMENT AND SENTENCING

Sentencing connotes a process for determining an appropriate sanction
after a finding of criminal responsibility. Punishment and sentencing
are conceptually distinct, although punishment has been the most
common element of sentencing throughout history. Punishment is a
social institution, and is determined by the cultural patterns of the

2   J.W.C. Turner, *Russell on Crime*, 12th ed., vol. 1 (London: Stevens & Sons, 1964)
    at 18.

day.[3] As an intentional infliction of pain or burden, punishment involves some form of suffering and is inherently coercive and intrusive. It is imposed in answer to some antecedent event or to achieve some consequential goal. As a tool, punishment fits neatly into the coercive and instrumental objectives of the criminal law. Beyond the crime-control goals of punishment, it can also, and often does, serve other purposes: political, social, economic, religious, and moral. However, the process of responding to violations need not necessarily be restricted to punishment. Treatment of the offender is distinct from punishment, as is compensation for a victim. Different communities from time to time have employed compensatory techniques rather than punitive ones. Recently, there has been much discussion about restorative justice which envisages a greater use of restoration, reconciliation, and compensation within the sentencing process. While a transition from punishment to reconciliation may seem attractive, the punitive sanction remains the principal tool of sentencing.

As part of a modern legal system, sentencing should be fair, just and principled both in terms of its procedures and its sanctions. It ought to be imposed in public by an institution which can be held accountable for its decisions. Available sanctions ought to have some contemporary legitimacy at least to the extent of popular acceptance. There should also be some confidence that the sanction actually achieves its ostensible goal, at least to some degree. These are some of the tests which we might wish to apply to modern systems of sentencing. Throughout history, however, punishment by the state with all the coercive power of the state behind it has often been the source of terrible harm and the instrument of oppressive tyranny. Thus, it is necessary to examine, and from time to time to re-examine, the justifications for punishment by the state and the legitimacy of the actual forms of punishment.

## FURTHER READINGS

GARLAND, D., *Punishment and Modern Society: A Study in Social Theory* (Oxford: Clarendon Press, 1990)

---

3    See the excellent and provocative discussion in D. Garland, *Punishment and Modern Society: A Study in Social Theory* (Oxford: Clarendon Press, 1990), particularly at 193–203. See *ibid.* at 249–60 for a discussion of the reciprocal influences that punishments have on culture.

# CHAPTER 2

# A BRIEF HISTORY OF PUNISHMENT AND SENTENCING

## A. A BRIEF HISTORY OF PUNISHMENT

As background to a discussion of the Canadian sentencing system, it is useful to consider how punishment has evolved over time. While imprisonment seems to be the most common anchor for current sentencing systems, this has not always been the case. Up to the beginning of the nineteenth century, most penal codes included hundreds of capital offences. Moreover, sentences often involved various attacks on the offender's body. Understanding the history of change, and the factors which have influenced it, is a worthwhile exercise given the conceptual and pragmatic link between the available forms of punishment and the nature of the sentencing process. A detailed exposition is beyond the scope of this book but a brief historical account will provide a helpful backdrop.

### 1) Punishment in Ancient Communities[1]

The common forms of punishment in ancient communities were capital punishment, physical mutilation, confiscation of property, exile, and

---

1    For a discussion of Mesopotamia, Egypt, Greece, Israel, Assyria, Babylonia, and Rome, read E.M. Peters, "Prison Before the Prison: The Ancient and Medieval Worlds" in N. Morris & D.J. Rothman, eds., *The Oxford History of the Prison* (New York: Oxford University Press, 1995) at 3.

loss of civil status. Capital punishment took many forms. An offender might be stoned to death (lapidation) or thrown from a cliff (precipitation). In ancient Greece, an offender could be bound to a stake to suffer a long, public death. This was the precursor to crucifixion.[2] There is evidence of the existence of prisons at least from the time of Socrates. These places served mostly to hold people pending trial or execution, and to encourage debtors to pay their obligations. Greek prisons also provided the place for executions and torture, which was inflicted, for the most part, on slaves.

In the Roman Republic,[3] from 509 BC onward, the death penalty was the usual punishment for crime although conviction for some offences was followed by orders for compensation. The type of execution depended on the offence and often bore some symbolic relation to essential qualities of the offence, although that linkage may no longer be visible. A person convicted of arson would suffer death by burning, and most thieves were hanged. The penalty for perjury was precipitation and death by clubbing was prescribed for anyone convicted of "writing scurrilous songs" about a Roman citizen. Being buried alive was the penalty for a vestal virgin who violated her oath of chastity. A gruesome punishment was devised for someone convicted of murdering a member of their immediate family: the offender was placed in a large sack with an ape, dog, or serpent, and thrown into the sea. As an alternative to execution, many convicted offenders were offered exile. Prisons, usually located underground, existed in Rome but were not used as places of long-term confinement. Magistrates had the power to imprison temporarily, but most prisoners were debtors or those awaiting execution.

From the middle of the second century BC, courts were used to adjudicate guilt for some offences, but sanctions were stipulated expressly in statutes. This marked the beginning of the evolution from private to public conceptions of the criminal law. After the Republic, the range of punishments reflected this change and took on a more exemplary and deterrent tone. Exile became a compulsory rather than optional penalty for certain offences. Some offenders were forced to work in mines, while

---

2    If the crime invoked a religious dimension, like homicide, the execution might include a dedication to the gods consisting of a ritual curse and other consequences like forbidding burial, or destruction of the offender's home. Other sanctions included fines and confiscation of property. Another range of punishments involved public shaming or denunciation, accompanied by civil disabilities and sometimes imposed posthumously. Exile was also an available sanction. See Peters, *ibid.* at 4–8.

3    *Ibid.* at 14–23.

others were compelled to participate in gladiatorial combat. Similar public exhibitions of the consequences of non-conformity included being thrown into a pit with beasts, burning, and crucifixion.

## 2) Punishment in the Middle Ages

Throughout the Middle Ages, sanctions can be traced by category back to their ancient sources: death, mutilation, loss of property, denial of status as citizen, and confinement. However, the criminal law was enforced by various institutions and individuals including the sovereign, local lords, the church, and local courts. Understandably, this resulted in variations on the common themes. In England, Henry II began building prisons but these were generally intended for debtors, trespassers, and those convicted of contempt and other lesser offences. During this period, the majority of crime resulted in much harsher penalties:

> Punishment in English criminal law was intended to be quick and public to serve as a deterrent to other crime. Thus, forms of punishment ranged from shaming display — the pillory, mutilation, branding, public stocks, and ducking stools — to severe and aggravated capital punishments — hanging, drowning, burning, burial alive, or decapitation — and any of these could be preceded by the infliction of torments before the execution itself.[4]

On the continent,[5] imprisonment was little used. It was usually restricted to confinement for those who could not pay fines or as an alternative to capital punishment. In France, some thefts and the offence of blasphemy resulted in imprisonment, as did "break and enter by night," but the sentence of two years close confinement for the latter offence was followed by exile. Italian courts relied, for the most part, on capital punishment, fines, exile, and instruments of public shame. Imprisonment for short periods was prescribed for a very small number of offences, including the curious offence of masquerading as a physician. Conversely, life imprisonment was available for some heretics who recanted their heresy.

One curious aspect of punishment which arose in the Middle Ages started with the argument that members of the clergy were only

---

4    *Ibid.* at 35.
5    For a discussion of punishment in Europe in the Middle Ages, see generally P. Spierenburg, "The Body and the State: Early Modern Europe" in Morris & Rothman, eds., above note 1 at 48.

answerable under ecclesiastical law. Consequently, English courts began the practice of recognizing what was known as "benefit of clergy"[6] which had the result of permitting someone to avoid death, the usual common law punishment for felonies. Soon the test for clerical status became one of literacy. As a result, the claim of benefit of clergy expanded beyond those who were in fact members of clerical orders. This expansion was recognized by statute in 1487 but limited so that lay men could take its benefit only once: those granted benefit of clergy for murder were branded with an "M" on their thumb so that they could easily be identified if charged a second time. Until 1623, the benefit of clergy was applicable only to men. Eventually, the application of the literacy test became irrelevant and was formally abandoned by statute in 1706. Soon, statutes distinguished between capital and non-capital offences by prescribing those which carried the "benefit of clergy" and those which did not, thus saving individuals from the gallows because of the nature of their criminality rather than their literacy.

## 3) Europe Before the Birth of the Penitentiary

Using the birth of the modern penitentiary between the late eighteenth and early nineteenth century as a benchmark, certain historical developments from earlier in the modern period are especially interesting. First, the Greek notion of civil disability evolved into civil consequences which extended beyond the offender to his or her family. In England, the disabilities which flowed from a conviction for treason and other felonies were known as attainder,[7] corruption of the blood, and outlawry.[8] Essentially, those convicted were dispossessed and excluded from the benefits

---

6    See J.M. Beattie, *Crime and the Courts in England, 1660–1800* (Princeton, N.J.: Princeton University Press, 1986) at 141–46.

7    See J. Crankshaw, *The Criminal Code of Canada and the Canada Evidence Act, 1893* (Montreal: Whiteford & Theoret, 1894) at 769, where he defined attainder as "the status, or, according to the old law, the taint, or stain, or corruption of blood of one condemned, by the judgement of the court for treason or felony." The consequences of attainder were the forfeiture of real and personal property, the "corruption of the blood" so that nothing could pass by inheritance to or from the offender, and the inability to bring a suit in court. Accordingly, attainder applied to the offender and corruption of the blood was the consequence suffered by his heirs.

8    *Ibid.* at 610. Crankshaw explained that outlawry applied when an accused could not be apprehended but an indictment had been found: "Outlawry being a punishment inflicted by the law upon an offender, for contumacy, in refusing to render himself amenable to justice." Once the indictment was found, it subjected the offender to attainder and forfeiture.

of the legal order — their property was confiscated and they were disconnected from the community. Furthermore, they could neither inherit property nor convey property to their heirs; this was known as "corruption of the blood," both "upwards and downwards."[9]

Secondly, the use of punishment as public spectacle grew but also began to attract criticism. Punitive spectacles included both public executions and the public infliction of corporal punishment. The act of execution was not restricted to hanging, decapitation, or garroting. These were the more merciful forms. In many cases, torture and ritual accompanied public death, as best exemplified by the execution of the regicide Damiens, the detailed report of which Foucault quotes at the beginning of his classic work, *Discipline and Punish*.[10] Corporal punishment also included various forms of branding and mutilation, used ostensibly to permit judges to identify recidivists but also intended to encourage public shame. By the eighteenth century, members of the elite classes, immersed in the Enlightenment, were becoming uncomfortable with these harsh public displays. It had also become apparent that onlookers were not passively receiving any moral deterrent message from the public execution or infliction of injury.

Thirdly, throughout Europe different forms of convict labour had become popular forms of punishment. These were really manifestations of bondage. Well-known examples were the Dutch *rasphouse*, the German *zuchthaus* and the English bridewell.[11] They derived not from views on crime but from attitudes about poverty, especially the fear of the itinerant poor. Initially, it was beggars and vagrants who were confined in workhouses or compelled to row in galleys. By the sixteenth century, forced work was becoming an acceptable form of sanction for criminal offences. In some countries (Spain, for example), the model expanded to include public works like mining, road building and repair, and collecting human waste door to door. Soon, institutions were built with the sole purpose of providing a place for forced labour. As the imperial European world was expanding to include vast colonies abroad, it was not long before the idea of transporting convicts arose. Ostensibly as a new and merciful response to offenders, King

---

9    See G.W. Burbidge, *A Digest of the Criminal Law of Canada (Crimes and Punishments)* (Toronto: Carswell, 1890) at 22–23.
10   M. Foucault, *Discipline and Punish: The Birth of the Prison*, trans. A. Sheridan (New York: Vintage Books, 1979) at 3–5.
11   See Spierenburg, above note 5 at 64–72.

James I issued a decree in 1615 which authorized indentured servitude in the Americas as a penalty. Large-scale transportation to the Thirteen Colonies began in 1718.[12]

## 4) The Birth of the Penitentiary

The late eighteenth century can be credited with two processes which shaped the context for modern sentencing systems: One was the almost universal movement away from capital punishment as a common penal sanction; the other was the birth of the modern penitentiary. There is a continuing academic debate about the engine which drove the development of the penitentiary. A number of historical factors that related directly to the state of punishment probably made some contribution, at least in terms of providing the right circumstances. There can be no doubt that the penitentiary was, to some extent, influenced by the development of the workhouses in England and Europe. Politically, the increased difficulty in transporting convicts and the expanding problem of the hulks (convict ships) festering in England's estuaries created a need for an alternative and, hence, an impetus to consider large-scale places of confinement. The efforts of John Howard (whose *The State of the Prisons in England and Wales*, published in 1777, recounted the disorder and poor conditions of England's jails) and the religious views of the Quakers promoted a place of confinement characterized by clear rules, rigid discipline, and opportunities for religious inculcation and penitence. More recently, writers like Foucault,[13] Ignatieff,[14] and Melossi and Pavarini[15] have placed the genesis for the modern penitentiary not as part of an evolving debate about punishment but within the larger political economy and culture of the Industrial Revolution.

Regardless of the disputes about origins, by the mid-nineteenth century, massive walled institutions could be seen in North America and Europe. Various architectural forms were used. In England, prior to building the first penitentiary, an architectural competition was con-

---

12   As a result of "An Act for the further preventing of Robbery, Burglary, and other Felonies, and for the more effectual Transportation of Felons" (1717), 4 Geo.1, c.11. See the discussion in L. Radzinowicz & R. Hood, *A History of the English Criminal Law*, vol. 5 (London, Stevens: 1986) at 465–89.

13   Above note 10.

14   M. Ignatieff, *A Just Measure of Pain: The Penitentiary in the Industrial Revolution, 1750–1850* (New York: Pantheon, 1978).

15   D. Melossi & M. Pavarini, *The Prison and the Factory: Origins of the Penitentiary System*, trans. G. Cousin (London: Macmillan, 1981).

ducted which attracted entries from the leading architects of the day, including John Soane, who had designed the Bank of England building and St. James Palace. He did not get the contract. Many of the early penitentiaries followed the popular radial design initiated by Blackburn, who designed nineteen English county prisons in the late eighteenth century. This concept was adopted and refined by Haviland in Pennsylvania with the construction of the Eastern State Penitentiary.[16]

The biggest debates around the building of the first penitentiaries concerned the conceptual bases for ordering the internal lives of the prisoners. This affected all aspects of prison organization and administration. There were two basic models. What became known as the "Pennsylvania" or "separate system" involved keeping prisoners confined separately at all times. Prisoners would work, eat, and pray separately and alone. A penitentiary structured around separation required an intricate design to permit prisoners to exercise outside and still remain alone. The competing model was based on the structure of the Auburn Penitentiary in upstate New York where prisoners were confined separately but came together for work, study, and prayer. However, they were prohibited from communicating with each other, orally or otherwise — hence the name "silent system." This model has also been called the "congregate system" because it did not require solitary confinement.

While Auburn and Pennsylvania dominated the debates, there were other conceptual models available. Foucault has described what he called the "Geneva model," which involved the prisoner progressing through four stages as the sentence proceeded, each accompanied by a different form of confinement and activity.[17] Jeremy Bentham enlivened the controversy with his unsuccessful attempt to persuade the British government to adopt "the Panopticon."[18] Designed by his brother, this proposed circular penitentiary provided for discipline through constant surveillance, and fiscal integrity through the prisoners' productivity. Prisoners would be confined separately but would be visible at all times of the day.

---

16  N.B. Johnston, *Eastern State Penitentiary: Crucible of Good Intentions* (Philadelphia: Philadelphia Museum of Art, 1994).

17  See Foucault, above note 10 at 245–46. The four stages were (1) intimidation through strict solitary confinement; (2) work in isolation; (3) moral education by attending lectures; and (4) working together with others.

18  For a detailed discussion of the progress of Bentham's penal obsession, see J. Semple, *Bentham's Prison: A Study of the Panopticon Penitentiary* (Oxford: Clarendon Press, 1993).

Although the model was ultimately rejected,[19] Bentham's other work substantially influenced the debate about punishment.

In Upper Canada, the Commissioners who advised the legislature on the construction of the Provincial Penitentiary were drawn into the debate between the Pennsylvania and Auburn models.[20] Before reporting, they visited American penitentiaries at Auburn, Sing Sing, Blackwell's Island, and Connecticut. A cholera epidemic cancelled their trip to the Eastern State Penitentiary in Pennsylvania. Ultimately, they chose the Auburn congregate model and hired the Deputy Warden of Auburn to assist with the construction. Various factors have been offered over the years in an effort to explain the genesis of the Provincial Penitentiary at Kingston which opened in 1835: fear of rising crime rates and the influx of destitute immigrants,[21] concern about a moral malaise that might nurture crime, the inadequate conditions of the local jails, and the influence of the penitentiary movement in the United States and England. A number of influential Tories supported the building of the penitentiary.[22] Recent analysis suggests that the Auburn model was selected for Kingston because the Commissioners were attracted to the potential revenues that could be generated by congregate convict labour.[23]

During this time, the debate between proponents of the separate and congregate models was in full flood in England. In 1835, a committee of the House of Lords issued a report favouring the separate system.[24] Soon after, a group of inspectors were appointed to oversee the

---

19   The concept was employed in modified form at Stateville Penitentiary in Illinois which opened in 1925: see J. Jacobs, *Stateville, The Penitentiary in Mass Society* (Chicago: University of Chicago Press, 1977) at 15–16. Other circular institutions were built in Spain, Holland, and Cuba: see N. Johnston, *The Human Cage: A Brief History of Prison Architecture* (New York, Walker & Co. 1973) at 20–21.

20   See the excellent discussion of the origins of the Kingston Penitentiary in P. Oliver, *Terror to Evil-Doers: Prisons and Punishments in Nineteenth-Century Ontario* (Toronto: University of Toronto Press, 1998) at 86–135.

21   Now, there seems to be agreement amongst historians that statistically Upper Canada was not suffering a crime problem but that crime was an issue of public conncern: see J.M. Beattie, *Attitudes Towards Crime and Punishment in Upper Canada, 1830–1850: A Documentary Study* (Toronto: Centre of Criminology, University of Toronto, 1977) at 1–8.

22   Chief Justice John Beverley Robinson favoured a penitentiary because it fit his conception of a modern justice system that required swift but fair punishment: see Oliver, above note 20 at 101–5.

23   *Ibid.* at 110.

24   See R. McGowen, "The Well-Ordered Prison: England, 1780–1865" in Morris & Rothman, eds., above note 1 at 100–01.

developing prison system, two of whom were ardent advocates of the separate system. When they decided to build Pentonville Prison in north London, it was not surprising that they chose the separate model, although the man responsible for the construction, Sir Joshua Jebb, had doubts about this approach.[25] The prison opened in 1842 with 520 separate cells. Guards wore padded shoes to enhance silence and could not speak with prisoners. The prisoners wore hoods when not inside their cells. Each was given a number, and had a separate exercise yard and a separate stall in the chapel. The construction and engineering were "ingenious," especially with respect to lighting, ventilation and plumbing, and served as a model for other prisons in England and elsewhere. Pentonville has been described as a monument to the separate system.

> It represented "the apotheosis of the idea that a totally controlled environment could produce a reformed and autonomous individual."[26]

Pentonville was the only example of the separate system attempted in England. There were two reasons for this. First, most of the western world had rejected the separate system and the debilitating solitary confinement which characterized it. Secondly, Jebb had risen in influence and in 1850 was made the Chairman of the Board of Convict Prisons. Adding insult to injury for the Pentonville planners, public outcry over alleged luxury for convicted prisoners resulted in a decision to cement-close the individual toilets in each cell, requiring prisoners to continue the practice of "slopping out" each day.

## 5) The Changing Focus of Punishment

At the end of the eighteenth century, most sentences were directed at the body of the offender either in the form of execution or mutilation. Exclusion was also a dominant feature, achieved through transportation, banishment, and civil disability. The birth of the penitentiary provided a change in course, to stipulated periods of deprived liberty during which, optimistically, some reformative process would take place. Initially, the engines of reformation were thought to be penitence, discipline, and hard labour. Later, the rehabilitative ideal replaced these regimes with psychological, vocational, and education programs. In the twentieth century, various factors produced a renewed

---

25  See L. Radzinowicz & R. Hood, above note 12 at 490–98.
26  See McGowen, above note 24 at 101.

interest in fines and the new sanction, probation. Now, at the beginning of the twenty-first century, we are in the midst of a debate about the overuse of imprisonment and the continuing search for non-custodial alternatives. One can anticipate that various disparate factors like rapidly expanding budgets, the enthusiasm for restorative justice, and dissatisfaction about the state of criminal justice in aboriginal communities will combine to encourage new community-based alternatives with a large role for members of the community, both as contracted service providers and volunteers.

## B. A BRIEF HISTORY OF SENTENCING IN CANADA

The criminal law in Canada, including the law of sentencing, now derives almost entirely from the *Criminal Code*. Enacted in 1892, the first comprehensive *Code* owed a great deal to English antecedents. When Sir John Thompson introduced it in Parliament, he said:

> The Bill is founded on the draft code prepared by the Royal Commission in Great Britain in 1880, on Stephens' Digest of the Criminal Law, the edition of 1887, Burbidge's Digest of the Canadian Criminal Law of 1889, and the Canadian Statutory Law. The efforts at the reduction of the criminal law of England into this shape have been carried on for nearly sixty years, and although not yet perfected by statute, those efforts have given us immense help in simplifying and reducing into a system of this kind our law relating to criminal matters and relating to criminal procedure. . . .
>
> I would further explain that the Bill aims at a codification of both common law and statutory law . . . , but that it does not aim at completely superseding the common law, while it does aim at completely superseding the statutory law relating to crimes.[27]

Thompson added that it was his intention that the Bill would encourage uniformity of punishment for "various offences of something like the same grade." In setting out the history of sentencing in Canada, it is helpful to use the first *Criminal Code* as the watershed.

---

27   *House of Commons Debates* (12 April 1892) at 1312–13 (Sir J. Thompson).

# 1) Before the First *Criminal Code*

Prior to 1892, the criminal law of England as it existed at specific dates applied in the various parts of Canada.[28] The link to English law remains significant historically since it provides the explanation for much of our current scheme, which in many respects has not changed substantially since 1892. At the turn of the nineteenth century, English criminal law included over 200 capital offences and provided for various corporal penalties and civil disabilities. Many of the forms of corporal and public punishment used in England, like the pillory and branding, were also available in Canada but fell into disuse by the 1830s.[29] In 1800, the legislature of Upper Canada ensured that local courts had discretion to impose a "moderate pecuniary fine" rather than the punishment of "burning in the hand" or other "lasting mark of disgrace and infamy" in response to a non-capital felony conviction.[30] Another alternative was whipping, in private or publicly, which was made available except in cases of manslaughter or where the offender was a woman. The same enactment provided for imprisonment with hard labour for a period of six months to two years in the "House of Correction." Recognizing the applicability of the English law of transportation, it also provided that an Upper Canadian court could substitute banishment for the same number of years. Of course, a banished offender who returned before the expiration of the term of banishment would, upon conviction, suffer death.[31] Transportation, usually to New South Wales,

28  For Ontario, the relevant date was September 17, 1792. In Quebec, it was the law of England as of 1764. In the maritime provinces of Nova Scotia, New Brunswick, and Prince Edward Island, there is some uncertainty but 1758, the date of the first legislative assembly in Nova Scotia which included the other two future provinces at the time, is arguably the correct point. English criminal law applied in British Columbia as of 1858, while 1870 was the relevant date for Manitoba, Saskatchewan, Alberta, and the two territories. See the discussion in Burbidge, above note 9 at 10–13.

29  See J.A. Edmison, "Some Aspects of Nineteenth-Century Canadian Prisons" in W.T. McGrath, ed., *Crime and Its Treatment in Canada*, 2d ed. (Toronto: MacMillan, 1976) 347 at 350–51.

30  See Stat. U.C. 1800, c. 1, s. 3.

31  *Ibid.*, ss. 5, 6.

Van Diemen's Land, or Bermuda, was often an alternative to capital punishment and was also used in cases with political dimensions.[32] While it may be difficult to determine exactly what the legislators of the day understood by the term "House of Correction," it is clear that few institutions satisfied their expectations. It was enacted in 1810 that all common gaols would be constituted as houses of correction for the following purposes:

> . . . that all and every idle and disorderly person, or rogues and vaga-bonds, and incorrigible rogues, or any other person or persons who may by Law be subject to a House of Correction, shall be committed to the said Common Gaols. . . .[33]

In 1830, the Justices of the Peace in Newcastle ordered that a new gaol be built given that the existing facility was "untenable."[34] The order was quashed on certiorari by Chief Justice John Beverley Robinson who held that only the legislature could commit public funds to build a prison. He did not doubt that a new gaol was needed and expressed some optimism that the legislature would respond to the situation.[35] The deplorable condition of local gaols was one factor which led in 1831 to the appointment of a commission to consider whether a penitentiary ought to be built. The subsequent report, criticizing various aspects of sentencing and describing imprisonment in the local gaols as "inexpedient and pernicious in the extreme,"[36] led to the building of the Provincial Penitentiary at Kingston.

---

32  The most dramatic example of the use of transportation was after the 1837 rebellion. It appears that 150 prisoners from Upper and Lower Canada were shipped to British penal colonies in New South Wales and Van Diemen's Land: see F.M. Greenwood, ed., *Land of a Thousand Sorrows: The Australian Prison Journal of the Exiled Canadien Patriote François-Maurice Lepailleur* (Vancouver: University of British Columbia Press, 1980); and F. Landon, *An Exile from Canada to Van Diemen's Land: Being the Story of Elijah Woodman, Transported Overseas for Participation in the Upper Canada Troubles of 1837–38* (Toronto: Longmans, Green, 1960).

33  Stat. U.C. 1810, c. 5.

34  See *R. v. Upper Canada* (1830), Draper 204 (U.C.K.B.).

35  Chief Justice Robinson, an influential Tory, had been a supporter of the need to build a provincial penitentiary as an element of an expanding justice system: see Oliver, above note 20 at 87, 135.

36  See *Report of a Select Committee on the Expediency of Erecting a Penitentiary*, Journal of the House of Assembly of Upper Canada (1831), Appendix at 211–12.

An enactment in Upper Canada in 1833 not only dramatically reduced the availability of the death penalty but also provided a framework for other penalties. After that date, the only capital crimes were murder, treason, rape and carnal knowledge of a girl under ten years of age, robbery, burglary, arson, buggery, and bestiality.[37] The regime for non-capital offences provided that offenders

> . . . shall be liable to be banished, or to be transported beyond the seas for life, or for such term not less than seven years, . . . or imprisoned and kept to hard labour, or in solitary confinement in the Common Gaol, or in any Penitentiary, or House of Correction, that may be provided for such purposes, for any term not exceeding fourteen years.[38]

The only specific offence dealt with by this section was manslaughter, for which the prescribed penalty was a fine or imprisonment for a term less than twelve months. The pillory and whipping, in public or private, were made available, by themselves or in addition to another punishment, for the offences of forgery, uttering and personation.[39]

A number of important penal statutes were passed within the few years after the merger of Upper and Lower Canada into the Province of Canada by *The Union Act, 1840.* In part, they represented an attempt to develop an appropriate penalty scale. Many of their details were quickly varied, probably reflecting the transitional nature of the period. It was a time of flux due to the changing political structure and also because of the demise of transportation as an available penalty. In 1841, the penalty scheme included imprisonment at hard labour in the penitentiary for life, imprisonment in the penitentiary for a term of at least seven years, and confinement in another prison for a term up to two years.[40] (Some attribute the current two-year split between the provincial and federal incarceration regimes to the use of two years as the

---

37   Stat. U.C. 1833, c. 4, ss. 1–11. Section 25 abolished benefit of clergy ensuring that thereafter capital offences would be those for which death was an expressly prescribed penalty — all others would be non-capital.

38   *Ibid.*, s. 25.

39   *Ibid.*, s. 26.

40   *An Act for improving the Administration of Criminal Justice,* 1841 (Can.), 4–5 Vict., c. 24, s. 30. Although in 1841 seven years was the common minimum for penitentiary confinement, some examples existed of offences for which the available term of imprisonment was between two and seven years: see note 48, below.

cap for non-penitentiary incarceration.[41]) In 1842, to "better [...] proportion the punishment of such offenders to the guilt of the offence,"
the minimum penitentiary term was reduced to three years imprisonment.[42] This enactment also provided that offences previously punished by transportation would be punishable by imprisonment for a
like term.[43] An interesting provision by today's standards empowered
courts to order solitary confinement for periods during a term of
imprisonment so long as each period was no longer than one month
and the total not greater than three months in a year.[44] On the progres-
sive side, the punishment of the pillory was abolished in 1841.[45]

During this period, specific statutes prescribed the penalties for
crimes of larceny, offences against the person, and "malicious injuries
to property."[46] They provide an interesting glimpse into the legislators'
sense of what was important. Setting fire to a dwelling-house was punishable by death, while arson in relation to a church or ship was punishable by life imprisonment, imprisonment in the penitentiary for
seven years or more, or imprisonment in another prison for up to two
years.[47] Imprisonment for a minimum of seven years in the penitentiary
or a maximum of two years in a prison applied to the destruction of

---

41   While this may hold water as far as the adoption in Canada of what is now the
     "two years less a day" dividing line, a recent detailed historical analysis situates
     the real source in a 1706 English statute, *An act for repealing a clause in an act,
     intituled, "An act for the better apprehending, prosecuting, and punishing felons that
     commit burglaries, house-breaking, or robberies in shops, ware-houses, coach-houses,
     or stables, or that steal horses,"* 1706 (U.K.), 5 Anne, c. 6: see M. Campbell, "A
     Most Vexatious Burden": Jurisdiction in Canadian Correctional Law (LL.M.
     Thesis, Faculty of Law, McGill University, 1997) [unpublished].
42   *An Act for better proportioning the punishment to the offence, in certain cases, and for
     other purposes therein mentioned,* 1842 (Can.), 6-7 Vict., c. 5, s. 2.
43   *Ibid.,* s. 4.
44   See *An Act for consolidating and amending the Laws in this Province relative to
     Offences against the Person,* 1841 (Can.), 4-5 Vict., c. 27, s. 36 [*Offences Against the
     Person Act*].
45   *Administration of Criminal Justice Act,* above note 40, s. 31.
46   See, respectively, *An Act for consolidating and amending the Laws in this Province,
     relative to Larceny and other Offences connected therewith,* 1841 (Can.), 4-5 Vict., c.
     25; *Offences Against the Person Act,* above note 44; and *An Act for consolidating and
     amending Laws in this Province relative to Malicious Injuries to Property,* 1841
     (Can.), 4-5 Vict., c. 26 . If no specific punishment was provided for a felony not
     punishable by death, the offender became liable to imprisonment in the
     Penitentiary at hard labour for a term of "not less than seven years" or
     imprisonment in "any other prison or place of confinement for any term not
     exceeding two years": *Administration of Criminal Justice Act,* above note 40, s. 24.
47   *Malicious Injuries to Property Act, ibid.,* ss. 2, 3.

silk, woollen, linen, or cotton, or equipment used in their manufacture, or threshing machines or engines. Damage to a "lock, sluice, flood-gate or other work on any navigable river or canal" or public bridge was punishable by up to four years imprisonment — the enactment does not indicate where that term would be served.[48] Damaging or destroying plants, roots, or fruits grown in a garden, nursery, or orchard resulted in a fine.[49] This hierarchy fits neatly into, and exemplifies, the nineteenth century notion of proportionality. Similarly, punishments for offences against the person started with death for murder, rape, sodomy, and unlawful carnal knowledge of a girl under the age of ten, through imprisonment for life or a lesser period for manslaughter[50] or assault with intent to maim or disfigure, and a "summary power of punishment" consisting of fines with imprisonment in default for "common assaults and batteries."[51]

Confederation in 1867 affected sentencing substantially. First, the criminal law power was vested in the federal sphere.[52] Secondly, the legislative authority over the implementation of sentences was split between the federal and provincial jurisdictions. Section 91(28) of the *Constitution Act, 1867*, placed the responsibility over penitentiaries within the federal domain, while section 92(6) gave the provinces authority over the "establishment, maintenance, and management of public and reformatory prisons." When constitutional meetings began in 1864, the early drafts had given the provinces responsibility for penitentiaries, but this was changed at the last minute, and the power became a federal one. The Canadian Sentencing Commission's 1987 report, suggested that influence may have been brought to bear at the London Conference by Lord Carnarvon who was, at the time, the British Colonial Secretary. Carnarvon had chaired a House of Lords Committee which inquired into the state of discipline in British prisons, and became an advocate of strict discipline and isolation as a result. The Commission suggested:

---

48    *Ibid.*, ss. 12, 13.
49    *Ibid.*, s. 21. See also ss. 20 and 22, in which fines were attached to the damage or destruction of "a tree, sapling, or shrub, or any underwood" and cultivated roots or plants used for food.
50    Interestingly, the fine option provided in an earlier statute was still available for a manslaughter conviction: see *Offences Against the Person Act*, above note 44, s. 7.
51    *Ibid.*, ss. 3, 7, 11, 15, 16, 17, & 23.
52    See *Constitution Act, 1867* (U.K.), 30 & 31 Vict., c. 3, reprinted in R.S.C. 1985, App. II, No. 5, s. 91(27).

Lord Carnarvon may have insisted that the federal government have authority over penitentiaries in order to ensure that Canadian institutions enjoyed the same conditions that prevailed in English jails.[53]

Regardless, the real question remains why the participants did not foresee the difficulties generated by split authority, and move other corrections and sentence-related matters firmly into the federal sphere as well. This would have avoided many of the current controversies, which are exacerbated by financial and political issues.

In 1869, the new Canadian government followed the English lead and consolidated all existing criminal and penal statutes. However, as well as the initiative, much of the substance also came from across the ocean.[54] The Sentencing Commission has described the impact of the English acts of 1861 on Canadian sentencing:

> Since the Canadian *Consolidation Acts* of 1869 were themselves a carbon copy of the 1861 English criminal legislation, it follows that the penalty structure derived from Stephen's *Draft Code* was already embodied in the Canadian criminal law. The penalty scale of six months, two, five, seven, ten and fourteen years of incarceration, of life imprisonment and of capital punishment, which allegedly passed from Stephen's draft into the Canadian *Criminal Code*, had already, in fact, been in use since the *Consolidation Acts* of 1869.[55]

While this is true, it did not undermine the impact of the *Criminal Code, 1892*,[56] which has provided the structure and much of the substance of sentencing for over a hundred years.

## 2) The First *Criminal Code*

The Sentencing Commission has observed that the first *Code* "embodied a rationale of retribution and deterrence" attributable to Stephen, who is well known to have advocated the view that people ought to hate criminals.[57] Certainly, the first *Code* now seems antiquated with its emphasis on capital punishment and imprisonment. Still, a number of

53   Canadian Sentencing Commission, *Sentencing Reform: A Canadian Approach* (Ottawa: Supply and Services Canada, 1987) [*Report of the Canadian Sentencing Commission*] at 31.

54   See the Canadian statutes in 1869 (Can.), 32 & 33 Vict., cc. 18–36, and compare with the English acts in 1861 (U.K.), 24 & 25 Vict., cc. 94–100.

55   *Report of the Canadian Sentencing Commission*, above note 53 at 32.

56   Above note 53.

57   S.C. 55–56 Vict., c. 29.

significant elements, especially technical prerequisites, continue to find expression in the current *Code* often with little change. For example, section 932 provided that whenever "different degrees or kinds of punishment" are available, the sentence shall be "in the discretion of the court." A virtually identical provision appears as section 718.3(1) of the current *Criminal Code*. The provision for consecutive sentences in section 954 of the *Criminal Code, 1892*, contains much of the language now found in section 718.3(4) which, because of its archaic nature, continued to cause problems until 1997.[58] The residual punishment of imprisonment for five years for an indictable offence when no specific penalty is prescribed appeared in section 951(1) of the *Criminal Code, 1892*, and now appears in section 743 in almost the same form.

The *Code* confirmed the abolition of the common law disabilities of outlawry, attainder, and corruption of the blood. While capital punishment continued to play a prominent role in the *Criminal Code, 1892*, its applicability as a mandatory penalty had been reduced to murder[59] and treason.[60] The penalty of death was still available for rape in the discretion of the trial judge who could also sentence the convicted person to life imprisonment.[61] The procedure for executions was described in detail, including the condition of separate confinement pending execution, a prohibition on visits, and a statement of who could be present at the execution. The execution was to take place "within the walls of the prison." The execution of a pregnant woman was suspended when the court received a report from a physician that she was "with child of a quick child."[62]

The major form of punishment was imprisonment prescribed with maxima that varied from life down through the already entrenched scheme of fourteen, ten, seven, five, and two years, or twelve and six months. The Sentencing Commission commented, with respect to the *Criminal Code, 1892*, that

---

58  See the comments of Lamer J. in *R. v. Paul*, [1982] 1 S.C.R. 621; and the discussion in Chapter 6, below. The "*Paul* problem" was removed by the *Criminal Law Improvement Act, 1996*, S.C. 1997, c. 18, s. 141(c), which amended s. 718.3(4)(a) of the *Criminal Code*, R.S.C. 1985, c. C-46, to make the operative date the time of sentencing, not conviction, as had previously applied. See the discussion in Chapter 4, below.

59  *Criminal Code, 1892*, above note 56, s. 231.

60  *Ibid.*, s. 65.

61  *Ibid.*, s. 267.

62  See s. 730, *ibid.*, which also provided: "If upon the report of any of them [one or more registered medical practitioners] it appears to the court that she is so with child execution shall be arrested till she is delivered of a child, or until it is no longer possible in the course of nature that she should be so delivered."

> . . . the punishment for a particular offence cannot be determined by examining the offence independently of the whole structure of penalties for other offences. There is no natural connection between an offence and a particular number of years in jail. Hence, when a sentence is taken out of a penalty structure, there is nothing to impede doubling or halving it. Determining a particular punishment should always be an exercise involving comparison of the seriousness of the offence to other offences.[63]

Some examples show the sometimes curious assessment of respective gravity of offences at the end of the nineteenth century:

- manslaughter was punishable by up to life imprisonment[64] as was attempted murder,[65] breaking and entering a dwelling-house,[66] and abortion;[67]
- conspiracy to murder was punishable with up to fourteen years imprisonment[68] as was theft by a clerk, cashier, agent or attorney;[69]
- sending a letter containing a death threat was punishable by a sentence of imprisonment up to ten years;[70]
- attempted rape had a maximum penalty of seven years imprisonment,[71] the same maximum that applied to a woman using means to procure her own miscarriage;[72]
- setting a spring-gun or man-trap had a five year maximum;[73]
- attempted suicide was punishable by up to two years imprisonment;[74]
- common assault as an indictable offence had a one-year maximum or a fine "not exceeding one hundred dollars,"[75] while on summary conviction it was punishable by imprisonment for up to two months or a fine of twenty dollars;

---

63  *Report of the Canadian Sentencing Commission*, above note 53 at 34, replicating the argument of Charles Greaves, the drafter of the English consolidation of 1861.
64  *Criminal Code, 1892*, above note 56, s. 236.
65  *Ibid.*, s. 232.
66  *Ibid.*, s. 410.
67  *Ibid.*, s. 272. This offence referred to the person who administered the "drug or other noxious thing" or uses "any instrument or other means whatsoever" to procure a woman's miscarriage, not the woman herself who would be liable to prosecution under s. 273 and liable to imprisonment for up to seven years.
68  *Ibid.*, s. 234.
69  *Ibid.*, ss. 319, 320.
70  *Ibid.*, s. 233.
71  *Ibid.*, s. 268.
72  *Ibid.*, s. 273.
73  *Ibid.*, s. 249.
74  *Ibid.*, s. 238.
75  *Ibid.*, s. 265.

- cruelty to animals, including torture, fighting or negligent usage, was punishable on summary conviction by a fine of up to $50 or up to three months imprisonment, or both.[76]

The *Criminal Code, 1892,* contained few penalties other than imprisonment. Fines were available only when expressly stipulated.[77] The *Code* contained a list of indictable offences which could be tried summarily by a magistrate.[78] Except for theft and attempted theft, which were punishable on summary conviction only by imprisonment in the common gaol for up to six months, the other offences were punishable by a similar term of confinement, or a fine of up to $100, or both.[79] A general provision, which continued in effect until 1996, provided that a fine could be attached to, or imposed in the place of, a sentence of imprisonment if the offence was punishable by no more than five years imprisonment — however, if the offence was punishable by more than five years, a fine could only be imposed in addition to imprisonment.

On the corporal side, whipping was available as an added punishment for a limited number of sexual offences including incest, gross indecency with another male, and carnal knowledge, or attempted carnal knowledge, of a girl under the age of fourteen.[80] Section 957 provided:

> Whenever whipping may be awarded for any offence, the court may sentence the offender to be once, twice or thrice whipped, within the limits of the prison, under the supervision of the medical officer of the prison; and the number of strokes and the instrument with which they shall be inflicted shall be specified by the court in the sentence; and, whenever practicable, every whipping shall take place not less than ten days before the expiration of any term of imprisonment to which the offender is sentenced for the offence.

Whipping could not be inflicted on women.

---

76  *Ibid.*, s. 512.
77  Usually these were summary conviction matters like playing in a common gaming house which was punishable by a fine between $20 and $100: *ibid.*, s. 199. Certain indicatable offences, like manipulating the value of stocks, provided for terms of imprisonment and fines: see s. 201, *ibid.*, which provided for five years imprisonment and a fine of $500.
78  See Part LV "Summary Trial of Indictable Offences," *ibid.*, ss. 782–808. The list of offences in s. 783 bears a striking similarity to those currently in s. 553, offences within the absolute jurisdiction of a provincial court judge except that in 1892 various assaults were also included.
79  *Ibid.*, ss. 787, 788.
80  *Ibid.*, s. 958 (rep. by *An Act to amend the Criminal Code (sentencing) and other Acts in consequence thereof,* S.C. 1995, c. 22, s. 6).

The *Criminal Code, 1892*, contained two precursors to the modern probation scheme, both of which involved release upon entering into a recognizance with conditions. Under section 958, in addition to any other sentence imposed, the judge or magistrate could require the offender to enter into a recognizance "or to give security to keep the peace, and be of good behaviour for any term not exceeding two years. . . ." A person who refused to enter into a recognizance could be imprisoned for up to one year following the original term of imprisonment.

Modelled after the English *First Offenders Act, 1887*, a special form of release on conditions instead of other punishment had been enacted in Canada in 1889[81] and was included in the new *Code* as sections 971 to 974 under the heading "conditional release of first offenders in certain cases." This was a rudimentary and restricted form of suspended sentence with probation, and applied only if the offence in question was not punishable by more than two years imprisonment.[82] The court was empowered to give consideration to "the youth, character, and antecedents of the offender, to the trivial nature of the offence, and to any extenuating circumstances," and release the offender "on probation of good conduct" through a recognizance with or without sureties instead of imposing the usual form of punishment. As a pre-condition to release, the court had to be satisfied that either the offender or the surety had "a fixed place of abode or regular occupation. Conditions of release were that the offender appear in court when required and "keep the peace and be of good behaviour." If it subsequently appeared that the offender had breached a condition of the recognizance, a warrant could issue and the offender would be returned to court to receive judgment for the original offence or "answer as to his conduct since his release." In the absence of a professional probation service to monitor and supervise these conditional releases, their role was limited and discriminatory given the statutory pre-conditions.

## 3) Developments Since the First *Criminal Code*

Most of the changes instituted during the twentieth century will be addressed in separate chapters later in this book where the history will be more useful in dealing with the concept or mechanism under dis-

---

81   See ss. 176, 178, 269, and 270 respectively.

82   This was extended a few years later to first offenders subject to punishment by more than two years imprisonment but the suspended sentence required the prosecutor's consent in these cases: see S.C. 1900, c. 46, s. 3.

cussion. Here, I will sketch only briefly the major categories of change introduced since the *Criminal Code, 1892*.

In 1947, Parliament introduced preventive detention, empowering a court to confine offenders potentially for life.[83] This has evolved over the years, using terms like "habitual offender," "dangerous sexual psychopath," and "dangerous offender." Although it has been changed in many respects, courts still have the power to order indeterminate detention after convicting a person of a serious personal injury offence and upon being satisfied of future dangerousness.

The last hanging took place in Canada on December 11, 1962, at the Don Jail in Toronto. Capital punishment was finally abolished in 1976. The current homicide regime imposes mandatory life sentences for first- and second-degree murder.[84] For first-degree, the prisoner is not eligible for parole until twenty-five years have been served. This is subject to the very controversial provision, now section 745.6, which permits an application to a jury for a reduction of parole ineligibility after at least fifteen years have been served. The parole ineligibility period for second-degree murder is set by the trial judge after hearing the views of the jury, and can be anywhere between ten and twenty-five years. If it is more than fifteen years, the section 745.6 process is available. This provision was amended in early 1997 to preclude serial or multiple murderers from applying and to enable the Chief Justice of a province to screen out applications where there is no reasonable prospect of success.[85]

The availability of probation was gradually extended and formal provisions for supervision enacted in 1921.[86] This encouraged the creation of a professional probation service to replace the voluntary efforts provided up until then by religious and charitable groups. Ontario began appointing probation officers in 1922 but other provinces did not join in the practice immediately. This was the source of critical comment by the 1938 Archambault Commission, which supported an expansion of probation.[87] British Columbia established a probation service in 1946. Nationally, use of the sanction began to grow in the

---

83   See the discussion in Chapter 11, below.
84   See the discussion in Chapter 10, below.
85   See *An Act to amend the Criminal Code (judicial review of parole ineligibility) and another Act*, S.C. 1996, c. 34, s. 2(2). To avoid arguments about impermissible retrospectivity, the preclusion of multiple and serial murderers only applies where at least one killing occurs after the enactment was proclaimed in force, January 9, 1997.
86   *An Act to amend the Criminal Code*, S.C. 1921, c. 25. See the discussion in Chapter 8, below.
87   See Canada, *Report of the Royal Commission to Investigate the Penal System of Canada* (Ottawa: King's Printer, 1938) at 225–31 (Chair: J. Archambault).

1950s. Until the major revision of the *Criminal Code* in 1955 removed it, an impediment to the use of suspended sentences with probation was the requirement of the prosecutor's consent if the offence was punishable by imprisonment for more than two years.[88]

An amendment in 1972 repealed the provisions which permitted whipping.[89] The same enactment introduced the new sanctions of absolute and conditional discharges,[90] which ameliorated the harshness of some prosecutions by enabling judges to make a finding of guilt but, instead of registering a conviction, impose a discharge with or without conditions. This would leave the offender, at least in theory, without a criminal record. At the same time another moderating provision was enacted, permitting sentences of imprisonment not longer than ninety days to be served intermittently.[91] Usually, the sentence was served on weekends to permit the offender to continue working or attending school. During the interim periods, the offender would be subject to a probation order. Another sanction which arose around the same time was the community service order. As a condition of a probation order, the offender was required to perform community service by devoting a stipulated number of hours of work or by performing a specific function.[92] The community service was usually directed to a charitable agency, public undertaking, or specified needy group. Since it was not specifically authorized by the *Criminal Code*, but was generated through the residual probation order power,[93] it is difficult to trace the source of the community service order to a particular date. Certainly, the acceptance of its constitutionality and efficacy by the Ontario Court of Appeal in 1976 encouraged trial judges to use it in appropriate cases.[94]

---

88   *Criminal Code*, S.C. 1953-54, c. 51, which did not re-enact the previous s. 1081(2).
89   See *Criminal Law Amendment Act, 1972*, S.C. 1972, c. 13, s. 70.
90   *Ibid.*, s. 57.
91   *Ibid.*, s. 58. See the discussion in Chapter 9, below, at 9(H).
92   *Ibid.*, s. 58. See the discussion in Chapter 9, below, at 9(H).
93   Before the 1996 amendments to the *Criminal Code*, s. 737(h) provided that a probation order could contain "such other reasonable conditions as the court considers desirable for securing the good conduct of the accused and for preventing a repetition by him of the same offence or the commission of other offences."
94   See *R. v. Shaw* (1977), 36 C.R.N.S. 358 (Ont. C.A.), involving charges of trafficking in LSD.

The manner in which sentences of imprisonment were administered changed substantially in 1959 with the establishment of the National Parole Board.[95] Amendments in 1970 ensured that prisoners whose release had been revoked for breaching a condition, including committing a new offence, were not only recommitted to confinement but also lost all remission.[96] The same enactment introduced the mandatory supervision regime which meant that federal prisoners released due to earned and statutory remission were subject to conditions just like parolees and could have their release suspended and revoked.[97] In 1986, the Board was given the power to detain prisoners beyond their mandatory supervision release date until warrant expiry if the Board was satisfied that the prisoner, if released, was likely to commit an offence causing death or serious harm before warrant expiry.[98] The *Parole Act* and *Penitentiary Act* were replaced in 1992 with a single statute, the *Corrections and Conditional Release Act*.[99] A major change that accompanied the new act was the abolition of remission for federal prisoners. Mandatory supervision was replaced with statutory release which occurs, subject to detention, after the prisoner has served two-thirds of his or her sentence.[100]

## 4)  The 1996 Reforms: Bill C-41

After two decades of public, political, and academic debate about the future of sentencing in Canada, the government of the day introduced Bill C-41 which it characterized as sentencing reform. In light of the ambitious work of the Law Reform Commission and the Sentencing Commission, many of the participants in the sentencing debates were disappointed by this legislation. It contained only a few new things. Its bulk was due to the fact that it consisted, for the most part, of a re-numbering

---

95  For a detailed history of parole, see D.P. Cole & A. Manson, "Canadian Parole Legislation and Practice: 1800–1977" in *Release from Imprisonment: The Law of Sentencing, Parole and Judicial Review* (Toronto: Carswell, 1990) 159–88.

96  *Criminal Law Amendment Act, 1968–69*, S.C. 1968–69, c. 38, s. 102. See also *Marcotte v. Canada (Deputy A.G.)*, [1976] 1 S.C.R. 108; and *Howley v. Canada (Deputy A.G.)* (1976), [1977] 2 S.C.R. 45.

97  See *Criminal Law Amendment Act, 1968–69*, above note 97, s. 101(1).

98  See *An Act to amend the Parole Act and the Penitentiary Act*, S.C. 1986, c. 42. See also *Cunningham v. Canada*, [1993] 2 S.C.R. 143. Currently, the detention provisions are in the *Corrections and Conditional Release Act*, S.C. 1992, c. 20, ss. 129–32.

99  S.C. 1992, c. 20.

100  *Ibid.*, s. 127.

of previously enacted provisions. It did make technical adjustments to fines and probation, authorized adult diversion, and also introduced a new alternative called the conditional sentence. This option, available when there is no minimum penalty, permits a judge who has concluded that a fit sentence would be imprisonment for less than two years to order that the sentence be served in the community if satisfied that doing so would not endanger the safety of the community. This provision has been extremely controversial with respect to its potential scope and the applicable methodology.[101]

Of primary importance was the insertion into the *Criminal Code* of a statement of the purpose of sentencing:

> 718. The fundamental purpose of sentencing is to contribute, along with crime prevention initiatives, to respect for the law and the maintenance of a just, peaceful and safe society by imposing just sanctions that have one or more of the following objectives:
>
> (a) to denounce unlawful conduct;
> (b) to deter the offender and other persons from committing offences;
> (c) to separate offenders from society, where necessary;
> (d) to assist in rehabilitating offenders;
> (e) to provide reparations for harm done to victims or to the community; and
> (f) to promote a sense of responsibility in offenders, and acknowledgment of the harm done to victims and to the community.[102]

While much of this language is reminiscent of the traditional rhetoric of sentencing, the Supreme Court has recognized that underlying the statement of purpose, objectives, and principles is a Parliamentary intention to reduce the use of incarceration. A concomitant aspect of this new direction is the encouragement of restorative justice principles.

---

101   *An Act to amend the Criminal Code (sentencing) and other Acts in consequence thereof*, 1st Sess., 35th Parl., 1994 (first reading 13 June 1994).

102   The idea for the inclusion of a statement of purpose, objectives and principles is usally credited to the influential 1982 publication by the Department of Justice, *The Criminal Law in Canadian Society* (Ottawa: Government of Canada, 1982). However, the Ouimet Report relied on the American Model Penal Code and recommended that the *Criminal Code* be amended to "provide Canadian courts with statutory direction on their approach to sentencing . . .": see Report of the Canadian Committee on Corrections, *Toward Unity: Criminal Justice and Corrections* (Ottawa: Queen's Printer, 1969) at 191 (Chair: R. Ouimet).

## 5)  Conclusion

Regardless of their source, the applicable principles and rules of sentencing have pragmatic effect. In Canada, many changes to the sentencing framework have not been the product of measured discussion and a balanced approach. Instead, they have been quick reactions to specific events or a changing public mood. On other occasions, however, amendments have occurred after a lengthy public debate or to correct a perceived deficiency. The current process is the sum of all these changes going back to the period before the first *Criminal Code* and must be understood as the total of a series of historical antecedents. The abbreviated account here demonstrates the many sources of both the language and the mechanisms currently in effect. The next step in understanding the context of sentencing is to survey the philosophical underpinnings which have influenced, criticized, and sometimes motivated the evolving approaches to sentencing.

## FURTHER READINGS

BEATTIE, J.M., *Crime and the Courts in England, 1660–1800* (Princeton, N.J.: Princeton University Press, 1986)

CANADIAN SENTENCING COMMISSION, *Sentencing Reform: A Canadian Approach* (Ottawa: Supply and Services Canada, 1987)

FOUCAULT, M., *Discipline and Punish: The Birth of the Prison* (New York: Vintage, 1979)

IGNATIEFF, M., *A Just Measure of Pain: The Penitentiaries in the Industrial Revolution 1750–1850* ( London: Penguin, 1978)

MELOSSI, D., & M. PAVARINI, *The Prison and the Factory: Origins of the Penitentiary System* (Totowa, N.J.: Barnes and Noble, 1981)

MORRIS, N., & D. ROTHMAN, eds., *The Oxford History of the Prison* (New York: Oxford University Press, 1995)

OLIVER, P., *Terror to Evil-Doers: Prisons and Punishments in 19th Century Ontario* (Toronto: University of Toronto Press, 1998)

RADZINOWICZ, L., & R. HOOD, *A History of the English Criminal Law*, vol. 5 (London: Stevens & Sons, 1986)

REPORT OF THE CANADIAN COMMITTEE ON CORRECTIONS, *Toward Unity: Criminal Justice and Corrections* (Ottawa: Queen's Printer, 1969)

*Report of the Royal Commission to Investigate the Penal System in Canada* (Ottawa: King's Printer, 1938)

SEMPLE, J., *Bentham's Prison: A Study of the Panopticon Penitentiary* (Oxford: Clarendon Press, 1993)

# CHAPTER 3

# THE JUSTIFICATIONS FOR PUNISHMENT

## A. INTRODUCTION

Punishments throughout history have served a number of political, economic, religious, and moral objectives. Still, the most commonly offered goal of state punishment is crime control. Because of the relationship between citizens and the state, punishments inflicted by the state on its citizens have understandably been the subject of debates which have attracted philosophers, lawyers, political theorists, and social scientists for centuries. Their purpose has been to find a convincing philosophical or empirical justification for punishment. It is important to explore these debates because of the central relationship between sentencing and punishment. As well, we find the philosophical justifications for state punishment moving into the legal sphere. For decades, they have crept into judges' explanations for specific punishments imposed on convicted persons. Now, they are also embodied in the *Criminal Code*'s new statements of purpose and objectives. It will be helpful to consider the traditional justifications and to try to understand their role and relevance in the current regime of sentencing.

In the past, most theoretical arguments have fallen into one of two schools, "retributivist" or "consequentialist." Retributivist proponents argue that the justification for punishment flows directly from the offence. In other words, the violation justifies the penal response. Consequentialist theories, often described as utilitarian, are premised on the need to produce some effect on the offender or in the community.

31

More recently, thoughtful observers have rejected a single theoretical rationale in favour of justificatory theories which borrow from both schools. In this chapter, I offer a brief and abbreviated explanation of the most common justificatory arguments and their corollaries.

## B. RETRIBUTIVIST THEORIES

There are two key aspects to any retributivist theory. First, is the notion of desert: the guilty deserve to suffer. Most retributivist approaches start with this basic proposition. It is not, however, a self-evident principle, although Stephen seemed to think so when he said in 1883 that it is "morally right to hate criminals."[1] It is important to ask whether the statement that X ought to be punished because she deserves it says any more than the circular propostion that X ought to be punished because she ought to be punished. The concept of desert, to be useful, must have more meaning than this tautology. The second key aspect of retributivism is the notion that it is the state's obligation to impose punishment. This completes the basic retributivist idea: the criminal deserves the punishment and it is the state's duty to impose it. In her summary of retributivist justifications, Nicola Lacey observes that desert "thus operates as both a necessary and a sufficient condition for justified punishment."[2]

The Biblical statement of retributivism, described as "lex talionis," is captured by the reference to "an eye for an eye." This encompasses the idea that a person who commits a certain prohibited act and causes harm must be punished. The full quotation is "life for life, eye for eye, tooth for tooth, hand for hand, foot for foot"[3] and was used in the context of explaining that the penalty for being a false witness should be the same as what was intended for the subject of the perjury. This is a rudimentary form of proportionality: the offence must be met with a proportionate penalty, not a lesser one than is deserved, nor a harsher one for some exemplary purpose like deterrence. It also suggests that offences can be ranked in terms of gravity, based on the harm caused or potentially caused. While this approach may seem attractive in its simplicity, it does not take into account questions of responsibility, excuse, or mitigation, which are central to modern criminal law.

1   See J.F. Stephen, *A History of Criminal Law of England*, vol. II (London: Macmillan, 1883) at 81.
2   N. Lacey, *State Punishment: Political Principles and Community Values* (London: Routledge, 1988) at 16.
3   Deut. 19:21.

Flowing from his view of people as self-determining actors who exercise free will, Kant developed a retributivist theory which was premised on the idea that punishment can never be administered merely as a means for promoting another social goal. Thus, punishment for deterrent purposes, whether individual or general, is unacceptable because it treats the individual as a means. Instead, people should be treated as ends which involves characterizing them as responsible moral agents whose personal welfare matters. Kant also argued that an equality must be achieved between the offence and the punishment. In total, the kind and extent of punishment must derive from the act committed after taking into account certain attributes of the actor. Kant would incorporate a number of factors into the penal calculus to determine the gravity of the offence and the appropriate punishment. Responsibility can vary based on the actor's intention. Relative gravity depends on the nature of the right violated, which may be imputed from the harm caused. While both of these factors are important in determining the kind and extent of appropriate punishment, it is also necessary to consider the situation of the offender. The offender's personal characteristics and circumstances must be taken into account to assist the court "in ensuring an equal balance between the effect of the criminal deed on society and the effect of the punishment on the offender."[4]

Kant considered that it was a "categorical obligation" for the state to impose the deserved penalty and carried this notion to its extreme ends in his often-quoted tale of the "last murderer." He argued that even at the point of the complete break up of a civil society, it was the state's duty to inflict death on someone convicted of murder. The argument assumes that the members of the society are disbursing to different parts of the world, never to communicate with each other again. If only two people remain, the "last murderer" and another person, it would be the duty of that other person to execute the murderer. To leave the murder unpunished would render all members of the society participants in the murder, or in Kant's words "accomplices in this public violation of legal justice."[5] Rupert Cross dismissed the argument:

> The weakness of Kant's position is that it does not follow from the fact that State action would be intrinsically right that it must be carried out. No doubt the execution of the last murderer could be described as

---

4    S. Young, "Kant's Theory of Punishment in a Canadian Setting" (1997) 22 Queen's L.J. 347 at 355.

5    I. Kant, *The Metaphysical Elements of Justice: Part I of the Metaphysics of Morals*, trans. J. Ladd (Indianapolis: Bobbs-Merrill, 1965) at 102.

"just" and he could properly be said to have had his deserts, but how could this last act of the hypothetical State be said to have been justified? . . . Surely most people would say that if, *per impossibile*, they were certain that a convicted criminal would never commit another crime, that failure to punish him would not in any way weaken the deterrent effect of the threat or example of punishment, and that it would not militate in any degree against the condemnation by society of the convict's crime, punishment would not be justified for, by inflicting it, the State would be allocating to itself the role of the Deity. There is force in the remark attributed to a judge "I don't punish, that is done by a higher power; I only protect society."[6]

There is little support today for Kant's exhortation to impose punishment even in the absence of any discernible benefit. Even those who argue that the moral education which flows from the imposition of punishment is sufficient regardless of the absence of other benefits could not accept the "last murderer" proposition since only the executioner would know for sure that the penalty had been carried out.

Another form of retributivist theory was offered by Hegel. Although it has often been criticized as insufficient, when viewed in the light of the recent emphasis on denunciation and arguments about the expressive or communicative nature of punishment, it may be making a modest comeback.[7] Hegel argued that the purpose of imposing punishment in response to crime was "to annul the crime, which otherwise would have been held valid, and to restore the right."[8] In other words the retributive process of punishment ought to consist of the annulment of the wrong and the re-assertion of the right or value which had been violated. This suggests that "punishment has the consequence of restoring a moral principle"[9] and suggests that denunciation can provide a legitimate justification of punishment. Like Kant who employed

---

6    R. Cross, *The English Sentencing System* (London: Butterworths, 1971) at 93.

7    See, for example, D. Garland, *Punishment and Modern Society: A Study in Social Theory* (Oxford: Clarendon Press, 1990), who does not mention Hegel, but whose chapter "Punishment as a Cultural Agent: Penality's Role in the Creation of Culture" at 249, *ibid.*, is a more nuanced account of a similar idea. See discussion below.

8    See G.W.F. Hegel, *Philosophy of Right*, trans. T.M. Knox (Oxford: Clarendon Press, 1942) at ¶99.

9    See T. Honderich, *Punishment: The Supposed Justifications* (London: Hutchinson, 1969) at 37. In Honderich's critique of Hegel's views on punishment, he makes interesting comparisons to the attraction to denunciation expressed both by Stephen and Lord Denning. For this linkage, he credits H.L.A. Hart's discussion of retribution and denunciation in *Law, Liberty, and Morality* (Oxford: Oxford University Press, 1963) at 60–69.

a principle of equality, Hegel argued for an "identity" between the harm caused and the subsequent penalty. This was not a matter of strict equality — rather, "the two injuries are equal only in respect of their implicit character, i.e. in respect of their value."[10] Again, one can distill from "identity" some notion of proportionality. It has been suggested that rehabilitation also appears in the retributive theory described in the *Philosophy of Right*. Hegel remarks that the imposition of a penalty on the offender is "a right established within the criminal himself."[11] Is this simply recognition of the offender as a rational moral agent, or does this imply that reformation is a potential consequence of some forms of punishment and that the offender has a right to claim it?[12] If Hegel intended to encompass a right to reformation, then his approach was not premised completely on retribution, but represented a merger of retributivist and consequentialist theories.

Retributivist theories have come in many forms but they all share the basic characteristic that their justificatory rationale comes from the crime committed. R.A. Duff in his 1986 book *Trials and Punishments* offers this account of retributivist theories:

> . . . or has the label 'retributivist' been applied to such a diversity of views and principles that it now lacks any unambiguous or unitary meaning? . . . Some talk of the payment of a debt incurred by crime, or of the restoration of a balance disturbed by crime; others of the expiation, atonement, or annulment of crime; others of the denunciation of crime: and we cannot suppose that these are simply different ways of expressing the same idea. But such accounts do share what can usefully be called a retributivist perspective on punishment: for they all find the sense and the justification of punishment in its relation to a past offence.[13]

According to Kant, a pure retributivist must be prepared to argue that the justification for punishment exists regardless of, and even in the absence of, consequences. While Hegel would also refer to the offence to determine the penalty, one can argue that his form of retribution includes some consideration for restoration and reformation.

---

10   Hegel, above note at ¶101.
11   *Ibid.* at ¶100 (emphasis omitted).
12   Honderich calls this interpretation a "curious reading": see Honderich, above note 9 at 39.
13   R.A. Duff, *Trials and Punishments* (Cambridge: Cambridge University Press, 1986) at 4 [*Trials and Punishments*].

## 1) Retribution and Vengeance

The conceptual relationship between retribution and vengeance has often captured the attention of philosophers. In 1968, the British Columbia Court of Appeal became involved in the debate in the case of *R. v. Hinch*:

> Reference was made before us to "retribution" as being one of the considerations involved in sentencing. I am of the opinion, with respect, that in those cases where the term "retribution" is used it is loosely equated with the word "punishment" for I cannot believe that "vengeance," a common meaning of the term "retribution," was ever intended. The application of such a meaning involves a loss of that objectivity which is essential to the exercise of the judicial process.[14]

The court concluded that the term "retribution" should be excluded from sentencing discourse because of its apparent affinity with vengeance.

Hegel relied on the distinction between public and private prosecutions to explain the difference between punishment as just retribution and punishment as vengeance. He argued that punishment, as an instrument of justice, had to be freed from subjective interest and the contingency of individual might. A more comprehensive and compelling argument can be found in Robert Nozick's *Philosophical Explanations*.[15] Nozick explained five ways in which punishment as desert differs from revenge:

1. Retribution responds to an offence, a wrong; revenge may flow from a triggering event or circumstance but this need not be a wrong;
2. Retribution is limited in its extent by the seriousness of the offence, whereas there are no internal limits on the amount of revenge inflicted;
3. Revenge is personal (as Hegel had argued), while the agent of retribution has no personal tie to the victim;
4. Revenge carries a self-satisfied tone or pleasure upon inflicting suffering upon another, while retribution need not involve any special emotional tone; and
5. Retribution derives from a general principle, imposing deserved punishment in response to an offence, which is usually clear and known; there need be no generality to revenge. It occurs when and how the seeker of revenge decides.[16]

---

14   *R. v. Hinch*, [1968] 3 C.C.C. 39 at 43, Norris J.A. (B.C.C.A.).
15   R. Nozick, *Philosophical Explanations* (Cambridge, Mass.: Belknap Press, 1981).
16   *Ibid.* at 366–68.

Nozick recognized that penalties can sometimes be inflicted for mixed motives, or that events may be linked in ways that, while not causal, generate confusion about their interrelationship. Accordingly, he offered a complex proposition which encompassed nine characteristics of retribution. Only if all are present could one say that a penalty inflicted after a wrong had been committed was intentionally imposed in response to the wrongfulness of the act.[17]

A more recent and pertinent discussion of the distinction between retribution and vengeance was provided by Chief Justice Lamer in *R. v. M.(C.A.)*, which involved the sentencing of a man convicted of a series of horrible physical and sexual assaults committed on his children over a period of years.[18] The appeal specifically raised the question of whether there should be a judicially imposed limit of twenty years imprisonment on fixed-term cumulative sentences when life imprisonment is not available. It also forced the Supreme Court to address some of the fundamental concepts that shape our sentencing system. For the court, Lamer C.J.C. said:

> . . . retribution bears little relation to vengeance, and I attribute much of the criticism of retribution as a principle to this confusion. As both academic and judicial commentators have noted, vengeance has no role to play in a civilized system of sentencing. . . . Vengeance, as I understand it, represents an uncalibrated act of harm upon another, frequently motivated by emotion and anger, as a reprisal for harm inflicted upon oneself by that person. Retribution in a criminal context, by contrast, represents an objective, reasoned and measured determination of an appropriate punishment which properly reflects the *moral culpability* of the offender, having regard to the intentional risk-taking of the offender, the consequential harm caused by the offender, and the normative character of the offender's conduct. Furthermore, unlike vengeance, retribution incorporates a principle of restraint; retribution requires the imposition of a just and appropriate punishment, and *nothing more.*[19]

This judicial opinion conforms neatly with the views of Nozick.

---

17  *Ibid.* at 369.
18  [1996] 1 S.C.R. 500. See the discussion of this case in Chapter 5, below.
19  *Ibid.* at 557–58.

## 2) Just Deserts

At the centre of many debates about sentencing reform in various jurisdictions over the past twenty years has been the notion of "just
deserts," a retributivist approach to sentencing. The major prolific and
articulate proponent of "just deserts" has been Andrew von Hirsch,
starting with his 1976 book entitled *Doing Justice: The Choice of Punishments*. However, the genesis of the idea can be traced to some very
important analytical observations by H.L.A. Hart. In *Punishment and
Responsibility*, Hart considered the issue of the justifying aims of punishment and observed:

> What is needed is the realization that different principles (each of
> which may in a sense be called a "justification") are relevant at differ-
> ent points in any morally acceptable account of punishment.[20]

This led him to pose some specific questions: What justifies the general
practice of punishment? To whom may punishment be applied? How
severely may we punish? One could argue that retribution as a general
justifying aim is different from retribution as it relates to distribution
and issues of severity; this latter form of retribution does not seek to justify the infliction of pain but rather to quantify the amount of pain. This
distinction was put another way by von Hirsch, who said that it "was
pointed out a quarter of a century ago, by H.L.A. Hart, that one can use
the notion of crime prevention to explain the existence of punishment
without being compelled to rely on it to decide how much to punish."[21]

Desert is the focus of von Hirsch's argument for determining the
appropriate punishment. However, he does not accept that it must be
either the determining factor or a limit on the amount of punishment.
Instead, he argues that the role of desert and proportionality is more
complex. There are, according to von Hirsch, two basic questions: (1)
how crimes should be punished relative to each other; and (2) the specific level or severity of punishment for a specific crime. These questions
represent the "*ordinal* and *cardinal* magnitudes of punishment."[22] Desert
determines the first question, but it only serves as a limit in answering
the second. The von Hirsch approach requires a system to gauge the relative gravity of its offences by assessing harm and culpability:

---

20   H.L.A. Hart, *Punishment and Responsibility: Essays in the Philosophy of Law*
(Oxford: Clarendon Press, 1968) at 3.

21   See A. von Hirsch, *Past or Future Crimes: Deservedness and Dangerousness in the
Sentencing of Criminals* (New Brunswick, N.J.: Rutgers University Press, 1985) at 48.

22   *Ibid.* at 39.

Harm refers to the injury done or risked by the criminal act. Culpability refers to the factors of intent, motive, and circumstance that determine how much the offender should be held accountable for his act. Culpability, in turn, affects the assessment of harm. The consequences that should be considered in gauging the harmfulness of an act should be those that can fairly be attributed to the actor's choice. This militates, for example, against including in harm the unforeseeable consequences of the act, or the consequences wrought by other independent actors who happen to choose similar actions.[23]

Then, a penalty scale must be developed by anchoring the specific punishments for at least some offences. The others will fit on the scale depending on their relative gravity to the anchored offences. The points on the anchored scale must be appropriately spaced to reflect different levels of seriousness exemplified by the different offence points. Von Hirsch accepts that anchoring is an imprecise exercise but that much can be learned from the penal traditions of the jurisdiction. Normative considerations and some preventive strategies, like selective incapacitation, may also be applicable to the issue of finding the anchoring points.

The Canadian Sentencing Commission seemed to be impressed with "just deserts."[24] In advocating what was essentially a "just deserts" or proportionality-based model, it defended von Hirsch and said:

> The view that "just deserts" is simply a rediscovery of retributivism is incorrect. Andrew von Hirsch has always argued that if punishment was a useless instrument for controlling crime, one could not justify its existence on purely retributivist grounds. Without the support of utilitarian considerations, retributivism becomes a circular argument or is reduced to the blind assertion that crimes ought to be punished.[25]

This comment accepts that there must be some concomitant or derivative crime prevention benefit to justify a just desert scheme. In his more recent work, von Hirsch has emphasized the role of censure. In terms of the multi-layered effect of the focused expression of disapprobation which is central to the sentencing function, he considers censure to be more important than prevention in his sentencing theory.[26]

23  Ibid. at 64–65.
24  Canadian Sentencing Commission, Sentencing Reform: A Canadian Approach (Ottawa: Supply and Services Canada, 1987) at 129–31 [Report of the Canadian Sentencing Commission].
25  Ibid. at 143.
26  See A. von Hirsch, Censure and Sanctions (Oxford: Oxford University Press, 1993).

Regardless of the rank attached to crime prevention, one has to ask whether a model that assumes a crime prevention benefit still qualifies as a pure retributivist model. More significantly, does the use of crime prevention in explaining a model undermine the centrality of proportionality?

Michael Tonry has offered a number of basic criticisms of "just deserts."[27] He argues that the process of categorizing like offenders and offences is both over-simplified and over-inclusive. Real cases cannot be conveniently or fairly grouped to produce categories of "like-situated offenders."[28] Moreover, the costs to individuals of imprecise objectification are too great since the same imprecision characterizes the quantification of deservedness and thereby determines punishment. Tonry argues that, by the same token, as fault is usually individualized for responsibility purposes by taking into account excuses, formal mitigation, and derivative responsibility, so, for sentencing purposes, the issue of culpability should also be tailored to the individual. Then, there is the issue of whether society is sufficiently just or equal to justify applying desert-determined penalties across the board. Given the disproportionate number of offenders from disadvantaged and marginalized backgrounds, can one justify making generic assessments of deservedness and imposing "like" penalties? Tonry also argues that a "just deserts" model violates what he calls the principle of parsimony which states that the appropriate penalty should be the least intrusive and restrictive required to fairly respond to the offence. In Tonry's view, the "challenge is not to decide between proportionality and parsimony, but to balance them in ways that preserve important elements of each."[29] He concludes his critique with the serious question of whether it can be legitimate to impose an "illusion of equality of suffering" on individuals who have not been the recipients of equal treatment in most other aspects of their lives. These important questions need to be addressed before anyone accepts "just deserts" as a model for fair and ethically consistent sentencing reform.

---

27  See M. Tonry, "Proportionality, Parsimony, and Interchangeability of Punishments" in A. Duff, S. Marshall, R.E. Dobash, & R.P. Dobash, eds., *Penal Theory and Practice: Tradition and Innovation in Criminal Justice* (Manchester: Manchester University Press, 1994) at 59.
28  Commenting on what he called "illusory proportionality," Tonry remarked that neither "offenders nor punishments come in standard cases": *ibid.* at 69.
29  *Ibid.* at 80.

# C. CONSEQUENTIALIST OR UTILITARIAN JUSTIFICATIONS

These approaches to sentencing find their justificatory force in the assumed benefit that the sentence will produce for society. That benefit may be as simple as incapacitation; the offender represents a risk of future harm and, therefore, incarceration is supported by the benefit to the community of removing that risk for the period of the sentence. Rehabilitation produces a social benefit, by reforming the offender so that a violator of the community's norms becomes a productive participant in the community's structures. Deterrence is a more amorphous concept. Specific or individual deterrence refers to the beneficial impact on the offender: that is, punishment delivers a lesson to the offender which deters the person from future criminality. General deterrence assumes that the punishment provides a lesson to others who will consequently be deterred in the future. Recently, utilitarian goals have been subjected to scrutiny. Empirical studies, discussed below, have questioned the assumptions upon which some approaches rest, and consequently question the validity of the justification itself. Moreover, one must ask whether the assumed benefit is worth the societal and individual cost.

A recurrent question which entertains philosophers is the situation of the innocent. If the justification for punishment does not derive from the offence but from some future benefit to society, why not pursue the benefit regardless of guilt? Why should a community not implement deterrent, rehabilitative, and incapacitative programs without, or regardless of, a conviction for a criminal offence? Retributivists need an offence to justify punishment, but do consequentialists? If we put the possibility of beneficial consequences aside for a moment, we will remember that we are discussing the criminal justice system. It invokes the word "justice" for a reason. We expect that processes will be just and decisions well-grounded. While we might debate the fairness or justice of specific decisions, or challenge the ethics of particular santions, or question the competence of certain decision-makers, there are fundamental precepts which we must embrace. Surely we must agree that any scheme which encompasses punishing the innocent would be unacceptable. Any process that would choose individuals without fault, without blame, and without responsibility, and inflict pain upon them against their will for possible future benefit to others is not a process that can call itself just. It is necessary to keep this criticism in mind when assessing the utilitarian goals and their modern manifestations.

Utilitarianism is often attributed to the European Enlightenment, especially Mill's liberalism and the penal ideas of Beccaria and Bentham. However, Plato advocated a consequentialist basis of punishment in the fifth century BC. In his *Gorgias*, he put the following statement in Socrates' mouth:

> Everyone who is punished, and rightly punished, ought either to be benefited and become better, or serve as an example to others that they may behold these sufferings and through fear become better.[30]

Invoking a notion of curability, Plato argued that those who could be reformed should be improved by the infliction of pain while those who are not reformable should be made examples of by subjecting them to the "most terrible and painful and fearful suffering." Plato's deterrent concerns are directed both at the offender and others.

The utilitarianism emanating from eighteenth and nineteenth century Europe was much less harsh in its nature. Bentham offered twelve principles circumscribing the scope and content of punishment. In his view, punishment should:

1) be variable both in intensity and duration;
2) be equable, imposing a roughly equal degree of pain independent of circumstance;
3) be commensurable (that is, a greater offence should attract a greater penalty);
4) possess "characteristicalness," (that is, have some obvious connection with the crime, perhaps by analogy);
5) be exemplary to deter others;
6) be frugal (keeping a man inactive in prison is an expensive waste of productive power; shooting him is cheap, but "everything he might be made to produce is lost");
7) tend to reform the criminal, not encourage him in his vices;
8) prevent him repeating his crime;
9) be convertible to profit to compensate for the wrong;
10) be popular to avoid public resistance to the law;
11) be simply described and easily understood; and
12) be remissible for those unjustly convicted.[31]

---

30  Plato, *Gorgias*, trans. W.C. Helmbold (Indianapolis: Bobbs-Merrill, 1952) at ¶525.
31  J. Semple, *Bentham's Prison: A Study of the Panopticon Penitentiary* (Oxford: Clarendon Press, 1993) at 26–27. The twelve principles are from Bentham's *The Rationale of Punishment*, probably written in the late 1770s and first published in French by Etienne Dumont in 1811. It was not published in English until 1830: see J. Bentham, *The Rationale of Punishment* (London: R. Heward, 1830).

While some of the language is unusual, most of the concepts provide links, in very general terms, to contemporary ideas about discretion, proportionality, and fairness. It must be remembered that Bentham was writing during the transition from a punishment system premised on the death penalty to one employing imprisonment as its major instrument. Hence his concern to have offenders working and producing revenue, a central element of his Panopticon proposal. The notion of "remissibility" would ensure that death and mutilation not be available as a punishment.

During the nineteenth century, the work of Bentham, Beccaria, and Mill "played an important part in shaping the penal codes of this period, giving pride of place to deterrent measures and emphasizing the freedom of all rational individuals to obey the law."[32] At the beginning of the twentieth century, new attitudes towards crime and criminality developed which suggested that many offenders were destined to offend given their psychological, social, and economic backgrounds. This moved the utilitarian focus from deterrence to incapacitation and rehabilitation. The assumption was that many offenders could be assessed and classified in terms of both reformative and risk potential — the former points to treatment and training, while the latter justifies incapacitation.

## 1) Deterrence

Both in individual and general terms, this has been a prominent goal or justification of punishment with roots that can be traced back to Plato. But is it true that punishment does deter? Is there any empirical proof to support the proposition that punishment deters the individual and can deter others? There are some layers of subtlety to the question. First, one must distinguish between deterrence as a goal of punishment generally and as the operative factor in determining a specific punishment for a particular offender. Second, if there is evidence to support the existence of deterrent effects, is it the result of punishment or the larger process of detection, conviction, and sentencing? There are important differences between saying "I choose not to act this way because of the likelihood of arrest and public prosecution," compared to "I choose not to do this because I have experienced or heard about the punishment and that prospect deters me."

Until recently, most people have assumed that the fear of punishment motivates people to conform to legal strictures. Certainly, this would be the response of nineteenth century liberals: everyone will act

---

32    Garland, above note 7 at 208.

to increase their personal benefit, including the avoidance of pain. In other words, since punishment means the infliction of pain or imposition of burdens, people will make law-conforming choices to avoid punishment. However, the limited research suggests that the issue is more complex. The fact that most of the recent research has been directed to the issue of general deterrence suggests that there is little or no doubt about specific deterrence. But does specific deterrence actually work? The individual deterrence generated by a specific sanction should be demonstrated by a reduction in recidivism. Using incarceration as the yardstick, data shows, however, that for some offenders recidivism may increase with this sanction compared to a community-situated sentence with "appropriate correctional treatment."[33]

A recent meta-analysis conducted by Canadian criminologists attempted to examine the effects of incarceration on recidivism.[34] The authors reviewed fifty studies which involved a total of 336,052 offenders. They concluded that "[n]one of the analysis conducted produced any evidence that prison sentences reduce recidivism."[35] In fact, they found that prison produced a slight increase in recidivism with a tendency for "lower risk offenders to be more negatively affected by the prison experience."[36] They offered the following policy implications:

- prisons should not be used "with the expectation of reducing criminal behaviour";
- the excessive use of imprisonment has "enormous cost implications";
- it is important to determine who is being adversely affected by imprisonment and this requires "repeated, comprehensive assessments of offenders' attitudes, values, and behaviours" during incarceration; and
- incapacitation should be the primary justification of imprisonment.[37]

While noting the need for more discriminating empirical research that would provide richer data about the effects of imprisonment assessed in relation to specific risk factors and internal prison conditions and situations, the report raises serious questions about the usually assumed

33   See Canadian Centre for Justice Statistics, *A Review of the National and International Literature and Recommendations for a National Study on Recidivism* (Ottawa: Statistics Canada, 1997), quoted by Rosenberg J.A. in R. v. *Wismayer* (1997), 5 C.R. (5th) 248, 115 C.C.C. (3d) 18 (Ont. C.A.).

34   See P. Gendreau, C. Goggin, & F.T. Cullen, *The Effects of Prison Sentences on Recidivism* (Ottawa: Solicitor General, 1999).

35   *Ibid.* at 18.

36   *Ibid.* at 2.

37   *Ibid.*

effect of incarceration. This suggests that penal responses need to be well-tailored to the specific offender, or courts run the risk of producing unwanted results.

The mass of general deterrence research has not produced definitive answers. During the 1970s in the United States, the National Research Council's Academy of Behavioral and Social Sciences established an expert panel to examine the deterrence issue. Its influential report, published in 1978, summarized its conclusion with the often-quoted statement that it could not "assert that the evidence warrants an affirmative conclusion regarding deterrence."[38] Daniel Nagin, a member of the panel's staff, provided a more detailed conclusion to his review of deterrence literature:

> The past decade has witnessed a burgeoning of analyses directed at testing the deterrence hypothesis for non-capital sanctions. In this critique over 20 published analyses are cited, and even this list is less than exhaustive. Yet, despite the intensity of the research effort, the empirical evidence is still not sufficient for providing a rigorous confirmation of the existence of a deterrent effect. Perhaps more important, the evidence is woefully inadequate for providing a good estimate of the magnitude of whatever effect may exist.
>
> . . . Certainly, most people will agree that increasing sanctions will deter crime somewhat, but the critical question is, by how much? There is still considerable uncertainty over whether that effect is trivial (even if statistically detectable) or profound. Any unequivocal policy conclusion is simply not supported by valid evidence.[39]

Nagin offered the pointed caution that anyone proposing new policies premised on deterrence should recognize the inadequacy of existing evidence to support their proposals. The Panel's views on deterrence found support in the Canadian Sentencing Commission, which undertook its own review of existing evidence and reported in 1987. The Commission accepted that "legal sanctions have an overall deterrent effect which is difficult to evaluate precisely."[40] It also agreed that studies supported the view that whatever deterrent effect existed, it was more due to certainty of punishment than severity of punishment.

---

38 National Research Council, Panel on Research on Deterrent and Incapacitative Effects, *Deterrence and Incapacitation: Estimating the Effects of Criminal Sanctions on Crime Rates*, A. Blumstein, J. Cohen, & D. Nagin, eds. (Washington: National Academy of Sciences, 1978) at 7.
39 *Ibid.* at 135–36.
40 *Report of the Canadian Sentencing Commission*, above note 24 at 136–37.

In 1999, a group of well-respected scholars at the University of Cambridge Institute of Criminology published a report on recent deterrence literature.[41] Their review found that there is some correlation between certainty of punishment and the rate of crime but no evidence of any statistically significant correlation between the severity of punishment and crime.[42] Both of these conclusions are consistent with earlier research. The report speculates that the "uncertain and seemingly limited effects" of severity on crime can be attributed to the following factors:[43]

- information about changes in penalties is not communicated as efficiently or quickly as information about changes in the likelihood of apprehension which can be observed directly from an increased police presence and other surveillance activities;
- more severe penalties are always contingent and contingent future costs are discounted; and
- the threshold effect that occurs as penalties rise.[44]

In summary, the evidence seems clear that some general deterrent effect accompanies the process of arrest, conviction, and punishment but it is probably linked to certainty and not to severity. In other words, assuming the existence of general deterrence, an increase in sentence severity is not likely to generate a proportionate increase in deterrence.

## 2) Incapacitation

Essentially, this refers to the use of imprisonment to incapacitate offenders who are considered to represent future risks. "Collective incapacitation" refers to a strategy which calls for the incarceration of all persons who commit a certain offence. The more popular form is known as "selective incapacitation" where individuals are assessed to determine the risk that they pose. The validity of this goal of sentencing depends on the ability of the sentencing system to predict dangerousness accurately. Another variation on the incapacitation theme involves consid-

---

41   See A. von Hirsch, A.E. Bottoms, E. Burney, & P.-O. Wilkström, *Criminal Deterrence and Sentence Severity: An Analysis of Recent Research* (Oxford: Hart, 1999).

42   *Ibid.* at 45.

43   *Ibid.* at 47–48.

44   This refers to the idea that a point is crossed at which those who are deterrable will be deterred but those unaffected by deterrence are still not deterrable. Thereafter, as the penalty increases, the increase is unnecessary for those who are deterrable and useless for those who are not.

ering the extent of recidivism which can be associated with specific offences that are carefully defined to include the elements and external circumstances which are believed to have the most direct and significant relation to recidivism. These are targeted for incarceration. This approach is known as "categorical incapacitation."

Excluding assaults while in prison, it is self-evidently true that the imprisonment of offender "X" reduces crime in the community to some extent because "X" is not there to commit crime. The extent of the reduction is speculative since it requires knowing how much crime "X" would commit. Accordingly, the question is not whether incapacitation works but rather how much incapacitation is warranted by reliable information available to the sentencer and how much a community can afford. The Panel on Research on Deterrent and Incapacitative Effects had no difficulty accepting that there is a reasonable presumption that imprisonment produces an incapacitative effect but its extent depends on knowing certain unknowables: (1) how much crime would the incarcerated have committed; and (2) how much would have been committed by others if the incarcerated were not available to be the perpetrators.

Advocates of incapacitation need to address the inherent difficulties associated with generalizations about recidivism and the controversies over predictions of dangerousness. Included in the Panel's report is a critique by John Monahan of prediction research in which he rejects clinical prediction by concluding that it will be wrong two times out of three.[45] Over fifteen years later, he recognized improvements in actuarial prediction through the use of better predictor variables. He and his co-author offered the following comment:

> If an actuarially valid array of risk markers for violence could be reliably identified, clinicians could be trained to incorporate these factors into their routine practice, and the accuracy of clinical predictions of violence among the mentally disordered would be commensurately increased. Such an increase in predictive accuracy would not obviate the profound questions of social policy . . . or of professional ethics . . . that attend any preventive use of the state's police power.[46]

---

45   See J. Monahan, "The Prediction of Violent Criminal Behavior: A Methodological Critique and Prospectus" in National Research Council, Panel on Research on Deterrent and Incapacitative Effects, above note 38 at 244.

46   J. Monahan & H.J. Steadman, eds., *Violence and Mental Disorder: Developments in Risk Assessment* (Chicago: University of Chicago Press, 1994) at 13.

The authors add that improving predictive tools so that fewer individuals would be erroneously confined as "dangerous" and fewer people would be victimized by people erroneously released would be "no small thing."

## 3) Rehabilitation

This goal is premised on a therapeutic view of criminality which suggests that some people are amenable to treatment or training, enabling them to become constructive participants in the community rather than violators of its laws. The argument is simply that a sanction which reforms the offender and prevents future crime is justifiable. There are two distinct aspects to rehabilitative approaches. First, there is the custodial issue which relates to the choice of sanction: Should a person be allowed to pursue a community-based sentence based entirely on rehabilitative goals regardless of other penal considerations? Second, with respect to imprisonment, do correctional programs produce rehabilitation and thereby reduce future crime?

As a general justification for punishment, the rehabilitative rationale was thrown into doubt in the mid-1970s by Robert Martinson, a sociologist at City College in New York. He was engaged with other researchers in an assessment of studies which evaluated the rehabilitative effects of various methods of correctional programming.[47] Martinson published a premature report of this enormous study without the concurrence of his co-researchers. Using the deceptive title of "What Works?,"[48] the pessimistic article soon became known in the field as "Nothing Works!" His point, however, was that none of the evaluation studies which his research had considered revealed a program that could claim it successfully rehabilitated offenders. This is not to say that some offenders did not receive rehabilitative benefits, sometimes long-lasting and substantial. However, success is difficult to measure[49]

---

47  This was eventually published as D. Lipton, R. Martinson, & J. Wilks, *The Effectiveness of Correctional Treatment: A Survey of Treatment Evaluation Studies* (New York: Praeger, 1975). This study examined evaluations of programs categorized into the following groups: probation, imprisonment, parole, casework and individual counselling, skill development, individual psychotherapy, group methods, milieu therapy, partial physical custody, medical methods, and leisure-time activities.

48  R. Martinson, "What Works? Questions and Answers About Prison Reform" (1974) 35 Pub. Interest 22.

49  The study by Lipton, Martinson, & Wilks, above note 47, assessed the effects of programs on recidivism, institutional adjustment, vocational adjustment, educational achievement, drug and alcohol readdiction, personality and attitude change, and community adjustment.

and could not be guaranteed. Given the variability of human conduct and human nature this conclusion should have come as no surprise. While the study cast doubt on how much rehabilitation could be expected within a coercive environment, the principal researchers found that some programs benefited some people. Later, Martinson publicly clarified his earlier remarks, indicating that when the set of assessments was expanded beyond the tight criteria used by the "Effectiveness of Correctional Treatment" study, one found evidence of programs that produced benefits and programs that were harmful, depending on the context and the kind of offenders.[50] One form of programming which received Martinson's support was parole supervision. The "nothing works" misnomer did a lot of damage, fitting neatly into the emerging "law and order" landscape. However, by the end of the 1980s there was empirical and conceptual support for re-injecting some enthusiasm into the rehabilitative objective.[51] This does not mean that imprisonment can be justified by a rehabilitative goal, but that there is value in including rehabilitative programs into the systemic context. More importantly, since one of the concerns about rehabilitation in prison is the effect of the coercive environment, there is greater support for the position that non-custodial sentences can legitimately be premised on rehabilitative goals.[52]

# D. MERGED THEORIES

It now seems clear that any attempt to construct a single monochromatic justification for punishment in general will be so riddled with defects that it will fail to provide a persuasive premise. The need to blend justifications is not new. In 1764, Beccaria said:

---

50  R. Martinson, "New Findings, New Views: A Note of Caution Regarding Sentencing Reform" (1979) 7 Hofstra L. Rev. 243. Whether this should be considered as clarification or recantation is debatable.

51  See, for example, T. Palmer, *A Profile of Correctional Effectiveness and New Directions for Research* (Albany: State University of New York Press, 1994).

52  See the discussion of the Sentencing Commission which accepted that sentences could be "individualized" to pursue rehabilitative goals but cautioned that this "legitimate practice" should not "be used to cover up evidence of unwarranted disparity in the imposition of custodial sentences": *Report of the Canadian Sentencing Commission*, above note 24 at 139.

The aim, then, of punishment can only be to prevent the criminal committing new crimes against his countrymen, and to keep others from doing likewise. Punishments, therefore, and the method of inflicting them, should be chosen in due proportion to the crime so as to make the most efficacious and lasting impression on the minds of men, and the least painful impressions on the body of the criminal.[53]

This eighteenth century argument combines deterrence, desert, and restraint. It reflects the position that tangible consequences ought to be the fundamental objective but that proportionality is essential to ensure that punishment does not exceed what is deserved. Utilitarians cannot precipitously pursue social ends without regard for guilt or differential levels of culpability. They cannot seek exemplary or rehabilitative objectives which involve infringements of liberty beyond the degree warranted by the gravity of the offence.

The attraction of merged theories was solidified by H.L.A. Hart's *Punishment and Responsibility*,[54] where he demonstrated both the inadequacies and irreconcilability of consequentialist and retributivist justifications. He began his discussion of merged models with the observation that most contemporary forms of retributive theory recognize that any theory of punishment purporting to be relevant to a modern system of criminal law must allot an important place to the utilitarian conception that the institution of criminal punishment is to be justified as a method of preventing harmful crime, even if the mechanism of prevention is fear rather than the reinforcement of moral inhibition.[55] While this statement spoke only to deterrence and crime prevention, Hart was aware that other utilitarian grounds could also be rolled into a justificatory theory along with retributive aims.

In 1974 Norval Morris published *The Future of Imprisonment*,[56] in which he described a form of merged theory. He argued that imprisonment must be guided by the principle of parsimony, that the least restrictive sanction needed "to achieve defined social purposes should be imposed."[57] However, it can never be based on a prediction of future dangerousness and must always be limited in severity by desert. He has extended this basic approach combining parsimony and desert to

53   C. Beccaria, *On Crimes and Punishments*, trans. J. Grigson (New York: Marsilio, 1996) at 49.
54   Above note 20.
55   *Ibid.* at 235–36.
56   N. Morris, *The Future of Imprisonment* (Chicago: University of Chicago Press, 1974).
57   *Ibid.* at 59–60.

encompass "intermediate sanctions."[58] R.A. Duff, a leading contemporary writer in the philosphy of punishment, believes that the two schools of thought can be merged to produce an integrated model:

> We may portray punishment as essentially goal-directed, thus abandoning the traditional retributivist's insistence that it must be justified without reference to any further goals which it may serve: but we may also insist that it is *internally* related to its justifying goals, thus rejecting the consequentialist view that the relationship is purely contingent.[59]

According to him, a system of punishment must satisfy the demands of both justice and utility. It must efficiently pursue consequences which are sufficiently substantial to justify it, but it must also be rooted firmly in a conception of desert that recognizes the "intrinsic demands of justice." This does not, however, resolve the debate about whether desert can be a justificatory engine so long as the system can be shown to produce beneficial consequences, or whether it ought to be used solely as a mediating or constraining device that limits sanctions which are determined by utilitarian goals. For Duff, in common with other contemporary thinkers, the ultimate answer may lie in a slightly different direction that focuses on the expressive role of the sentence.

# E. COMMUNICATIVE THEORIES

Beyond the debate about utility and desert, and the efforts to develop merged theories as a third category of justifications, we are seeing recognition of another kind of theoretical approach that focuses on the expressive medium of sentencing. In some ways, von Hirsch's recent emphasis on censure as a supplement to the normative retributive thrust of his just deserts approach is a form of communicative or expressive theory. It was recently characterized in this way by Tony Bottoms.[60]

Duff in his 1986 book *Trials and Punishments* explained the potential expressive role of punishment:

---

58   See N. Morris & M. Tonry, *Between Prison and Probation: Intermediate Punishments in a Rational Sentencing System* (New York: Oxford University Press, 1990).

59   *Trials and Punishments*, above note 13 at 7. See also R.A. Duff, "Penal Communications: Recent Work in the Philosophy of Punishment" (1996) 20 Crime & Just. 1 ["Penal Communications"].

60   See A. Bottoms, "Five Puzzles in von Hirsch's Theory of Punishment" in A. Ashworth & M. Wasik, eds., *Fundamentals of Sentencing Theory: Essays in Honour of Andrew von Hirsch* (Oxford: Clarendon Press, 1998) 53 at 84–89.

Punishment, we may say, expresses condemnation: it denounces and formally disapproves the criminal's act; it disavows that act as one which is not to be tolerated or condoned. . . . Though this condemnation is expressed to the criminal himself, punishment may also communicate to the public at large (and especially to potential criminals) a reminder of the wrongness of the criminal's conduct, and to the victims of crime an authoritative disavowal of such conduct. But if we are to avoid the charge that in punishing a criminal we are simply using him as a means to some communicative purpose which is directed at others, its essential expressive aim must be that of communicating to the criminal himself a proper condemnation of his crime.[61]

This description encompasses a number of relevant concepts, principally desert, denunciation, and deterrence. It also includes victims and their need to hear disavowal. Significantly, Duff recognized that the expression of punishment is done on behalf of the community, not simply by an agent of the state, and is directed to the offender as a rational and responsible member of that community. Perhaps he was using the notion of community as a springboard for the inclusion of consequences like reparation, restoration, and rehabilitation as important elements of an expressive theory. In later work, Duff expanded his ideas and developed a "communicative account of punishment, as a penitential process that aims to bring the offender to repent her crime and, through her repentance, to repair those relationships that it damaged."[62] In so doing, he accepted the inherent difficulty in setting levels of punishment. However, Duff is not a philosopher who ignores the actual context of sentencing. His answer to this problem lies in the "principle of penal parsimony" and leads him to argue for an overall strategy of reducing the levels of punishment, especially the use and length of prison sentences.[63]

Another major influence on current thinking about punishment which can also be described as a communicative theory[64] has been David Garland's *Punishment and Modern Society*.[65] Garland argues that punishment must be viewed as a social institution which is influenced by prevailing cultural patterns and also influences those cultural pat-

---

61   *Trials and Punishments*, above note 13 at 235–36.
62   "Penal Communications," above note 59 at 88, and 51–67.
63   *Ibid.* at 67. He describes this approach as a "decremental strategy."
64   Duff prefers "communicative" to "expressive" since expression does not necessarily capture the need for both expression and reception which are both included in the notion of communication: *ibid.* at 32.
65   Garland, above note 7.

terns. In terms of punishment, what is tolerable, what is humane, what is expedient, will be culturally determined. At the same time, the social institution of punishment will be a cultural agent through a process of "social signification." The expressive meanings of the forms of punishment and the imposition of punishment in response to deviance and harm will have resonance throughout a community:

> In the course of its routine activities, punishment teaches, clarifies, dramatizes, and authoritatively enacts some of the basic moral-political categories and distinctions which help form our symbolic universe. It routinely interprets events, defines conduct, classifies action, and evaluates worth, and, having done so, it sanctions these judgments with the authority of law, forcefully projecting them on to offenders and the public audience alike.[66]

In some ways, this is reminiscent of the Hegelian "annul the crime and restore the right" approach discussed earlier in this chapter. Garland accepts that the principal meaning conveyed by punishment is "a symbolism of censure, condemnation, and reprobation" (annulment) but that this is accompanied by other meanings that convey "a dramatic, performative representation of the way things officially are and ought to be" (restoration).[67]

The process of signification which Garland describes requires us to think of punishment as a complex social institution with impacts beyond what happens to a particular offender or set of offenders and "helps define the nature of our society, the kinds of relationships which compose it, and the kinds of lives that it is possible and desirable to lead there."[68] Thus any evaluation of a form of punishment must transcend the one-dimensional instrumental questions of crime control and invoke broader more complex criteria, such as those that we would ordinarily apply to other integral social institutions. As Garland explains:

> we need an enriched form of penological thinking which considers penality as an institution through which society defines and expresses itself at the same time and through the same means that it exercises power over deviants.[69]

While Garland's linking of punishment to culture may seem to lack practical implication, one need only think about the constant debates

---

66   *Ibid.* at 252.
67   *Ibid.* at 265.
68   *Ibid.* at 287.
69   *Ibid.* at 291.

about crime and punishment taking place in our legislatures and in the media. These must be viewed as discourses which engage an important social institution and necessarily must transcend the banality of snippets of crime statistics, or an account of the inherent tragedy of a specific offence. A clear example is provided by disputes over the utility of capital punishment. These controversies engage deeply held and broadly influential attitudes that are only partly about crime — they are also about ideology, morality, religion, class, and race. In similar but less self-evident ways, debates about conditional sentences, fines, penitentiaries, boot camps, parole, and other aspects of the penal landscape need to be understood as manifestations of broader themes.

## FURTHER READINGS

ASHWORTH, A., & M. WASIK, eds., *Fundamentals of Sentencing Theory: Essays in Honour of Andrew von Hirsch* (Oxford: Clarendon Press, 1998)

CANADIAN SENTENCING COMMISSION, *Sentencing Reform: A Canadian Approach* (Ottawa: Supply and Services Canada, 1987)

DUFF, R.A., S. MARSHALL, & R. DOBASH, eds., *Penal Theory and Practice: Tradition and Innovation in Criminal Justice* (Manchester: Manchester University Press, 1994)

DUFF, R.A., *Trials and Punishment* (Cambridge: Cambridge University Press, 1986)

GARLAND, D., *Punishment and Modern Society: A Study in Social Theory* (Oxford: Clarendon Press, 1990)

HART, H.L.A., *Punishment and Responsibility: Essays in the Philosophy of Law* (New York: Oxford University Press, 1968)

HONDERICH, T., *Punishment: The Supposed Justifications* (London: Penguin, 1976)

LACEY, N., *State Punishment: Political Principles and Community Values* (London: Routledge, 1988)

MORRIS, N., *The Future of Imprisonment* (Chicago: University of Chicago Press, 1974)

MORRIS, N., & M. TONRY, *Between Prison and Probation: Intermediate Punishments in a Rational Sentencing System* (New York: Oxford University Press, 1990)

NOZICK, R., *Philosophical Explanations* (Cambridge, Mass.: Belknap Press, 1981)

PALMER, T., *A Profile of Correctional Effectiveness and New Directions for Research* (Albany: State University of New York Press, 1994)

TONRY, M., *Sentencing Matters* (New York: Oxford University Press, 1996)

SHAW, G.B., *The Crime of Imprisonment* (New York: Greenwood Press, 1946).

VON HIRSCH, A., *Censure and Sanctions* (Oxford: Oxford University Press, 1993)

VON HIRSCH, A., A. BOTTOMS, E. BURNEY, & P-O. WILKSTROM, *Criminal Deterrence and Sentence Severity: An Analysis of Recent Research* (Oxford: Hart Publishing, 1999)

VON HIRSCH, A., *Past or Future Crimes: Deservedness and Dangerousness in the Sentencing of Criminals* (New Brunswick, N.J.: Rutgers University Press, 1985)

# CHAPTER 4

# JUDICIAL DISCRETION AND THE METHODOLOGY OF SENTENCING

## A. THE SOURCE OF SENTENCING DISCRETION

Sentencing in Canada is, in the vast majority of cases, discretionary. Before the nineteenth century, most felonies were capital offences. The move away from the pervasive use of capital punishment relied originally on transportation, and then on imprisonment. When long-term imprisonment became available as a substitute for transportation, terms of penal servitude equal to the terms of transportation were prescribed. In England, these were originally set at seven-year intervals.[1] While it took a series of English statutes to reduce the periods of penal servitude,[2] the Canadian *Act for better proportioning the punishment to the offence* reduced the minimum penitentiary term for Upper and Lower Canadian offenders in 1842 to three years.[3] It also provided that,

---

1   The 1841 Canadian statute provided for penitentiary imprisonment for terms of at least seven years: see *An Act for improving the administration of Criminal Justice in this Province, 1841* (Can.), 4-5 Vict., c. 24, s. 24.

2   See L. Radzinowicz & R. Hood, *The Emergence of Penal Policy in Victorian and Edwardian England*, vol. 5 of *A History of English Criminal Law and Its Administration from 1750* (London: Stevens & Sons, 1986) at 244–46, explaining how the minimum period went from seven to three (1857), to five (1864), and finally back to three years (1879).

3   See *An Act for better proportioning the punishment to the offence, in certain cases, and for other purposes therein mentioned, 1842* (Can.), 6-7 Vict., c. 5, s. 2.

for various offences, imprisonment in common gaols or houses of correction could be ordered for terms up to and including two years.[4]

The set of punishments was refined in the *Criminal Code, 1892*, which made available various "degrees or kinds" of punishment and placed the choice between them "in the discretion of the the court."[5] Of course, the *Criminal Code, 1892*, borrowed heavily from the draft code prepared by Sir James Fitzjames Stephen for the English Parliament in 1879. In relation to sentencing, one of its purposes was to prescribe proportionate punishments by abolishing minimum punishments and by entrenching the discretion of judges, allowing them substantial latitude to mitigate the punishment.[6] While Stephen's draft did little to reduce maxima, Radzinowicz and Hood have commented that his "overriding objective was to expand rather than confine judicial discretion."[7] This approach was embodied in the *Criminal Code, 1892*.

# B. THE CURRENT FRAMEWORK FOR DISCRETION

Now, with the exception of the small but expanding group of offences that carry minimum penalties, sentencing in Canada continues to be discretionary. Section 718.3 of the *Criminal Code* provides:

> 718. 3.(1) Where an enactment prescribes different degrees or kinds of punishment in respect of an offence, the punishment to be imposed is, subject to the limitations prescribed in the enactment, in the discretion of the court that convicts a person who commits the offence.

Murder carries with it a mandatory penalty of life imprisonment;[8] the most common mandatory minimum sentence applies to subsequent

---

4    For a discussion of the range of sentences available in Canada prior to the *Criminal Code, 1892* (Can.), 55-56 Vict., c. 29, see Chapter 2, above.

5    *Ibid.*, s. 932.

6    Bill 178, Criminal Code (Indictable Offences) Bill, first reading May 14, 1878. See the discussion in L. Radzinowicz and R. Hood, *A History of English Criminal Law*, vol. 5 (London: Stevens, 1986) at 738–39.

7    *Ibid.*

8    See *Criminal Code*, R.S.C. 1985, c. C-46, s. 235. Parole ineligibility is set at twenty-five years for first-degree and a minimum of ten years for second-degree: see s. 745, *ibid*. For a detailed discussion of murder sentencing see Chapter 10, below.

convictions for impaired driving;[9] and the 1996 firearms legislation resulted in minimum punishments of four years imprisonment for stipulated offences committed with firearms.[10] However, for most offences, the *Code* stipulates only a maximum term of imprisonment, and leaves the determination of the kind and extent of punishment to the sentencing judge. The maxima are unrealistic because they are rarely imposed and do not reflect the comparative gravity of the offence, as the following table illustrates:

| Offence | Maximum Available Sentence |
|---|---|
| Manslaughter, s. 236 | Life imprisonment |
| Death by criminal negligence, s. 220 | Life imprisonment |
| Attempted murder, s. 239 | Life imprisonment |
| Kidnapping, s. 279 | Life imprisonment |
| Robbery, s. 344 | Life imprisonment |
| Aggravated sexual assault, s. 273 | Life imprisonment |
| Breaking & entering (home), s. 348(1)(d) | Life imprisonment |
| Accessory after fact to murder, s. 240 | Life imprisonment |
| Perjury re: offence punishable by life, s. 132 | Life imprisonment |
| Sexual assault with a weapon, s. 272(2) | Fourteen years |
| Criminal breach of trust, s. 336 | Fourteen years |
| Public Servant refusing to deliver property, s. 337 | Fourteen years |
| Discharging firearm with intent, s. 244 | Fourteen years |
| Perjury, s. 132 | Fourteen years |

---

9   See *ibid.*, s. 255(1)(a). Other examples of mandatory penalties for subsequent sentences, although they rarely arise, are ss. 202(2)(b) & (c) for bookmaking, and ss. 203(e) & (f) for placing bets on behalf of another.

10  See *Firearms Act*, S.C. 1995, c. 39, ss. 141–50, establishing the four-year minimum sentences for using a firearm in the course of the following *Criminal Code* offences: s. 220 (criminal negligence causing death); s. 236 (manslaughter); s. 239 (attempted murder); s. 244 (causing bodily harm with intent); s. 272 (sexual assault with a weapon); s. 273 (aggravated sexual assault); s. 279 (kidnapping); s. 279.1 (hostage-taking); s. 344 (robbery); and s. 346 (extortion). It also created a mandatory one-year sentence for illegally importing or exporting a restricted or prohibited weapon: s. 103(2).

| Offence | Maximum Available Sentence |
|---|---|
| Impaired driving causing death, s. 255(3) | Fourteen years |
| Aggravated assault, s. 268 | Fourteen years |
| Counterfeiting stamps, s. 376 | Fourteen years |
| Making counterfeit money, s. 449 | Fourteen years |
| Possession of counterfeit money, s. 450 | Fourteen years |
| Counselling or aiding suicide, s. 241 | Fourteen years |
| Incest, s. 155 | Fourteen years |
| Impaired driving causing bodily harm, s. 255(2) | Ten years |
| Sexual assault, s. 271 | Ten years |
| Fraudulent use of computer service, s. 342.1 | Ten years |
| Theft over $5000, s. 334(a) | Ten years |
| Breaking & entering (not a home), s. 348(1)(e) | Ten years |
| Fraud over $5000, s. 380(1)(a) | Ten years |
| Bestiality, s. 160 | Ten years |
| Bodily harm by criminal negligence, s. 221 | Ten years |
| Assault causing bodily harm, s. 267 | Ten years |
| Personation with intent, s. 403 | Ten years |
| Mischief to property over $5000, s. 430 | Ten years |
| Destroying title documents, s. 340 | Ten years |
| Theft of credit card, s. 342 | Ten years |
| Forgery, s. 367 | Ten years |
| Uttering forged document, s. 368 | Ten years |
| Abduction by parent, s. 283 | Ten years |
| Sexual touching of young person, s. 151 | Ten years |
| Illegal importing/exporting weapons, s. 103 | Ten years |
| Criminal breach of contract, s. 422 | Five years |
| Knowingly buying military stores, s. 420 | Five years |
| Assaulting a peace officer, s. 270 | Five years |

| Offence | Maximum Available Sentence |
|---|---|
| Assault, s. 266 | Five years |
| Uttering death threat, s. 264.1 | Five years |
| Defamatory libel, s. 300 | Five years |
| Infanticide, s. 237 | Five years |
| Impaired driving, s. 255 | Five years |
| Fraud re: manipulation of stock exchange, s. 382 | Five years |
| Bigamy, s. 291 | Five years |
| Polygamy, s. 293 | Five years |
| Dangerous driving, s. 249 | Five years |
| Sexual exploitation of young person, s. 153 | Five years |
| Carrying concealed weapon, s. 90 | Five years |
| Communicating race hatred, s. 319 | Two years |
| Cheating at play, s. 209 | Two years |
| Driving while disqualified, s. 259 | Two years |
| Obscene performance, s. 169 | Two years |
| Carrying weapon at public meeting, s. 89 | Six months |
| Witchcraft, fortune telling, s. 365 | Six months |

The rarity of maximum sentences is obvious when one compares the maxima with actual sentencing patterns. A greater cause for concern is the false impression of comparative gravity of offences: one need only read any part of the list to see that the sets of offences with common maxima include disparate offences and extend across a broad range of harm, blameworthiness, and societal importance.

Sentencing discretion, exercised on an individual basis, encompasses the threshold decision of whether to impose a custodial or non-custodial penalty. Depending on the answer, it continues to the subsequent questions of choosing between non-custodial sanctions, determining the length of a custodial response, or sometimes combining the two. As broad as this discretionary function is, it must be exercised with some degree of consistency. More importantly, its hallmark must be fairness with due regard both to similar cases and the individual circumstances of the offender. This is the challenge which the *Criminal*

*Code* presents: maintaining discretion, encouraging creativity, and still ensuring consistency and fairness.

# C. THE EXERCISE OF SENTENCING DISCRETION

## 1) The Traditional Approach

If the *Criminal Code* has provided little guidance to judges, it is legitimate to ask how judges reach their decisions about sentencing. How do they decide whether to incarcerate or not, and for how long? How do they choose between available non-custodial options? For many years, the task of articulating principles was left entirely to the judiciary. In 1964, the Chief Justices of the provinces and various trial level judges attended a sentencing conference in Toronto. The meeting was opened by Cartwright J. of the Supreme Court of Canada, who said:

> I do not think it is an overstatement to say that not only the public but the Courts and Counsel are disturbed by the apparent inconsistencies between the sentences imposed in many cases where not only is the crime the same but the surrounding circumstances are, on their face, very similar. The Bench and Bar also are concerned over the difficulty of finding a uniform and authoritative statement as to all the factors, and the relative importance of these factors, which should influence the decision of the tribunal of first instance in imposing sentence and those which should guide the appellate courts in reviewing sentences.[11]

Clearly, by 1964 the judiciary had not succeeded in developing principles which adequately guided discretion.

Canadian judges recognized the need to develop principles to guide the exercise of discretion. Essentially, they adopted a pragmatic approach in which they borrowed from the philosophical justifications of punishment in general. The set of justifications became the set of potential purposes of a sentence. Accordingly, the judge must consider the circumstances of the offence and the offender to determine which objectives should be pre-eminent or subordinate in a particular case. The Canadian approach was described by Mackay J.A. in *R. v. Willaert*:

---

11 Centre of Criminology, University of Toronto, *Proceedings of the National Conference of Judges on Sentencing* (Toronto: Centre of Criminology, University of Toronto, 1964) at 1.

> . . . the true function of criminal law in regard to punishment is in a wise blending of the deterrent and reformative, with retribution not entirely disregarded, and with a constant appreciation that the matter concerns not merely the Court and the offender but also the public and society as a going concern. Punishment is, therefore, an art — a very difficult art — essentially practical, and directly related to the existing needs of society. A punishment appropriate today might have been quite unacceptable 200 years ago and probably would be absurd 200 years hence. It is therefore impossible to lay down hard and fast and permanent rules.[12]

This suggests an individualized discretionary process without "hard and fast" rules. Instead, the judge relies on his or her experience to select the appropriate purpose for the sentence. In a similar vein, McLennan J.A. stated in 1966 that the "fundamental purpose of any sentence of whatever kind is the protection of society."[13] He added that courts should consider "prevention, deterrence, and reformation" but that the relative weight would be as variable as the array of cases and their individual facts. Striking the same chord, Culliton C.J.S. in *R. v. Morrissette* noted that the difficulty lay in deciding which principle should be emphasized. He remarked that "the circumstances surrounding the commission of an offence differ in each case so that even for the same offence sentences may justifiably show a wide variation."[14]

These comments reflect the acceptance of a sentencing methodology which is guided by the choice of objective, or objectives, which suit the circumstances of the case. In essence, this is an amalgam approach where all the objectives of punishment are translated into the potential purposes of the individual sentence. An amalgam is defined as a plastic mixture of substances. This metaphor captures both the combination of factors and the basic fluidity of the methodology: it is inherently amorphous. While the approach enables a judge to make a choice and give an explanation for it, it offers little guidance to direct the judge to a particular path, or to tell the judge how far the path should be followed.

When the Canadian Sentencing Commission reported in 1987, the problems raised by Cartwright J. in 1964 had not been solved. The Sentencing Commission found that one of the major defects of the sentencing process was the degree of unwarranted disparity. Relying on a number of studies, including Hogarth's *Sentencing as a Human*

---

12  (1953), 105 C.C.C. 172 at 176 (Ont. C.A.).
13  *R. v. Wilmott* (1966), [1967] 1 C.C.C. 172 at 177 (Ont. C.A.).
14  (1970), 1 C.C.C. (2d) 307 at 309 (Sask. C.A.).

*Process,*[15] it accepted that sentences are closely related to the individual judge's experience and sentencing philosophy. Consequently, it concluded that, notwithstanding judicial efforts to expound principles of sentencing, "at the moment . . . there is no consensus on how sentencing should be approached."[16]

This damning characterization was, in some ways, accurate. Certainly, there was no structured process that would guarantee similar results in similar cases most of the time. However, it would be an exaggeration to suggest there was no common ground amongst sentencing judges. Many Canadian judges apply an undeclared and untested sense of the usual range of sentence applicable to different offences and subcategories of offences.

## 2)   Ranges, Tariffs, and Individualization

While there has been much debate over what judges should be doing, it is surprising that there are also disputes over what, in fact, they have been doing. The 1982 *Canadian Sentencing Handbook* prepared by the Canadian Association of Provincial Court Judges advocated the "blending imperative" from *Willaert.*[17] This approach suggests that judges must consider the relevant purposes of sentencing to craft the sanction which reflects the most appropriate purpose or combination of purposes for the offence. In the same section, however, the *Handbook* says that a sentencer will likely not go wrong by imposing the "usual" sentence in the "run-of-the-mill case." This suggests that some norms exist within the practice of sentencing even if they are not formally articulated. Of course, the *Handbook* explains the importance of giving due consideration to aggravating and mitigating factors, and unusual circumstances. However, it does clearly suggest some operating concept of range.

In England, D.A. Thomas has argued that the Court of Appeal has constructed, over the years, a tariff applicable to most offences. There has been controversy over whether the "tariff" was intentionally developed by the Court of Appeal or is the product of Thomas' observations of the Court's sentencing activity. Still, Thomas' account is persuasive.

---

15   J. Hogarth, *Sentencing as a Human Process* (Toronto: University of Toronto Press, 1971).

16   Canadian Sentencing Commission, *Sentencing Reform: A Canadian Approach* (Ottawa: Supply and Services Canada, 1987) at 77 [*Report of the Canadian Sentencing Commission*].

17   Canadian Association of Provincial Court Judges, *Canadian Sentencing Handbook*, looseleaf (Ottawa: Canadian Association of Provincial Court Judges, 1982) at 23–24 [*Canadian Sentencing Handbook*].

It is also consistent with the traditional Canadian approach discussed above. By "tariff," he does not mean a precisely prescribed sentence but rather a range of sentences. The applicability of the tariff depends on the nature of the offence; specific characteristics of the offender may operate to preclude the tariff in favour of an individualized response. A "tariff" response applies to cases where the nature of the offence requires a sanction that reflects general deterrence or denunciation. In these cases, the interests of rehabilitation are subordinated: some examples are rape, robbery, wounding, trafficking, perjury, arson, and blackmail.[18] Conversely, there are categories of offenders for whom an individualized approach is indicated: here, Thomas refers to youthful offenders, mentally ill offenders, and what he describes as intermediate and inadequate recidivists.[19] The individualized sentence would be motivated by utilitarian concerns, while the tariff is more clearly a retributive response. When cases do not fit clearly into one approach or the other, the court must choose which one is most appropriate to the circumstances of the individual case. Thomas maintains that the "overriding principle" is proportionality.

Although not formally adopted and sanctioned by appellate courts, there is some evidence that a similar methodology — choosing between tariff or individualized — is employed by many judges in Canada. Of course, the word "tariff" never appears but phrases like "usual range,"[20] "ordinary range,"[21] or "appropriate range"[22] are commonly heard. They often appear in appellate court decisions considering the adequacy or severity of a sentence especially when the court wants to make a statement about the comparative gravity of an offence, its prevalence, or the goals of deterrence or denunciation. One can assume that judges who use this phrase have a sense of what it means. This sense would come from their own experience and the collective experience of local judicial colleagues. Sometimes, it would filter down from remarks made by an appellate court. The *Canadian Sentencing Handbook* said:

---

18    *Ibid.* at 15.

19    *Ibid.* at 17–25.

20    See, for example, *R. v. MacPherson* (1995), 16 M.V.R. (3d) 152 (B.C.C.A.) (dangerous driving causing death); *R. v. Vaudreuil* (1995), 98 C.C.C. (3d) 316 (B.C.C.A.) (manslaughter where the victim is a child); *R. v. Douglas* (1989), 51 C.C.C. (3d) 129 (Ont. C.A.) (conspiracy to traffic in cocaine); and *R. v. Wood* (1988), 43 C.C.C. (3d) 570 (Ont. C.A.) (manslaughter by stabbing).

21    See, for example, *R. v. H.(W.)* (1993), 84 C.C.C. (3d) 465 (Ont. C.A.) (sexual assault on a spouse's child); and *R. v. B.(J.)* (1990), 36 O.A.C. 307 (C.A.) [*B.(J.)*] (sexual assault by person *in loco parentis*).

22    See, for example, *R. v. Brown* (1990), 53 C.C.C. (3d) 521 (Sask. C.A.).

Some help in understanding what is proportional and not excessive can be gained by having regard to the range of punishment usually imposed in similar cases reasonably contemporaneous in point of time. Such ranges are not published, but some indications can be obtained from the judgments of the court of appeal from time to time, from the practice of other courts and from counsel experienced in the courts.[23]

Of course, there are many cases in which the "usual range" would be rejected in favour of an individualized approach, but there can be no doubt that the idea of "range" has been around for a long time although not formally sanctioned, precisely articulated, or carefully examined. It has provided a guide for the proper individualization of a sentences in two ways. First, it indicates the usual kind of punishment: custodial or non-custodial. Then, with respect to the quantum of punishment, after considering aggravating or mitigating factors relevant to the particular offence and offender, the concept of usual range gives some sense of proportionality and parity.

A classic example of an attempt by an appellate court to establish a new range or norm for a particular offence was provided by the British Columbia Court of Appeal in 1968 in R. v. Adelman.[24] The court allowed a Crown appeal from a suspended sentence for simple possession of marijuana. It concluded that the prevalence of the offence had become so great that severe punishment was necessary to help bring it under control. In the Court's view, lenient sentences had not adequately reflected the seriousness of the problem. After referring to the sentences in other marijuana possession cases, the Court stated:

> In recent years there has been a strong movement across this country for greater uniformity in sentences. For various reasons complete uniformity is almost impossible of production, but every effort should be made by the Judges and Magistrates in British Columbia to avoid the creation of serious disparity in sentences. . . . It is not right that the nature and extent of the penalty for possession of marijuana or, for that matter, for any other offence, should depend on the accident of the location of the offence or the accident of the identity or personality of the convicting Judge or Magistrate. . . . The lower Courts must have all due regard to the policy that has been laid down by this Court concerning punishment of particular types of offences and the severity of punishment that would be appropriate in the absence of special circumstances.[25]

---

23  *Canadian Sentencing Handbook*, above note 17 at 27.
24  [1968] 3 C.C.C. 311 (B.C.C.A.).
25  *Ibid.* at 322.

It imposed a term of imprisonment of six months solely for the purpose of entrenching a new range of sentence for simple possession of marijuana. This case shows how an appellate court can mandate a penalty range. Whatever term is used, range or tariff, the Court of Appeal had set a new norm which subordinated individualized concerns in favour of an exemplary sentence. The decision in *Adelman* was sufficiently influential that, in the interest of striving for national uniformity, the appellate court in Newfoundland increased a sentence for trafficking in marijuana to eighteenth months.[26] Fortunately, the norm for marijuana sentencing dropped dramatically over the next two decades. By 1984, the British Columbia Court of Appeal was endorsing conditional discharges for possession.[27]

An appellate court can direct a sentencing trend in the opposite direction or can act to inhibit a newly observed trend. Clearly, this was what the British Columbia Court of Appeal did in the *Sweeney* package of cases dealing with the offences of dangerous driving and impaired driving causing death.[28] In that province, the sentences for this category of offence had been slowly moving upward so that sentences in the six- to eight-year range were not rare. From a panel of five, one other judge agreed with Wood J.A. that the assessment of culpability could not be based solely on the fortuitous consequences of a death or even multiple deaths but rather should be determined by the blameworthiness of the conduct. Wood J.A. held that the higher sentences could only be justified by persistent drunk driving, most often shown by individuals with chronic alcohol problems who continued to drive after drinking. This decision has been interpreted as stemming the tide of "creeping incrementalism" which had been encouraging sentences to "drift too high."[29] It serves as another example of an appellate court's efforts to mandate the appropriate range.

## 3) Starting Points

The *Criminal Code* gives appellate courts a broad authority to set sentencing standards within their territorial jurisidiction through the sentence appeal process, which requires a consideration of the "fitness

---

26   See *R. v. O'Neill* (1973), 13 C.C.C. (2d) 276 (Nfld. S.C. (A.D.)).

27   See *R. v. Brown*, [1984] B.C.J. No. 1489 (C.A.) (QL), in which the court substituted a conditional discharge for a $1000 fine for marijuana possession.

28   See *R. v. Sweeney* (1992), 11 C.R. (4th) 1 (B.C.C.A.).

29   This phrase was used by Lambert J.A. in his recent discussion of *Sweeney* in *R. v. Mafi* (2000), 142 C.C.C. (3d) 449 at 457 (B.C.C.A.).

of the sentence."[30] Over time, a systematic assimilation of appellate decisions will provide guidance for the exercise of sentencing discretion. Traditionally, this guidance has taken the form of broadly articulated ranges and occasional statements indicating presumptions of incarceration. Accordingly, sentencing discretion has continued to cover a wide area. This encourages individualization but also may permit disparity. Appeals are expensive and time-consuming; it is not realistic to assume that all errors, or even a large portion of them, will reach the appellate level. One way in which appellate courts have attempted to structure trial-level discretion is the "starting point" approach.

In the late 1970s, a number of appellate courts led by the Alberta Court of Appeal began to articulate appropriate sentences for types of offences to provide sentencing judges with a place to start the consideration of what would be fit. The earliest example was a crude effort to ensure that leniency did not creep into drug sentencing in Alberta. The Court of Appeal filled its docket with various kinds of drug cases and offered samples of the kind of stern sentences that ought to be imposed in Alberta.[31] This was soon followed by sentencing directions for Nova Scotia in robbery cases involving youthful offenders.[32] When the Alberta Court of Appeal addressed the issue of robbery by youthful offenders, it refined its general methodology by recognizing the broad range of conduct encompassed by the offence of robbery. It chose a number of cases that represented a narrowly defined sub-category of robbery: "unsophisticated armed robbery of unprotected commercial outlets" committed by youthful offenders who caused no physical harm.[33] The court set the starting point at three years. In dealing with seven offenders, the harsh impact of the three-year starting point was clear. Five of the youthful offenders were sent to the penitentiary. Only an eighteen-year-old with no previous record and an exceptionally inept criminal who had taken $20 were given sentences of less than two years. While individual factors were considered, it took a lot to move significantly off the norm. Clearly, starting points had moved the range of sentences for young persons committing unsophisticated robberies up the penalty scale.

---

30   See *Criminal Code*, above note 8, s. 687(1); and the discussion of sentence appeals in Chapter 12, below.

31   See *R. v. Sprague* (1974), 19 C.C.C. (2d) 513 (Alta. C.A.).

32   See *R. v. Hingley* (1977), 19 N.S.R. (2d) 541 (S.C.A.D.); and *R. v. Owen* (1982), 50 N.S.R. (2d) 696 (C.A.).

33   See *R. v. Johnas* (1982), 32 C.R. (3d) 1 (Alta. C.A.).

As the kinds of offences covered by starting points expanded, the Alberta Court of Appeal also developed a clearer and more refined explanation of the approach. In *R. v. Sandercock*,[34] the court addressed the issue of sexual assault. It described the three stages of the starting point approach. First, offences were categorized into "archetypical" cases described with as much precision as possible. Then, a starting sentence would be attached to the category. Lastly, the sentencing court would apply the relevant mitigating and aggravating factors to vary the sentence up or down from the starting point. Applying this methodology, the court defined the category of "major sexual assault" as being cases where "a person, by violence or threat of violence, forces an adult victim to submit to sexual activity of a sort or intensity such that a reasonable person would know beforehand that the victim likely would suffer lasting emotional or psychological injury, whether or not physical injury occurs."[35] The starting point was set at three years for a mature accused with no prior convictions and previous good character. In the circumstances of the case, which involved planning and stalking by an offender with a prior record for violence, the resulting sentence was four-and-a-half years imprisonment.

The Alberta Court of Appeal argued that the *Sandercock* methodology was not a rigid method of producing uniform sentences but rather a flexible way of ensuring a uniform approach[36] which would limit disparity but, at the same time, leave discretion unfettered. While it might achieve these goals, it would also encourage a higher penalty scale. This would result both from the three-year starting point itself and also the removal of the traditionally accepted mitigating factors of previous good character and absence of record. By weaving these factors into the definition of the archetypical offence, they would no longer have any mitigating effect.

---

34   (1985), 22 C.C.C. (3d) 79 (Alta. C.A.).

35   *Ibid.* at 84.

36   The "uniformity of approach" idea, while not attributed by the Alberta Court of Appeal, likely came from *R. v. Bibi* (1980), 2 Cr. App. R. (S) 177 (C.A.), an appeal from a three-year sentence for importing marijuana. The appeal arose at a time when prisons were "dangerously overcrowded." The Lord Chief Justice said that in many cases, the deterrent and punitive needs of justice can be served "equally justly and effectively by a sentence of six or nine months imprisonment as by one of eighteen months or three years." In reducing the sentence to six months, he observed: "We are not aiming at uniformity of sentence; that would be impossible. We are aiming at uniformity of approach": *ibid.* at 179.

Over the next decade, the starting point approach was extended to a large number of offences.[37] Manslaughter presented an obstacle for the new regime — the court concluded that the offence description covered so many routes to culpability that it was not amenable to the starting point approach.[38] With respect to sexual assault, the three-year starting point was picked up by some jurisdictions[39] and rejected by others.[40] A comparison of the number of penitentiary sentences imposed for sexual assaults reflected a substantially higher rate of penitentiary incarceration in the provinces that followed *Sandercock*.[41]

In England, the Court of Appeal has been issuing sentencing guidelines judgments and the early ones used an approach similar to Alberta's starting point methodology.[42] Guidelines judgments have increased since 1988 when the prosecution was, for the first time, given the ability to appeal against a sentence considered to be "unduly lenient."[43] The more recent cases show a tendency to offer ranges instead of starting points. In *Re Attorney General's Reference (No. 17 of 1990)*,[44] the Court of Appeal spoke of "the range of sentences which a judge could properly consider" when dealing with sexual assaults on young children. Similarly, in *Re Attorney General's Reference (No. 10 of 1994)*,

---

37  See, for example, *R. v. S.(W.B.)* (1992), 73 C.C.C. (3d) 530 (Alta. C.A.), which established a four-year starting point for sexual offences against children within a relationship of trust; *R. v. Brown* (1992), 73 C.C.C. (3d) 242 (Alta. C.A.) and *R. v. Ollenberger* (1994), 29 C.R. (4th) 166 (Alta. C.A.) (inter-spousal assaults); *R. v. Getty* (1990), 104 A.R. 180 (C.A.) (set three years as the starting point for minimal scale trafficking in hard drugs); *R. v. Honish* (1990), 100 A.R. 79 (C.A.) (setting four and a half years as the starting point for wholesale commercial trafficking of hard drugs); and *R. v. Matwiy* (1996), 178 A.R. 356 (C.A.) [*Matwiy*] (setting an eight-year starting point for home invasions).

38  *R. v. Tallman* (1989), 68 C.R. (3d) 367 (Alta. C.A.).

39  Manitoba adopted *Sandercock* in *R. v. Price* (1989), [1990] 1 W.W.R. 37 (Man. C.A.), when it increased a two-year sentence for sexual assault to four years. It also adopted the four-year starting point for sexual assaults against children within a family unit: see *R. v. D.(C.)* (1991), 75 Man. R. (2d) 14 (C.A.).

40  See the Ontario Court of Appeal decision in *R. v. Glassford* (1988), 42 C.C.C. (3d) 259 at 265. See also *B.(J.)*, above note 21, where the court spoke of a three- to five-year range for sexual assaults on children. The Alberta Court of Appeal in *R. v. S.(W.B.)*, above note 37 at 551, characterized this as "not far different from" a starting point.

41  See A. Manson, "*McDonnell* and the Methodology of Sentencing" (1997), 6 C.R. (5th) 277 at 283.

42  See, for example, *R. v. Turner* (1975), 61 Cr. App. R. 67 (C.A.) (fifteen-year starting point for bank robberies); and *R. v. Billam* (1986), 82 Cr. App. R. 347 (C.A.) (five years for rape).

43  See *Criminal Justice Act 1988* (U.K.), 1988, c. 33, s. 36(1).

44  (1991), 92 Cr. App. R. 288 (C.A.).

a case involving imitation firearms and intent to rob, it used the phrase "acceptable range of sentences open to a trial judge."[45] A variation on the range theme arose in *Re Attorney General's Reference (No. 3 of 1994)*, when the court used the terminology of "normal level of sentencing" in articulating a range of three and a half to seven years for robberies of small premises like filling stations and off-licences.[46]

More recently, Lord Bingham examined a hierarchy of firearms offences and the sentences imposed in various cases, and spoke against a "rigid formulaic" approach which would necessarily produce injustice in some cases.[47] Instead, he offered a series of guidelines cast in terms of escalating presumptions of custody. Depending on the specific offence and whether stipulated factors were present in ways that were "adverse" to the accused, the sentences would be custody, custody of considerable length, or custody near the maximum. This signals a very different and more flexible approach than the use of precise starting points.

## 4) Starting Points and the Supreme Court: *R. v. McDonnell*

In 1997, the Supreme Court heard an appeal in a sentencing case which questioned the legitimacy of the starting point approach.[48] The accused pleaded guilty after a preliminary inquiry to two counts of sexual assault, one on a sixteen-year-old foster child and the other on a fourteen-year-old baby-sitter. In one case, he returned home intoxicated and found the foster child asleep on a sofa. Without consent, he removed her pants and assaulted her, including partial vaginal penetration with his penis. In the other case, a sleeping baby-sitter awoke to find the accused on top of her after he had removed her underwear. He was fondling her pelvic and vaginal area. The sentencing judge did not consider either assault to be a major sexual assault within the *Sandercock* definition. She concluded that the offences were spontaneous and attributable to drunkenness. Taking into account the accused's expression of remorse, his good character, his stable employment history, his record of community involvement, and his apparent desire to quit drinking, she sentenced him to twelve months on one count and six months on the other, to be served concurrently and to be followed by two years probation. On appeal, both offences were characterized as major sexual assaults. In allowing the appeal, the Alberta Court of

45   (1995), 16 Cr. App. R. (S) 285 (C.A.).
46   (1995), 16 Cr. App. R. (S) 176 (C.A.).
47   *R. v. Avis*, [1998] 2 Cr. App. R. (S) 178 (C.A.).
48   *R. v. McDonnell*, [1997] 1 S.C.R. 948 [*McDonnell*].

Appeal noted the breach of trust, penetration, and "presumed psychological harm." It varied the sentence for the first offence to four years and added one year consecutive for the second offence. McDonnell appealed to the Supreme Court.

In the Supreme Court, the five-four majority decision allowing the appeal and restoring the original sentence was written by Sopinka J. Applying the recently articulated standard of deference,[49] he concluded that the trial judge did not fail to consider relevant factors and the sentences were not demonstrably unfit. Given the nature and circumstances of the assaults, the latter conclusion is controversial.[50] However, it was in the course of addressing whether the trial judge committed an error in principle that the Supreme Court's analysis centred on the starting point regime. While the Court of Appeal found error in the trial judge's failure to characterize the offences as "major sexual assaults" in *Sandercock* terms, Sopinka J. objected to the use of a "judicially created category of assault for the purposes of sentencing."[51] He concluded that a sentencing judge's failure to place an offence into a category carved out by the appellate court can never, by itself, be a reversible error. His reasons were principally[52] the relationship of deference which an appellate court owes to the sentencing court and the holding in *Frey* v. *Fedoruk*.[53]

These two arguments reflected the source of the majority's concerns but did not capture the essential problem inherent in the starting point approach: the constraint on discretion without Parliamentary authority. First, deference arises from the granting of authority to sentencing judges to assesses the relevant factors and circumstances, not the manner in which they apply legal standards. Secondly, *Frey* v. *Fedoruk*, which signalled the end of common law offences in Canada, was not a sentencing case. Its potential relevance was the concern about usurping Parliament's authority. Accordingly, the issue which should have attracted the court's attention was the problem of constraint on discretion, not

---

49   See R. v. *Shropshire*, [1995] 4 S.C.R. 227; and R. v. *M.(C.A.)*, [1996] 1 S.C.R. 500. See also the discussion in Chapter 12, below.

50   See Manson, above note 41 at 285–86.

51   *McDonnell*, above note 48 at 974.

52   Sopinka J. also expressed concern about some remarks by the Court of Appeal which may have suggested that, in the case of a major sexual assault, psychological harm could be assumed: *ibid.* at 975–78. However, it is not clear that the Court of Appeal intended any presumption that would remove the need to prove harm, and, in any event, Sopinka J. accepted that there was evidence of psychological harm in the case. See the discussion of harm in Chapter 5, below.

53   [1950] S.C.R. 517.

the use of offence categories for sentencing purposes. Distinct offence categories for sentencing purposes are common and useful: bank robberies, thefts by employees, wife assault, assaults on children. Rigid starting
points establish quasi-minimum sentences which intrude on individualization and thereby usurp the function of Parliament. Of course, it can
be argued that starting points do not mandate a specific response. However, that has been their effect: to increase the number and length of
sentences of imprisonment through raising the bar and discounting oth-
erwise-applicable mitigating factors.

McLachlin J. in dissent supported the use of the starting point
approach. She concluded that it is "theoretically sound and marks an
advance in the need to find a principled approach to the dual goals of
individualization of sentences and the need for uniformity and consistency."[54] While these are laudable objectives, the history and evolution
of starting points does not bear out the conclusion either that they
were developed for, or have been used for, these purposes. Certainly,
the early examples were pointed efforts to ratchet upward the applicable penalty scales. As far as individualization is concerned, the practice
of neutralizing mitigating factors through the definiton of the archetypical case, as was done in *Sandercock* with previous good character
and absence of a record, suggests that starting points have not promoted this goal. The empirical results indicate how difficult it is to
depart substantially from the norm.

Ultimately, Sopinka J. returned to the issue of the legitimacy of
starting points and concluded that they could have a guiding role but
could not be a rigid tariff. He said:

> . . . I do not disagree with McLachlin J. that appellate courts may set
> out starting-point sentences as guides to lower courts. Moreover, the
> starting point may well be a factor to consider in determining
> whether a sentence is demonstrably unfit. If there is a wide disparity
> between the starting point for the offence and the sentence imposed,
> then, assuming that the Court of Appeal has set a reasonable starting
> point, the starting point certainly suggests, but is not determinative
> of, unfitness. In my view, however, the approach taken by McLachlin
> J. in the present case places too great an emphasis on the effect of
> deviation from the starting point. . . . Deviation from a starting point
> may be a factor in considering demonstrable unfitness, but does not
> have the significance McLachlin J. gives it.[55]

---

54    *McDonnell*, above note 48 at 1008.
55    *Ibid.* at 981.

This contemplated a diluted form of starting point that provides guidance but does not entrench a template that will trigger appellate intervention if it is not applied.

## 5) Starting Points After *McDonnell*

Since *McDonnell*, the Alberta courts have continued to consider starting points[56] but their role has been unclear. In *R. v. Waldner*,[57] Berger J.A. summarized the lessons from *McDonnell* and, particularly, the inability of an appellate court to rely solely on deviation from a previously articulated starting point as a ground for intervention. He went on to offer the view that *McDonnell* "greatly diminishes the value and utility of the starting point sentence which, for some time now, has placed undue constraints upon the sentencing discretion that trial judges must have and which Parliament has conferred upon them."[58]

While this may be a fitting comment, the starting point trend has only been bruised, not beaten. In the subsequent case of *R. v. G.(D.W.)*,[59] the use of starting points as guidelines for trial courts was resurrected by relying on both the majority and dissenting opinions in *McDonnell* and the more recent Supreme Court decision in *R. v. Stone*.[60] In that case, Bastarache J. confirmed that appellate courts can "fix ranges" as guidelines for lower courts and that this function could also

---

56   See, for example, *R. v. Chung* (1999), 232 A.R. 193 (C.A.), an appeal by the Crown against sentences imposed for trafficking in cocaine. The court relied on a 1990 starting point of 4 1/2 years for commercial trafficking to increase the sentences to eight and five years respectively given the large, ongoing, and interprovincial nature of the trafficking enterprise. See also *R. v. Pyykonen* (1999), 232 A.R. 274 (C.A.), in which the offenders appealed unsuccessfully against 6 and a half year global sentences arising from a home invasion. The trial judge had refered to the eight-year starting point used in the 1996 case of *Matwiy*, above note 37, but the Court of Appeal held that this was not an error since he had only compared the cases factually and did not rely on the starting point.

57   (1998), 15 C.R. (5th) 159 (Alta. C.A.).

58   *Ibid.* at 169. See also *R. v. Beaudry*, [2000] A.J. No. 1080 (Alta. C.A.) in which Berger J.A. wrote for the majority upholding a conditional sentence for trafficking in cocaine in the face of starting point judgments indicating a penitentiary term. He commented that "a starting point, standing alone, is not much of a guideline."

59   (1999), 244 A.R. 176 (C.A.). See also the more recent case of *R. v. Ostertag*, [2000] A.J. No. 965 (Alta. C.A.) in which five years was stipulated as the starting point for lower level here in trafficking. For a unanimous court, Veit J. (ad hoc) stated that "starting point sentencing does not create minimum sentences as a by-product" of the attempt to achieve "greater uniformity" amongst offenders (at para. 12).

60   [1999] 2 S.C.R. 290.

include starting points.[61] Moreover, he added the caution that when doing so, courts should be clear in describing the category of offence to which the guideline applied. Certainly, the fact that *Criminal Code* offences apply to broad bands of conduct which can be committed by a variety of offenders, producing almost infinite consequences, has always meant that appellate sentencing advice can only be practicable if the offence category is described with sufficient detail to be useful. Viewed in this way, Bastarache J.'s requirement of clarity is a helpful admonition but it does not reverse the *McDonnell* ruling on the relationship between guidelines and sentencing discretion. Certainly, clear guidelines, whether cast in terms of ranges or starting points, are being encouraged as tools to avoid disparity but they cannot usurp the role of individualization.

## D. CODIFIED PRINCIPLES OF SENTENCING

While Parliament may be removed from the daily activity of the criminal courts, it has the legislative responsibility to determine the nature of criminal culpability and the methods of criminal punishment. As experienced as judges may be, there are institutional limits on their ability to alter the substance of sentencing. It seems clear that unstructured discretion has produced unwarranted disparity. Still, there are only a small number of ways in which Parliament can define, structure, or limit sentencing discretion. The use of minimum and maximum sentences has been the traditional way in Canada although, as we have seen, there are very few minimum sentences. This relatively unobtrusive form of guidance has done little to structure discretion. Currently, many American jurisdictions have implemented statutory guidelines. This controversial approach provides presumptive sentences from which judges can depart only with explanations and in limited circumstances.[62]

Another vehicle, less intrusive than guidelines, is to codify principles to guide the discretion of sentencing judges. The utility of this approach depends on the degree of clarity and the scope of applicability of the principles. Obviously, little help is provided by instructing judges to be fair and equitable and to take into account all relevant circumstances. Such instructions, while appropriate, are too abstract and nebu-

---

61   *Ibid.* at 411–12.
62   In the United States, a new sentencing jurisprudence which deals only with the issue of departures from statutory guidelines is developing: see, for example, M.S. Gelacak, I.H. Nagel, & B.L. Johnson, "Departures Under the Federal Sentencing Guidelines: An Empirical and Jurisprudential Analysis" (1996), 81 Minn. L. Rev. 299.

lous to structure discretion: Judges would still be left without real guidance. However, one can imagine some statements of principle which would produce specifically intended results. One example would be a statement that separate convictions for distinct events or transactions should warrant consecutive offences subject to an overriding consideration of total harshness. This example reflects, in general terms, usual sentencing practice but would still lead to some controversies over what is a transaction or what is too harsh. However, it would shape discretion whenever a judge is faced with multiple convictions.

This discussion may remind some of the nineteenth century debates about the comparative advantages of the common law versus a codified criminal law, but there is a marked difference. A *Code* which deals with responsibility and offences must be universal and complete. There cannot be openings where the *Code* tells the trial judge: "This one is tough; it's your call." Sentencing is, however, inherently difficult; there is a recognized need for discretion to accommodate events and circumstances which come forward in infinitely variable shapes and sizes.

## 1) Efforts to Entrench Sentencing Principles

In 1984, a statement of principles was included in Bill C-19,[63] a first attempt at sentencing reform which died on the House of Commons order paper. The project was embraced by the Sentencing Commission in 1987 but the Commission employed a different perspective. Bill C-19 had anchored its process on sentencing discretion coupled with a statement of purpose and applicable principles including the requirements that the sentence be both proportionate and the "least onerous alternative appropriate in the circumstances."[64] The Commission argued that proportionality should be the "paramount principle governing the determination of a sentence" with the principle of restraint listed as the second most significant factor.[65] The version which finally surfaced in Bill C-41 in 1995 bore some similarity to both of its predecessors but was substantively and structurally different.

---

63  Bill C-19, *Criminal Law Reform Act, 1984*, 2d Sess., 32nd Parl., 1984 (first reading 7 February 1984). Section 199 repealed the previous Part XX and replaced it with a new part, which added some new provisions and re-numbered the old ones. The proposed s. 645(1) defined the purposes of sentencing; s. 645(2) prescribed that sentences were within the discretion of the sentencing court; and s. 645(3) outlined the principles which governed how the discretion was to be exercised.

64  *Ibid.* See proposed s. 645(3)(a) & (c).

65  *Report of the Canadian Sentencing Commission*, above note 16 at 154.

## 2) The 1996 Amendments

Effective September 3, 1996, for the first time statements of purpose, objectives, and principles were inserted in the *Criminal Code*. The purpose of sentencing, as explained in section 718, is "to contribute, along with crime prevention initiatives, to respect for the law and the maintenance of a just, peaceful and safe society" through the imposition of "just sanctions." This is followed by a recitation of the ostensible objectives of sentencing consisting of the usual array (denunciation, deterrence, incapacitation, rehabilitation, and reparation) with one new addition in section 718(f): "to promote a sense of responsibility in offenders, and acknowledgment of the harm done to victims and to the community." Section 718.1 establishes the principle of proportionality described under the sub-heading "Fundamental principle":

> 718.1 A sentence must be proportionate to the gravity of the offence and the degree of responsibility of the offender."

This is followed by a list of principles, clearly non-exhaustive, with the sub-heading "Other sentencing principles":

> 718.2 A court that imposes a sentence shall also take into consideration the following principles:
> (a) a sentence should be increased or reduced to account for any relevant aggravating or mitigating circumstances relating to the offence or the offender, and, without limiting the generality of the foregoing,
> (i) evidence that the offence was motivated by bias, prejudice or hate based on race, national or ethnic origin, language, colour, religion, sex, age, mental or physical disability, sexual orientation, or any other similar factor,
> (ii) evidence that the offender, in committing the offence, abused the offender's spouse or common-law partner or child,
> (iii) evidence that the offender, in committing the offence, abused a position of trust or authority in relation to the victim, or
> (iv) evidence that the offence was committed for the benefit of, at the direction of or in association with a criminal organization.
> shall be deemed to be aggravating circumstances;
> (b) a sentence should be similar to sentences imposed on similar offenders for similar offences committed in similar circumstances;
> (c) where consecutive sentences are imposed, the combined sentence should not be unduly long or harsh;
> (d) an offender should not be deprived of liberty, if less restrictive sanctions may be appropriate in the circumstances; and

(e)  all available sanctions other than imprisonment that are reasonable in the circumstances should be considered for all offenders, with particular attention to the circumstances of aboriginal offenders.

Proponents of the Sentencing Commission recommendations were disappointed especially by the lower authority given to the principle of proportionality.[66] Rather than proportionality being the engine of sentence determination, it became simply a brake. It was described by Rosenberg J.A. as a concept "rooted in notions of fairness and justice" which ensured that an offender was not "unjustly dealt with for the sake of the common good."[67] Other criticisms have been directed to the absence of any definition given to the set of mitigating circumstances. When Bill C-41 was before Parliament, the entire debate was consumed by misdirected and specious attacks on section 718.2(a)(i) because of the inclusion of "sexual orientation." Appellate courts had, for some time, used the sentencing process to reflect the societal importance of respecting the "dignity, privacy, and person" of other members of the community.[68] The provision was nothing new but its proposed codification distracted the Bill C-41 debate.

## 3)  The Effect of the Codification of Principles

At first, there was a debate amongst judges as to whether the entrenchment of codified principles changed the sentencing context. The view that the amendments merely restated the previously applied principles was offered by Sherstobitoff J.A. in R. v. McDonald,[69] one of the early and important conditional sentence cases. Relying on the general approach advocated by the Saskatchewan Court of Appeal in Morrissette, he held that the entrenched statement did not change the bases upon which sentencing had always proceeded. Even the new sections 718.2(d) and (e) did not, in his view, support the proposition that Parliament had intended to "make major changes to the principles of sentencing." Vancise J.A. responded by arguing that the legislation reflected

---

66  See the criticisms in J.V. Roberts & A. von Hirsch, "Statutory Sentencing Reform: The Purpose and Principles of Sentencing" (1995) 37 Crim. L.Q. 220 at 230–32.

67  R. v. Priest (1996), 110 C.C.C. (3d) 289 at 297–98 (Ont. C.A.).

68  See, for example, R. v. Ingram (1977), 35 C.C.C. (2d) 376 (Ont. C.A.) (racially motivated assaults; R. v. Lelas (1990), 58 C.C.C. (3d) 568 (Ont. C.A.) (racially motivated mischief to property); and R. v. Atkinson, Ing and Roberts (1978), 43 C.C.C. (2d) 342 (Ont. C.A.) (assault motivated by hatred over gays).

69  [1997], 113 C.C.C. (3d) 418 (Sask. C.A.).

"the stated policy of the government that imprisonment should be used as a last resort."[70] When new sentencing issues reached the Supreme Court, the argument was raised and resolved — through the statements of purpose, objectives, and principles, Parliament had issued new directions to sentencing judges.

## 4) Codification and the Supreme Court Decision in R. v. *Gladue*

In 1999, the case of *R. v. Gladue*[71] came before the Supreme Court requiring an interpretation of section 718.2(e) and the phrase "with particular attention to the circumstances of aboriginal offenders." A twenty-year-old aboriginal woman had pleaded guilty to manslaughter after the stabbing death of her husband. She had been sentenced to three years imprisonment. Evidence had been adduced that she had been recently diagnosed as suffering from a hyperthyroid condition which would produce exaggerated reactions to emotional situations. The offence took place in Nanaimo where the couple lived. The sentencing judge inquired whether their previous home in Alberta was in an aboriginal community and was advised that it was "just a regular community." Accordingly, the judge found no reason to take aboriginal background into account. The majority of the British Columbia Court of Appeal dismissed the sentence appeal but held that the application of section 718.2(e) was not precluded because an aboriginal offender does not live on a reserve. The dissent by Rowles J.A. argued that section 718.2(e) represented a recogniton of the systemic discrimination which aboriginal offenders had suffered within the criminal justice system as evidenced by the disproportionate degree of incarceration. Accordingly, she would have reduced the sentence to two years less a day.

While the immediate issue was the scope of section 718.2(e), and the phrase "with particular attention to the circumstances of aboriginal offenders," the case also raised the more general issue of whether the new statutorily-entrenched principles of sentencing were simply a codification of already accepted principles. Here, Cory and Iacobucci JJ., writing for a unanimous Supreme Court, explained that the determination of Parliamentary intention and legislative purpose required an examination of both intrinsic factors and "admissible extrinsic" evi-

---

70   *Ibid.* at 434.
71   [1999] 1 S.C.R. 688 [*Gladue*].

dence dealing with legislative history and context.[72] Accordingly, the ensuing analysis included excerpts from statements in the House of Commons by the Minister of Justice, data and findings from official inquiries,[73] and academic research.[74] They noted the high and rising rate of incarceration in Canada compared to other industrialized democracies and the even more disturbing rate of incarceration of aboriginal people. They concluded that the newly amended Part XXIII went beyond codifying recognized principles:

> . . . the government position when Bill C-41 was under consideration was that the new Part XXIII was to be remedial in nature. The proposed enactment was directed, in particular, at reducing the use of prison as a sanction, at expanding the use of restorative justice principles in sentencing, and at engaging in both of these objectives with a sensitivity to aboriginal community justice initiatives when sentencing aboriginal offenders.[75]

Consequently, the elements included in sections 718 and 718.2, and in particular sections 718.2(d) and (e), translated the theoretical principle of restraint into a direction to sentencing judges to look for alternatives and avoid imprisonment whenever an alternative would satisfy the objectives of sentencing.

The role of section 718.2(e) in relation to aboriginal offenders was the focus of the decision. Subsequently, it has been the source of controversy as a result of the suggestions, especially in the media, that the Supreme Court has authorized a different standard of sentencing for aboriginal offenders. This view misunderstands the import of the decision. Throughout, Cory and Iacobucci JJ. emphasized the role of individualization as it applies to all offenders but they refined it with respect to aboriginal offenders expressly to include two questions

---

72   *Ibid.* at 704, relying on *Re Rizzo & Rizzo Shoes Ltd.*, [1998] 1 S.C.R. 27; and *R. v. Chartrand*, [1994] 2 S.C.R. 864.

73   Cory and Iacobucci JJ. included material from the *Report of the Canadian Sentencing Commission*, above note 16; the House of Commons, Standing Committee on Justice and Solicitor General, *Report of the Standing Committee on Justice and Solicitor General on Its Review of Sentencing, Conditional Release and Related Aspects of Corrections: Taking Responsibility* (Ottawa: The Committee, 1988); and the Royal Commission on Aboriginal Peoples, *Bridging the Cultural Divide: A Report on Aboriginal People and Criminal Justice in Canada* (Ottawa: The Commission, 1996): see *Gladue*, above note 71 at 717–22.

74   See especially M. Jackson, "Locking Up Natives in Canada" (1989), 23 U.B.C. L. Rev. 215.

75   *Gladue*, above note 71 at 714.

which, in the non-aboriginal context, are usually present although implicit or subliminal: how did background contribute to the offence? what is the community's view of the appropriate sanction?

These are not novel considerations. Specifically with respect to section 718.2(e) and aboriginal offenders, Cory and Iacobucci JJ. said the sentencing judge must consider:

> (A) The unique systemic or background factors which may have played a part in bringing the particular aboriginal offender before the courts; and

> (B) The types of sentencing procedures and sanctions which may be appropriate in the circumstances for the offender because of his or her particular aboriginal heritage or connection.[76]

This requires and legitimizes a consideration of aboriginal background, with respect both to understanding the offence and choosing a fit sentence in order that restraint may reduce the use and extent of incarceration. The major aspect of section 718.2(e) is its enhancement of the principles of restraint by requiring that sentencing judges consider and reject all available options before turning to imprisonment. While this principle applies to all offenders, the inclusion of the specific reference to aboriginal offenders in section 718.2(e) ensures that a background, including historical and systemic discrimination, and the availability of culturally based sanctions, will be considered within the decision-making process.

# E.  CONCLUSION

Discretion continues to be the hallmark of sentencing in Canada. The *Criminal Code* now contains statements of purpose, objectives, and principles, which are more than a mere codification of accepted sentencing principles — they are intended to be a remedial response to the fact of over-incarceration. The principle of restraint is an entrenched guiding principle. Proportionality also is now included in the *Criminal Code* as a "fundamental principle" of sentencing, but the 1996 attempt at sentencing reform did not adopt the Sentencing Commission's view that a more instrumentally directed model was needed to ensure certainty and predictability while reducing disparity. Appellate efforts to constrain discretion by imposing rigid starting points have been

---

76   *Ibid.* at 737–38.

rejected by the Supreme Court, but appellate guidelines, whether in the form of starting points or ranges, are being encouraged.

Two other important methodological points have been confirmed and refined by the most recent Supreme Court of Canada sentencing decisions.[77] First, the role of individualization as the primary mode of sentencing has gained ground. The myriad circumstances in which offences can be committed and the infinitely varied characters of the people who commit them require that sentencing be approached with an open mind. The analytical process of refining prinicples and the concomitant need to develop new sentencing resources, particularly at the community level, should encourage judges to see every offender as an individual for whom the fit sentence may not be pulled from a mould. Of course, proportionality and parity will inevitably produce similar sentences for similarly situated offenders. However, this does not foreclose creativity to achieve individual results on a principled basis.

Second, the importance of the sentencing judge's discretion has been re-enforced by the entrenchment of deference as the guiding principle of appellate review.[78] As a result, counsel must be vigilant to ensure that options are carefully canvassed and the factual basis clearly laid out at the trial level. While errors can be rectified on appeal, it will become increasingly hard to reverse discretionary choices.


## FURTHER READINGS

CANADIAN SENTENCING COMMISSION, *Sentencing Reform: A Canadian Approach* (Ottawa: Supply and Services Canada, 1987)

COLE, D., & A. MANSON, *Release from Imprisonment: The Law of Sentencing, Parole and Judicial Review* (Toronto: Carswell, 1990)

GREEN, R.G., *Justice in Aboriginal Communities: Sentencing Alternatives* (Saskatoon: Purich Publishing, 1998)

HOGARTH, J., *Sentencing as a Human Process* (Toronto: University of Toronto Press, 1971)

MANSON, A., "*McDonnell* and the Methodology of Sentencing" (1997) 6 C.R. (5th) 277

---

77   Here, I am referring to *Gladue, ibid.*; and *R. v. Proulx*, [2000] 1 S.C.R. 61, discussed in detail in Chapter 9, below.

78   See the discussion in Chapter 12, below.

RADZINOWICZ, L., & R. HOOD, *A History of the English Criminal Law*, vol. 5 (London: Stevens & Sons, 1986)

ROBERTS, J., & A. VON HIRSCH, "Statutory Sentencing Reform: The Purpose and Principles of Sentencing" (1995) 37 Crim. L.Q.

ROYAL COMMISSION ON ABORIGINAL PEOPLES, *Bridging the Cultural Divide: A Report on Aboriginal People and Criminal Justice in Canada* (Ottawa: Canada Communication Group, 1996)

# CHAPTER 5

# SUBSTANTIVE PRINCIPLES OF SENTENCING

## A. THE ROLE OF PRINCIPLES

In the last chapter, we considered the evolution of sentencing discretion and how the entrenchment of statements of purpose and general principles in sections 718 to 718.2 of the *Criminal Code* were intended to provide a framework for the exercise of discretion. In this chapter, we begin an examination of the principles, rules, and factors that a judge needs to consider to properly exercise sentencing discretion. Some are now included in the *Code* while others remain within the arena of the common law. It is important to remember the distinction drawn by H.L.A. Hart between the set of ideas which provide justifications for punishment in general, and the relevant principles which justify an individual sentence imposed on a specific offender for a particular offence. Canadian judges continue to consider the amalgam of justificatory objectives in an attempt to determine which one, or combination, deserves priority in a given case. The process of choosing the right objective may be difficult depending on the gravity of the offence, the harm caused, and the antecedents of the offender, but it is a misnomer to refer to the objectives in section 718 as "principles." The principles of sentencing are the analytical concepts which refine and shape the process of choosing objectives. This chapter examines the primary substantive principles: proportionality, parity, and restraint. Chapter 6 examines the narrower rules which provide responses to specific sentencing problems, and Chapter 7 discusses factors which can apply to aggravate or mitigate a sentence. In sum, these principles and rules provide the framework for assessing gravity, and for determining which options are reasonable in the circumstances and whether the case falls at the low or high end for quantum purposes.

## B. PROPORTIONALITY

Under the heading "fundamental principle," section 718.1 provides:

> A sentence must be proportionate to the gravity of the offence and the degree of responsibility of the offender.

The idea of proportionality is now a central element in Canadian sentencing but its origins are far from recent. In the eighteenth century, Beccaria argued that punishments "should be chosen in due proportion to the crime so as to make the most efficacious and lasting impression on the minds of men, and the least painful impressions on the body of the criminal."[1] Judges and philosophers have maintained the prominence of proportionality although, from time to time, we have witnessed egregious examples of its failures, especially with respect to capital punishment. In *R. v. Wilmott*, an often-quoted sentencing case, McLennan J.A. reinforced the currency of Beccaria's approach and spoke of the need to ensure a "just proportion" between the offence and the subsequent penalty.[2] Recently, from a philosophical perspective, the role of proportionality has been promoted by the interest in "just deserts" models of sentencing. Von Hirsch, the prominent "just deserts" theorist, has explained the reason for the current focus on proportionality:

> It is because the principle embodies, or seems to embody, notions of justice. People have a sense that punishments scaled to the gravity of the offenses are fairer than punishments that are not. Departures from proportionality — though perhaps eventually justifiable — at least stand in need of defence.[3]

In *R. v. Priest*, a case that raised important questions about sentencing youthful offenders for an apparently prevalent offence, Rosenberg J.A. also relied on fairness as the underpinning of proportionality and was

---

1   C. Beccaria, *Of Crimes and Punishments*, trans. J. Grigson (New York: Marsilio, 1996) at 49.
2   [1967] 1 C.C.C. 172 at 179 (Ont. C.A.).
3   A. von Hirsch, "Proportionality in the Philosophy of Punishment" (1992) 16 Crime & Just. 55 at 56.

careful to point out that this ensured that an individual is not sacrificed "for the sake of the common good."[4]

## 1) Gravity of the Offence

While the promotion of fairness might be the underlying rationale for arguments about proportionality, its elements are more complex. Proportionality is a relative concept which consists of two dimensions, both of which are measures of gravity. First, the sentence for an offence must properly reflect the relation in terms of gravity that the offence generally bears to other offences. By definition, some crimes are more blameworthy than others. In this respect, an individual sentence can be placed on a scale of punishments at a point where it is in close proximity to offences of similar blameworthiness but perceptibly distant from those that are distinctly more or less blameworthy. Second, the sentence must reflect the various degrees of seriousness which might apply to the range of conduct covered by the offence. This includes the quantum of harm caused or potentially caused, and the degree of participation.

Gravity is a common word that masks some difficult sentencing problems. It is a compendious description that encompasses three elusive concepts: harm, potential harm, and blameworthiness. For sentencing purposes each generates its own problems of proof, theoretical justification, and conceptual coherence.

## 2) Proportionality and Blameworthiness

While there may be controversies surrounding the precise content of proportionality, there is no dispute about its central role in sentencing in Canada — even before it was entrenched as a "fundamental principle" in the *Criminal Code*, the Supreme Court of Canada confirmed its prominence. The need for a proportionate relation between punishment and blameworthiness was included as a principle of fundamental justice in *R. v. Martineau*, thereby raising it to a matter of constitutional significance.[5] More recently, proportionality was at the centre of the discussion of the role of retribution in sentencing by Lamer C.J.C. in *R. v. M.(C.A.).*[6] He argued that retribution provides the "conceptual link" between criminal liability and the eventual sanction, and that

---

4    (1996), 110 C.C.C. (3d) 289 at 298 (Ont. C.A.).
5    [1990] 2 S.C.R. 633 at 645–46.
6    [1996] 1 S.C.R. 500 [*M.(C.A.)*].

proportionality determines its measure. Distinguishing retribution from vengeance, he stated:

> Retribution in a criminal context, by contrast, represents an objective, reasoned and measured determination of an appropriate punishment which properly reflects the *moral culpability* of the offender, having regard to the intentional risk-taking of the offender, the consequential harm caused by the offender, and the normative character of the offender's conduct. Furthermore, unlike vengeance, retribution incorporates a principle of restraint; retribution requires the imposition of a just and appropriate punishment, and *nothing more.*[7]

This suggests two important observations. First, proportionality must be a central feature of a constitutional sentencing system. Second, at the individual level, proportionality must be present but will take the form of a complicated calculus. At least in its Canadian conception, it includes the element of restraint, which provides a brake for retributivist zeal.

## 3) Proportionality and Harm

Certainly, harm caused (or at least harm risked) is a factor encompassed by gravity. The question is whether all harm actually done can be attributed to the offender for sentencing purposes, or whether there are limits on the consequences which can fairly be taken into account. Looking at the *Criminal Code*, an argument can be mounted that the provisions contemplate including all harm, without qualification. The terms "harm done" or "loss suffered" appear in sections 718(e), 722(1), and 722(4).[8] These provisions provide a statutory opportunity for victims to explain in their own terms the consequences to them of the offence. They are used without any modifier or qualification beyond the fact that they must arise or result from the commission of the offence. Indeed, the definition of victim includes someone who has "suffered physical or emotional loss as a result of the commission of the offence."[9] Again, the provision can be interpreted as including any consequential harm as long as it can be linked causally to the offence.

Sentencing jurisprudence has not resolved this issue. In R. v. *Petrovic*,[10] a man had been abusing his wife, both verbally and physically,

---

7   *Ibid.* at 557–58.
8   Harm, damage and loss are also used as triggering factors for the use of restitution orders as provided by s. 738(1) of the *Criminal Code*.
9   Section 722(4)(a), *ibid.*
10   (1984), 13 C.C.C. (3d) 416 (Ont. C.A.).

during a social night out with friends. Upon returning home, he assaulted her again by slapping her repeatedly. Later, she jumped from the apartment balcony and killed herself. The husband was convicted of assault causing bodily harm and sentenced to five years imprisonment. The Court of Appeal concluded that the sentence was, to some extent, influenced by the suicide. Given that there was no offence charged in relation to the death, the court held that the sentencing judge erred by considering the actual result of the assault rather than relying only on the probable result. It reduced the sentence to two years. This was different from cases where the consequence of death is included in the charge but at trial causation cannot be proven.[11] The *Petrovic* case was a situation where causation was apparent but there was no criminal culpability in relation to the consequence. It seems that the court was saying that only consequences which fit within the scope of a probable result of the criminal act will be relevant in determining a fit sentence.

The argument that only probable consequences should be attributed to an offender is an attractive one because it seems to link consequences to culpability and state of mind. This would be consistent with the analysis of Wood J.A. in a series of sentencing cases dealing with impaired driving causing death and bodily harm.[12] The creation in 1985 of new offences that incorporated consequences and higher penalty ranges raised the question of what factors should lead to a high-end sentence when death or serious bodily harm had been caused. Wood J.A. concluded that moral culpability was the key. Since consequences are fortuitous, he grounded culpability in the offender's conduct, especially a record of persistent alcohol abuse combined with driving. About consequences in general, he said:

> As a society, we long ago opted for a system of criminal justice in which the moral culpability of an offence is determined by the state of mind which accompanies the offender's unlawful act. Thus the consequences of an unlawful act when either intended, or foreseen and recklessly disregarded, aggravate its moral culpability. But consequences, which are neither intended nor foreseen and recklessly

---

11   See, for example, *R. v. Brown*, [1991] 2 S.C.R. 518, where the charges included criminal negligence causing death but the jury convicted only of dangerous driving *simpliciter*. The Supreme Court held that the sentencing must proceed on a factual basis consistent with the verdict. Accordingly, the death could not be considered.

12   See *R. v. Sweeney* (1992), 71 C.C.C. (3d) 82 (B.C.C.A.).

ignored, cannot aggravate the moral culpability of an unlawful act, except and to the extent that Parliament so decrees.[13]

The opinion of Wood J.A. was written before the Supreme Court of Canada confirmed the constitutionality of crimes for which culpability is based on a form of negligence.[14] After this development, one might argue that the Wood approach could be updated to limit relevant consequences to intended, foreseen, and recklessly disregarded results for offences based on subjective fault, plus reasonably foreseeable consequences for offences based on conduct that is a marked departure from the standard of a reasonable person in the circumstances. On the other hand, given the importance of harm to gravity, and the centrality of gravity to proportionality, a preferable view would be to use the simpler approach of restricting harm to intended, foreseen, or reasonably foreseeable consequences for all offences. This position is reflected in the recent *Youth Criminal Justice Act*.[15]

But the jurisprudence has not consistently restricted the set of relevant consequences to what is probable or reasonably foreseeable. Occasionally, one sees attempts to include actual consequences which do not appear to meet this threshold. In *R. v. Phillips*,[16] a man was charged with first-degree murder after a police officer was stabbed and died. Officers had been called on two occasions during the same evening to a rural residence because of the accused's violent conduct. After the second incident, Phillips fled to the bush. He was pursued by a group of people including police officers. In the dark, he attacked and killed one of his pursuers, who was a police officer. By rejecting first-degree murder and returning a verdict of guilty to second-degree, the parole ineligibility issue had to proceed on the basis that Phillips did not know that the deceased was a police officer. The Court of Appeal held that the "unforeseen" consequence that a police officer had died could be considered on sentencing. Because it was unforeseen, it did not trigger the deterrence objective, but it did raise the issue of denunciation because of the community value inherent in the need to protect the lives of police officers.

---

13    *Ibid.* at 97.
14    See *R. v. Creighton*, [1993] 3 S.C.R. 3; *R. v. Gosset*, [1993] 3 S.C.R. 76; *R. v. Finlay*, [1993] 3 S.C.R. 103; and *R. v. Naglik*, [1993] 3 S.C.R. 122.
15    Bill C-3, *An Act in respect of criminal justice for young persons and to amend and repeal other acts*, 2d Sess., 36th Parl., 1999 (2d reading 23 November 1999). Section 37(3)(b) requires a youth court judge to take into account "the harm done to victims and whether it was intended or reasonably foreseeable."
16    (1999), 138 C.C.C. (3d) 297 (Ont. C.A.).

The *Phillips* decision does not stand for the proposition that, in all cases, unforeseen circumstances can be attributed to the offender. The issue comes back to culpability. Given the importance of subjective foresight in murder cases, the Court of Appeal was required to address the focused issue of whether the special status of the victim was relevant even though the jury was not persuaded beyond a reasonable doubt that the offender knew he was stabbing a police officer. While the court's conclusion was directed to the issue of actual foresight, the circumstances of the case make it clear that the death of a police officer was a reasonably foreseeable consequence even if Phillips did not subjectively foresee it at the time of the stabbing. Whether attributable consequences are determined by the set of results which can be circumscribed by the test of reasonable foreseeability was not the issue which the court in *Phillips* was required to decide, but the decision can be reconciled with that view.

In *R. v. M.(C.A.)*, Lamer C.J.C. said that it is the "element of 'moral blameworthiness' which animates the determination of the appropriate quantum of punishment for a convicted offender as a 'just sanction.'"[17] The relationship between moral blameworthiness and harm must be a function of the relevant culpability standard. Using manslaughter as an example, death will, with the exception of provocation cases, have been unintended. While it remains the pivotal consideration for sentencing, it is not viewed in a vacuum but rather as a function of the conduct which produced it. This covers the spectrum from a punch to a vicious beating so long as the act or conduct meets the test of objective foresight of bodily harm. Culpability is reduced as the prospect of death diminishes in relation to the violence which produced it — the less violent the act, the less culpable the offender. When the prospect of harm falls below the level of reasonably foreseeable bodily harm, the offence is no longer manslaughter. At that point, it would be wrong to take a consequential death into account. Accordingly, even in the most compelling case, where a death has resulted from an offence, a careful understanding of the intersection of culpability and harm precludes taking into account an actual consequence which does not meet the reasonably foreseeable test. Of course, Parliament can expand the scope of attributable consequences. Arguably, this is the case with manslaughter itself where the culpability standard has been interpreted to be only reasonable foresight of bodily harm. If proportionality is a constitutional obligation, the gravity of an offence for punishment

---

17   *M.(C.A.)*, above note 6 at 557.

purposes must be linked to culpability and the kinds of consequences which may reasonably be expected.

## 4) Actual Harm and Potential Harm

The issue of potential harm also depends on the nature of the offence and the relevant culpability standard. In cases where conduct without consequences is in issue, as is the case with dangerous driving or impaired driving where there are no injuries, the punishment should be determined by the nature of conduct in relation to the potential for reasonably foreseeable consequences. Accordingly, the absence of consequences is less important than the quality of the driving, or the degree of intoxication, or the number of previous acts of impaired driving. Similarly, when the offence involves a threat, culpability will be a function of the threatened consequences, including both the physical and psychological harm that would likely occur if the threat was carried out. Accordingly, in a case of a threatened sexual assault, the offence is automatically one of sexual assault causing bodily harm because of the presumed likelihood of psychological harm resulting from a sexual assault. However, when the offence involves a consequence and not a threat, the extent of the consequence, including any psychological harm, must be proven if it is to be taken into account.[18] Sopinka J. in *McDonnell* went further and suggested that allegations of physical or psychological harm should result in charges under the *Criminal Code* offences which expressly include bodily harm like assault causing bodily harm or sexual assault causing bodily harm.[19] These *obiter* comments would, if followed, mean that a sentencing court could not take into account a broken nose unless the charge was assault causing bodily harm. Encouraging more serious charges is not a necessary answer so long as the Crown is required to make timely disclosure and is held to the burden of proof beyond a reasonable doubt that applies to all aggravating factors. In subsequent decisions, courts have not followed the Sopinka view. It has been expressly rejected by the Alberta Court of Appeal which has held that a sentencing court is not precluded from considering actual psychological harm when the Crown has charged only sexual assault *simpliciter*.[20]

---

18   See *R. v. McDonnell*, [1997] 1 S.C.R. 948 at 976–77, Sopinka J. See the full discussion of this case in Chapter 4, above.

19   *Ibid.* at 977.

20   See *R. v. Almon* (1999), 250 A.R. 157 (C.A.).

## 5) Proportionality and the Degree of Participation

The Canadian law of party or accessorial liability makes all parties equally culpable with the principal actor or actors. In other words, for responsibility purposes, everyone is equally guilty whether they are perpetrators, aiders, abettors, or parties under section 21(2) of the *Criminal Code*. This is not the case, however, for sentencing purposes, where a more individualized approach is taken. Proportionality requires the sentencing court to determine, acknowledge, and take into account the relationship of the offender to the offence and other participating offenders. This is a large part of what is meant by "degree of responsibility" in section 718.1. Of course, it also encompasses any form of diminished or impaired responsibility that can mitigate blameworthiness, especially for offences that require subjective fault. The focus is always on individual culpability for the offence as committed.

When dealing with parties, the issue can become clouded. As a general rule, there ought to be a distinction between the sanctions imposed on perpetrators and those with a lesser level of complicity. However, this assumes that the distinction is meaningful. If the appropriate sanctions for the offence for all participants fall at a low level, there is likely no need to impose different sanctions simply to exhibit a distinction. Also, there may be cases where the distinction between perpetrator and party does not reflect a difference in blameworthiness or at least show the perpetrator is clearly more blameworthy. Assume a shoplifting where A encourages B to steal an object and offers to act as lookout. B is the perpetrator and A is both an abettor and aider. It would be wrong to assess B with a higher level of blameworthiness, given A's central role.

Aside from formal legal characterizations as parties, there may be other distinctions in responsibility between participants which are pertinent for proportionality purposes. For example, the distinction between leader and follower can be a relevant consideration. Similarly, in crimes involving financial gain, distinctions between participants in the amount of benefits actually received or anticipated are relevant because it is assumed that this reflects differential degrees of responsibility.[21] Where multiple parties are involved in a crime of violence, distinctions can be drawn based on the actual harm caused by each

---

21  See *R. v. Gaudet* (1998), 125 C.C.C. (3d) 17 (Ont. C.A.), where an eight-year sentence for a large-scale fraud was upheld against the accused who was characterized as the leader and who received a larger share of the money; two other co-accused received sentences of five years.

participant but it is not always the case that greater harm caused means a greater sentence. Common intention or the degree of encouragement can equalize sentences regardless of distinctions in harm actually caused. Similarly, the existence of a substantial record for crimes of violence can distinguish between co-accused even to the extent of justifying a greater sentence for the person who caused less harm.[22]

Another degree of participation issue has been noted in conspiracy cases. Given that conspiracy prosecutions usually mean that the offence has not been completed, responsibility depends on whether the Crown can establish an agreement. Sometimes, very little in the way of an overt act is sufficient. In terms of sentencing, degree of participation is an important distinguishing feature but can be difficult to determine depending on the extent of the evidence indicating who played leadership roles and who played subordinate ones. Courts have recognized that a relationship with a major participant may result in acts which constitute membership in the conspiracy and that such "situational" involvement warrants a lower order sentence. It is not necessary to show any form of duress or compulsion to qualify for this mitigating consideration.[23]

## C. PARITY

Section 718.2(b), one of the recently entrenched principles of sentencing, requires a court to take into consideration the principle that

> a sentence should be similar to sentences imposed on similar offenders for similar offences committed in similar circumstances.

This is a re-statement of the traditionally accepted principle of parity which, by itself, is an attempt to bring the rule of law to sentencing. Offenders who are equally blameworthy ought to receive approximately the same punishment. Punishments cannot be identical but only approximately the same given sentencing discretion, individualization, and the recognition that cases are rarely identical.

---

22   In *R. v. Cece and Taylor*, the jury returned verdicts of guilty to second-degree murder for both co-accused; the one who actually stabbed the police officer was sentenced to life with no parole eligibility for sixteen years while the other offender received a sentence of life with no parole eligibility for eighteen years. The explanation for the distinction was the record for crimes of violence: see J. Gadd, "Police Killers Whisper Apologies to Widow: Cece and Taylor Sentenced to Long Prison Terms" *Globe and Mail* (22 January 2000) A1.

23   See *R. v. Valentini* (1999), 43 O.R. (3d) 178 at 209, Rosenberg J.A. (C.A.).

The promotion of parity is often discussed using the converse term "disparity," which has been a concern during the decades of discussions about sentencing reform in Canada.[24] When one considers not only the individualized nature of decision making, but also the recently imposed standard of deference that appellate courts owe to the trial judge's sentencing decisions, it is clear that a "considerable latitude for disparity"[25] is expected and condoned across the system. The legitimate concern is about unwarranted disparity, meaning variations of a substantial degree which cannot be justified by reference to differences in individual circumstances.

At the simplest level, there should not be disparity between co-accused with similar backgrounds because the offence will be empirically identical. However, co-accused are not always dealt with at the same time by the same judge. By itself, the difference between a guilty plea and a trial may create a distinction depending on timing, effect on witnesses, and sincerity of remorse. More importantly, when co-accused are tried separately, the factual basis of sentencing may differ depending on such things as what facts formed the basis of a guilty plea, evidentiary rulings, or findings of fact. Accordingly, it is not always easy to achieve parity between co-accused.

Beyond the situation of co-accused, the set of distinctions which may produce disparity expand substantially. Not only will two offenders rarely be similar, but offences occur in myriad circumstances producing infinite consequences. For sentencing purposes, it is necessary to characterize the essential elements of an offence and to weed out distinctions which are irrelevant. For example, when dealing with crimes of violence, the age of a victim is relevant in distinguishing between an assault on a child compared to an assault on an adult but unlikely to be significant if one victim is twenty-four years old and the other twenty-nine years old. Accordingly, offences need to be carefully characterized before comparison with other sentences is meaningful. From an appellate perspective, comparison for the purpose of reducing disparity invokes the standard of deference which applies generally to appellate review. Accordingly, the Supreme Court has held that "a court of appeal should only intervene to minimize the disparity of sentences where the sentence imposed by the trial judge is in substantial

---

24   See Canadian Sentencing Commission, *Sentencing Reform: A Canadian Approach* (Ottawa: Supply and Services Canada, 1987) at 71–76.

25   As was observed by Vancise J.A. in *R. v. Laliberte* (2000), 143 C.C.C. (3d) 503 at 538 (Sask. C.A.) [*Laliberte*].

and marked departure from the sentences customarily imposed for similar offenders committing similar crimes."[26]

The principle of parity makes other sentencing decisions relevant. A sentencing judge needs to know what sanctions have been imposed on similar offenders for committing the offence in similar circumstances. Here, some practical issues can arise. For some offences, sentencing attitudes have changed over time. Accordingly, what was appropriate twenty years ago may no longer be helpful. As well, sentencing decisions can have a local aspect. As Lamer C.J.C. said in *R. v. M.(C.A.)*:

> . . . sentences for a particular offence should be expected to vary to some degree across various communities and regions in this country, as the "just and appropriate" mix of accepted sentencing goals will depend on the needs and current conditions of and in the particular community where the crime occurred.[27]

This is often the case with sentences involving community sanctions which can reflect not only local attitudes but also local resources. This does not mean that they should be dismissed for parity purposes. Instead, it means that sanctions need to be equated to take account of differences in resources.

The way in which sentencing decisions are communicated can also present a practical problem. An absence of facts in many sentencing decisions, or the reports of them, can preclude useful comparisons. A sentencing judge needs an adequate factual account to determine whether another case and another offender are sufficiently similar for parity purposes. Many sentencing decisions are too devoid of facts to be useful — this is especially true of digest services where the whole decision is not provided.

---

26  *M.(C.A.)*, above note 6 at 567.
27  *Ibid.* See also the comments of Vancise J.A. in *Laliberte*, above note 25 at 538, where he noted that the Supreme Court has recognized: "sentences will vary across various communities and regions because the accepted sentencing goals depend upon the needs and current conditions in the community where the crimes occur. The corollary of this proposition is that less disparity should be tolerated within a particular community. Indeed, it can be argued that disparity is not in and of itself a bad thing. It reflects the individualized nature of sentencing."

# D. RESTRAINT

A major aspect of the 1996 amendments was the entrenchment of the principle of restraint in sentencing. This is achieved through three specific provisions. Within section 718, the statement of purpose and objectives, the objective of "separation" (a euphemism for imprisonment) is qualified by the phrase "where necessary." Section 718.2(d), the correlative provision, provides that "an offender should not be deprived of liberty, if less restrictive sanctions may be appropriate in the circumstances." To add some methodological bite to restraint, section 718.2(e) requires a sentencing judge to consider "all available sanctions other than imprisonment that are reasonable in the circumstances." These provisions exist to discourage imprisonment when another less onerous sanction will also satisfy the relevant sentencing principles.

Restraint means that prison is the sanction of last resort.[28] However, the 1996 amendments go beyond expressing this fiat. Restraint also means that when considering other sanctions, the sentencing court should seek the least intrusive sentence and the least quantum which will achieve the overall purpose of being an appropriate and just sanction. Moreover, the Supreme Court has interpreted the recent amendments as imposing on sentencing judges the obligation to expand the use of restorative justice principles.[29] While this is a change in direction of general applicability, it has special meaning when courts are responding to aboriginal offenders.[30]

## 1) Restraint and Aboriginal Persons

In recognition of the dramatic over-incarceration of aboriginal persons in Canada,[31] Parliament added a special direction to section 718.2(e): "with particular attention to the circumstances of aboriginal offenders." The Supreme Court was required to interpret this direction in R. v. Gladue,[32] a case involving a young aboriginal woman who had been sentenced to three years for manslaughter for the stabbing of her husband.[33] In her detailed dissenting judgment in the British Columbia Court of Appeal, Rowles J.A. canvassed a wide range of literature in

---

28  See R. v. Gladue, [1999] 1 S.C.R. 688 at 709, 715–19 [Gladue].
29  Ibid. at 714.
30  Ibid. at 727–31.
31  Ibid. at 719–23.
32  Above note 28.
33  See Chapter 4(D)(4) for details of the case.

order to document the systemic discrimination experienced by aboriginal people within the criminal justice system. In the Supreme Court, the unanimous judgment written by Cory and Iacobucci JJ. followed the conceptual path set by Rowles J.A.[34] They agreed that one function of section 718.2(e) was to redress the inordinate incarceration of aboriginal people:

> It is reasonable to assume that Parliament, in singling out aboriginal offenders for distinct sentencing treatment in s.718.2(e), intended to attempt to redress this social problem to some degree. The provision may properly be seen as Parliament's direction to members of the judiciary to inquire into the causes of the problem and to endeavour to remedy it, to the extent that a remedy is possible through the sentencing process.[35]

In its application of the principle of restraint in relation to aboriginal offenders, the decision in *Gladue* requires judges to consider the "unique systemic or background factors" which may have contributed to the offence; the availability and appropriateness of any sentencing procedures or alternatives within the aboriginal community or culture that might provide an alternative to incarceration; as well as the circumstances of the offender as an aboriginal person. The decision was careful to point out that section 718.2(e) did not automatically mandate a reduction in sentence because the offender is an aboriginal person. Particularly when dealing with offences that are "more serious and violent," the objectives of "separation, denunciation, and deterrence" will likely dominate the decision making whether the offender is an aboriginal or non-aboriginal offender.[36] This was demonstrated in the subsequent decision in *R. v. Wells*,[37] in which the Supreme Court rejected a conditional sentence for an aboriginal offender convicted of sexual assault. Iacobucci J. confirmed that the role of section 718.2(e) is to require a "different *methodology* for assessing a fit sentence for an aboriginal offender" and not to mandate a necessarily different result.[38] He emphasized that restraint in terms of finding alternatives to incarceration when reasonable applies to all offenders.

---

34   Although it did not result in a reduction of the sentence: *ibid.* at 740–41.
35   *Ibid.* at 722.
36   *Ibid.* at 728–34.
37   [2000] 1 S.C.R. 207.
38   *Ibid.* at 229.

# FURTHER READINGS

CANADIAN SENTENCING COMMISSION, *Sentencing Reform: A Canadian Approach* (Ottawa: Supply and Services Canada, 1987)

MORRIS, N., *The Future of Imprisonment* (Chicago: University of Chicago Press, 1974)

MORRIS, N., & M. TONRY, *Between Prison and Probation: Intermediate Punishments in a Rational Sentencing System* (New York: Oxford University Press, 1990)

VON HIRSCH, A., "Proportionality in the Philosophy of Punishment" (1992) 16 Crime and Justice 55

# CHAPTER 6

# RULES OF SENTENCING

## A. INTRODUCTION

Principles reflect broad concepts of general applicability while rules address specific problems. Given the array of offences in the *Criminal Code*, the various procedural requirements, and the infinite variety of circumstances in which offences can be committed, it should be no surprise that the principles of sentencing are not sufficiently precise to resolve the myriad problems which can arise. Over the years, answers have evolved to address specific questions. I consider these to be the rules of sentencing even though they are sometimes referred to as principles, a name I reserve for the larger and more abstract concepts discussed in Chapter 5. Some rules are contained in the *Code* and others are found in the jurisprudence of sentencing. Some are common and others are arcane. This chapter examines the set of rules available to resolve most of the problems which judges and lawyers will encounter.

## B. MULTIPLE SENTENCES: THE CONSECUTIVE/CONCURRENT ISSUE

### 1) The General Rule

At common law, a sentence commenced when imposed but judges had the power, in certain circumstances, to add one term of imprisonment to another.[1] The first rule is reflected by the current section 719(1) which provides:

> A sentence commences when it is imposed, except where a relevant enactment otherwise provides.

The ability to postpone a sentence was included in the English Draft Code of 1879 which found its way, along with its archaic language, into our *Criminal Code, 1892*.[2] The approach to multiple sentences, whether imposed by the same or subsequent judges, is governed by a combination of statutory provisions and common law jurisprudence. Generally, there is power to make a sentence consecutive to one previously imposed but this is usually a discretionary decision subject to a few common law principles. There are, however, some *Code* offences which require a consecutive sentence. For example, under sections 85(1) and (2) it is an additional offence to commit certain stipulated indictable offences with a firearm or imitation firearm.[3] Minimum punishments of one year and three years are mandated depending on whether the offence is a subsequent one or not. Section 85(4) requires that all sentences must be served consecutively to the sentence for the underlying offence and any other sentences previously imposed.

## 2) The *Paul* Problem

Until recently, there were situations in which a consecutive sentence was not legally permissible because of the sequence in which multiple convictions were registered. This situation arose from the Supreme Court's interpretation in *R. v. Paul*[5] of the archaic language in the enabling provision that existed at the time, the predecessor to the current

---

1    See *R. v. Wilkes* (1770), 4 Burr. 2427, 98 E.R. 327.
2    The code as drafted by Stephen became the *Criminal Code* (Indictable Offences Bill) of 1878. This led to the 1879 "Report of the Royal Commission Appointed to Consider the Law Relating to Indictable Offences, with an Appendix containing a Draft Code embodying the Suggestions of the Commissioners," C. 2345, Parl. Papers (1878–79), Vol. 20, p. 169, discussed in L. Radzinowicz & R. Hood, *A History of English Criminal Law*, vol. 5 (London: Stevens, 1986) at 739–40.
3    Section 85(1) of the *Criminal Code*, R.S.C. 1985, c. C-46, deals with firearms in the commission of all indictable offences except for the ten which carry mandatory minimum sentences of four years if a firearm is used: ss. 220, 236, 239, 244, 272, 273, 279, 279.1, 344, & 346. Section 85(2) deals with imitation firearms used in the commission of all indictable offences.
4    See ss. 85(3)(a), (b), & (c) of the *Criminal Code*.
5    [1982] 1 S.C.R. 621.

section 718.3(4). As a result, the key date for determining whether the sentence for offence B could be made consecutive to the sentence for offence A was the date of conviction for offence B. The only sentences to which the sentence for offence B could be made consecutive were sentences extant as of the date of conviction. For example, if a person was convicted of offence A on January 1 but not sentenced until February 1, a conviction for offence B registered on January 15 could not result in a sentence consecutive to that for offence A, since on the date of conviction, the offender was not subject to a previously imposed sentence. This historical anomaly, which resulted in a number of illegal consecutive sentences, was eliminated by an amendment[6] effective June 16, 1997. Now, the operative date is the date of a subsequent sentence. However, consecutive sentences imposed prior to June 16, 1997, are not remedied by the new amendment and there may still be some prisoners serving aggregate terms that include *Paul* problems.

## 3)  Section 718.3(4) and the Date of Sentencing

Now, section 718.3(4) resolves the issue by making the date of sentencing the relevant date. It provides:

> Where an accused
> (a)  is sentenced while under sentence for an offence, and a term of imprisonment, whether in default of payment of a fine or otherwise, is imposed,
> (b)  is convicted of an offence punishable with both fine and imprisonment and both are imposed, or
> (c)  is convicted of more offences than one, and
>> (i)   more than one fine is imposed,
>> (ii)  terms of imprisonment for the respective offences are imposed, or
>> (iii) a term of imprisonment is imposed in respect of one offence and a fine is imposed in respect of another offence,
> the court that sentences the accused may direct that the terms of imprisonment that are imposed by the court or result from the operation of subsection 734(4) shall be served consecutively.

---

6   *Criminal Law Improvement Act, 1996*, S.C. 1997, c. 18, s. 141.

This provision should cover most multiple offence situations, whether convictions are imposed by the same judge or different judges. It makes the date of sentencing the relevant date[7] so that a judge can consider whether to order the consecutive service of a sentence of imprisonment in relation to any sentences of imprisonment extant at that time. It even incorporates imprisonment that may result from default of payment of a fine, but a specific order is required dealing with the default term to make its service consecutive.[8]

## 4) The Transaction Concept

In exercising discretion over whether to order terms to be served concurrently or consecutively, the sentencing judge should ordinarily be governed by the principle that sentences which are part of the same event or transaction ought to be served concurrently but offences which are discrete in time or nature can be the subject of consecutive terms. The *Kienapple* principle ensures that multiple convictions are not entered when the elements of contemporaneous offences overlap.[9] However, when there are multiple convictions for related offences, there is a real concern about double punishment. It is generally assumed that culpability is aggravated by the fact that more than one offence has been committed. While this mutual aggravation of culpability may increase individual sentences, it should not be compounded by making them consecutive. Accordingly, when related convictions can be considered to be parts of the same transaction or event, they should ordinarily result in sentences served concurrently. In this way, it is the transaction which determines the sanction.

An analogy can be drawn to pleading rules in criminal procedure where the single transaction concept is also used to ensure that, in general, each count in an indictment applies to a single transaction.[10] For this purpose, courts have noted that "single transaction" is not synonymous with a single incident, occurrence, or offence.[11] Multiple offences can be included within the single transaction concept if there is continuity between them in the sense of forming part of an ongoing transaction.

---

7  See *R. v. Johnson* (1998), 131 C.C.C. (3d) 274 (B.C.C.A.).
8  See the discussion in Chapter 9, below, dealing with fines and imprisonment in default of payment. The 1996 amendments have attempted to make this consequence less frequent than it had previously been.
9  See *R. v. Kienapple*, [1975] 1 S.C.R. 729.
10  See s. 581(1) of the *Criminal Code*.
11  See *R. v. Selles* (1997), 116 C.C.C. (3d) 435 (Ont. C.A.).

A similar approach can be taken to grouping events together to consider whether concurrent sentences are appropriate. Exceptions to the single transaction concept occur when other principles intervene to distinguish elements of the event. For example, violence used against a police officer who has interrupted an offence or is attempting an arrest immediately after an offence is usually treated distinctly from the original offence.[12]

## 5) The Totality Principle

The global effect of consecutive sentences cannot produce excessive punishment, regardless of the number of offences. This is known as the totality principle, and is now entrenched in the *Criminal Code*:

> section 718.2(c) where consecutive sentences are imposed, the combined sentence should not be unduly long or harsh.

In determining whether a merged sentence is excessive, courts usually consider the age and rehabilitative prospects of the offender. Even when there is little evidence of positive rehabilitative prospects, total sentences should not be so long as to crush optimism about eventual re-integration. It is also relevant to consider the relative gravity of the underlying offences. For example, it would be extremely unusual if a string of "theft under" convictions, no matter how long, would warrant a penitentiary term of imprisonment.

There has been some controversy over how to calculate individual sentences when the totality principle operates to cap the global sentence. One method would be to artificially reduce the duration of the component sentences so that when grouped together consecutively they add up to the appropriate global sentence. This has been rejected by most courts which prefer to impose appropriate individual sentences and then order that some, or all of them, be served concurrently to reach the right global sentence. The latter method is preferable because it ensures frankness in that each conviction will generate an appropriate sentence, whether served concurrently or consecutively. Moreover, the impact of individual sentences will be preserved even if an appeal intervenes to eliminate some of the elements of the merged sentence.

---

12   See, for example, *R. v. Austin* (1980), 2 Cr. App. R. (S) 203 (C.A.).

## 6)  Bill C-251

In 1999, the House of Commons passed Bill C-251 which, as well as dealing with murder sentences,[13] also addressed multiple convictions for sexual assault. It provided that a person sentenced for more than one offence of sexual assault would be required to serve each component sentence consecutive to all others. This removal of sentencing discretion was, according to the supporters of the bill, necessary to respect the needs of individual victims. Apparently, as explained by the back-bencher who introduced the bill, some victims feel that their suffering is discounted by a global sentence. Other than the context of debates over Bill C-251, there does not seem to be any evidence, empirical or conceptual, that the need for mandatory consecutive sentences is a real issue. The proposal is constitutionally suspect on a number of grounds encompassed by sections 7 and 12 of the *Charter*.[14] Certainly, proportionality, individualization, and restraint would be subverted unjustifiably by mandatory consecutive sentences. Also, at some point the global sentence will be grossly disproportionate so as to implicate the guarantee against cruel and unusual punishment in section 12 of the *Charter*. If the legislation is passed into law, one can expect that judges will deliberately avoid its impact by reducing the duration of individual sentences to ensure a sensible global sentence.

# C.  YOUTHFUL OFFENDERS, FIRST OFFENDERS, AND FIRST CUSTODIAL SENTENCES

## 1)  General Approach

While these three qualities are distinct, they should be considered together because they often arise in the same context and they have a common source. The general principle that applies to youthful offenders and first offenders and the issue of a first custodial sentence stems

---

13  Bill C-251, *An Act to amend the Criminal Code and the Corrections and Conditional Release Act (cumulative sentences)*, 1st Sess., 36th Parl., 1999. Bill C-251 was reinstated as Bill C-247 in the 2d Session of the House of Commons, and referred to committee by the Senate on May 18, 2000. It provides that, if a person kills more than one victim, the periods of parole ineligibility applicable to the life sentences can be added to each other to a maximum of fifty years. At the time of writing, the bill had not passed the Senate.

14  *Canadian Charter of Rights and Freedoms, Part 1 of the Constitution Act, 1982*, being Schedule B to the Canada Act 1982 (U.K.), 1982, c. 11 [*Charter*].

from a combination of restraint and the notion that a lack of experience with the world warrants leniency and optimism for the future. Restraint also combines with optimism when considering a first custodial sentence in the sense that courts will attempt to limit the incarceration.

## 2) Presumption Against Incarceration

There is a presumption against incarceration for youthful offenders, especially if they are first offenders. While restraint ought to apply to all offenders, special care should be taken with youthful offenders to explore all alternatives and only incarcerate when the gravity of the offence requires it.[15] This often results in suspended sentences with terms of probation. Although these are viewed as lenient community sanctions, the potential net-widening effect that can be generated by a breach of condition raises the question of whether one ought to encourage greater use of modest fines, assuming an ability to pay. The sanction should always be the minimum intervention that is adequate in the circumstances.[16]

In *R. v. Leask*,[17] three offenders under the age of twenty had been sentenced to one year of imprisonment for a brutal assault on a stranger. Quoting from the earlier Ontario decision in *R. v. Demeter*,[18] the majority of the Manitoba Court of Appeal held that the paramount sentencing consideration for youthful first offenders was their immediate rehabilitation. Recognizing that some days in custody had already been served, the court set aside the sentences of imprisonment and levied substantial fines of $6000 on two offenders and ordered the third who could not pay a fine to perform 500 hours of community service.

## 3) First Custodial Sentence

Given the range of offences committed by youthful offenders, incarceration may sometimes be considered. Dealing specifically with a robbery, the Ontario Court of Appeal has said:

A first sentence of imprisonment especially for a first offender should be as short as possible and tailored to the individual circum-

---

15   See *R. v. Priest* (1996), 110 C.C.C. (3d) 289 at 294–96 [*Priest*]; and *R. v. Stein* (1974), 15 C.C.C. (2d) 376 (Ont. C.A.).
16   See *Priest, ibid.* at 295.
17   (1996), 112 C.C.C. (3d) 400 (Man. C.A.).
18   (1976), 32 C.C.C. (2d) 379 (Ont. C.A.).

stances of the accused rather than solely for the purpose of general deterrence."[19]

This dictum was applied recently in a case of administering a noxious substance to a child to reduce a sentence of imprisonment of two years less a day to time served plus three years probation.[20] The offender was thirty-one years old but the need to limit the duration of custody was applicable because it was her first custodial sentence. Accordingly, she was treated in a similar fashion to a youthful offender. The combination of youth and a first custodial term can have a substantial impact. In *R. v. Childs*, these factors resulted in a reduction of a twenty-five-year term for six offences including robbery, kidnapping, and extortion to a total sentence of twelve and a half years.[21] The offender was twenty-two years old.

## 4) Who Is a Youthful Offender?

How old is a youthful offender? Since the *Young Offenders Act* standardized the age of adult responsibility at eighteen years, the term "youthful offender" refers to a narrower group of young adults than it did before. But when does someone cease to qualify? In *R. v. Priest*, Rosenberg J.A. suggested that the issue was one of maturity and not a particular chronological age.[22] The British Columbia Court of Appeal seemed to consider a married twenty-five-year-old with two children who committed a robbery with a firearm and a mask as a youthful offender[23] — on the other hand, the Quebec Court of Appeal has held that a twenty-seven-year-old was too mature to argue that he was entitled to the leniency that might attach to "youthful folly."[24] When the Alberta Court of Appeal in 1982 decided as part of its starting point approach to consider a group of robberies committed by youthful

---

19   *R. v. Hayman* (1999), 135 C.C.C. (3d) 338 at 346 (Ont. C.A.) [*Hayman*], citing the decision in *R. v. Vandale* (1974), 21 C.C.C. (2d) 250 (Ont. C.A.).

20   *Hayman, ibid.*

21   (1984), 52 N.B.R. (2d) 9 (C.A.).

22   Above note 15.

23   See *R. v. Campbell* (1981), 64 C.C.C. (2d) 336 (B.C.C.A.), which allowed a Crown appeal against a suspended sentence and imposed a term of one-year imprisonment.

24   *R. v. Lafrance* (1993), 87 C.C.C. (3d) 82, Bisson C.J.Q. in dissent (Que. C.A.). The majority upheld a ninety-day intermittent sentence for possession of cocaine for the purposes of trafficking imposed at trial on the twenty-seven-year-old first offender. This was based largely on rehabilitative prospects which Otis J.A. said, at 94, "were best left to the privileged position of the sentencing judge."

offenders, the ages varied from sixteen to twenty-three years.[25] Perhaps it is safe to conclude that, subject to a finding of experience and maturity that disentitles an offender from inclusion in the group, youthful offenders will usually be between eighteen and twenty-five years old. This represents a potentially large number of offenders. In 1998, this group of offenders was the object of a significant minority of *Criminal Code* charges: 19.6 percent of violent offences; 25.6 percent of property offence charges; 20 percent of *Criminal Code* driving offences; and 26 percent of other *Criminal Code* charges.[26]

# D. MAXIMUM SENTENCES

## 1) The General Rule

With the exception of murder, which requires a mandatory sentence of life imprisonment, all *Criminal Code* offences have a stipulated maximum sentence.[27] The general rule is that the maximum sentence is reserved for the worst offence committed by the worst offender.[28] The threshold has also been cast in terms of whether the offence falls into a "category for which no other sentence is appropriate."[29]

However, the issue is not simply whether a sentencing court can imagine worse circumstances. It may be that the crime is sufficiently vile or heinous to warrant the maximum sentence even if it cannot be described as the worst. For example, the "stark horror" of an attempted murder may be sufficient to justify the maximum sentence of life imprisonment even though the circumstances do not satisfy the rubric of "worst offence by the worst offender."[30] However, the imposition of a maximum sentence is, and ought to be, rare. Few situations arise where a lesser term will not adequately protect society and also reflect an appropriate degree of denunciation. Even cases where the offender's record seems to demonstrate incorrigibility that suggests a maximum

---

25　See *R. v. Johnas* (1982), 2 C.C.C. (3d) 490 (Alta. C.A.).

26　Statistics Canada, Canadian Centre for Justice Statistics, *Canadian Crime Statistics 1998* (Ottawa: Statistics Canada, 1998) at 62–65.

27　See the table in Chapter 4, above, for examples of maxima from life to six months.

28　See *R. v. Reimer* (1990), 59 C.C.C. (3d) 136 (Man. C.A.), in which a life sentence for three counts of criminal negligence causing death was reduced to six years.

29　*R. v. Hynes* (1991), 64 C.C.C. (3d) 421 at 426 (Nfld. C.A.) [*Hynes*].

30　*R. v. Mesgun* (1997), 121 C.C.C. (3d) 439 (Ont. C.A.).

sentence for reasons of individual deterrence and protection of the public, consideration must be given to whether the case meets the "worst case" standard.[31] Especially in cases where the maximum is life imprisonment, usually for crimes against the person, the principal justification for a maximum sentence is a finding of dangerousness based on a record of violence and the consequential need to address public protection.[32]

## 2)  No Cap for Fixed-term Sentences

A question related to the issue of maximum sentences is whether there is a notional cap which can be imposed on the length of a fixed-term sentence. In other words, is there a judicially created maximum that limits the length of a fixed sentence? In *R. v. M.(C.A.)*, the offender had pleaded guilty to a lengthy list of sexual and physical assaults inflicted upon his children over a period of years.[33] The sentencing judge described the pattern of conduct as "egregious" and concluded that it transcended the "parameters of the worst case." However, none of the offences was punishable by life imprisonment. Earlier jurisprudence in British Columbia had held that when life imprisonment was available as a maximum punishment but the trial judge decided not to impose it, there was a "qualified ceiling" of twenty years on the fixed term used in its place. Here, the sentencing judge ruled that he was not bound by this cap since he was dealing with the cumulative effect of a number of consecutive sentences when life imprisonment was not available. Taking into account the totality principle, he imposed a combination of consecutive and concurrent sentences which totalled twenty-five years. On appeal, the majority concluded that the qualified ceiling of twenty years applied equally to this situation and varied the term

---

31  See, for example, *R. v. Ko* (1979), 50 C.C.C. (2d) 430 (B.C.C.A.), in which a life sentence for heroin trafficking was reduced to fourteen years.

32  See *R. v. Horvath* (1982), 2 C.C.C. (3d) 196 (Ont. C.A.). For a survey of the case law, see *R. v. Cooper* (1997), 117 C.C.C. (3d) 249 at 266–68 (Nfld. C.A.). For a time, the view was expressed that prosecutors should commence dangerous offender applications rather than seek a life sentence, based on the notion that the dangerous offender process provided greater safeguards including early parole reviews: see, for example, *R. v. Pontello* (1977), 38 C.C.C. (2d) 262 (Ont. C.A.). This is heard much more rarely now that it is clear that prisoners with the "dangerous offender" label are viewed with great caution by the National Parole Board and are likely to serve long periods in custody.

33  [1996] 15 C.R. 500 [*M. (C.A.)*].

to twenty years imprisonment. One reason for the cap, according to Wood J.A.,[34] was the recognition that parole ineligibility on fixed terms was one third of the sentence, to the limit of seven years, on a sentence of twenty-one years or more. This was the same ineligibility period that applied to life sentences imposed other than for murder. Accordingly, so the argument went, this suggested Parliament's intention to limit fixed-term sentences to around twenty years since beyond that point release would be in the hands of the National Parole Board after seven years anyway.

In the Supreme Court, the unanimous decision written by Lamer C.J.C. dealt with a number of important sentencing issues including the respective roles of retribution and denunciation. He rejected the existence of a qualified ceiling on fixed terms. In so doing, he concluded that it would be a perversion of the purpose and function of the *Corrections and Conditional Release Act* to find that the intricate parole eligibility mechanisms also operated to restrict sentencing discretion. He found nothing absurd in the operation of the parole eligibility rules, including the possibility that by reason of pre-sentence custody, a person serving a sentence of life as a maximum could be eligible for parole before a co-accused serving a twenty-year sentence.[35] It was unlikely that the prisoner with the more serious sentence would actually achieve conditional release before his mythical co-accused. In rejecting a de facto limit on fixed sentences, he commented:

> The bastion which protects Canadians from unduly harsh fixed-term sentences is not found in the mechanics of the *Corrections Act* but rather in the good sense of our nation's trial judges. For many of the lesser crimes presently before our courts, a single or cumulative sentence beyond 20 years would undoubtedly be grossly excessive, and probably cruel and unusual. In other circumstances, such a stern sentence would be both fitting and appropriate. In our system of justice, the ultimate protection against excessive criminal punishment lies within a sentencing judge's overriding duty to fashion a "just and appropriate" punishment which is proportional to the overall culpability of the offender.[36]

---

34   Rowles J.A. concurred, but reached her conclusion because the sentencing judge did not find that confinement beyond twenty years was necessary to protect society and, even if protection of society was the dominant consideration, lengthy sentences should not be used as "an expedient alternative to dangerous offender proceedings": *R. v. M.(C.A.)* (1994), 28 C.R. (4th) 106 at 125 (B.C.C.A.).

35   *M.(C.A.)*, above note 33 at 551–52.

36   *Ibid.* at 552.

While the advancing age of an offender might suggest that both the "utilitarian and normative" goals of sentencing would dissipate at some point, in other situations the only limit on sentencing discretion is the principle of proportionality. Still, as Lamer C.J.C. noted, the examples of provincial appellate courts upholding sentences beyond twenty years are few and far between. The Supreme Court restored the original twenty-five-year sentence noting the "disturbingly high" degree of violence, the extent of the psychological damage, and the offender's dim prospects for rehabilitation. Although the law permits fixed terms beyond twenty years, it seems clear that their imposition would be rare.

# E. PRE-SENTENCE CUSTODY

## 1) The General Rule

While this issue has gone through a rocky history, section 719(3) of the *Criminal Code* now provides:

> In determining the sentence to be imposed on a person convicted of an offence, a court may take into account any time spent in custody by the person as a result of the offence.

The language of this provision is cast in discretionary terms, as distinct from the English statute which requires credit toward subsequent sentence of imprisonment.[37] Notwithstanding "bail reform," it is clear that there are large numbers of remand prisoners[38] who, depending on the offence and their personal circumstances, spend considerable time in custody prior to disposition either as a result of a detention under section 515(5) or (6), or an inability to meet the conditions of a release order. The rationale for taking these custodial periods into account was expressed by Laskin J.A. in *R. v. Rezaie*:

> Although this section is discretionary, not mandatory, in my view a sentencing judge should ordinarily give credit for pre-trial custody. At least a judge should not deny credit without good reason. To do so offends one's sense of fairness. Incarceration at any stage of the criminal process is a denial of an accused's liberty.[39]

---

37  See *Criminal Justice Act 1967* (U.K.), 1967, c. 80, s. 67 (as am. by *Criminal Justice Act 1991* (U.K.), 1991, c. 53, Sch. 11, para. 2).

38  In 1998–99, 104,975 remand prisoners were admitted to custody in Canada: see "Adult Correctional Services in Canada, 1998–99" *Juristat* 20:3 (June 2000) at 5. This amounts to approximately 50 percent of all provincial and territorial admissions.

39  See, for example, *R. v. Rezaie* (1996), 112 C.C.C. (3d) 97 at 104 (Ont. C.A.) [*Rezaie*].

## 2) Extent of Credit

Judicial views on the extent of the credit which should be given for pre-sentence custody have changed over time. In the 1947 case of *R. v. Sloan*, the Ontario Court of Appeal held that a sentence could not be antedated but accepted that a sentencing judge could consider pre-sentence custody by giving credit for "the whole or part of the period" served.[40] While courts have accepted that there is no strict formula for translating pre-sentence custody into a credit, it has become common to see a "two-for-one" or double-time credit. The rationale has been based on the combined effect of two factors: the inapplicability of remission provisions[41] to these periods, and the general absence of programs and amenities in remand facilities.[42]

## 3) Articulating the Sentence

There is no power to antedate a sentence[43] to take into account pre-sentence custody. Similarly, there is no power in correctional authorities to make administrative deductions from a sentence once imposed. It is important that sentences be correctly and accurately structured and communicated.

---

40  (1947), 87 C.C.C. 198 at 199 (Ont. C.A) [*Sloan*].
41  Since 1992, federal prisoners no longer receive remission but are subject to detention, ordinarily entitled to statutory release after serving two-thirds of their sentence: see s. 127 of the *Corrections and Conditional Release Act*, S.C. 1992 c. 20. Provincial prisoners continue to be eligible for fifteen days remission for each month served (a one-third credit): see *Prisons and Reformatories Act*, R.S.C. 1985, c. P-20, s. 6(1).
42  In unusual circumstances, the second basis, the unavailability of programs, has been held not to apply. For example, in *R. v. Schoenhalz* (1999), 121 B.C.A.C. 138 (C.A.) [*Schoenhalz*], a nineteen-year-old woman spent seventeen months in pre-sentence custody. The British Columbia Court of Appeal agreed that a double credit for the pre-sentence custody was not required since the time was spent at Burnaby Correctional Centre for Women where she upgraded her education, and participated in both religious and cognitive therapy programs.
43  At common law, a sentence commenced when imposed or when the convicted person was taken into custody upon execution of a warrant of committal: see *Bowdler's Case* (1848), 12 Q.B. 612, 116 E.R. 999. Due to the inclusion of ambiguous language in both the *Penitentiary Act* and the *Prisons and Reformatories Act* prior to 1969, a number of appellate decisions dealt with the issue of antedating. The Ontario view was that there was no power to antedate: see *Sloan*, above note 40. A majority of the British Columbia Court of Appeal concluded that the statutory language permitted a sentence to begin on the date of conviction but no earlier: see *R. v. Wells*, [1969] 4 C.C.C. 25, Tysoe J.A., Bull J.A. dissenting (B.C.C.A.). The ambiguous phrase has been repealed leaving the position clear that there is no power to antedate.

There will be situations where, by reason of pre-sentence custody, the ultimate sentence will not warrant additional imprisonment even though incarceration would ordinarily be expected. In these cases, judges should avoid using the phrase "time served,"[44] although that is essentially what is happening. Instead, clarity and frankness require an explanation of the effect of pre-sentence custody on the sentence which would otherwise be warranted. This ensures that everyone appreciates the kind of sentence that the offence usually produces. A similar caution applies to sentences of imprisonment which have been substantially reduced by pre-sentence custody. One often hears media reports which mention only the actual sentence without regard for a lengthy period of pre-sentence custody: this kind of incomplete information can generate unnecessary and ill-informed criticism. Judges cannot control how a sentence will be reported by the media, but they can ensure that it is properly explained in court.

## 4) Pre-sentence Custody and Life as a Maximum

When a trial judge characterizes a case as being within the category of "worst case," it is a discretionary decision whether pre-sentence custody should apply to reduce the sentence below the maximum. If the available maximum is a fixed term, consistency would suggest that in most cases credit should be given for the pre-sentence custody. However, the same reasoning need not apply to life as a maximum. A trial judge may be less inclined to give credit for pre-sentence custody. It is important to note that sentences of life imprisonment are treated differently than other offences for parole eligibility purposes. In cases of life imprisonment as a maximum punishment, custodial periods after arrest are included in calculating parole eligibility.[45] This does not apply to other sentences and can produce anomalous results. Assume two co-accused, both of whom served two years in pre-sentence custody, are convicted of manslaughter. If they receive sentences of life and twenty-one years respectively, the prisoner serving life will be eligible for parole after five years while the other offender must serve seven years before parole eligibility.[46] This can be avoided by ensuring

---

44  See *R. v. Coutu* (1997), 12 C.R. (5th) 324 at 330–31, Ryan J.A. (B.C.C.A.).
45  This is the combined effect of ss. 746 and 745(d) of the *Criminal Code*.
46  The "lifer" will be subject to a seven-year eligibility date starting from the date of arrest while eligibility for the prisoner serving twenty years will be six years eight months from the date of sentencing.

that distinctions between offenders are properly reflected by distinct sentences, including taking parole eligibility into account.[47] However, in the uncommon situation where this systemic unfairness may appear, it should only be rectified by reducing the sentence on the second prisoner. It would be doubly unfair to do otherwise.

## 5) Pre-sentence Custody and Minimum Sentences

With minimum sentences, the issue of pre-sentence custody can also produce anomalies that may appear unfair. In a situation where the *Criminal Code* stipulates a mandatory minimum — if the sentence cannot be reduced below that minimum, how does a sentencing judge deal with two co-accused with similar backgrounds, where one has served a substantial period of pre-sentence custody while the other was at liberty on judicial interim release? A number of courts have addressed the issue as a result of the recent addition of mandatory minimum sentences of four years for using a firearm in the commission of ten stipulated offences.[48] While courts have consistently rejected arguments that these sentences violated section 12 of the *Charter*,[49] concern has been expressed about whether, in the circumstances of a particular case, the inability to reduce a minimum sentence to reflect pre-sentence custody could have an unfair result. Recognizing this problem, some courts suggested that a constitutional exemption would remedy the situation if it arose.[50] However, it is difficult to understand why the very real potential of gross disparity arising from an apparent inability to give credit does not qualify as a reasonable hypothetical according to the

---

47   This is an exception to the general view that judges should not consider parole eligibility: see the discussion, below, at 6 (F)(2).

48   See *Firearms Act*, S.C. 1995, c. 39, ss. 141–50, establishing the four-year minimum sentences for using a firearm in the course of the following *Criminal Code* offences: s. 220 (criminal negligence causing death); s. 236 (manslaughter); s. 239 (attempted murder); s. 244 (causing bodily harm with intent); s. 272 (sexual assault with a weapon); s. 273 (aggravated sexual assault); s. 279 (kidnapping); s. 279.1 (hostage-taking); s. 344 (robbery); and s. 346 (extortion).

49   See, for example, *R. v. Morrisey* (1998), 124 C.C.C. (3d) 38 (N.S.C.A.) [*Morrisey No. 2*]; and *R. v. W.(L.W.)* (1998), 17 C.R. (5th) 45 (B.C.C.A.) [*W.(L.W.)*].

50   See *R. v. Lapierre* (1998), 123 C.C.C. (3d) 332 at 346–47 (Que. C.A.); *Morrissey No. 2, ibid.* at 57–58; and *W.(L.W.), ibid.* at 61.

*Goltz* mode of analysis.[51] As well, there has yet to be an authoritative pronouncement by the Supreme Court of Canada on the availability of this kind of constitutional exemption.

A different answer was provided by the Ontario Court of Appeal in *R. v. McDonald* where Rosenberg J.A. applied statutory interpretation principles to reconcile section 719(3) with the mandatory minimum sentence of four years imprisonment for robbery with a firearm as required by section 344(a).[52] He analysed the legislative history of section 719(3), which was enacted as part of the *Bail Reform Act*, and found it to be ambiguous and uncertain as to whether the section was intended to apply to situations where the *Criminal Code* mandated a minimum sentence. He noted that the language of section 344(a) uses the phrase "minimum punishment." Relying on the general interpretive principle that an ambiguity in a penal statute should be resolved in favour of the person whose liberty was at stake, he concluded that the interaction of sections 719(3) and 344(a) encompassed a proper credit for pre-sentence custody even if it would reduce the sentence actually pronounced to less than four years, because the total punishment (including the punitive element of pre-sentence custody) would still meet the mandated standard. After the judgment in *McDonald*, the British Columbia Court of Appeal convened a five judge panel to re-hear the minimum sentence issue decided in *Wust* as it related to the question of pre-sentence custody.[53] The Court agreed with the statutory interpretation approach of Rosenberg J.A. and upheld a sentence of two years less a day for kidnapping in light of the substantial period of pre-sentence custody. The Crown appealed *Wust* to the Supreme Court.

The Supreme Court of Canada[54] adopted the analysis in *McDonald* and the distinction between punishment and sentence. Speaking for a unanimous court, Arbour J. held that pre-sentence custody could reduce the sentence below four years and that an interpretation of sections 719(3) and 344(a) which did not permit credit would "reward

---

51   For s. 12 *Charter* analysis, while the first issue is whether the case before the court presents a grossly disproportionate sentence, the second consideration is whether a reasonable hypothetical situation would meet this standard: see *R. v. Goltz*, [1991] 3 S.C.R. 485. The concurring decision of Arbour, J. in *R. v. Morrisey*, (2000) 148 C.C.C. (3d) 1 (S.C.C.), questioned the appropriateness of the *Goltz* approach for offences like manslaughter with a firearm where it is not possible to imagine what examples may in fact occur in the future. She preferred making a finding of validity while still keeping open the prospect of finding gross disproportionality in a future case.
52   (1998), 127 C.C.C. (3d) 57 (Ont. C.A.).
53   See *R. v. Mills* (1999), 133 C.C.C. (3d) 451 (B.C.C.A.).
54   See *R. v. Wust* (2000), 143 C.C.C. (3d) 129 (S.C.C.) [*Wust*].

the worst offender and penalize the least offender," a result that could not be countenanced.[55] With respect to calculating the appropriate credit for pre-sentence custody, she did not endorse a "mechanical formula" but said that a credit of two-for-one is "entirely appropriate."[56] However, she added the comment that a different ratio might properly apply if the offender had been detained in a facility with full access to "educational, vocational, and rehabilitation programs." Clearly, she was responding to the argument that one of the reasons for a credit greater than one-for-one is the absence of constructive programs. The issue, however, is a larger one and encompasses the general conditions in local detention centres and jails.[57] Sentencing judges should be cautious about reducing credit simply because a prisoner had access to some form of programming without knowing more about the stresses and conditions of the daily environment. Given the usual limited level of resources expended on detention before trial, in most jurisdictions a judge is well-advised to apply a standard credit beyond one-for-one.

During the course of interpreting the relevant provisions in a way that was consistent with proper sentencing principle, Arbour J. made the following important observation on the potential harm that mandatory minimum sentences can generate:

> Even if it can be argued that harsh, unfit sentences may prove to be a powerful deterrent, and therefore still serve a valid purpose, it seems to me that sentences that are unjustly severe are more likely to inspire contempt and resentment than to foster compliance with the law. It is a well-established principle of the criminal justice system that judges must strive to impose a sentence tailored to the individual case.[58]

The recognition of the counter-productive nature of over-zealous sentences is a worthwhile caution for both legislators and judges.

---

55   *Ibid.* at 147.
56   *Ibid.* at 148.
57   As noted by Arbour J., *ibid.* at 147, with reliance on a quotation from G.T. Trotter, *The Law of Bail in Canada* (Scarborough, Ont.: Carswell, 1992). See also the discussion of *Schoenhalz*, above note 42.
58   *Wust*, above note 54 at 139.

# F.  CONDITIONAL RELEASE ISSUES

## 1)  Considering Conditional Release in Determining the Sentence

Since the establishment of the National Parole Board in 1959,[59] Canadian courts have not been consistent on the issue of whether early release can be considered in determining the original sentence. Muddled arguments about general deterrence and rehabilitation have produced decisions that support treating potential release as a relevant factor.[60] Other decisions have recognized that any consideration of early release to increase a sentence undercuts Parliamentary intention in providing forms of early release.[61] On reading more recent cases, with the exception of the rehabilitation issue which I will discuss below, the weight of authority favours the proposition that parole and statutory release should not be considered. In *R. v. Oliver*, the Newfoundland Court of Appeal concluded succinctly that sentencing judges should not consider potential post-sentencing decisions and that it was "inappropriate to adjust sentences on the assumption that they will not be carried out or to foil the impact of programs sanctioned by Parliament or the Legislature."[62] If there is any doubt about the correctness of this view, one only needs to consider some of the current realities about conditional release. The Supreme Court in *R. v. M.(C.A.)* recognized that conditional release does not reduce a sentence, or its deterrent or denunciatory impact, but merely changes the conditions under which it is served.[63] On the effects of conditional release, Lamer C.J.C. observed:

> But even though the conditions of incarceration are subject to change through a grant of parole to the offender's benefit, the offender's sentence continues in full effect. The offender remains under the strict control of the parole system, and the offender's liberty remains significantly

---

59   For a history of parole and other forms of conditional release in Canada, both before and after 1959, see D.P. Cole & A. Manson, "Canadian Parole Legislation and Practice: 1800–1977" in *Release from Imprisonment: The Law of Sentencing, Parole and Judicial Review* (Toronto: Carswell, 1990) at 159.

60   See *R. v. Wilmott*, [1967] 1 C.C.C. 172 at 186–87 (Ont. C.A.).

61   See *R. v. Bailey*, [1970] 4 C.C.C. 291 at 305 (Ont.C.A.). See also *R. v. Pearce* (1974), 16 C.C.C. (2d) 369, Dubin J.A. dissenting (Ont. C.A.).

62   (1997), 147 Nfld. & P.E.I.R. 210 at 223, Cameron J.A. (Nfld. C.A.). See also *R. v. Ross* (1989), 74 Sask. R. 230 (C.A.).

63   *M.(C.A.)*, above note 33 at 545.

curtailed for the full duration of the offender's numerical or life sentence. The deterrent and denunciatory purposes which animated the original sentence remain in force, notwithstanding the fact that the conditions of sentence have been modified. The goal of specific deterrence is still advanced, since the offender remains supervised to the extent and degree necessary to prevent possible crime, and since the offender remains under the shadow of re-incarceration if he or she commits another crime. As well, the goal of denunciation continues to operate, as the offender still carries the societal stigma of being a convicted offender who is serving a criminal sentence.[64]

As well, recent data show that parole is granted to substantially less than half the prisoners who apply.[65] The remainder must wait at least until their statutory release dates.[66] While the comments of Lamer C.J.C. quoted above apply equally to prisoners on statutory release, since 1986 prisoners may be denied release entirely and held in confinement until their warrant expiry date.[67] All of these factors support the view that sentencing and conditional release are integrated but discrete functions. It would be unfair to permit opinions about parole or other forms of conditional release, whether ill-informed or not, to interfere with principled sentencing discretion.

## 2)  Increasing Parole Ineligibility

Traditionally, with the exception of second-degree murder, the issue of parole eligibility has been dealt with by the relevant conditional release statute or, in the early years, its regulations. This ensured that minimum periods of incapacitation with the concomitant denunciatory effects were standardized rather than individualized. It recognized that sentencing looks backward in time to the offence, the offender, and her background, while parole looks forward and attempts to assess risk. It

---

64   *Ibid.*

65   Between 1996 and 1999, the full parole granting rate for the National Parole Board varied from 40 percent to 44 percent: see "Adult Correctional Services in Canada, 1998–99," above note 38 at 14. If one excludes the "accelerated parole release" candidates (non-violent, first-time penitentiary prisoners), the granting rate for the remainder is less than 25 percent.

66   With the abolition of remission in the federal system, this arises after service of two-thirds of a penitentiary sentence, pursuant to s. 127 of the *CCRA*, above note 41.

67   The detention provisions are set out in ss. 129–32 of the *CCRA, ibid.*

seemed appropriate that the minimum custodial period required before one could have access to that process would be set by legislators and not judges. Generally, that minimum period has been one-third of the sentence to a maximum of seven years. When the *Parole Act* was replaced by Part II of the new *Corrections and Conditional Release Act* in 1992, the *Criminal Code* was amended to permit sentencing judges, in some circumstances, to increase the period of parole ineligibility.

Section 743.6 now authorizes a judge to entertain increasing parole ineligibility to "one half of the sentence or ten years, whichever is less" in two situations. In the first category are sentences of more than two years imprisonment, including life as a maximum punishment,[68] for offences prosecuted by indictment which are included in Schedules I and II of the *Corrections and Conditional Release Act*.[69] These long lists of offences are those which can subject a penitentiary prisoner to detention until warrant expiry date. Schedule I contains a huge array of *Criminal Code* offences from assault to manslaughter, from invitation to sexual touching to rape. Originally, it did not include the offence of "break and enter and commit" contrary to section 348(1)(b)[70] but this group of offences was added in 1995.[71] Schedule II is a list of narcotics offences involving trafficking,[72] importing, and possession of proceeds. The statutory test for increasing parole ineligibility for the first category is whether the court is satisfied,

> . . . having regard to the circumstances of the commission of the offence and the character and circumstances of the offender, that the expression of society's denunciation of the offences or the objective of specific or general deterrence so requires . . .

The second category of offences for which parole ineligibility can be increased are the "criminal organization offences" which were enacted

---

68   See *R. v. Shorting* (1995), 102 C.C.C. (3d) 385 (Man. C.A.), where the majority held that the power to increase parole ineligibility applies to life as a maximum, permitting an increase from the ordinary threshold of seven years up to ten. It must be noted that for life sentences, the calculation of the parole eligibility period commences on the date of arrest not the date of sentencing.

69   See s. 743.6(1) of the *Criminal Code*.

70   See *R. v. Nichol* (1995), 102 C.C.C. (3d) 441 (Ont. C.A.).

71   See *An Act to amend the Corrections and Conditional Release Act, the Criminal Code, the Criminal Records Act, the Prisons and Reformatories Act and the Transfer of Offenders Act*, S.C. 1995, c. 42, s. 67.

72   Including possession for the purposes of trafficking: see *R. v. Dankyi* (1993), 86 C.C.C. (3d) 368 (Que. C.A.) [*Dankyi*].

in 1997.[73] While this group of offences does not carry with it the statutory test in section 743.6(1), both provisions are governed by section 743.6(2) which provides that the paramount principles when considering increasing parole ineligibility are denunciation and deterrence, including specific deterrence.

In applying this new power, appellate courts seem to be divided into two camps which disagree about whether an increase in parole ineligibility should be an exceptional order or not. In *R. v. Dankyi*, Fish J.A. of the Quebec Court of Appeal characterized the "conceptual foundation" of the provisions as "elusive" but concluded that it could only be used as an "exceptional measure" upon clearly articulated reasons.[74] The Ontario Court of Appeal applied this decision in *R. v. Goulet*[75] when considering the sentence appeal of a twenty-one-year-old offender sentenced to three years for possession of cocaine for the purposes of trafficking. The trial judge had increased the parole ineligibility to half of the sentence. At the sentencing hearing, the local police chief testified that there had been twenty drug-related stabbings in the previous six months and that, in his experience, there was a connection between crack cocaine use and violence. The court struck out the order and agreed with Fish J.A. that an increase was an exceptional measure that should be reserved for exceptional circumstances. In discussing the kinds of cases where an increase might be appropriate, the court observed that the circumstances of the offence will rarely justify an increase. In the ordinary case, the offence context might justify a longer sentence but should not be used to increase parole ineligibility unless it exhibited "unusual violence, brutality, or degradation" that compelled a strong expression of societal denunciation.[76] The offender's background might also support considering an increase. Here, the reasoning entered a speculative area and included issues such as whether the offender would be deterred or rehabilitated within the

---

73    *Ibid.*, s. 743.6(1.1) (enacted by *An Act to amend the Criminal Code (criminal organizations) and to amend other Acts in consequence*, S.C. 1997, c. 23, s. 18). Section 2 of the *Criminal Code* defines a "criminal organization offence" as an offence under s. 467.1 or an indictable offence "committed for the benefit of, at the direction of or in association with a criminal organization" that carries a punishment of at least five years imprisonment, including a conspiracy or attempt to commit such an offence, or being an accessory after the fact or counsellor.

74    Above note 72.

75    (1995), 97 C.C.C. (3d) 61 (Ont. C.A.).

76    See also *R. v. Smith* (1995), 37 C.R. (4th) 360 (Ont. Gen. Div.), in which Watt J. held that the degree of violence justified a ten-year sentence for manslaughter but not an increase in parole ineligibility.

normal parole ineligibility period. However, the court was adamant that only "clear evidence" could satisfy the sentencing judge. As an example of a case where an increase would have been justified, reference was made to R. v. *Faulds*,[77] involving an armed robbery of a Brinks truck by two offenders — both had penitentiary records and one was on parole at the time of the offence.

*Goulet* has been followed in a number of cases as authority for the proposition that parole ineligibility should be increased only in exceptional circumstances.[78] However, the appellate courts of Alberta, New Brunswick, and Newfoundland disagree. In R. v. *Matwiy*, a case dealing with an armed home invasion, the trial judge had imposed sentences of ten years imprisonment with an increase in parole ineligibility to one half.[79] The offender had a record of "break and enter and commit" and was on parole from a penitentiary sentence at the time of the offence. After considering both *Goulet* and *Dankyi*, the court turned to the Supreme Court decision in R. v. *Shropshire*[80] dealing with the issue of parole ineligibility for second-degree murder where Iacobucci J. rejected any exceptional circumstances requirement for an increase beyond the statutory minimum of ten years. The court concluded that the appropriate standard to justify using section 743.6 was as follows:

> As a general rule an order under s. 741.2 [now 743.6] increasing parole ineligibility should not be made. However, where the trial judge is satisfied, having regard to the circumstances of the offence and the circumstances and character of the accused, that the objectives of the expression of society's denunciation or specific or general deterrence so require, the judge may make the order increasing parole ineligibility.[81]

While this may not seem controversial, the court also, relying on *Shropshire*, rejected the need for any "special circumstances, unusual circumstances or particularly aggravating factors." Subsequently, other appellate courts have joined in this approach.[82]

---

77   (1994), 20 O.R. (3d) 13 (C.A.).
78   See, for example, R. v. *Ferguson* (1995), 64 B.C.A.C. 211 (C.A.); and R. v. *Osborne* (1996), 110 C.C.C.(3d) 161 (Ont. C.A.) [*Osborne*].
79   (1996), 105 C.C.C. (3d) 251 (Alta. C.A.).
80   [1995] 4 S.C.R. 227.
81   *Matwiy*, above note 79 at 268.
82   See, for example, R. v. *Cormier* (1999), 140 C.C.C. (3d) 87 (N.B.C.A.); and R. v. *Dodd* (1999), 139 C.C.C. (3d) 2 (Nfld. C.A.).

The analogy to second-degree murder, where the need for exceptional circumstances has been rejected, is not apt. As Charron J.A. has pointed out,[83] the setting of parole ineligibility is an essential part of the normal second-degree murder sentencing process while sentencing for other offences does not generally implicate section 743.6. As she said, it is "exceptional in nature" and, accordingly, ought to require exceptional circumstances.[84] She is correct in distinguishing the second-degree murder situation. Section 745.4 authorizes the sentencing judge in a second-degree murder case to substitute a number of years greater than ten "as the judge deems fit in the circumstances." By comparison, section 743.6 only permits a judge to increase parole ineligibility for offences that it covers if "satisfied" that the objective of denunciation or deterrence "so requires." The mental element for second-degree murder sets the minimum standard of blameworthiness and Parliament has stipulated the commensurate period of incapacitation which meets that standard. Over time, judges can be expected to develop criteria which respond to situations of increased culpability and can increase parole ineligibility accordingly. However, section 743.6 does not apply to a single offence with a defined mental element but encompasses a vast array of offences, which can be committed in an infinite variety of ways. Parliament cannot have the same expectation about the judicial development of distinctions in culpability over this set of crimes as it does for second-degree murder.

If there is any question about whether second-degree murder is indeed different, look at how the *Corrections and Conditional Release Act* deals with parole and compassionate claims. Section 121(1) of that Act permits a prisoner to apply for parole before reaching her eligibility date in certain stipulated compassionate circumstances. This provision, formerly known as parole by exception, can apply notwithstanding an order under section 743.6 but cannot apply to a life sentence for murder. The distinction is not based on the life sentence, since sentences of life as a maximum are covered, but applies because the offence is murder. For murder, the minimum period of incarceration as set by the sentencing

83   *Osborne*, above note 78 at 165–67.
84   Also see the more recent decision of the same court, but a differently constituted panel, in R. v. *Demedeiros*, [1999] O.J. No. 1523 (C.A.).

judge is sacrosanct.[85] This suggests that when Parliament puts its mind to parole ineligibility, murder is viewed differently than other offences.

Regardless of *Shropshire*, increasing parole ineligibility for scheduled offences should be justified only when something exceptional requires an intervention into the normal parole process. This is a form of increased punishment[86] which should be imposed with restraint. It ensures not only a postponement of potential re-integration, regardless of what may happen in the future, but can also delay access to the scarce resources of correctional programming.[87] Sentencing judges should be slow to consider an increase without an application from the Crown and certainly not without some notice to the offender.[88] While many aggravating factors will justify an increased sentence, few will justify an increase in parole ineligibility. Section 743.6 should be reserved for offences of brutality or degradation that compel added denunciation, or offenders whose history of incarceration and release makes the normal parole eligibility an undoubtedly incongruous element of their sentence. Even when the principal characteristic of a case is its violence, courts must be careful to distinguish between enhanced culpability, that justifies a lengthy sentence, and a factor that bears on parole eligibility.[89]

## 3) The Anomaly of Parole Revocation

Clearly, an offence committed while on conditional release is an aggravating factor.[90] Since the statutory codification of parole in 1959 and mandatory supervision in 1970, the statute governing federal prisoners has authorized the National Parole Board to revoke the conditional release of a prisoner who commits a new offence. With the enactment of the *Corrections and Conditional Release Act* in 1992, this discretionary power was extended to statutory release, the successor to mandatory

---

85 Subject perhaps to a s. 12 *Charter* claim as in R. v. *Latimer* (1998), 131 C.C.C. (3d) 191 (Sask. C.A.). While the Saskatchewan Court of Appeal rejected this argument, the Supreme Court granted leave and the case was argued in June of 2000. Judgment has been reserved.

86 As noted by LaForest J. in R. v. *Chaisson*, [1995] 2 S.C.R. 1118.

87 Because of a general shortage of programmes, places are often allocated based on the proximity of potential release.

88 The absence of notice can provide a successful ground of appeal: see *Rezaie*, above note 39.

89 See, for example, R. v. *Davis* (1999), 117 O.A.C. 81 (C.A.), upholding a sixteen-year sentence for robbery, sexual assault with a weapon and kidnapping, but setting aside the order increasing parole ineligibility. It called this aspect a "close one."

90 See the discussion in Chapter 7 at 7(D)(4).

supervision. During this period, many decisions held that the court which sentences the prisoner for the new offence should apply the totality principle to the term that would be created by adding the new sentence to the remanet. This created the apparent anomaly that the parole status both aggravated and mitigated the new sentence.[91] While curious, a second look makes it clear that the two factors are based on different concepts. An offence by a parolee may be more blameworthy but a merged term of imprisonment should still not be excessive or harsh. Totality still plays a role, although it may be of reduced importance in light of the gravity of the subsequent offence.[92]

Without going into detail about how sentences involving revocations of conditional release are calculated,[93] there are some significant features for those involved in the sentencing process. Suspension is the temporary status during which the offender is returned to custody pending a determination of whether the suspension should be cancelled, or the release revoked or terminated. When a person on parole or statutory release is convicted of a new offence, whether the conditional release will be revoked or terminated is within the discretion of the National Parole Board, subject to its statutory mandate.[94] However, as a consequence of amendments enacted in 1995,[95] if an offender

---

91   This was noted by Donald J.A in *R. v. Bueger* (1994), 48 B.C.A.C. 266 (C.A.), where he said: "Care must be taken to avoid the inconsistency involved in treating the commission of the offense on parole as an aggravating circumstance on the one hand, and, on the other, mitigating the penalty because of the consequences of parole revocation."

92   See *R. v. Moore* (1995), 59 B.C.A.C. 207 (C.A.), where the court dismissed an appeal against a five-year sentence for criminal negligence causing bodily harm which had resulted in a revocation of mandatory supervision. The accused had fired fifteen shots from a semi-automatic rifle at the offices where his parole officer worked. The Court of Appeal was of the view that the added penalty arising from the revocation of his mandatory supervision was "of little or no significance" in the circumstances.

93   See Canada, Solicitor General, *Sentence Calculation: A Handbook for Judges, Lawyers and Correctional Officers*, 2d ed. (Ottawa: Supply and Services Canada, 1999).

94   See *CCRA*, above note 41, ss. 135(1), (3), & (5). The statutory issue is whether the offender will "present an undue risk to society" by re-offending if re-released. Instead of revocation the remedy of termination is available in situations where the reasons for suspension were "beyond the offenders' control."

95   See *An Act to amend the Corrections and Conditional Release Act, the Criminal Code, the Criminal Records Act, the Prisons and Reformatories Act and the Transfer of Offenders Act*, S.C. 1995, c. 42, s. 50(7). See also s. 91, a transitional provision, which made s. 135(9.1) of the *CCRA*, above note 41, applicable only to additional sentences imposed after the provision came into force on January 24, 1996 (see S.I./96-10, C. Gaz. 1996.II.828).

receives an additional sentence of imprisonment as a result of an offence committed while on conditional release, the conditional release is automatically revoked regardless of whether the sentence is to be served concurrently or consecutively.[96] All revocations establish a new statutory release date of two-thirds of the term required to be served, from the date of recommitment to custody on suspension or revocation.[97] Consequently, all offenders, will have a new "statutory release date" (SRD). However, whether the offender's "parole eligibility date" (PED) changes depends on whether a new sentence is imposed. A new consecutive sentence will always change the PED[98] while a new concurrent sentence may not, depending on the date of imposition and its length in relation to the pre-existing sentence.[99] Accordingly, for sentencing purposes, when dealing with a person on conditional release, the first question is the status in terms of the National Parole Board's discretion. If not revoked as a matter of discretion, any additional sentence of imprisonment will result in automatic revocation. The totality principle is relevant both to the length of an additional sentence, when merged with the remanct (pre-existing sentence), and to whether it is to be served consecutively or concurrently, since both factors will affect ultimate release.

# G.  ISSUES RELATING TO PREVIOUS CONVICTIONS

## 1)  Escalations and Jumps in Custodial Terms

These two related concepts apply when the offender has a previous record for a related offence and was sentenced to a term of incarceration for the most recent offence. Assuming that there is not a significant gap[100] between the current offence and the preceding one, there is a prevalent attitude that the instant offence must receive an escalated penalty. This flows from a simplistic view of individual deterrence: if a pound of penal medicine did not work, we had better try two pounds this time. While the concept of proportionality does not negate the relevance of prior offences or the issue of individual deterrence, it does

---

96  See the *CCRA*, above note 41, ss. 135(9.1) & (9.2).

97  *Ibid.*, s. 127(5).

98  *Ibid.*, s.120.1(1).

99  *Ibid.*, s. 120.2(1).

100  See the discussion of gaps in Chapter 7(B)(13).

ensure that the sanction cannot be inordinate and inequitable when compared to the gravity of the offence. Also, the *Criminal Code* now formally respects the principle of restraint. Accordingly, sentences cannot simply continue to escalate. It may be that a recidivist thief should go to jail, but proportionality and restraint often persuade appellate courts to reduce sentences that seem to be a product of local frustration rather than a measured approach to finding the appropriate sanction.[101] The most dramatic rejection of automatic escalation is the situation of the intermediate recidivist.[102] For this category of offender the recognition of important life changes can even contradict the argument for custody, let alone an escalation of custody.

The "jump principle" suggests that when an escalation in the duration of custody is warranted, it should occur by moderate steps not substantial jumps. In other words, a previous sentence of one month for an offence of similar gravity might be followed by a three- to six- month term but not an eighteen-month sentence. There is some judicial acceptance of this approach. In *R. v. Robitaille*,[103] the British Columbia Court of Appeal heard an appeal involving a total sentence of nine years, consisting of seven years for robbery and two years consecutive for using a firearm in the commission of the robbery. The offender was thirty-nine years old with a record going back twenty years that showed an escalating involvement in crimes of violence. In the past, he had received penitentiary sentences of two and three years for robberies. His counsel argued that the jump principle suggested that the next level after three years was a five-year term not a seven-year sentence for robbery. Lambert J.A. commented that the jump principle should only apply where rehabilitation is a significant sentencing factor since it manifests a concern not to discourage the offender from making positive rehabilitative efforts. In the instant case, involving a robbery with a sawn-off shotgun of a jewellery store by an offender with a long record for break and enter and robbery, the predominant sentencing factor was protection of the public. The appeal was dismissed.

---

101   See *R. v. Leonard* (1990), 85 Sask. R.300 (Sask C.A.) in which the court noted a gap of ten years in a long record to reduce a sentence of two years less a day to one year imprisonment.

102   See the discussion in Chapter 7(B)(13).

103   (1993), 31 B.C.A.C. 7 (C.A.).

## 2) Intention to Seek a Greater Punishment by Reason of Previous Convictions

Section 727(1) of the *Criminal Code* requires the Crown to notify the offender of its intention to seek a greater punishment by reason of previous convictions. This does not mean that any time the Crown wants to use a record of previous convictions to seek a harsher sentence that it needs to serve notice. The notice requirement applies to the small number of sentencing provisions that require a minimum penalty or mandatory penalty by reason of previous convictions. The most common is impaired driving, where fourteen days imprisonment is the minimum sentence for a second offence and ninety days for a subsequent offence.[104] Increased penalties also arise in the context of *Criminal Code* mandated driving prohibitions.[105] Also, the mandatory weapons prohibition imposed by section 109(1) increases from ten years for a first offence to life for a subsequent offence.[106] If proper notice is not served, or if service is not proven, the court may still consider the previous convictions but is not bound by any mandatory *Code* requirement. In impaired driving cases, prosecutors usually exercise their discretion and do not prove service of the notice if the previous conviction is more than five years old. Even for more recent convictions, whether the Crown proves service of the notice is often a subject of a negotiated plea arrangement. If service of the notice is not proven, the judge is free to exercise sentencing discretion according to ordinary principles which may or may not result in a term of imprisonment.

The notice requirement is relatively recent but its origins can be traced to a conflict apparent in the *Criminal Code, 1892.* The existence of offences for which greater penalties applied for subsequent convictions generated a pleading problem: a charge should give notice of this consequence, but it would be unfair if the indictment disclosed the details of previous convictions to a jury. Sections 628 and 676 of the

---

104   See ss. 255(1)(a)(ii) & (iii) of the *Criminal Code.*
105   Section 259(1)(b) of the *Criminal Code* provides for a driving prohibition of between six months and three years for a second impaired driving offence; s. 259(1)(c) requires driving prohibitions from between one year and three years for subsequent offences.
106   See ss. 109(2) & (3). The applicability of the notice requirement to these prohibitions was confirmed in *R. v. Jobb* (1988), 43 C.C.C. (3d) 476 (Sask. C.A.).

*Criminal Code, 1892*,[107] provided an unsatisfactory procedure. The substance of a previous charge could be included in the indictment charging the subsequent offence but without "otherwise describing the previous offence or offences." If found guilty of the subsequent offence, the accused would be asked "whether he was so previously convicted as alleged in the indictment." If admitted, the sentencing would proceed but if the accused denied the allegation or stood mute, the jury would hear evidence and make a finding. This was amended in the 1955 revisions to provide that no indictment make any mention of previous convictions.[108] At the same time, the predecessor to section 727(1) was enacted. Section 572(1) provided:

> Where an accused is convicted of an offence for which a greater punishment may be imposed by reason of previous convictions, no greater punishment shall be imposed upon him by reason thereof unless the prosecutor satisfies the court that the accused, before making his plea, was notified that a greater punishment would be sought by reason thereof.[109]

Consequently, the potential prejudice which might flow from the jury or judge learning of a previous conviction was removed but the accused would still have notice of all possible consequences.

The notice provision in the *Criminal Code, 1955*, was, as it is today, skeletal in the sense that it provides no details of the kind of notice that would be satisfactory. Surprisingly, courts have not been concerned to require specificity. Oral notice can be satisfactory[110] but most jurisdictions employ written notice which, in impaired driving cases, is usually served along with the other breathalyzer paperwork.[111] There is, however, no "reasonable notice" component to section 727(1) and courts

---

107   The antecedents of these provisions can be traced to English statutes: *An Act to consolidate and amend the Statute Law of England and Ireland relating to Larceny and other similar Offences, 1861* (U.K.), 24 & 25 Vict., c. 96; *The Prevention of Crimes Act, 1871* (U.K.), 34-35 Vict., c. 112, s. 9; and s. 494 of the *English Draft Code, 1878*.

108   See *Criminal Code*, S.C. 1953-54, c. 51, s. 571.

109   *Ibid.*, s. 572(1). This provision is virtually identical to the current s. 727(1). Section 572(2) of the 1955 *Code* bears the same relation to the current s. 727(2).

110   See *R. v. Bolley*, [1966] 3 C.C.C. 57 (B.C.S.C.).

111   Section 258(7) of the *Criminal Code* requires the Crown to give the accused reasonable notice of the intention to use a certificate provided for by ss. 258(1)(e), (f), (g), (h), or (i), and a copy of the certificate if the certificate is to be admitted into evidence. Unlike s. 727(1), this provision has a "reasonable notice" component.

have not inserted one. Accordingly, the only timing requirement is that it be effected before plea. Notice served the morning of trial has been considered satisfactory so long as the plea had not yet been entered at the time.[112] Looking at the content of the notice, courts have demanded very little specificity. A notice must indicate "clearly and unequivocally" that the Crown will be seeking a greater penalty and is deficient if it only indicates that a greater punishment "may" be imposed.[113] It need not specify the previous convictions[114] or provide any details of the greater penalty which might be sought.[115] In *R. v. Monk*, the Ontario Court of Appeal even held that the notice need not even indicate whether the Crown is alleging a single previous conviction or multiple previous convictions.[116] One would have thought that the requirement that the notice be given before plea indicated an intention to ensure that an accused person had sufficient information to obtain advice and make an informed decision about how to plead. Surely, one would think that fairness would include the scope of the potential penalty within the set of information that an accused should have before plea.[117] Yet, courts have not required the prosecution to go this far. One can perhaps justify the reluctance to place rigid standards on the section 727(1) notice requirement given the difference between it and other statutory notice provisions[118] which make something admissible that would otherwise not be admissible.[119]

While section 727(1) may not create a new and easy mode of proof that lessens the Crown's burden, it can have substantial implications for an accused. While it is true that an accused can be taken to know his or her own record,[120] an accused cannot be taken to understand the nuances of prosecutorial policy which may affect whether an old record is proven. *R. v. Urquhart* provides an excellent example of the

---

112   See *R. v. Boufford* (1988), 46 C.C.C. (3d) 116 (Ont. Dist. Ct.) [*Boufford*].

113   See *R. v. Riley* (1982), 69 C.C.C. (2d) 245 (Ont. H.C.).

114   See *R. v. Pidlubny* (1973), 10 C.C.C. (2d) 178 (Ont. C.A.).

115   See *R. v. Bear* (1979), 47 C.C.C. (2d) 462 (Sask. C.A.).

116   (1981), 62 C.C.C. (2d) 6 (Ont. C.A.).

117   Wilson J. in dissent argued that this was a principle of fundamental justice encompassed by s. 7 of the *Charter*: see *R. v. Lyons*, [1987] 2 S.C.R. 309 at 379–81.

118   See, for example, s. 189(5) of the *Criminal Code*, which deals with intercepted private communications; s. 258(7), which deals with breathalyzer and other alcohol certificates; and s. 667(4), which deals with proof of previous convictions. These all require "reasonable notice."

119   Borins D.C.J., as he then was, made this distinction in *Boufford*, above note 112 at 120–22.

120   This point was also made in *Boufford*, *ibid.* at 124.

need for clarity.[121] A plea arrangement was made on the basis that the notice would only apply to a single previous conviction. However, the entire record was filed and the presiding judge considered that a 1984 conviction also had to be considered. Consequently, the instant offence was a third conviction and a mandatory ninety-day sentence was imposed contrary to the understanding between the parties. Although varied on appeal to fourteen days, this indicates the need for frankness in the notice. It can always be amended to reflect a plea arrangement, so that the *Urquhart* misunderstanding will not occur. While the courts are concerned that an accused not be misled,[122] it seems wrong not to require the Crown to specify what set of enhanced consequences it intends to seek before the accused enters a plea. How else can the plea be characterized as informed?

## H. REHABILITATIVE PROSPECTS

An older line of cases has held that in situations where the offender has treatment needs that can be met in a custodial setting, a sentence can be fashioned to permit the completion of therapy.[123] More recent decisions have accepted a rehabilitative objective only so long as the sentence remains within the acceptable range for the kind of offence in issue.[124] The early cases emanate from an era in which the liberal rehabilitative ideal was prominent in sentencing and correctional thinking. Even then, however, informed systemic observers like Professor Norval Morris expressed concern that proportionality apply to limit a well-meaning rehabilitative sentence to its proper range.[125] Now, sentencing judges ought to be concerned about the speculative nature of many treatments especially if they are implemented behind prison walls without adequate linkages to post-release continuity. Imprisonment represents a gross intrusion by the state into an individual's liberty and good intentions should take a back seat to the principles of proportionality and restraint. It is the entrenchment of restraint which suggests that longer sentences, even within an acceptable range, should not be

---

121   (1984), 52 N.B.R. (2d) 9 (C.A.).

122   See *Pidlubny*, above note 114; and *R. v. Reid*, (1970) 5 C.C.C. 368 (B.C.C.A.).

123   See, for example, *R. v. Robinson* (1974), 19 C.C.C. (2d) 193 (Ont. C.A.).

124   See, for example, *Hynes*, above note 29 (schizophrenic who harassed neighbour while not taking medication).

125   See N. Morris, *The Future of Imprisonment* (Chicago: University of Chicago Press, 1974) at 12–20.

imposed solely for rehabilitative purposes. This is consistent with the provisions which specify that treatment may only be imposed as a condition of probation if the offender consents.[126] At the same time, the optional conditions for conditional sentences permit mandatory treatment orders regardless of consent.[127] The distinction suggests that a sentence which is not inherently punitive should not coerce treatment. In other words, rehabilitative concerns alone cannot support a sentence with coerced treatment as its objective. Accordingly, while rehabilitation may form part of a punitive sentence, the length of the deprivation of liberty should not be determined by this goal.

## FURTHER READINGS

Manson, A., "Charter Violations in Mitigation of Sentence" (1995) 41 C.R. (4th) 318

Ruby, C., *Sentencing*, 5th ed. (Toronto: Butterworths, 1999)

Solicitor General Canada, *Sentence Calculation Handbook: A Handbook for Judges, Lawyers and Correctional Officials*, 2nd ed. (Ottawa: Supply and Services Canada, 1996)

Thomas, D.A., *Principles of Sentencing*, 2nd ed. (London: Heinemann, 1979)

---

126  See *Criminal Code*, s. 732.1(3)(g).
127  *Ibid.*, s. 742.3(2)(e).

# CHAPTER 7

# AGGRAVATING AND MITIGATING FACTORS

## A. THE ROLE OF AGGRAVATING AND MITIGATING FACTORS

The traditional Canadian amalgam approach to sentencing requires the judge to reflect all relevant objectives while emphasizing any one that is, in the circumstances, predominant. It also encompasses an important role for mitigating and aggravating factors. Generally, the nature of the offence will provide a good indication to the court about whether to consider the punitive objectives of denunciation and deterrence. These objectives may appear appropriate as the inherent gravity of the offence increases. Issues of rehabilitation and the impact of, or need for, incapacitation are reflected in the individual characteristics of the offender. The potential for reparation or restoration raises questions about the victim and the community, and a potential relationship for the offender in that context. The circumstances of the case may highlight certain objectives but regardless of that focus, section 718.2(e) of the *Criminal Code* requires the judge to consider all available sanctions that are reasonable. Proportionality and parity are important considerations as are recent sentencing practice and any appellate guidelines for similar offences. As the judge begins to narrow the decision to a range of begins options and begins to consider questions like quantum, the presence of mitigating or aggravating factors becomes the lever that shifts the balance toward one option or another, up or down a quantum range. In great measure, they fine-tune the sentencing decision.

Section 718.2(a) now entrenches the common law by requiring judges to increase or reduce a sentence by taking into account aggravating or mitigating circumstances relevant to the offence or the offender. The *Criminal Code* lists a few examples of aggravating circumstances, some of which were clearly encompassed by the common law and others which were applied previously but not without controversy: curiously, there are no examples of mitigating factors. However, over the years, the common law has recognized dozens of factors which can have a mitigating or aggravating effect. In the following discussion, most available factors are included with authorities and some consideration of their underlying rationale. Aggravating and mitigating factors are often taken for granted in the sense that courts rarely debate their applicability or premises. For the most part, the underlying premises which explain the applicability of an aggravating or mitigating factor relate to two large categories:

1. The gravity of the offence in terms of the culpability of the offender and the consequential harm which was caused; and

2. The ways in which character, past conduct, and post-offence conduct implicate a particular objective of sentencing.

The second category involves the presence or absence of factors which either diminish or enhance the significance of a relevant sentencing objective. In other words, they may relate to rehabilitative prospects, the context for re-integration, the relevance of individual deterrence, and the utility of specific options or conditions. This includes the amorphous set of factors represented by the ledger of pro-social conduct which courts take into account in mitigation.

# B. MITIGATING FACTORS

## 1) First Offender

The status of being a first offender is a significant mitigating factor. The fact that the offender has not been found guilty by the criminal process before generates a number of favourable inferences, with rehabilitative prospects always at the forefront of consideration. First, being a first offender suggests that the conviction itself constitutes a punishment. It is assumed that the offender will respond positively to the deterrent effects of the process of arrest, charging, finding of guilt, and imposition of sanction. This discounts any special need for individual deterrence and suggests that a lenient response is in order. Being a first offender is also consistent with demonstrating good character prior to the offence. Although it does not guarantee a non-custodial sentence, there is both a presumption against custody and a significant reducing effect if custody is mandated.

## 2)   No Prior Record Advanced

Occasionally, a case will go forward with no record of previous convictions being advanced even though a previous conviction exists. It may be unrelated or stale. Regardless, defence counsel should be careful not to characterize the offender as a "first offender" if she is not. Still, the judge who deals with a case where no mention is made of any prior record must treat the offender as if she is a "first offender."

## 3)   Prior Good Character

Good-character evidence during a trial when responsibility is at stake is usually limited to reputation in the community. For sentencing purposes, character is much broader and will often include achievements and opinions attributed to relatives, friends, associates, and acquaintances. It is usually directed to showing that the offence is out of character. In this way, evidence of conduct which shows values antithetical to those which ordinarily underlie the particular offence will be helpful. Accordingly, evidence of honesty and generosity will be relevant to a crime of dishonesty. Similarly, evidence of compassion will be relevant to a crime of violence.

Claims of prior good character are often misconceived. For example, it is often confused with a claim about standing in the community. While this is often put forward, it has a nebulous and questionable basis as a mitigating factor, more suited to showing re-integrative potential. For some offences, evidence of a person's pro-social community commitment through volunteer work is not mitigating when the offence arises from those activities. Assaulting children involved in the volunteer activity is an obvious example. In general, courts have found that good-character claims are inappropriate when dealing with offences committed in the dark corners of people's lives. With respect to sexual offences, the Supreme Court has recognized that they are usually perpetrated in private, out of sight and knowledge of friends and associates. Accordingly, evidence of good community reputation has little probative value.[1] While this conclusion was directed to the use of character evidence at trial, it applies equally to sentencing issues.

---

1   See *R. v. Profit*, [1993] 3 S.C.R. 637, accepting the dissent below of Griffiths J.A. at (1992), 11 O.R. (3d) 98 (C.A.).

## 4) Guilty Plea and Remorse

The reason that a guilty plea is usually considered to be a mitigating factor is because it implies remorse and an acknowledgement of responsibility by the offender. The extent of the mitigating value is affected by the timing of the guilty plea: the earlier, the better. This is especially true if one intends to include consideration for the victims as an added element. Avoiding the need to have a victim testify is a legitimate dimension of remorse but gets little credence if a guilty plea is entered only after hearing the witness at the preliminary hearing. Convenience to the court by saving its time is not a reason for mitigation. While this is a systemic benefit, it would be wrong to give the impression that forego-ing the constitutional right to plead not guilty will garner credit simply because it makes the judge's life easier. The court is a public institution exercising an important public function and a guilty plea must reflect more than time-saving to support mitigation. In this sense, it ought to be communicated as an acceptance of responsibility.

Of course, a guilty plea is not the only way to show remorse. Sin-cere apologies and other efforts at reparation can convey a stronger message than simply the guilty plea. Moreover, remorse can be indi-cated even after a trial. The right to compel the Crown to prove its case does not entirely remove the opportunity to show remorse although it may diminish it.[2]

## 5) Evidence of Impairment

Impairment of judgment can be a mitigating circumstance. Sentencing ought to respond proportionately to culpability; intended consequences should be treated more severely than those caused negligently. This is a principle of fundamental justice.[3] Accordingly, evidence that an accused was suffering from impaired judgment can be very significant.

Within the criminal law generally, voluntary intoxication has been the subject of variable and inconsistent treatment. In the nineteenth century, it was not considered a factor that could mitigate fault[4] but, in this century, it became an accepted defence to a crime of specific

---

2   If, however, there has been misconduct in the defence, as for example a threat to a witness, this will preclude a claim of remorse: see *R. v. Sawchyn* (1981), 60 C.C.C. (2d) 200 at 210 (Alta. C.A.).

3   See *R. v. Martineau*, [1990] 2 S.C.R. 633 at 645–46 [*Martineau*].

4   See *D.P.P. v. Beard*, [1920] A.C. 479 at 494 (H.L.).

intent.[5] During the same period, it was accepted as a mitigating factor on sentencing. However, this has changed. Kerans J.A. has said:

> Drunkenness generally should not be a mitigating factor. Nevertheless, the fact that an assault is totally spontaneous can offer mitigation, and sometimes drunkenness is a factor in determining whether the attack is spontaneous or whether the likely consequences were fully appreciated.[6]

This puts intoxication in its proper place as a factor that can distinguish between a planned offence and one generated spontaneously with little regard for consequences.[7] Moreover, with respect to crimes of violence where there is a history of drunken violence, intoxication is an aggravating circumstance.

However, there are other situations where emotional, physical, and psychological impairment can mitigate culpability because they affect judgment. Cool and deliberate choices are more culpable than those clouded by depression, medication, and extraordinary stress. Gambling addiction has been recognized as a mitigating background factor especially with respect to thefts and frauds. In R. v. Horvath,[8] a former bank manager was convicted of thefts totalling almost $200,000 from her employer and fraud in the amount of $35,000 from another financial institution. She was a thirty-six-year-old married woman with a child. She had become pathologically addicted to video lottery terminals and would leave work at the end of the day to gamble until late at night. She lost money and incurred huge debts. Then, she started stealing from her employer using an elaborate scheme involving fictitious and actual accounts. The trial judge heard expert evidence about her gambling addiction and her efforts to deal with it, and sentenced her to a conditional sentence of two years less a day in duration. The Crown appealed arguing that the amount stolen and the breach of trust required a custodial sentence. For the court, Bayda C.J.S. dismissed the appeal. He said:

> Perhaps the factor that carries most weight in assessing the gravity of the offences in this particular case is the one that generated those offences. The offences were the products of a distorted mind — a

5   See R. v. Daviault, [1994] 3 S.C.R. 63 [Daviault], which also carved out a small space in respect of general-intent offences in cases of drunkenness akin to automatism. See also s. 33.1 of the Criminal Code.

6   R. v. Sandercock (1985), 22 C.C.C. (3d) 79 at 88 (Alta. C.A.).

7   The limited potential for a mitigating effect with respect to sexual assault was recognized by Sopinka J. in dissent, in Daviault, above note 5 at 119–20. See also McLachlin J. in dissent in R. v. McDonnell, [1997] 1 S.C.R. 948 at 1011.

8   (1997), 117 C.C.C. (3d) 110 (Sask. C.A.) [Horvath].

mind seriously diseased by a disorder now recognized by the medical community as a mental disorder. The acts committed at the command of that mind were not acts of free choice in the same sense as are the acts of free choice of a normal mind. A pathological gambler does not have the same power of control over his or her acts as one who does not suffer from that complex disease. Accordingly, where those acts constitute criminal offences, the moral culpability — moral blameworthiness — and responsibility are not of the same order as they would be in those cases where the mind is not so affected.[9]

*Horvath* highlights the ability of an addiction to reduce culpability enough to warrant a conditional sentence, even in a case aggravated by a breach of trust. Of course, this mitigating effect of a gambling addiction has its limits. The offender in *Horvath* had no prior record and was making serious efforts to address her problem. In cases where there is a prior record, courts have not been so sympathetic to the gambling addiction factor.[10]

While many courts have followed the *Horvath* approach to proven gambling addictions for breach of trust thefts[11] and even for robbery,[12] the Alberta Court of Appeal has rejected conditional sentences in cases of substantial thefts from employers.[13] It has held that the proven gambling addiction did not constitute an exceptional circumstance that warranted a conditional sentence. This view does not seem to give proper weight to the basis for using a gambling addiction in mitigation. The gambling addiction does not serve as an excuse but it does diminish culpability if it has affected the offender to the point where there is little or no free will, as described in *Horvath*. Then, blameworthiness has been substantially reduced, and this should be reflected in the sentence.

## 6)  Employment Record

A good employment record is always a mitigating factor although its impact may be diminished or even superceded by the nature of the offence. The reason why courts respond favourably to a good work

---

9   *Ibid.* at 129.

10   See, for example, *R. v. Harris* (1990), 105 N.B.R. (2d) 361 (Q.B.).

11   See *R. v. Lloyd*, [1998] S.J. No. 639 (C.A.) (QL); *R. v. Russell* (1998), 126 Man. R. (2d) 313 (C.A.); and *R. v. Cleary* (1998), 161 Nfld. & P.E.I.R. 234 (Nfld. S.C. (T.D.)).

12   See *R. v. Sanderson* (1997), 115 Man. R. (2d) 205 (C.A.), where a conditional sentence was imposed for robbery committed by a person with a gambling addiction.

13   See *R. v. Holmes*, [1999] A.J. No. 862 (C.A.); *R. v. McIvor* (1996), 106 C.C.C. (3d) 285 (Alta. C.A.).

record is because it demonstrates pro-social responsibility and conformity to community norms which are the antithesis of crime. Accordingly, the offender is considered to be more redeemable with more promising rehabilitative prospects particularly if the record is consistent over a long period of time. However, courts should be careful not to turn the absence of a good work record into an aggravating factor. Many offenders, especially those with little training and education, have diminished opportunities for work. Moreover, many offences are committed in places with high unemployment. In these situations, offenders should not be prejudiced. However, lawyers should consider finding out about community volunteer work or even a pattern of assistance to family and friends. These facts can serve the same mitigating purpose.

## 7) Collateral or Indirect Consequences

As a result of the commission of an offence, the offender may suffer physical, emotional, social, or financial consequences. While not punishment in the true sense of pains or burdens imposed by the state after a finding of guilt, they are often considered in mitigation. However, careful distinctions need to be made.

When an offender suffers physical injury as a result of an offence, this may be relevant for sentencing purposes especially if there will be long-lasting effects. This kind of consequence may bear on a number of sentencing goals like individual and general deterrence. Certainly, this is the result when an offender is seriously injured after a driving offence. Given the general familiarity with automobiles as part of modern life, the direct conduct/consequence image plays a communicative role consistent with traditional sentencing objectives. This is not the case when the personal injury arises from uncommon conduct that is purely criminal, such as might occur during a robbery.

The loss of employment or professional qualifications will often be ,raised as relevant collateral consequences. However, there is a difference between situations where the specific criminal act results in disqualification from a profession or employment, and those situations where employment is lost as a result of personal or community responses that stigmatize the offender. The latter scenario should be taken into account because it[14] flows from the criminal process; disqualification is

---

14   See, for example, *R. v. Vinson* (1981), 3 Cr. App. R. (S) 315 (C.A.), where a sentence of two years for sexual assaults was reduced to nine months in light of the "catastrophic" personal results. Also see the dissent of Brooke J.A. in *R. v. Gorman* (1971), 4 C.C.C. (2d) 330 at 332 (Ont. C.A.).

a more difficult issue. Careful distinctions are required. Some mitigation may be available if the disqualification arises from an offence which is not centrally related to professional responsibility. For example, there is a difference between a surgeon who is struck off the professional roll for criminal negligence causing death after performing surgery while intoxicated, and a physician who commits an offence of dishonesty regarding his medicare billings. The former receives no sympathy for losing a profession which his conduct shows he was ill-suited to perform while the loss of livelihood for the latter arises from conduct unrelated to patient care.[15] Another example is a police officer who is convicted of an offence related to policing. A conviction for assaulting a prisoner will likely end a career and should not generate any mitigation when the officer is being sentenced for the assault. An off-duty offence may also end a law enforcement career, but this factor would be viewed in a different light depending on the nature of the offence.

The mitigating effect of indirect consequences must be considered in relation both to future re-integration and to the nature of the offence. Burdens and hardships flowing from a conviction are relevant if they make the rehabilitative path harder to travel. Here, one can include loss of financial or social support. People lose jobs; families are disrupted; sources of assistance disappear. Notwithstanding a need for denunciation, indirect consequences which arise from stigmatization cannot be isolated from the sentencing matrix if they will have bearing on the offender's ability to live productively in the community. The mitigation will depend on weighing these obstacles against the degree of denunciation appropriate to the offence.

Some indirect consequences are so inevitably linked to an offence that they seem to be part of the punishment and cannot be considered mitigating. Realism has to be brought to the analysis.[16] For example, losing a year in school is a relevant mitigating indirect consequence when it is put in the context of a short custodial sentence, but if the exclusion from school arises from an assault on a teacher, it has little or no mitigating effect. The point is simply that indirect consequences must be viewed in the light of the offence itself. Where the consequence is so directly linked to the nature of an offence as to be almost inevitable, its role as a mitigating factor is greatly diminished.

---

15   See *R. v. Richards* (1980), 2 Cr. App. R. (S) 119 (C.A.), where a physician made false financial returns.

16   For example, the old joke of the person charged with killing his parents who seeks mercy because he is an orphan.

## 8) Post-offence Rehabilitative Efforts

Progress in dealing with personal problems, and efforts to improve or repair one's social situation, are always given mitigating credit.[17] There may be concerns that such efforts are self-serving but they warrant credit because they show both a recognition of personal difficulties and a commitment to remedying them. Of course, one needs to show sincerity and motivation — this can usually be done through material from a treatment program, job, family, or friends. At the sentencing stage, some credit will be given for rehabilitative plans but it is always preferable if an offender is already participating and achieving some degree of progress rather than simply explaining their plans for the future. Regrettably, not all communities have appropriate resources available locally. Moreover, not all treatment facilities are available at public expense. Accordingly, there is a real opportunity for the privileged offender to gain an advantage over the non-privileged. This does not diminish the mitigating effect of an offender's sincere rehabilitative efforts. However, it does mean that courts should be sensitive to these resource difficulties and be prepared to credit time and energy spent looking for appropriate resources and attempting to qualify for them as important factors. These efforts are a first step to reform since they reflect introspection and a commitment to change. The extent of the mitigating effect of post-offence efforts will obviously depend on sincerity, actual progress, and relevance to the offence. In cases of drug and alcohol abuse, where the offence is closely linked to the addiction, courts should be cautious about imposing a sentence which may disrupt the rehabilitative progress. More to the point, the absence of progress is not as critical as the fact that efforts at treatment show some interest in change. It is an accepted part of dealing with drug addiction that hard-core addicts will fail a number of times along the road to recovery.

## 9) Unrelated Meritorious Conduct

Some courts have accepted the mitigating effect of acts of charity or bravery unrelated to the offence. The basis is that such conduct suggests something positive about the offender which should enhance the courts' view of rehabilitative prospects. Also, this conduct is the kind of community involvement which one wants to encourage. This is

---

17   See, for example, *R. v. Bonneteau* (1994), 93 C.C.C. (3d) 385 at 394 (Alta. C.A.); *R. v. H.(W.)* (1993), 84 C.C.C. (3d) 465 at 467, 469–70 (Ont. C.A.); and *R. v. Alderton* (1985), 17 C.C.C. (3d) 204 at 212 (Ont. C.A.).

sometimes referred to as "moral credit."[18] Examples are
from drowning[19] or attempting to rescue people trap
Such conduct can have taken place before or after the o

## 10) Acts of Reparation or Compensation

Reflecting the common law, two of the potential objectives of a sentence are now described in sections 718(e) and (f) as follows:

> (e) to provide reparations for harm done to victims or to the community; and
> (f) to promote a sense of responsibility in offenders, and acknowledgment of the harm done to victims and to the community.

For the same reasons that a sentence may be directed to these ends, an offender is entitled to some mitigating credit for acts of reparation or compensation done prior to sentencing. It may be impossible to know whether an act is purely self-interested or really reflects remorse and a concern to rectify harm done. Absent contradictory evidence, the benefit of any doubt should always go to the offender. Obviously, some harm is more easily rectified and some offenders are in a better position to take steps to repair damage. Still, these are steps which should be encouraged. While lawyers may want to encourage the repair of a broken window, they should exercise some caution in advising offenders. A victim may harbour some residual fear of the offender. In the absence of an organized and responsible attempt at reconciliation, damage should be repaired by a third party and not the offender personally.

## 11) Provocation and Duress

Any situations which reduce the degree of culpability or moral blameworthiness present relevant mitigating circumstances. The defence of duress or compulsion is limited by section 17 of the *Criminal Code* both in terms of qualifying offences and factual pre-conditions.[21] Accordingly,

---

18  See N. Walker & N. Padfield, *Sentencing: Theory, Law, and Practice*, 2d ed. (London: Butterworths, 1996) at 52–53.
19  See *R. v. Keightley*, [1972] Crim. L. Rev. 262 (C.A.), where a sentence of eighteen months for fraud was cut in half in recognition of the offender's heroism.
20  See *R. v. Reid* (1982), 4 Cr. App. R. (S) 280 (C.A.).
21  The requirement of "immediacy" has been found to be unconstitutional in *R. v. Langlois* (1993), 80 C.C.C. (3d) 28 (Que. C.A.); and *R. v. Ruzic* (1998), 128 C.C.C. (3d) 97 (Ont. C.A.). *Ruzic* was appealed to the Supreme Court of Canada and is on reserve at the time of writing.

ere will be situations where there is evidence of compulsion but no defence to the charge. Because it can be considered less blameworthy to act under threat than of one's own initiative, these situations can mitigate a sentence. The common case is a drug courier who argues that a threat was made to encourage his or her participation. If there is no defence of duress, there may still be facts that support its use for sentencing purposes.[22]

Acts or words which provoke a violent response are in the same category. In cases of murder, provocation under section 232 reduces the offence to manslaughter. For all other forms of assault, provocation is not a partial defence but can provide mitigation on sentencing. Again, the premise is straightforward. Punching someone is an assault but it is a less blameworthy assault if it was provoked by an insult, threat, violent gesture or other form of offensive or wrongful conduct. At some point, the response is so disproportionate to the provocation that the provocation becomes irrelevant. Conversely, the provocation may have been so severe and the retaliation so slight that the mitigating effect produces a discharge.

In *R. v. Stone*,[23] the offender was convicted of manslaughter after being charged with the murder of his wife. Evidence of provocation had been placed before the jury. In imposing a sentence of seven years for manslaughter, the trial judge took into account the provocation evidence. On appeal, it was argued by the Crown that this constituted a double counting since the provocation evidence had already resulted in mitigating the offence from murder to manslaughter. For the court,[24] Bastarache J. rejected this argument and commented:

> In reaching a sentence which accurately reflects a particular offender's moral culpability, the sentencing judge must consider all of the circumstances of the offence, including whether it involved provocation. Indeed, . . . to ignore the defence of provocation accepted by the jury, and the evidence upon which that defence was based, would be to ignore probative evidence of an offender's mental state at the time of the killing.[25]

---

22  See the discussion in Chapter 8 relating to establishing the factual premise for sentencing in a situation where a defence was rejected or not raised at trial.

23  [1999] 2 S.C.R. 290.

24  Although there was a 5/4 split on the issue of automatism and whether non-insane automatism ought to have been left with the jury, the court was unanimous on the sentencing point: *ibid.* at 350, Binnie J.

25  *Ibid.* at 406.

Accordingly, provocation was relevant in determining the level of moral culpability. At the same time, the fact that the killing occurred in the context of a spousal relationship was a relevant aggravating factor.[26]

## 12)  Delay in Prosecution or Sentencing

Before discussing delay by authorities, it is necessary to say something about delays by victims in coming forward. It is not uncommon to find a case on a docket alleging an offence that was committed decades before, usually a serious charge involving physical or sexual abuse of the victim when the victim was a child. Regardless of the attitude at the time of the offence towards assaults on children, these matters are taken very seriously today. Often these offences involve a breach of trust which is now recognized in the *Criminal Code* as an aggravating factor[27] and a custodial sentence of some length is usually sought for denunciatory and deterrent purposes.

But what about the delay in bringing the charges forward? By itself, the intervening period does not mean very much and will not be considered as a mitigating factor.[28] However, delay may present corollaries which can be mitigating. They are often raised in the context of submissions for a conditional sentence. For example, a lengthy period with no repetition of offending is an important mitigating factor.[29] This, of course, is enhanced to some extent by evidence of productive social integration in terms of employment and family during that period. The extent of its influence is affected by the gravity of the offence and is diminished by a lack of remorse or denial that the offence was a serious matter.[30] The age of the offender can play a role. On the one hand, through the passage of time, the offender may have become elderly. While this is not mitigating, it may be accompanied by ill-health or infirmity which ought to be considered because of the inherent hardships of incarceration. From a different perspective, if offences were committed when the offender was very young, exemplary conduct

---

26   See s. 718.2(a)(ii) of the *Criminal Code*, page 131; and the discussion below at 148–9, 157.

27   See s. 718.2(a)(iii), *ibid.*

28   See, for example, the decision of Romilly J. in *R. v. L.(C.)*, [1998] B.C.J. No. 61 (S.C.) (QL).

29   See, for example, *R. v. Anderson* (1998), 128 C.C.C. (3d) 478 (B.C.C.A.).

30   See *R. v. E.(R.J.)*, [1999] B.C.J. No. 691, Romilly J. (S.C.).

during adulthood will be a serious mitigating factor.[31] These examples demonstrate how the passage of time may produce changes that are relevant mitigating factors. While the ability of the justice system to reach back into time for the subject matter of prosecutions may cause some to grimace, we do not have limitations on prosecutions and no automatic benefit accrues to offenders because of the passage of time.

There are *Charter* issues arising from delay. A prosecution may have moved slowly but not enough to constitute a violation of section 11(b) (the guarantee of trial within a reasonable time) to support a stay. Some courts have held that excessive delay which can be attributed to either the police or the prosecution may be a mitigating factor even if it was insufficient to produce a section 11(b) breach.[32] To some extent, this question is enmeshed in the debate about whether a *Charter* breach that does not produce a stay as a remedy can be resurrected at the sentencing stage in mitigation.[33] However, given the recognition that any prosecution produces burdens and stress, and impinges on liberty,[34] it is not necessary to engage in that controversy to argue that a deliberate or unnecessary expansion of the period during which these factors operate is akin to added punishment. Accordingly, it is appropriate to give it a mitigating effect.

The second issue is whether delay in relation only to sentencing can produce a section 11(b) breach which leads to a stay rather than simply a mitigating consideration. The Supreme Court has concluded that section 11(b) includes the right to be sentenced within a reasonable time.[35] McLachlin J., as she then was, noted the potential adverse effects of living in "suspense" pending sentencing, and held:

> Delay in sentencing extends the time during which these constraints on an individual's liberty are imposed. While the sentencing judge may take them into account, there is no certainty that this will occur. It follows that delay in sentencing may prejudice the accused's liberty interest.[36]

---

31   See, for example, *R. v. M.(D.E.S.)* (1993), 21 C.R. (4th) 55 (B.C.C.A.), which occurred prior to the conditional sentencing regime. It is discussed in Chapter 9 dealing with probation and electronic monitoring.

32   See *R. v. L.(W.)* (1996), 3 C.R. (5th) 138 (Ont. C.A.); and *R. v. Bosley* (1992), 18 C.R. (4th) 347 (Ont. C.A.).

33   See A. Manson, "*Charter* Violations in Mitigation of Sentence" (1995), 41 C.R. (4th) 318.

34   See *R. v. Rahey*, [1987] 1 S.C.R. 588 at 610.

35   See *R. v. MacDougall*, [1998] 3 S.C.R. 45 [*MacDougall*]; and *R. v. Gallant*, [1998] 3 S.C.R. 80 [*Gallant*].

36   See *MacDougall, ibid.* 62–63.

For the purpose of section 11(b), she applied the usual tests[37] and concluded that, in the absence of any indicia of prejudice, the bulk of the delay occasioned by judicial illness could not be considered unreasonable. Accordingly, stays were not warranted. What is significant, however, is the recognition that delay can be an appropriate mitigating factor since it extends the ordinary impact of a sentence. Regardless of a section 11(b) claim, one can argue that any deliberate, unnecessary, or unreasonable delay ought to be a mitigating factor.

While pre-charge delay has no bearing on an accused's section 11(b) rights to a speedy trial, some courts have taken deliberate delay into account in mitigation of sentence.[38] This flows from the proposition that it is in everyone's interests, including the offender's, to proceed expeditiously to determine responsibility and impose a fair sanction. This kind of claim usually occurs when an offender is already serving a sentence of imprisonment and needs to resolve an outstanding charge before proceeding with release plans. From the offender's perspective, the authorities should not be able to arbitrarily postpone release by sitting on a warrant or evidence. Given the recognized interest in sentencing within a reasonable time, an example of deliberate or negligent delay which may prolong a term of imprisonment should generate mitigating consideration, including the possibility of a concurrent sentence even if otherwise not warranted.

## 13)  Gap in Criminal Record and the Intermediate Recidivist

These are related factors which serve to place an offender's record into a context which has bearing on rehabilitative prospects. By definition, a recidivist is someone with a long record of previous convictions. A significant gap in that record, especially one that occurs just prior to the instant offence, indicates an ability to conform to legal norms for a substantial period of time. Notwithstanding the cynical view that a charge-free period does not mean a crime-free period, a significant gap shows a rehabilitative potential. Of course, the effect of the gap is relative but it would be enhanced if it included a period of good employment or responsible domestic relations. How the mitigation is applied depends on the nature of the offence. Where it can legitimately be concluded that imprisonment is the only reasonable alternative, a significant

---

37   As set out in R. v. Morin, [1992] 1 S.C.R. 771.

38   See, for example, R. v. Simon (1975), 25 C.C.C. (2d) 159 (Ont. C.A.); and R. v. Fairn (1973), 12 C.C.C. (2d) 423 at 440–41 (N.S. Co. Ct.).

gap should be an important argument against an automatic escalation of the duration of imprisonment.

The "intermediate recidivist" is a category described by D.A. Thomas[39] which includes an offender with a record who has arguably reached a point in life where a corner can be turned. For example, there may be a recent record of constructive employment with good prospects, a new domestic relationship, long-awaited success in dealing with an addiction or other personal difficulty, or a combination of these kinds of significant and potentially reformative life events. Notwithstanding the record, and depending on the nature of the instant offence, a court should give very serious consideration to a non-custodial sanction that will enhance the prospect of solid rehabilitation rather than frustrate it. One vehicle which may be particularly well-suited to this category of offender is the conditional sentence.[40] There may be serious factual issues about the extent to which these significant life events have occurred, but courts are equipped to deal with issues of disputed fact and credibility. While sincerity may be a hard issue, courts should not be shy to address it.

A good example of the intermediate recidivist, although that label was not used, can be found in the case of *R. v. McLeod*,[41] an offender with a long criminal record and a long-standing problem with prescription drugs. At the age of thirty, facing another drug offence and a charge of breach of probation, he experienced a number of positive changes. He returned to school and finished grades eleven and twelve before entering a college program. He attended church and A.A., and did volunteer work at his school. The trial judge imposed a non-custodial sentence consisting of a two-year probation period with electronic monitoring for the first six months. The Crown appealed, seeking a term of imprisonment in light of the offences and the offender's record. Vancise J.A. wrote a lengthy decision supporting the non-custodial sentence. Recognizing the apparent change in the offender's life, he held that a fit sentence is one that is neither excessive nor inadequate judged on the merits of the particular case, taking into account the circumstances and the characteristics of the offence. In his view, intensive

---

39   D.A. Thomas, *Principles of Sentencing*, 2d ed. (London: Heinemann, 1979) at 20–22.
40   See Conditional Sentences, in Chapter 9, below.
41   (1993), 81 C.C.C. (3d) 83, Vancise J.A. (Sask. C.A.). While this case might be characterized as an example of post-offence rehabilitative efforts, the age of the offender and the extent of the positive life changes qualify it as an example of the intermediate recidivist.

probation supervision aided by a period of electronic monitoring was a sufficient and appropriate sanction.

## 14)  The Test Case Scenario

Legislative provisions which have novel or ambiguous dimensions can generate good faith attempts to test their scope. With respect to non-violent crimes, an effort to create a test case for adjudicative purposes can result in a mitigated sentence.[42] Of course, just being one of the first individuals prosecuted is not the same as an offence which was the product of a will to test the legislation. However, given the costs, rigours, and uncertainties of protracted litigation, there can be a mitigating effect for an accused who decides to carry a case forward even if this decision arose after the charge.[43]

## 15)  Disadvantaged Background

There is little doubt that much of crime can be traced back to histories of poverty, abuse, and family dysfunction. While we applaud those who rise above the limiting and even crippling circumstances of their backgrounds, it is obvious that many cannot. The community must bear responsibility for its schools, hospitals, children's aid agencies, and other social institutions which intervene in the lives of young people. When these efforts do not succeed, some recognition to disadvantaged background must be paid within the sentencing process. Of course, the impact will depend on the gravity of the offences for which the offender is being sentenced. Still, it is incumbent on courts to consider the real life-experience of the offender and put the offences into context. For example, in R. v. George,[44] a dangerous offender case, the

---

42   See R. v. Turmel, [1995] O.J. No. 1302 (Prov. Div.), dealing with a prosecution for keeping a common gaming house under s. 201(1) of the Criminal Code where the accused attempted openly to run a small casino-like enterprise without violating the Code. See also R. v. Stewart (No. 2) (1983), 45 O.R. (2d) 185 (H.C.), where the accused was convicted of counselling the theft of confidential information. The case involved an analysis of whether the information was property. The offender was given an absolute discharge.

43   See, for example, R. v. Horseman, [1990] 1 S.C.R. 901. The majority held that the act of selling a bear hide warranted a conviction but that the offender had a license and sold the hide in good faith. Since the statute required a minimum fine, Cory J. concluded that a stay of proceedings was appropriate so that no financial burden would be imposed.

44   (1998), 126 C.C.C. (3d) 384 (B.C.C.A.).

British Columbia Court of Appeal had to consider the "pattern of aggressive behaviour" test in section 753(a)(ii). In doing so, it observed:

> The dangerous offender provisions may fall more heavily on the poor and disadvantaged members of our society if their childhood misconduct is counted against them. This appellant had to face school as an aboriginal foster child living in a non-aboriginal culture with an I.Q. at or near the retarded level, without having ever acquired a sense of discipline or self-control. It is understandable that any child with this background would get into a lot of trouble by lashing out aggressively when challenged by his or her environment.[45]

This demonstrates the importance of placing relevant factors into the proper light: prior record both as a young offender and adult, employment record, educational record, family contacts. All of these factors need to be contextualized by taking into account the impact on them of the offender's disadvantaged background. It is not that difficult beginnings provide some kind of sentencing credit, but they do often explain other factors which are relevant to sentencing in an aggravating way.

A history of abuse by the offender is a controversial factor. The New Brunswick Court of Appeal has rejected the mitigating effect of an offender's "personal tragedy" in relation to a sentence for sexual assault causing bodily harm.[46] The offender had been the victim of sexual abuse as a boy in the care of provincial institutions. He had a long record, and the assault, inflicted on the woman he had been living with, was described as a "prolonged and vicious sexual assault which included acts of cruelty and sadism." Within this context, his history of abuse as a youth was not given a mitigating role.[47]

Recently, the Ontario Court of Appeal considered an offender who had received two consecutive sentences of three-and-a-half and two-and-a-half years for two counts of aggravated sexual assault.[48] On top of this six-year sentence he had served nineteen months in pre-sentence custody. The offender was a young aboriginal man from Moose Factory and the case illustrates the important role that section 718.2(e) can play. It also has broader impact because the court relied on the nexus between the circumstances of the offences and the disadvan-

---

45   *Ibid.* at 391–92.

46   See *R. v. J.(R.K.)* (1998), 207 N.B.R. (2d) 24 (C.A.).

47   In imposing a six-year sentence, the court did consider as mitigating the twenty months of pre-sentence custody, and the offender's drug and alcohol problems which he was attempting to address.

48   See *R. v. Sackanay* (2000), 47 O.R. (3d) 612 (C.A.).

taged history which the offender presented. He was a drug addict who had committed two violent assaults on the same evening while in a continuous state of intoxication. The appeal was allowed and the two sentences made concurrent for a total of three and a half years.

## 16)  Mistaken Belief in the Nature of a Prohibited Substance

Currently, substantive criminal law has produced some complicated and sometimes contradictory ruling about when a mistaken belief can exonerate. For example, with drug offences, knowledge of the general nature of a substance as an illicit drug is sufficient for culpability even if the offender believes the substance was a less serious drug. There is still a controversy over whether the offence committed is the factually completed offence or an attempt at the intended offence.[49] For sentencing purposes, it is important to remember the central role of culpability as measured by blameworthiness. As a result, the offender's mental state should be the focus of sentencing attention. While the factual context cannot be ignored, a belief that a less serious offence was in progress is a mitigating factor. Accordingly, a belief that a transaction involved only a substance held out to be heroin should be distinguished from knowledge that a substance was heroin.[50] The Ontario Court of Appeal reached a different conclusion in an importing case where the offender believed the substance involved to be marijuana but where it was, in fact, cocaine. Finlayson J.A. concluded that the offender should be sentenced on the basis of participation in cocaine importing.[51] This is inconsistent with the principle of fundamental justice that recognizes greater blameworthiness in intended consequences compared to those which are negligently produced.[52] Some mitigating distinction

---

49   In *R. v. Kundeus* (1975), [1976] 2 S.C.R. 272, the majority held that trafficking in LSD was made out while the dissent of Laskin J. held that the proper conviction should have been for an attempt. There is a good argument that the reasoning in the recent decision in *Dynar* followed the Laskin approach: *United States of America* v. *Dynar*, [1997] 2 S.C.R. 462. See also A. Manson, "Annotation of *United States v. Dynar*" (1997), 8 C.R. (5th) 83.

50   See *R. v. Saddler*, [1995] O.J. 3112 at para. 8 (Prov. Div.) (QL); and *R. v. Masters* (1974), 15 CCC (2d) 142 at 143, Martin J.A. (Ont. C.A.).

51   *R. v. Madden* (1996), 104 C.C.C. (3d) 548 (Ont. C.A.). See also *R. v. Cunningham* (1996), 104 C.C.C. (3d) 542 at 546–48 (Ont. C.A.), where the same court rejected any mitigating effect when the offender did not know the quantity of drugs involved on the basis that she could not rely on her own "reckless disregard" for the truth as a mitigating factor.

52   See *Martineau*, above note 3.

should be drawn to reflect the mistaken belief, even if it has no impact on criminal responsibility but does reflect a reduced level of blameworthiness. More recently, in *R. v. Sagoe*[53] the same court considered a situation where the offender had been convicted of possession of heroin for the purposes of trafficking. She maintained that she did not know that the substance was heroin. In reducing the sentence from two years to six months, the court commented:

> The trial judge appears to have thought that it was irrelevant that the appellant was wilfully blind to the nature of the narcotic involved, as opposed to having knowledge that it was heroin. This is not correct. Although the appellant had to be sentenced as being in possession of heroin for the purpose of trafficking, the fact that she did not know it was heroin was a mitigating factor.[54]

Combined with her passive role in the offence and the absence of any personal benefit, the original two-year sentence was reduced to six months. This case reflects a recognition that the proper basis for assessing culpability for sentencing purposes is the factual context known to the offender.

# C. STATUTORY AGGRAVATING FACTORS

## 1) The *Code*'s Aggravating Factors

The *Code* now provides in section 718.2(a) that the following circumstances are "deemed" to be aggravating factors:

> 718.2(a)(i) evidence that the offence was motivated by bias, prejudice or hate based on race, national or ethnic origin, language, colour, religion, sex, age, mental or physical disability, sexual orientation, or any other similar factor,
>
> (ii) evidence that the offender, in committing the offence, abused the offender's spouse or common-law partner or child,
>
> (iii) evidence that the offender, in committing the offence, abused a position of trust or authority in relation to the victim, or

---

53   [1998] O.J. No. 4721 (C.A.) (QL).

54   *Ibid.* at para. 6. Given that the panel consisted of Finlayson, Laskin, and Rosenberg JJ.A., this may represent a change in direction from, or at least a softening of, the approach in *Madden*.

(iv) evidence that the offence was committed for the benefit of, at the direction of or in association with a criminal organization.

While there is ample support for the view that subsections (i) through (iii) were recognized by the common law before statutory entrenchment, their inclusion in the *Code* serves to alert all participants to the aggravating role which these factors play.[55] Their inclusion may give rise to some interpretation issues and it is relevant to note that these three were enacted as a package with a unifying theme — the importance of recognizing power imbalances as aggravating contexts for sentencing. In other words, the gravity of an offence is increased when it manifests an abuse of power against a vulnerable individual, or is motivated by a wrongful assertion of power. It is important to appreciate the background and intent of section 718.2(a)(i) to (iii) when considering the scope of their applicability. For example, the aggravating nature of offences against spouses goes beyond an intention to deter domestic violence. It would continue after separation and perhaps even after divorce so long as there was a continuing relationship that reflected the underlying concern about an imbalance of power. This would be the case where financial or child custody obligations continued between the former spouses.

An example of the use of section 718.2(a)(i) arose in *R. v. Miloszewski*,[56] dealing with the brutal killing of a Sikh caretaker at a temple by a group of self-avowed white supremacists. After they plead guilty to manslaughter, the judge heard evidence of the racist views and prior acts of the accused. He concluded:

> . . . I must also take into account Section 718.2(a)(i) of the *Criminal Code* in determining the appropriate penalties to impose upon these five accused. That section, as I have stated earlier, is not simply a re-affirmation of an existing principle. It is a direction to the Courts of this country, as expressed by Parliament, that a sentence ought to be increased if the offence was motivated by bias, prejudice or hate based on the enumerated factors.
>
> I have concluded that this was such a crime and the evidence for that finding is, in my respectful view, overwhelming. I have heard evidence of truly hateful and sickening comments made by all of the accused as they disparaged ethnic minorities, homosexuals and members

---

55   See *R. v. Atkinson* (1978), 43 C.C.C. (2d) 342 (Ont. C.A.). For a case dealing specifically with s. 718.2(a)(i) of the *Criminal Code*, see *R. v. Miloszewski*, [1999] B.C.J. No. 2710 (Prov. Ct.).

56   *Ibid.*

of the Jewish community. Clearly these views were fueled by hate, fear and ignorance. These are views which are antithetical to the principles upon which this country is based and which principles are adhered to by the overwhelming majority of our citizens. These are views which are alien to a tolerant, multi-cultural and civilized society.[57]

Notwithstanding two years in pre-sentence custody, evidence of remorse, and even a recantation of racism by two of the accused, the actual sentences ranged from twelve to fifteen years. The Crown had been seeking life sentences. Given the youth of the accused and the pre-sentence custody, the lengthy sentences manifest the aggravating role of section 718.2(a)(i).

## 2)  The *Controlled Drugs and Substances Act*

As of 1997, the primary statute dealing with drug offences is the *Controlled Drugs and Substances Act*.[58] Section 10(1) provides its own statement of sentencing purpose, which supplements the comparable statement in the *Code*:

Without restricting the generality of the *Criminal Code*, the fundamental purpose of any sentence for an offence under this Part is to contribute to the respect for the law and the maintenance of a just, peaceful and safe society while encouraging rehabilitation, and treatment in appropriate circumstances, of offenders and acknowledging the harm done to victims and to the community.

This is followed by a set of aggravating factors which apply to persons convicted of a "designated substance offence" which includes all offences in Part I except for possession. The aggravating factors in section 10(2) are as follows:

- the carrying, use or threat of use of a weapon, or use or threat of violence in relation to the commission of the offence, and
- trafficking in or near a school or other public place frequented by persons under eighteen.

If the judge is satisfied that one or more of these factors are present but does not sentence the offender to imprisonment, reasons are required for that decision.[59]

---

57    *Ibid.* at paras. 159–60.
58    S.C. 1996, c. 19, brought into force on May 14, 1997.
59    *Ibid.*, s. 10(3).

# D. JUDICIALLY RECOGNIZED AGGRAVATING FACTORS

## 1) Previous Convictions

The existence of a previous record can have bearing on a variety of sentencing factors. First, it relates to character, in the sense that it disentitles an offender to consideration as a first offender who is inexperienced or who has behaved out of character. Secondly, it can highlight a concern about individual deterrence. This can be very important with respect to crimes of violence especially where there is an indication of escalating offences. Thirdly, prior convictions include prior sanctions. Considering the nature of earlier sentences may shed light on what form of sanction would be appropriate or adequate in the instant case. A previous discharge, however, does not qualify as a previous conviction and cannot be used as a prior record.[60]

On the other hand, the relevance of previous convictions can require some clear distinctions and should not be overstated. It is important to consider the similarity of offences to determine whether there is any relevance to the offence before the court.[61] An impaired driving conviction has no relevance to a charge of theft but would be directly relevant to a charge of dangerous driving. It may have relevance, although more remote, to an assault if it is alleged that the assault has some relation to the abuse of alcohol.

The age of the previous convictions is another consideration. At some point, a record can become too stale to be considered. Of course, this is a function of the nature of the offences in question. A twenty-year-old conviction for "theft under" is unlikely to have any relevance to anything; a twenty-year-old murder conviction is very relevant if the instant offence is murder, but not so relevant if the instant offence is impaired driving. Similarly, the intervals between offences can be instructive. They may reveal a pattern of escalating conduct which suggests real risks or they may reveal significant gaps consistent with positive events within the offender's life that indicate strong rehabilitative prospects.[62] The story behind a record is sometimes more informative

---

60   See *R. v. Naraindeen* (1990), 80 C.R. (3d) 66 at 77–78 (Ont. C.A.).
61   See, for example, *R. v. Jones* (1991), 64 C.C.C. (3d) 181 (Sask. C.A.), where a 2 1\2 sentence for possession of Talwin for the purposes of trafficking contrary to the *Narcotic Control Act* was considered substantial but fit given the prior record for trafficking.
62   See the discussion of a "gap" as a mitigating factor, above, at 7(B)(13).

than simply totalling up convictions or looking for the longest period of incarceration previously imposed. However, a long list of related offences is always a seriously aggravating factor which cannot be ignored, although it may, in rare circumstances, be rebutted.[63]

Relevant previous conduct which may have amounted to an offence but was not prosecuted may be admitted on sentencing.[64] However, it must be proven if not admitted. This will usually require calling *viva voce* evidence, which must meet the *Gardiner* standard of proof beyond a reasonable doubt.[65] Courts must be careful only to sentence the offender for the convictions before the court. Previous acts only go to show character. If the sentencing relates to assaultive behaviour, other victims can be called to testify to previous assaults even if they have not been prosecuted, but the purpose is only to show an abusive or violent character.[66]

## 2)  Actual or Threatened Violence or Use of Weapon

Although consequences are important to gravity, so is the potential danger generated by an offender's conduct. Regardless of the nature of an offence, it is always graver when a weapon is used or threatened. Although distinctions can be made about whether a weapon was carried, brandished, or actually used, or about the nature of a weapon, the presence or threat of weapons is an aggravating factor. There are now a number of mandatory minimum sentences of four years for using a firearm in the commission of certain stipulated offences. Similarly, knives and other cutting weapons are serious aggravating factors.

## 3)  Cruelty or Brutality

Offences involving violence are always serious but there is another dimension to their gravity when there is evidence of cruelty or brutality. Clearly, the greater physical harm generated by an offence the more serious is the offence, but acts of cruelty, degradation, and humiliation go beyond this consideration. They demonstrate a propensity for harm often consistent with some underlying pathology, psychology, or deviance that makes individual deterrence an important focus of sentenc-

---

63   See the discussion of intermediate recidivist, above, at 7(B)(13).
64   See *R. v. Roud* (1981), 21 C.R. (3d) 97 (Ont. C.A.).
65   See the discussion of *R. v. Gardiner*, [1982] 2 S.C.R. 368, and the burden of proof in Chapter 8, below, at 8(c).
66   See, for example, *R. v. Inwood* (1989), 48 C.C.C. (3d) 173 (Ont. C.A.).

ing as well as denunciation. Recently, there have been examples of assaults committed with acid producing horrifying results. These disfiguring offences, whether threatened or carried out, are obviously very aggravated circumstances.[67] The duration of an assault as well as its nature can also be aggravating.[68]

## 4)  Offences While Subject to Conditions

If an offence is committed while the offender is subject to conditions, whether the conditions arise from bail, probation, parole, or statutory release, that fact is usually considered an aggravating factor even though a breach of condition may carry its own sanction. The argument is that by committing an offence in these circumstances the offender is, on top of the offence, showing disrespect for the processes of the law. However, the claim should not be overstated. The aggravating effect depends on the nature of the release, the nature of the new offence, and the time interval. For example, an impaired driving offence committed by a person released many years before from a sentence for murder should not be aggravated by the still extant parole conditions. However, had the release been recent, the aggravating role would be apparent. Similarly, if a serious offence, like dangerous driving or impaired driving causing death or bodily harm, was committed while someone was on probation, it would be considered aggravating and, in combination with other factors, could rule out a conditional sentence.[69]

## 5)  Multiple Victims or Multiple Incidents

Generally, blameworthiness is compounded as the number of incidents expands. This rationale applies to both violent and non-violent offences: a series of victims indicates a pattern which compounds the culpability. In *R. v. Stuckless*[70] the offender had been an employee of Maple Leaf Gardens and had used that role to seduce and assault dozens of young boys over two decades. The court noted the multiple victims

---

67   See, for example, *R. v. Szpala* (1998), 124 (3d) 430 (Ont. C.A.), where the offender received a ten-year sentence.

68   See, for example, *R. v. Murray* (1986), 31 C.C.C. (3d) 324 (N.S. S.C.(A.D.)), where a sentence of four years nine months was upheld for sexual assault with note taken of the two- to three-hour duration of the assault.

69   See, for example, *R. v. Biancofiore* (1997), 119 C.C.C. (3d) 344 (Ont. C.A.) [*Biancofiore*].

70   (1998), 127 C.C.C. (3d) 225 (Ont. C.A.).

and characterized his conduct as "individually and collectively, unconscionable." It raised the original sentence of two years imprisonment followed by three years probation to a sentence of five years. Aside from the aggravating effect of multiple victims for all assaults, for sexual assaults the number can result in a characterization of the offender as a predator who represents a substantial danger to the safety of others. This can make protection of the community the predominant factor in sentencing.

## 6) Group or Gang Activity

The entire basis of the law of parties is that it is necessary to criminalize the conduct of those who join in offences, or assist or encourage them, because deterring help and support may prevent crimes. Conversely, for sentencing purposes, the gravity of many offences is increased by group activity. Sometimes, it implies organized, planned, and continuous criminal activity; this is certainly the situation when the offence is based on financial gain.[71] In cases of violence, group activity may imply the brutality of a gang assault or may even invoke the unthinking violent potential of mob action.

Another aggravating aspect of group activity arose in *R.* v. *Kennedy*, where a nineteen-year-old and a fourteen-year-old young offender were convicted of sexually assaulting a fourteen-year-old girl.[72] They lured her over along with a friend, got her intoxicated, and raped her while she was unconscious. Both the victim and the young offender went to the same school and were part of the same peer group. After the offence, the victim was harassed and humiliated and eventually moved to another school. The court held that the need for deterrence was heightened when there was a group offence committed within an identifiable peer set, especially where it was likely that the offence would become public knowledge. As result of the aggravating factors,[73] the one-year sentence for the nineteen-year-old offender was considered demonstrably unfit.

---

71   See, for example, *R.* v. *Le* (1992), 76 C.C.C. (3d) 274 (Alta. C.A.), where a sentence of nine months imposed on a nineteen-year-old offender for extortion was increased to three years on the basis of proven gang activity.

72   (1999), 140 C.C.C. (3d) 378 (Ont. C.A.).

73   Among others, the court noted the group rape, the multiple acts, the disparity in age between the offender and the victim, the failure to use a condom, the planning, the degradation of the victim in front of her friend, and the victim's subsequent humiliation.

# 7) Impeding Victim's Access to the Justice System

Whatever culpability is inherent in an offence, that culpability is increased if there are any threats or physical efforts to stop the victim from complaining about the offence. The justice system needs to assure people that they can invoke its processes and therefore it must respond seriously to conduct intended to prevent someone from seeking its protection. In cases where a conditional sentence is being considered, threats of this sort over a period of time have persuaded appellate courts not to permit service of the sentence in the community.[74] When dealing with second-degree murder and the issue of parole ineligibility, threats to witnesses can be very significant. In *R. v. Michelle*,[75] the British Columbia Court of Appeal upheld a seventeen-year period of ineligibility where the trial judge had described the "terror" which the witness experienced from threats by the accused.

# 8) Substantial Economic Loss

Sentencing for frauds and thefts are influenced by the size of the loss.[76] In *R. v. Gaudet*,[77] thefts by senior executives of a trading company which "struck at the foundation of the securities trade" produced sentences of eight and five years imprisonment. This was considered the appropriate range for a fraud that netted the offenders over $9 million. The court considered all accused jointly liable for the entire loss.

It is interesting to consider how courts assess the magnitude of larger white-collar thefts. In *R. v. Ruhland*,[78] while apparently agreeing with the proposition that the magnitude of the fraud affected the sentences, the Ontario Court of Appeal reduced the sentences to the maximum reformatory term for offenders who had defrauded their own company. The trial judge had characterized the loss as being about $2.5 million. The Court of Appeal corrected this figure by noting that it was based on book value and not realizable value; accordingly, the

---

74  See, for example, *R. v. J. (B.)*, [1998] O.J. No. 3701 (C.A.) (QL), where the efforts to suppress a complaint persuaded the court to allow a Crown appeal from a conditional sentence and turn it into a sentence of incarceration for fifteen months.

75  (1998), 119 B.C.A.C. 163 (C.A.).

76  See, for example, *R. v. Gotkin* (1997), 116 C.C.C. (3d) 382 at 383 (Man. C.A.), where a suspended sentence was increased to a twelve-month conditional sentence because the "sentencing judge erred in failing to grasp the magnitude of the fraud."

77  (1998), 125 C.C.C. (3d) 17 (Ont. C.A.).

78  (1998), 123 C.C.C. (3d) 262 (Ont. C.A.).

judge had been using a magnified figure. In R. v. *Horvath*,[79] in review-ing a conditional sentence imposed on a former bank manager who had a gambling addiction and stole over $200,000 from financial insti-tutions, Bayda C.J.S. noted that the impact of the loss is relative to the victim's financial resources. A small loss to a senior citizen on a fixed income may be catastrophic while a large loss to a bank may be incon-sequential. He observed:

> The answer appears to be that the amount stolen is a relevant factor to consider but no weight can be assigned in an objective sense to a particular sum. The weight must be assessed differently in each case and will vary with the other circumstances of the case.[80]

## 9) Planning and Organization

Because blameworthiness is at the heart of sentencing, evidence of planning and pre-meditation is aggravating because it shows that the offender contemplated the offence and produced the harm in a calcu-lated and not spontaneous or precipitous way. In R. v. *Kelly*,[81] the offender was convicted of assaulting his estranged spouse after firing a shotgun through her door. At trial, he was sentenced to two years less a day. The Alberta Court of Appeal increased the sentence to four years. First, it was concerned to convey a strong message that community standards rejected domestic violence. Secondly, it noted that the assault did not occur in the heat of the moment since the offender had taken the shotgun with him. Some degree of planning went into the assault and this increased his culpability.[82] For similar reasons, with crimes of financial gain the degree of organization, planning, complex-ity, and continuity of transactions can all be considered aggravating. They show calculation and foreclose a claim of rash action or tempo-rary lapse of judgment.

---

79  Above note 8.
80  *Ibid.* at 129.
81  (1994), 90 C.C.C. (3d) 444 (Alta.C.A.).
82  See also R. v. *Plourde* (1985), 23 C.C.C. (3d) 463 (Que. C.A.), where a woman received a total of forty-two months for participating with two men in aggravated sexual assault and buggery of another woman. The court concluded, at 474, that the "crimes committed by the appellant were premeditated and that they involved violence which was out of the ordinary."

## 10)  Vulnerability of Victim

The sentencing process as an integral part of the administration of justice must be seen to provide some degree of protection for vulnerable members of the community, even if its actions are mostly symbolic. As well, crimes that are directed at vulnerable members of the community are considered more blameworthy. The usual categories of vulnerability include children,[83] the elderly, individuals who are physically or mentally challenged,[84] and people who are ill or injured. While the vulnerability of a victim often supports a claim for aggravation, the effect on culpability is increased even beyond that if there is evidence that the offender sought out vulnerable victims. A good example is concocting a plan to defraud the elderly.

## 11)  Status or Role of Victim

The role that a victim plays in the community might make them worthy of special attention when they are victimized by criminal acts: thus, the sentencing court acts to protect these roles through denunciation and deterrence. For example, in R. v. Phillips[85] the victim of a second-degree murder was a police officer. Because the jury had rejected the first-degree murder charge, the Ontario Court of Appeal began from the factual premise that the offender did not know that he was attacking a police officer. As a result, it concluded that there was no basis to increase parole ineligibility for deterrent reasons. Denunciation was relevant given the societal role of an on-duty police officer and it warranted an increased period of parole ineligibility. Assaults and shooting offences with police officers as victim usually get "high end" sentences.[86] Assaults on prison guards receive the same treatment.[87]

The converse situation is where a police officer is the accused and a prisoner, detainee, or suspect is the victim. In R. v. O'Donnell[88] a police officer was convicted of manslaughter after "deliberate or excessive force

---

83   See, for example, R. v. Stuckless, above note 70, and the exploitation of vulnerable young boys.

84   See, for example, R. v. McGovern (1993), 82 C.C.C. (3d) 301 (Man. C.A.), where the victim who was twelve at the time of the sexual assaults, was developmentally challenged. She was nineteen years old at trial and had a mental age of ten.

85   (1999), 138 C.C.C. (3d) 297 (Ont. C.A.).

86   See, for example, R. v. Peer, [1992] O.J. No. 1155 (Gen. Div) (QL); and R. v. Mantla (1985), 21 C.C.C. (3d) 136 (N.W.T. C.A.).

87   See, for example, R. v. Littletent (1985), 17 C.C.C. (3d) 520 (Alta. C.A.).

88   (1982), 3 C.C.C. (3d) 333 (N.S. S.C. (A.D.)).

was used" on a man being arrested. He was a manic depressive who was being a nuisance to traffic on a bridge. The Nova Scotia Court of Appeal increased the sentence from ten months to three years holding that

> The public expects a high standard of conduct on the part of trained police officers and any abuse of power on the part of the police must be resolutely constrained.[89]

The same reasoning would apply to a prison guard convicted of assaulting a prisoner.

Taxi drivers as victims represent another common situation where societal role is an aggravating factor. Here, the primary motivation is deterrence. Taxi drivers can be directed to travel anywhere and are vulnerable to robbery and threats from the back seat. Accordingly, the relative ease of a robbery attempt is counter-balanced by stiff sentences in an effort to deter. Another example is health-care providers, especially in controversial contexts like abortion clinics. These are the kinds of situations where violence can escalate, as has tragically been shown by the shooting of doctors. To provide some degree of protection, even if only symbolic, for those providing needed health care, courts take an aggravated view of any threats or acts of violence against health-care providers or patients.

## 12) Deliberate Risk-taking

Intentionally caused harmful consequences will play a large role in determining a fit sentence. When the crime is based on a form of negligence, deliberate risk-taking that results in harm is also an aggravated circumstance. In rejecting a conditional sentence for dangerous driving causing bodily harm in *R. v. Biancofiore*,[90] the Ontario Court of Appeal noted the applicable aggravating factors. One element which impressed the court was the offender's decision to leave his home at 2 a.m. after he and his friends had been drinking to take his brother's high-powered car for a ride. This was characterized as intentionally leaving a safe place to embark on a dangerous act. In other words, the offender had chosen to engage in a risky activity that endangered others.[91]

---

89   *Ibid.* at 371.
90   Above note 69.
91   See also *R. v. Johnson* (1996), 112 C.C.C. (3d) 225 (B.C.C.A.), where the offender had been drinking for two days before getting into a car to drive.

# E. FACTORS NOT TO BE TREATED AS AGGRAVATING

## 1) Not Guilty Plea and Conduct of Defence

Everyone charged with an offence in Canada has the constitutional right to plead not guilty and require the Crown to prove the allegation beyond a reasonable doubt. The majority of cases are resolved by guilty pleas often after discussions or negotiations between counsel, commonly known as plea bargaining. It may be that plea bargaining can, depending on various factors including problems in the Crown's case, produce a more lenient sentence than would likely result if sentencing proceeded without a negotiated resolution. However, this is very different than a threat that a not guilty plea will aggravate the sentence. No one should feel coerced to enter a not guilty plea for fear that a trial will prejudice their situation. A guilty plea has mitigating potential especially when it reflects remorse and saves witnesses from the ordeal of giving testimony, but the converse is not true.

Similarly, given the constitutional right to make full answer and defence, an offender should not be prejudiced as a result of the conduct of the defence. In R. v. Kozy,[92] the trial judge concluded that the accused had lied in his testimony during the trial and that this reflected on his character and showed lack of remorse. On this basis, a longer sentence was imposed. The Ontario Court of Appeal reduced the sentence to eighteen months from two years less a day, holding:

> Just as an accused should never apprehend that a penalty will flow from a plea of not guilty, there should also be no perceived impingement upon the manner of presenting the defence. This is so whether it be counsel's viciousness in attacking a complainant or lies told by the accused. The latter may lead to its own penalty on a trial and conviction for perjury, but within the trial for the offence of sexual assault both rank as tactics of the defence, however ill-conceived, and they are embraced within the right to full answer and defence. . . .[93]

The court noted that full answer and defence is both a statutory right and a *Charter* right which cannot be impaired by the apprehension that a penalty may follow a trial. If a court has concerns about the accused's testimony or how counsel conducted the trial, care should

---

92  (1990), 80 C.R. (3d) 59 (Ont. C.A.).
93  *Ibid.* at 64. See also *R. v. Paradis* (1976), 38 C.C.C. (2d) 455 at 462, Kaufman J.A. (Que. C.A.).

be taken to ensure they do not, and cannot be perceived as, aggravating the sentence.[94]

## 2)  No Evidence of Remorse

Although a guilty plea and other indicia of remorse are usually considered to be mitigating factors, this does not mean that an absence of remorse is an aggravating factor. If it did, anyone who denies guilt at the time of sentencing would be subjected to an increased sentence. Convictions are subject to appeal, and convicted persons are entitled to continue to deny guilt. We do not demand a public display of contrition. Of course, in some cases, a person can deny guilt and still express concern for loss suffered. This can occur where the offence is not disputed but the identity of the offender is in issue. For the most part, however, remorse requires an acceptance of guilt. If absent, it ought to be treated as a neutral factor. There may, however, be callous or vindictive expressions which go beyond an absence of remorse. These can legitimately be considered aggravating.

## 3)  Failure to Co-operate with Authorities

The law does not require confessions and it does not compel an accused person to divulge information about accomplices. While courts will give credit to an offender who assisted authorities, they ought not to contemplate penalizing an offender who does not. This is similar to the way remorse and guilty pleas are treated. With respect to a failure to assist, it arises from the right to remain silent. In *R. v. Wristen*,[95] a second-degree murder case, the Ontario Court of Appeal said:

> The appellant was not legally obliged to assist the police. He was entitled to exercise his right to silence and require the prosecution to prove the case against him beyond a reasonable doubt. Exercising this right is not an aggravating consideration on sentence.[96]

However, after accepting that principle, the court went on to uphold the increase in parole ineligibility to seventeen years even though the

---

94   See *R. v. Nastos* (1994), 95 C.C.C. (3d) 121 at 126 (Ont. C.A.), where Galligan and Weiler JJ.A. upheld a ninety-day intermittent sentence plus probation for sexual assault commenting: "An appropriate sentence cannot be increased to demonstrate a court's displeasure at the manner in which a defence was conducted."
95   (1999), 141 C.C.C. (3d) 1 (Ont. C.A.).
96   *Ibid.* at 30.

trial judge was influenced by the convicted man's efforts to conceal the killing of his wife. The deceased woman's body had never been found and her sisters had prepared victim impact statements in which they expressed regret that they could not conduct a proper funeral. The court noted that, with respect to parole eligibility and second-degree murder, section 745.4 of the *Criminal Code* directed the trial judge to consider the nature of the offence and its surrounding circumstances. Accordingly, it held that it was proper that the judge consider the efforts to hide the offence and the refusal to provide any information about the location of the body. Interestingly, the defence had been that the woman had just disappeared and that he was not responsible for her death. This position was apparently maintained throughout the appeal. It is true that the sentencing judge and the court of appeal must consider a fit parole ineligibility period on the basis of the conviction and all the circumstances which are inherent in it. They must accept that the accused killed his spouse and concealed her death. However, given the accused's denial of responsibility, how can he be expected to disclose the location of the body? When a failure to co-operate with authorities becomes a situation of callous disregard for the survivors or a victim, this is legitimately aggravating. It is this characterization which might support an increase in parole ineligibility, not simply the failure to assist the police.

## FURTHER READINGS

RUBY, C., *Sentencing*, 5th ed. (Toronto: Butterworths, 1999)

WALKER, N., & N. PADFIELD, *Sentencing: Theory, Law and Practice*, 2nd ed. (London: Butterworths, 1996)

# CHAPTER 8

# THE SENTENCING HEARING: ESTABLISHING THE FACTUAL BASIS FOR SENTENCING

## A. OVERVIEW OF THE PROCESS

The sentencing hearing takes place, as one would expect, after the finding of guilt. However, the criminal process is not completed until after there has been both a finding of guilt and a disposition.[1] Findings of guilt can be the product of a guilty plea, a decision of a judge sitting alone, or a jury verdict. Each situation provides a different context for approaching the factual basis for sentencing. With a guilty plea, the offender will have admitted the essential requirements of guilt but all other factors relevant to sentencing are left to the sentencing hearing. When a judge has convicted the offender, the judge has made findings of fact about the offence and perhaps even the offender. When a jury returns a verdict of guilty, the sentencing function is given to the presiding judge but the factual findings which provide the basis for the verdict are not disclosed. In each situation, the judge must establish a factual basis that provides the relevant information about the offence and the offender to permit the determination of a fair and fit sentence.

---

1   See, for example, *R. v. Lessard* (1976), 30 C.C.C. (2d) 70 (Ont. C.A.), in which it was held that a judge sitting alone could vacate a finding of guilt and permit the accused to adduce further evidence so long as the sentencing had not been completed. See also *R. v. Urbanovitch* (1985), 19 C.C.C. (3d) 43 (Man. C.A.) [*Urbanovitch*].

The sentencing process has always been characterized by informality. The procedural structure is only provided in skeletal form by the *Criminal Code* and the formal evidentiary rules which apply to fact-finding at trial do not apply with the same rigour at the sentencing stage. Generally, submissions from counsel play a major role. Crown counsel, as well as making submissions about the offence, will submit a criminal record, if one exists and is relevant. Defence counsel will provide the court with information about the offender by submissions, often supported by letters which will be filed as exhibits to the sentencing hearing. In some cases formal reports may be adduced. These may consist of a court-ordered pre-sentence report (PSR) or a victim impact statement (VIS). Occasionally, defence counsel will present expert opinion evidence in the form of a psychiatric assessment or other medical report. Witnesses can be called by either party but this is the exception and not the rule. Each counsel will end their submission with a sentencing recommendation. It is important that the judge know the position of the respective counsel especially on whether the sanction should be community-based or custodial. Similarly, it is helpful if the judge has an indication of their views on quantum although this will often be expressed only in term of broad ranges. Well-prepared defence counsel arguing for a community-based sanction will often present a structured proposal complete with material indicating the offender's suitability for, or acceptance into, any programs encompassed by the submission. Occasionally, counsel will present the judge with a joint submission, usually the product of some plea negotiation.

While the basic sentencing hearing in Canadian courts will be roughly the same throughout the country, there may be some variations in local practice. These may relate to how material is presented to the court, especially about existing alternatives and the suitability of the offender. More often, differences will be a function of the time available for sentencing. Particularly in large urban centres, some courts are expected to process large numbers of cases. Guilty pleas are entered and dispositions imposed in assembly line fashion. Adjournments to obtain better information are rare and judges rely principally on what counsel say. At the other end of the spectrum, sentencing in some aboriginal communities has moved to a circle process which can require many hours to complete.

# B. EVIDENCE AND THE SENTENCING HEARING

The combination of the recognized need for sentencing information and the time allocated to the sentencing function has contributed to an informal approach to evidence. In *R. v. Gardiner*,[2] the Supreme Court of Canada examined the issue of how evidence is adduced at the sentencing hearing. While the Court split on the question of its jurisdiction to hear sentence appeals,[3] Dickson J. for the majority discussed the general evidentiary context in order to deal with the particular issue of how disputed aggravating factors should be proven. He described the process and the need for information in the following terms:

> One of the hardest tasks confronting a trial judge is sentencing. The stakes are high for society and for the individual. Sentencing is the critical stage of the criminal justice system, and it is manifest that the judge should not be denied an opportunity to obtain relevant information by the imposition of all the restrictive evidential rules common to a trial. Yet the obtaining and weighing of such evidence should be fair. A substantial liberty interest of the offender is involved and the information obtained should be accurate and reliable.
>
> It is a commonplace that the strict rules which govern at trial do not apply at a sentencing hearing and it would be undesirable to have the formalities and technicalities characteristic of the normal adversary proceeding prevail. The hearsay rule does not govern the sentencing hearing. Hearsay evidence may be accepted where found to be credible and trustworthy. The judge traditionally has had wide latitude as to the sources and types of evidence upon which to base his sentence. He must have the fullest possible information concerning the background of the accused if he is to fit the sentence to the offender rather than to the crime.[4]

This is the authoritative statement of the evidentiary context for sentencing. It emphasizes the fundamental importance of background information and confirms the common law admissibility of hearsay material so long as it is credible and trustworthy. It also provides that

2   [1982] 2 S.C.R. 368 [*Gardiner*].
3   Laskin C.J.C., with Estey and McIntyre JJ. concurring, wrote a dissent arguing that the Supreme Court of Canada had no jurisdiction to entertain sentence appeals. For the majority, Dickson J., as he then was, held that the Supreme Court could hear sentencing issues so long as they dealt with points of law and not quantum.
4   *Gardiner*, above note 2 at 414.

the sentencing hearing, with its potentially substantial impact on liberty, is circumscribed by the constraints of accuracy and fairness.

In England, following the traditional practice where the police provided background information about offenders, an "antecedent report" is prepared for the court. These reports are expected[5] to contain the following:

- age, educational background, previous and present employment
- date of arrest, and whether in custody or out on bail
- previous convictions and sentences
- brief statement of family or domestic circumstances

Certainly, along with the circumstances of the offence, these are the basic factual necessities for sentencing. In Canada, most of the information about the offender is provided by defence counsel unless a PSR has been ordered. In some small communities where local police know residents well, the Crown may have information about the offender beyond a previous record but this is rare. There is no formal requirement for the submission of particular sentencing material.

Since the 1996 amendments, the *Criminal Code* now provides a basic framework. Section 723(1) requires the sentencing judge to provide both the offender and the prosecutor with an opportunity to make submissions "with respect to any facts relevant to the sentence to be imposed." This is followed by section 723(2) which provides that the sentencing judge "shall hear any relevant evidence presented by the prosecutor or the offender." This presents a number of important implications. The language is mandatory and should ensure due consideration for submitted material. Secondly, as is the case throughout the trial process, admissibility is subject to the constraint of relevance. For sentencing purposes, relevance is a broadly defined concept that will be determined in each case by the offence, the offender, and the range of available sentencing options. Thirdly, because section 723(2) does not simply say that the judge will hear relevant evidence but adds the qualification "presented by the prosecutor or the offender," it confirms that only these two parties have standing at the sentencing hearing.[6]

The remainder of section 723 addresses the judge's power to supplement sentencing evidence. While section 723(5) provides statutory recognition of the common law admissibility of hearsay material, it also empowers the sentencing judge "in the interests of justice" to compel the attendance of a person who has personal knowledge of the

---

5   See "Practice Note (Previous Convictions)," [1993] 4 All E.R. 863.
6   See the discussion of the role of victims, below, at 8(I).

matter, is reasonably available, and is compellable. The scope of this judicial power is unclear. If any sentencing evidence adduced at an informal hearing is disputed, it must be proven before the court can rely on it,[7] but section 723(5) does not require a dispute as a condition precedent to the judge's power to call a witness. Since any hearsay material that is not credible and trustworthy ought to be rejected, section 723(5) confirms the judge's ability to reject material, whether there is a challenge to it or not, if not satisfied that it meets this threshold. In addition, there may be situations where the hearsay addresses a subject which the judge considers important but it does not provide sufficient information. The judge can rely on section 723(5) and compel the attendance of the maker of the statement to obtain more information.

Sections 723(3) and (4) give additional new powers to sentencing judges which, while useful, have produced controversy over their scope. They provide:

(3) The court may, on its own motion, after hearing argument from the prosecutor and the offender, require the production of evidence that would assist it in determining the appropriate sentence.

(4) Where it is necessary in the interests of justice, the court may, after consulting the parties, compel the appearance of any person who is a compellable witness to assist the court in determining the appropriate sentence.

While sub-section (3) empowers the court to require the production of any evidence in whatever form, sub-section (4) is restricted to compelling *viva voce* evidence after consulting the parties. While these powers seem quite broad, they are consistent with the need to ensure full information for sentencing purposes. However, they should not be read as carte blanche to enter the arena. The adversary system usually relies on the parties to control the evidence placed before the court. Accordingly, the position of the parties ought to be canvassed before making any order that expands the factual context.[8] It may be that an apparent gap in information is attributable to a negotiated plea

---

7   See the discussion of disputed facts, below, at 8(C) and (D).

8   Note that s. 723(5) of the *Criminal Code* discussed above has no express consultation requirement. As a matter of fair practice, however, a judge should hear from the parties before exercising that power as well. In *R. v. Hrynkiw* (1999), 134 C.C.C. (3d) 349 (Ont. Gen. Div.), Stortini J. held that an order that an offender remain in custody pending sentencing made without hearing the offender's position was a breach of s. 7 of the *Charter*. He concluded, at 350, that "due process obliges the affording of an opportunity to be heard."

arrangement and the judge should be cautious about entering this terrain unwittingly.

These exceptional powers can supplement the evidence available to the sentencing judge but they must be interpreted and applied within the scope of the sentencing function. In *R. v. Hunter*[9] an aboriginal man pleaded guilty to an assault charge arising from cuts and bruises inflicted on his spouse. After the commission of the offence, he left his reserve and attended an anger management course in Calgary. However, he had to withdraw because his Band could not continue financing the program. At the sentencing hearing, it was apparent that alcohol played a major role in the offender's record for assaultive behaviour and that he would benefit from alcohol abuse treatment. However, no resources were available on his reserve. In response, the sentencing judge, who had been travelling to this community for some time, ordered the Chief Crown Prosecutor to commence an investigation into social conditions, political corruption, and financial management on the reserve. The Crown applied for certiorari to quash the order. At the heart of the matter was the scope of the judge's power to use sections 723(3) and (4) to compel evidence. These provisions were enacted as part of the 1996 amendments to Part XXIII of the *Criminal Code*, which also included section 718.2(e) that requires judges to consider all available sanctions before ordering imprisonment "with particular attention to the circumstances of aboriginal offenders." LoVecchio J. held that sections 723(3) and (4) enabled the judge to take charge of the sentencing process in order to fulfill the statutory obligations in Part XXIII. However, the power was not open-ended but required a "logical nexus or relevance" between the object of the production order and the issues before the sentencing. The court concluded that the sentencing judge's order should be severed, preserving the questions dealing with relevant issues and excising the parts of the order which had no nexus to the sentencing process. For example, questions dealing with the state of educational facilities on the reserve were excised since the accused was a forty-four-year-old man. Similarly, questions about the Chief's business activities were also excluded. On the other hand, some of the questions about social conditions on the reserve were maintained because they related to relevant sentencing factors like employment opportunities. The extent of domestic abuse, the incidence of drug and alcohol addiction, and suicide were also considered pertinent to the sentencing function. The questions about

---

9   (1997), 11 C.R. (5th) 156 (Alta. Q.B.).

policing resources was relevant to the prospect of a community-based sentence like a conditional sentence. Ultimately, the decision confirmed that the new powers in sections 723(3) and (4) were available to a sentencing judge of her own initiative so long as the matters pursued were relevant to the sentencing function. Moreover, with respect to the determination of relevance, deference was due to a sentencing judge with local experience.

The decision of the Supreme Court of Canada in R. v. *Gladue*[10] confirms the need, on occasion, for an aggressive approach like that employed in *Hunter*. When dealing with aboriginal persons, section 718.2(e) not only confirms the relevance of information about the background of aboriginal persons, it creates a duty on trial judges to ensure that they have appropriate material to consider:

> However, even where counsel do not adduce this evidence, where for example the offender is unrepresented, it is incumbent upon the sentencing judge to attempt to acquire information regarding the circumstances of the offender as an aboriginal person. Whether the offender resides in a rural area, on a reserve or in an urban centre the sentencing judge must be made aware of alternatives to incarceration that exist whether inside or outside the aboriginal community of the particular offender. The alternatives existing in metropolitan areas must, as a matter of course, also be explored.[11]

Whether the situation is one of an unrepresented accused or an unhelpful counsel, sections 723(3) and (4) are the vehicles for pursuing this duty, aside from any role that judicial notice may play.[12]

A case that illustrates how these provisions can be useful in relation to the issue of sentencing resources is R. v. *Frittaion*[13] in which Hill J. considered the appropriateness of a conditional sentence for a man convicted of assaulting his wife. During the course of the sentencing, the subject of electronic monitoring arose. The court was advised that, while the technical resources existed in Ontario, the Ministry of Correctional Services had decided that they would only be employed for post-sentence purposes like temporary-absence passes. Hill J. adjourned so that a senior Ministry official could attend to answer questions

---

10   [1999] 1 S.C.R. 688 [*Gladue*].
11   *Ibid.* at 732.
12   See the discussion of judicial notice, below, at 8(K).
13   (1997), 10 C.R. (5th) 394 (Ont. Gen. Div.). See also the discussion of the availability of electronic monitoring in R. v. *Patterson* (2000), 33 C.R. (5th) 45 (Ont. Ct.).

about electronic monitoring. During that attendance, the official acknowledged that if the judge expressly ordered the Ministry to use its electronic monitoring facilities as part of a sentence, the order would be followed. While not explicitly mentioned in the decision, it is clear that section 723(3) provides a judge with the power to obtain information about relevant sentencing options or programs which may be included in a court-ordered sanction.

# C. THE BURDEN AND STANDARD OF PROOF AT COMMON LAW

While it has long been accepted that a challenge to a factual submission required some degree of proof, for many years Canadian courts disagreed about the burden and standard of proof. In *R. v. Gardiner*,[14] the accused had pleaded guilty to assault causing bodily harm, which at the time carried a maximum penalty of five years. The victim of the assault was the accused's wife. She gave evidence at the sentencing hearing that he had viciously beaten her, threatened sexual mutilation, and forced her to engage in a sexual act with her paralysed son. The accused admitted that he had slapped her but testified that he blacked out and remembered nothing more of the evening. The judge ruled that the burden of proving the aggravated circumstance fell on the Crown but that the standard was the civil one of proof on a balance of probabilities. He preferred the evidence of the wife and did not consider that he needed to hear from the son. Using the aggravated circumstances, he sentenced the accused to four years and six months imprisonment.

When the case reached the Supreme Court, Dickson J., as he then was, analysed the proof question for the majority,[15] starting with a comparison to the criminal trial process. He observed:

> To my mind, the facts which justify the sanction are no less important than the facts which justify the conviction; both should be subject to the same burden of proof. Crime and punishment are inextricably linked. "It would appear well established that the sentencing process is merely a phase of the trial process." . . . Upon conviction the accused is not abruptly deprived of all procedural rights existing

---

14  Above note 2.

15  While there was a significant dissent by Laskin C.J.C., his disagreement was about the Supreme Court's jurisdiction to entertain appeals on sentencing issues and not with respect to the evidentiary questions addressed by Dickson J.

at trial: he has a right to counsel, a right to call evidence and cross-examine prosecution witnesses, a right to give evidence himself and to address the court.[16]

Consequently, he concluded that the criminal standard of proof beyond a reasonable doubt applied. While the issue before the court was proof of aggravating circumstances, nowhere did he suggest that a different standard should apply to mitigating circumstances. In fact, his use of the phrase "ordinary legal principles governing criminal proceedings, including resolving relevant doubt in favour of the offender" suggests that he considered that all disputes should be resolved in the manner that would apply at trial. In other words, if there was evidence that made an issue relevant, it was the Crown's burden to satisfy the court of the aggravated position.

Subsequent cases have clarified some but not all of the residual issues about proof of disputed facts. When the factual submission of Crown counsel is disputed, the court must provide an opportunity for the Crown to prove it. If this is declined, the submission cannot be considered and the version favourable to the offender must be accepted.[17] This approach has been applied to all circumstances of the offence. In R. v. Poorman, the Saskatchewan Court of Appeal applied it to two issues: whether the appellant was armed and whether he was provoked. Being armed is a matter of aggravation, and provocation is a mitigating factor, but both relate to the offence rather than the background of the offender. Another example of the *Gardiner* principle is *Canada (A.G.) v. Boulet*,[18] which also dealt with a mitigating motive. The Saskatchewan Court of Appeal examined a drug trafficking case where, at the sentencing stage, the accused put forward a mitigating motive. An incarcerated friend had been pressured by other prisoners and sought help in smuggling drugs into the jail. The Crown rejected this explanation but did not demand a formal hearing. Bayda C.J.S. concluded that the only onus on the offender was the "minimal" one of providing an account that was within the "bounds of reasonable possibility" and not "so manifestly false as to be incapable of belief." This is similar to the "air of reality" test that applies during the criminal trial. It is the Crown's obligation then to disprove the account. Bayda C.J.S. considered briefly whether disputes over mitigating personal circumstances deserved different treatment but did not offer a conclusion,

---

16    *Gardiner*, above note 2 at 415.

17    See *R. v. Poorman* (1991), 66 C.C.C. (3d) 82 (Sask. C.A.).

18    (1990), 58 C.C.C. (3d) 178, Bayda C.J.S. in dissent on the merits (Sask.C.A.).

although he suggested an affinity for a Commonwealth decision where the minimal onus approach was applied to mitigating personal circumstances.[19] Clearly, as far as the Saskatchewan Court of Appeal was concerned, all aspects of the offence, however characterized, had to be proven beyond a reasonable doubt by the Crown or the factor could not be applied to the offender's detriment.

An earlier Ontario case reached a different result. In *R. v. Holt*,[20] the accused was convicted of trafficking in heroin, totalling three-and-a-half ounces. The Crown characterized the accused as a "commercial level" trafficker while defence counsel submitted that he was a "small dealer" supporting his own habit. At the time of one of the sales to an undercover police officer, the accused had said that he was a "big time" dealer but his counsel characterized this as unrealistic bragging. No formal proof was offered on the question of the extent of his trafficking activities. The trial judge accepted that the accused had reformed his life and kicked his heroin addiction. Relying on the evidence of family support, he suspended sentence and placed him on probation for three years.

The Crown appealed and the sentence was varied on appeal to two years less a day in custody. In the course of that decision, Weatherston J.A. referred to *Gardiner* and commented that it did not support the proposition that, in the absence of proof beyond a reasonable doubt, "all possible mitigating facts must be assumed in favour of the accused." However, the actual decision about the quantum of the sentence was made regardless of whether the offender was a low-level dealer or not. Moreover, the facile interpretation of *Gardiner* without any supporting analysis seems off the mark for two reasons. First, the Crown was arguing for an aggravated account of the offence based on its commercial nature and ought to have been put to the proof. Secondly, as the Saskatchewan cases point out, it is not all mitigating circumstances that trigger the Crown's burden of proof but only those which meet the test of being within the bounds of reasonable possibility. It was within the trial judge's discretion to decide this issue and ask whether the Crown wanted an opportunity to prove its allegation. The ruling in *Holt* has been rejected by the Manitoba Court of Appeal which recognized that "commercialism" is an aggravating factor in drug offences that must be

---

19   See the views of Bray C.J. in *Law v. Deed*, [1970] S.A.S.R. 374, which dealt specifically with mitigating information about the offender and applied the same minimal onus of passing the "bounds of reasonable possibility." Bray C.J. went further and held that only when a submission fails to meet this test should any burden of proof be placed on the offender.

20   (1983), 4 C.C.C. (3d) 32 (Ont. C.A.).

proven by the Crown.[21] All in all, *Holt* is weak authority for the proposition that mitigating factors should be treated differently.[22]

# D. THE 1996 AMENDMENTS AND THE BURDEN OF PROOF

In 1984, an omnibus criminal law reform bill was placed before Parliament.[23] In an effort to codify the effect of *Gardiner*, it contained specific provisions dealing with the proof of sentencing facts.[24] The bill died on the order paper but these provisions were re-introduced almost verbatim as part of the 1996 sentencing amendments. As a result, their unrevised content has a stale quality that does not reflect either *Charter* or common law developments since the early 1980s.

Section 724(1) of the *Criminal Code* provides that, for sentencing purposes, "a court may accept as proved any information disclosed at trial or at the sentencing proceedings and any facts agreed on by the prosecutor and the offender." It does not explain what is required to accept something as "proved." It is followed by a provision dealing only with jury trials[25] and then section 724(3), a general provision which deals with disputes:

> Where there is a dispute with respect to any fact that is relevant to the determination of a sentence,
>
> (a) the court shall request that evidence be adduced as to the existence of the fact unless the court is satisfied that sufficient evidence was adduced at the trial;
>
> (b) the party wishing to rely on a relevant fact, including a fact contained in a presentence report, has the burden of proving it;
>
> (c) either party may cross-examine any witness called by the other party;
>
> (d) subject to paragraph (e), the court must be satisfied on a balance of probabilities of the existence of the disputed fact before relying on it in determining the sentence; and

---

21   R. v. *Gobin* (1993), 85 C.C.C. (3d) 481 (Man. C.A.). Only Lyon J.A. in dissent was impressed by *Holt*.

22   It was applied recently by Hill J. in R. v. *Holder* (1998), 21 C.R. (5th) 277 (Ont. Gen. Div.), discussed below.

23   See Bill C-19, *Criminal Law Reform Act, 1984*, 2d Sess., 32nd Parl., 1984 (first reading 7 February 1984).

24   *Ibid.*, s. 206.

25   See *Criminal Code*, s. 724(2).

(e) the prosecutor must establish, by proof beyond a reasonable doubt, the existence of any aggravating fact or any previous conviction by the offender.

This set of provisions goes beyond *Gardiner*. The combined effect of sections 724(3)(b) and (f) is to place a burden of proof on a balance of probabilities on an offender who wants the sentencing court to rely on a mitigating fact that is disputed. It makes no distinction between facts that are related to the offence, like motive, and personal mitigating factors about the offender.

While the discussion above indicates some degree of judicial controversy over the scope of the *Gardiner* principle as it relates to mitigating facts, there is no doubt about its status. It has now assumed a constitutional dimension. In *R. v. Pearson*,[26] the Supreme Court of Canada considered the constitutionality of a reverse-onus bail provision and concluded that the "reasonable bail" guarantee in section 11(e) of the *Charter* was not violated. In the course of that decision, Lamer C.J.C. commented on the scope of the presumption of innocence and the extent of the Crown's burden of proof at various stages in criminal proceedings. He noted that the Crown's burden is not only reflected in section 11(d) which guarantees the presumption of innocence but can also be found as part of a broader substantive principle in section 7 of the *Charter* which would extend to the sentencing stage. He commented:

> The interaction of s. 7 and s. 11(d) is also nicely illustrated at the sentencing stage of the criminal process. The presumption of innocence as set out in s. 11(d) arguably has no application at the sentencing stage of the trial. However, it is clear law that where the Crown advances aggravating facts in sentencing which are contested, the Crown must establish those facts beyond reasonable doubt. . . . The Court in *Gardiner* cited with approval at p. 415 the following passage from J.A. Olah, "Sentencing: The Last Frontier of the Criminal Law" . . . "because the sentencing process poses the ultimate jeopardy to an individual . . . in the criminal process, it is just and reasonable that he be granted the protection of the reasonable doubt rule at this vital juncture of the process."

> Although, of course, *Gardiner* was not a *Charter* case, the problem it confronted can readily be restated in terms of ss. 7 and 11(d) of the *Charter*. While the presumption of innocence as specifically articulated in s. 11(d) may not cover the question of the standard of proof

---

26  [1992] 3 S.C.R. 665 [*Pearson*].

174 THE LAW OF SENTENCING

of contested aggravating facts at sentencing, the broader substantive principle in s. 7 almost certainly would . . .[27]

## 1) Burden and Standard of Proof for Aggravating Factors

While it was characterized in *Pearson* as an issue of "proof of contested aggravating facts," all factors which tend to make an offence graver would have an aggravating effect on the ultimate sentence. Similarly, the rejection of a mitigating personal circumstance would also have an aggravating effect. In *R. v. Jones*,[28] dealing with whether the principle against self-incrimination applies during dangerous offender proceedings, Lamer C.J.C. capsulized the *Gardiner* position: "Gardiner held that disputed facts relied on by the Crown with respect to the penalty must be established according to the normal criminal standard of beyond a reasonable doubt."[29] This suggests that the principle ought to apply regardless of whether the fact is categorized as aggravating or mitigating, since any finding unfavourable to the offender may result in an aggravated penalty.

## 2) Burden and Standard of Proof for Mitigating Factors

With the exception of having no relevant previous record, which can be assumed if nothing is placed before the court, the sentencing process takes a neutral view of all other mitigating personal circumstances. Accordingly, every challenge by the Crown to a mitigating factor is an attempt to aggravate the penalty. It's like a bank account. Whether the bank is denying you an interest credit or imposing a new service charge, you end up with less money either way. Similarly, an offender moves up the penalty scale if a mitigating factor is denied or an aggravating factor accepted. Viewed from the liberty perspective, it is fair to expect the Crown to justify lengthier or larger sentences. However, an offender cannot expect that everything put forward in mitigation must necessarily be accepted. There must be a standard similar to the "air of reality" test that permits judges to reject mitigating claims without requiring the Crown to disprove them if they are implausible or apparently without foundation. Beyond an "air of reality" threshold, section 7 and the principle of fundamental justice reflected by *Gardiner* should require the Crown to play its usual adversarial role if it chooses to seek a graver

---

27  *Pearson*, above note 26 at 686.
28  [1994] 2 S.C.R. 229 [*Jones*].
29  *Ibid.* at 260.

penalty by disputing a material mitigating factor. At the very least, this ought to be the position with respect to facts about the offence.

Notwithstanding this argument about the *Gardiner* principle and mitigating facts, some cases have applied section 724(3) to mitigating facts without any section 7 challenge and without distinguishing between facts that relate to the offence and facts which are personal to the offender. In *R. v. Holder*,[30] the jury returned a verdict of guilty to drug importing, although the accused had given evidence at the trial that she was subjected to threats and acted under duress. Her counsel argued that the jury's rejection of the defence of duress could have been based on the existence of a safe avenue of escape and not whether she had been threatened. Accordingly, it was not a contradiction to use the threats as a mitigating circumstance with respect to sentence. Recognizing that he had to make an independent finding of fact, Hill J. ruled that section 724(3)(d) required that he be satisfied on a balance of probabilities that the evidence established the mitigating factor. As a result, he concluded that he was not satisfied that she had been subjected to threats, and that her account was "manifestly implausible." On the burden of proof issue, both counsel agreed that section 724(3)(d) applied and that it placed the burden of proof on the accused.[31] Beyond this consensus, Hill J. was persuaded that it was appropriate to have the accused prove a mitigating circumstance.

In reaching this conclusion, Hill J. relied on *Holt*,[32] a questionable authority, and also on recent case law from the English Court of Appeal, *R. v. Guppy*.[33] In *Guppy*, Hirst L.J. concluded that the accused should be required to prove "extraneous facts put forward in mitigation, which will usually be within the exclusive knowledge of the defendant . . . , and will have been raised by him entirely on his own initiative."[34] On its face, this seems to be a significant authority but

---

30  Above note 22.

31  In *Holder, ibid.* at 285, Hill J. said: "The parties further agreed, properly in my view, that, on the sentencing phase, the factual existence of some circumstances of the failed duress defence is properly considered a mitigating factor to be established by Ms. Holder."

32  Above note 20 discussed at 8(c). *Holt* has also been followed in *R. v. Saddler*, [1995] O.J. No. 3112, MacDonnell J. (Prov. Div.) (QL), in which he held that whether a person knew a substance was a narcotic or just a substance held out to be a narcotic, the accused must prove his version on a balance of probabilities.

33  (1995), 16 Cr. App. R. (S) 25 (C.A.) [*Guppy*].

34  *Ibid.* at 37. His only authority was the opinion of the editors of "the current edition of Archbold": see J.F. Archbold, *Pleading, Evidence and Practice in Criminal Cases*, rev. ed. by P.J. Richardson (London: Sweet & Maxwell, 1993).

there are a number of reasons why its applicability is dubious. The issue was not related to the facts of the offence but was whether, on appeal, the appellant had to give evidence to prove his claim that he was financially incapable of paying the million-dollar fine which accompanied the five-year term of imprisonment levied by the trial judge. Hirst L.J. distinguished this situation from those "where the issue goes directly to the facts and circumstances of the crime itself." In those situations, where disputes arise, the English courts are required to conduct what is known as a Newton hearing where the ordinary criminal burden and standard applies. Accordingly, with respect to a claim of duress, the English position is that the onus would be on the prosecutor to rebut.[35] This is consistent with Canadian authorities like *Poorman* and *Boulet*.[36] Moreover, *Guppy* deals with an issue of personal circumstances, not facts about the offence, and the underlying concern was that the prosecution would be unfairly prejudiced if required to disprove a claim that was solely within the knowledge of the accused. In fact, Hirst L.J. even remarked that the factual issue might not arise until "an adjourned sentencing hearing at which the prosecution would not be present."[37] This situation has no parallel in Canada.

Accordingly, the decision in *Guppy* does not resolve the problem of proof of mitigating factors as clearly as Hill J. has suggested. At the very least, there is ample authority for distinguishing between facts about the offence (including mitigating motives) and facts about personal circumstances, which suggest that section 724(3)(e) ought to have been applied in *Holder*. Although this would place the burden of proof on the prosecutor, given the judge's conclusion that the accused's account was "manifestly implausible," the Crown could have been relieved of any obligation of proof by applying an "air of reality" threshold. The same result would have been achieved without shifting the burden of proof. Still, the decision in *Holder* is significant because it illustrates why the use of the shifted burden in section 724(3)(d) requires *Charter* scrutiny.

Assuming that the *Gardiner* principle embedded in section 7 of the *Charter* does require the Crown to prove factors that will aggravate a sentence, and imposes only an "air of reality" obligation in respect of

---

35   See *R. v. Tolera*, [1999] 1 Cr. App. R. (S) 25 at 30, Lord Bingham C.J. (C.A.).
36   See the discussion at 8(c), above. Equally consistent is the English view that a Newton hearing is not required if the accused makes a claim that is "inherently incredible and defies common sense." This is the same as Bayda's minimal evidentiary onus.
37   See *Guppy*, above note 33 at 37–38.

mitigating claims, then sections 724(3)(b) and (d) appear to violate section 7. However, the Supreme Court has, on occasion, included a balancing function as part of its interpretation of the scope of section 7. As a result, it has incorporated concerns about public security along with the protection of fairness to the offender.[38] There is no empirical argument that the issue of proving mitigating factors has wrongly jeopardized anyone's safety and no reason why the issue is not simply one of interpreting the scope of the *Gardiner* principle.

If these provisions violate section 7, can they be saved by section 1? Here, it is worth noting that in *Reference re Motor Vehicle Act (British Columbia) s. 94(2)*,[39] Lamer J. concluded that section 1 could only justify a section 7 breach in extraordinary emergency situations while Wilson J. was of the view that a section 7 breach could never be justified. Still, a section 1 analysis requires, in the first instance, a showing that they are the product of a pressing and substantial legislative intention. Again, if one takes a focused look at the specific issue of proof of mitigating factors, no arguments or data seem to support this proposition. Moreover, if one pursues the second aspect of the *Oakes*[40] test and moves to proportionality, there is clearly a less intrusive answer, in the form of an evidentiary burden with an appropriate "air of reality" standard. This would be consistent with the Saskatchewan Court of Appeal's view of the common law situation.[41] Of course, in *R. v. Chaulk*, the Supreme Court upheld the reverse-onus provision dealing with a claim for a mental disorder exemption from criminal responsibility under section 16, on the apparent basis that insanity can be easily feigned.[42] Lamer J. re-stated the minimal impairment test in terms of "whether Parliament could reasonably have chosen an alternative means which would have achieved the identified objective as effectively."[43] Applying this test, section 16(3) was upheld even without empirical evidence that supported this concern. Perhaps the broad legislative intention and obvious public safety concerns made it easy to

---

38   See *Cunningham v. Canada*, [1993] 2 S.C.R. 143 at 153.
39   [1985] 2 S.C.R. 486.
40   *R. v. Oakes*, [1986] 1 S.C.R. 103. The *Oakes* test for justifying a *Charter* violation requires the state to show, on a balance of probabilities, that (1) the legislative objective was pressing and substantial, that is, sufficiently important to warrant overriding a constitutional right or freedom; and (2) that the means chosen were proportionate in terms of (a) rational connection; (b) minimal impairment; and (c) residual proportionality of benefits and deleterious effects.
41   See the discussion of *Boulet* and *Poorman* in 8(c), above.
42   [1990] 3 S.C.R. 1303.
43   *Ibid.* at 1341.

tempt the Supreme Court with this argument. It is unlikely that a similar result would apply to the sentencing provision.

Regardless of how mitigating facts must be proven, the substantive principles of sentencing that apply to the gravity of the offence and the offender's criminal background will ensure that public safety is not endangered by forced leniency. Ultimately, if judicial opinion finds a section 7 violation, there is little likelihood that sections 724(3)(b) and (d) can be saved. The remedy issue is not easy since the provision would need to deal with both mitigating and aggravating factors in an integrated way which implicates sections 724(3)(b), (d), and (e). The answer should begin with the invalidation of section 724(3)(d) combined with a ruling that the burden described in section 724(3)(b) can only be an evidentiary burden when the party seeking to prove the fact is the offender. A judicial resolution producing this result is necessary if offenders are to receive the benefit of the doubt at sentencing, as clearly stated in *Jones*.[44] The evidentiary burden can be defined in terms of an amplified "air of reality" test which permits judges to reject claims that are implausible, beyond the bounds of reasonable possibility, or lacking in apparent foundation.

# E.  FINDING FACTS AFTER A JURY VERDICT

## 1)  Discerning a Jury's Finding of Fact

Until the 1996 amendments, the *Criminal Code* was silent on how to establish the appropriate factual context for sentencing after a jury returns a verdict of guilty. While this is not a problem in most situations where the underlying factual findings are obvious, there are some offences, like manslaughter and sexual assault, where the Crown can place alternative avenues of criminal responsibility before the jury. As a result, a verdict of guilty does not provide an explanation of the basis upon which the jury acted. There may be other situations where the facts of an event are in dispute and it is not clear from the verdict the extent of aggravating factors which the jury found as facts. For example, there may have been a controversy over whether a weapon was used. Also, a case involving multiple parties may leave unanswered questions about what conduct the jury attributed to each participant. For many years, different views were applied to resolve these kinds of questions.

---

44    Above note 28.

In *R.* v. *Speid*,[45] the accused was convicted of manslaughter as a result of the death of his child. On the evidence, the jury may have convicted because he had assaulted the child personally or because he had failed to protect the child. Before sentencing, the trial judge asked the jury to answer a series of questions which would clarify which account formed the basis of the verdict. The Court of Appeal questioned this procedure but, since the conviction appeal was allowed, it was not necessary to rule on this sentencing issue. It did make reference to the English practice which discouraged delving into jury deliberations but appeared to condone an exception in manslaughter cases.[46] Ordinarily, though, judges were expected to reach their own conclusion on the facts. Soon after, Campbell J. faced a similar situation in *R.* v. *Lawrence*.[47] This was another case of child homicide in which the manslaughter conviction could have been based on an assault or a failure to prevent harm. The judge concluded that there was "no . . . basis to penetrate the deliberations of the jury by asking how they had reached their conclusion." Instead, he used his own judgment to determine the facts based on the evidence adduced at trial. He found that the accused had shaken the little girl to death and sentenced him to fourteen years. The conviction was reversed on appeal on evidentiary grounds without any discussion of the sentencing issue.[48]

Subsequently, the Supreme Court has resolved most of the jury verdict issues. In *R.* v. *Tempelaar*,[49] a jury convicted the accused of sexual assault after the trial judge had instructed it that a verdict of guilty could be premised either on the accused's touching of the victim's breast, or touching her crotch, or non-consensual intercourse. The judge toyed with the idea of having the jury indicate which version formed the basis of their verdict but decided to proceed with the sentencing in accordance with his own view. The offender was sentenced to thirty months imprisonment, and he appealed to the Ontario Court of Appeal. That court dismissed the appeal on the basis that "the trial judge was entitled to make up his own mind on disputed question of fact which were relevant to sentence." A further appeal to the Supreme Court of Canada was dismissed by Lamer C.J.C. in a one-sentence judgment: "We find no reason to depart from the laws as regards sentencing

---

45   (1985), 20 C.C.C. (3d) 534 (Ont. C.A.) [*Speid*].
46   See also *R.* v. *Tuckey* (1985), 20 C.C.C. (3d) 502 (Ont. C.A.).
47   (1987), 58 C.R. (3d) 71 (Ont. H.C.).
48   (1989), 52 C.C.C. (3d) 452 (Ont. C.A.).
49   [1995] 1 S.C.R. 760.

as it now stands, and has for many years." Consequently, notwithstanding doubt about how a jury reached its verdict, the responsibility for determining the factual context rested with the trial judge.

## 2) Reconciling the Sentence with the Verdict

The Supreme Court has also pronounced on the issue of reconciling the judge's view of the factual context with the verdict. In *R. v. Brown*,[50] the accused was charged with causing death by criminal negligence and dangerous driving causing bodily harm after a motor vehicle collision in which two people were killed and two injured. The jury found him not guilty of causing death or bodily harm but returned a verdict of guilty to the included offence of dangerous driving. The sentencing judge took into account the tragic consequences of the accused's driving and sentenced him to twelve months imprisonment. This was affirmed on appeal where a majority of the Saskatchewan Court of Appeal accepted the argument that the offender was "at least partly to blame" for the deaths and injuries. In dissent, Tallis J.A. disagreed on the issue of consequences and would have reduced the sentence to six months. In the Supreme Court, Stevenson J. concluded that the sentencing judge was "bound by the express and implied factual implications of the jury's verdict."[51] Applied to the case before the court, he held that the verdict of guilty to dangerous driving *simpliciter* negated the causal link between the driving and the consequences. Since Parliament had enacted separate offences involving the causing of death and bodily harm for which the offender had been acquitted, it was an error to consider the consequences when determining the fit sentence. The appeal was allowed and the sentence was reduced to six months, as Tallis J.A. had suggested.

The result of *Brown* is that the factual context for sentencing must be consistent with any fact which is inherent in the verdict. In other words, if the jury verdict must have been premised on a particular view of a factual or legal element, the sentencing must proceed on the same basis. If the issue is ambiguous, then *Tempelaar* confirms that it is the judge's role to consider the evidence adduced at trial and reach her own factual conclusions consistent with the verdict.

In some cases, the argument has been raised that an ambiguous verdict requires a judge to sentence on the version of the facts most

---

50   [1991] 2 S.C.R. 518.
51   *Ibid.* at 523.

favourable to the accused.[52] This was expressly rejected in *R. v. Gauthier (No. 2)*[53] where the British Columbia Court of Appeal, dealing with a verdict of guilty in a sexual assault case, relied on *Brown* and *Tempelaar* to reach the conclusion that

> The case law is clear. Where an evidential conflict at trial is left unresolved by the verdict of the jury, the trial judge must reach his or her own conclusions as to the facts surrounding the offence of which the accused was convicted applying the usual standard of proof in a criminal case.[54]

Accordingly, the judge must make independent findings to resolve ambiguities. However, when the evidence is dubious and does not permit a clear finding, doubts will be resolved in favour of the accused.

Difficult problems can arise especially when there is a combination of multiple parties and various premises that might support the verdict. Here, it must be remembered that, on the role of credibility, juries are charged that they can accept all, part, or none of the evidence of a witness. Sometimes, it is not easy to reconstruct the jury's factual premise. For sentencing, however, the judge cannot abdicate the responsibility of making an independent finding if the evidence permits.[55] In *R. v. Cooney*,[56] the accused was prosecuted for first-degree murder. The evidence indicated that he and another man had placed a magazine personal ad to lure the victim. The victim's bank card was taken and used at various bank machines. The victim was subsequently killed. The accused testifed and admitted that he had purchased the gun and was involved in using the card, but denied that he knew anything about the robbery, or that he participated in the killing. He said that he was elsewhere when the killing took place. The jury convicted him of manslaughter. The judge, without explaining which view of the facts she considered applicable, sentenced him to twelve years imprisonment.

On appeal, it was argued that the judge was obliged to determine the accused's involvement before sentencing him. Finlayson J.A., with Laskin J.A. concurring, held that the trial judge should have attempted

---

52   See, for example, *R. v. Fiqia* (1994), 162 A.R. 117 (C.A.), a sexual assault case where the conviction could have been based on a variety of sexual offences from touching to more serious intrusions. The majority relied on *Speid*, above note 45, for the conclusion that it was the trial judge's obligation to find the factual basis.
53   (1996), 108 C.C.C. (3d) 231 (B.C.C.A.).
54   *Ibid.* at 239.
55   See *R. v. Englehart* (1998), 124 C.C.C. (3d) 505 (B.C.C.A.).
56   (1995), 98 C.C.C. (3d) 196 (Ont. C.A.).

to make the findings of fact necessary to sentence the offender. By application of the *Gardiner* principle, if she was not satisfied beyond a reasonable doubt of the graver account, then she was "obliged to give the convicted accused the benefit of the doubt."[57] Since the trial judge had not set out the factual basis for her sentence, he proceeded to consider how the jury must have approached the case even though he found it difficult to formulate a theory that was consistent with the verdict. Ultimately, he concluded that the jury must not have been satisfied beyond a reasonable doubt that the offender was either the killer or was present at the killing. Accordingly, giving the benefit of the doubt to the offender, the sentence was reduced to eight years on the basis that liability must have been premised on section 21(2) common intention. In dissent, Galligan J.A. had no difficulty characterizing the offence as a botched robbery where the offender was present and actively involved. On this reading of the facts, he would have upheld the twelve-year sentence. This case illustrates the importance of the trial judge sifting the evidence, assessing credibility and making the necessary findings of fact. If not satisfied that the facts permit a clear finding, the burden of proof should resolve the matter with, as *Gardiner* confirmed, the benefit of the doubt going to the offender.

## 3) Re-litigation of Issues at a Sentencing Hearing

There have been examples of offenders attempting to re-litigate issues addressed at trial after the verdict for sentencing purposes. Courts have generally not been sympathetic. For example, in *R. v. Gauthier (No. 2)*, the British Columbia Court of Appeal in a sexual assault case upheld the trial judge's decision to exclude expert evidence intended to show that there had been no penile penetration.[58] Ryan J.A. concluded that the "notion that either the Crown or the defence could call evidence for the purpose of either minimizing or amplifying the facts after a verdict is rendered would lead to unseemly tactics and serious injustices."[59] In other words, if the issue is on the table at trial, the parties must stake out their turf at that stage. The difficulty here, of course, is that an accused may decide to exercise the constitutional right to put the Crown to the proof of his or her and remain silent. Does this mean that the accused cannot give evidence at the sentencing hearing to explain

57   *Ibid.* at 204.
58   Above note 53.
59   *Ibid.* at 241.

his or her conduct? In *R. v. Braun*,[60] the Manitoba Court of Appeal held that an accused who did not give evidence at trial could not give *viva voce* evidence at the sentencing stage after a verdict of guilty to manslaughter to show a less serious source of criminal responsibility. In this case, the proposed sentencing evidence would have contradicted evidence offered by the Crown at trial. In other words, since the matter was in issue at trial, that's where it should have been addressed.

## 4)  The 1996 Amendments

The 1996 amendments have codified and refined the Supreme Court decisions in *Tempelaar* and *Brown*. Section 724(2) now provides:

> (2)  Where the court is composed of a judge and jury, the court
>   (a)  shall accept as proven all facts, express or implied, that are essential to the jury's verdict of guilty; and
>   (b)  may find any other relevant fact that was disclosed by evidence at the trial to be proven, or hear evidence presented by either party with respect to that fact.

These confirm both the integrity of the verdict and the duty of the sentencing judge to find the sentencing facts so long as they are consistent with the verdict. They also deal with the question of how to respond if the evidence at trial is insufficient. Section 724(2)(b) allows the judge to "hear evidence presented by either party with respect to that fact." This seems to suggest that when a judge is not satisfied that the trial evidence fully canvassed a relevant sentencing factor, she should advise the parties and provide an opportunity for them to present evidence. Clearly, it contemplates additional evidence to that adduced at trial and, consequently, may contradict both *Braun* and *Gauthier*, discussed above. Those cases can be reconciled if section 724(2)(b) places the initiative on the trial judge. If the judge is satisfied with what was adduced at trial and can make a finding of fact, then the sentencing should be proceed on that basis. If, however, the evidence is unclear but the issue is material, then the parties can be given an opportunity to present new evidence, subject to the concern about the issue of "unseemly tactics." If the parties do not call additional evidence, the judge would apply the ordinary burden of proof to the issue.

---

60   [1995], 95 C.C.C. (3d) 443 (Man. C.A.).

## F. RECORD OF PREVIOUS CONVICTIONS

In many cases, the prosecutor will want to present a record of prior convictions to the court at the sentencing hearing. Usually, this includes the date and place of conviction, the nature of the offence, and the sentence. Specific details of a previous offence may be adduced, if relevant, but these can present additional problems of proof.[61] The common practice is for Crown counsel to give a copy of the record to defence counsel, or the offender personally if unrepresented, and ask whether the record is admitted.[62] If admitted, the record is made an exhibit to the sentencing. Since the document most often used will be a Canadian Police Information Centre (CPIC) printout, counsel should be careful to make sure that the portion indicating charges which have been withdrawn or resulted in acquittals has been deleted from the document before it is handed to the court.

Courts have consistently held that a record must be "unequivocally admitted" or properly proven before it can be relied upon for sentencing purposes.[63] Accordingly, if the record or any of its details are not admitted, the Crown can omit the controversial material or can proceed to prove it. Proof will likely require an adjournment: an application by the Crown for time to prove a record of previous convictions will not customarily be refused.[64]

### 1) Proving the Validity of the Record

Section 667(1)(a) of the *Criminal Code* provides that a certificate "setting out with reasonable particularity" the conviction and sentence of an offender, signed by the person who made the order, the clerk of the court, or a fingerprint examiner, is evidence of the prior record so long as there is proof that the accused before the court is the same person

---

61 Details of a previous offence may be admitted. Alternatively, they may be presented through reasons for judgment which, so long as there are no outstanding appeals, are *res judicata*. Statements of fact from an appellate factum or excerpts from a transcript are useful ways of explaining the facts of another offence but are not, without consent, admissible. Of course, any fact can be proven by *viva voce* evidence of someone with personal knowledge.
62 If the accused admitted a previous record during the trial, this constitutes an admission for sentencing purposes: *R. v. Protz* (1984), 13 C.C.C. (3d) 107 (Sask. C.A.).
63 See, for example, *R. v. Ronaghan* (1984), 13 C.C.C. (3d) 480 (P.E.I. S.C. in banco).
64 See *R. v. Veale*, [1984] A.J. No. 547 (C.A.), where it was held that the trial judge had erred in refusing the Crown an adjournment to prove a record.

referred to in the certificate. A fingerprint examiner is a "person designated as such for the purposes of this section by the Solicitor General of Canada."[65] Sections 667(1)(b) and (c) provide additional help in facilitating proof. Their combined effect is to ensure that evidence of a fingerprint comparison is proof, in the absence of evidence to the contrary, that the record belongs to the accused and that the fingerprint comparison can be adduced through a certificate. In fact, the entire process can be effected by two certificates prepared by a fingerprint examiner. Form 44 provides a certified record with a reproduction of fingerprints; form 45 provides the fingerprints of the accused, and a comparison with those in the respective Form 44, to certify that they belong to the same person. With leave of the court, an accused may seek the attendance of the fingerprint examiner for cross-examination[66] but the fingerprint comparison procedure will almost always provide conclusive admissible proof. The certificate procedure, however, must be strictly followed and offences clearly identified.[67] Section 667(1)(a) also provides for certificates prepared by judicial officers but these must be accompanied by some form of proof identifying the person named in the record as the accused before the court. It is unlikely that this can easily be adduced, especially if previous convictions come from various jurisdictions.

There may be other ways that the Crown can attempt to prove a previous record. In *R. v. Albright*,[68] the Crown sought a greater penalty in an impaired driving case after serving its notice of intention to do so but proceeded to prove the previous conviction by using a "Certified Extract of British Columbia Driving Record." The trial judge accepted this mode of proof and imposed the minimum three-month sentence for a subsequent offence. In the Supreme Court of Canada, it was argued that the *Criminal Code* procedure was exhaustive. For a unanimous court, Lamer J., as he then was, rejected this contention and held that the *Code* procedure provided "sufficient evidence" but was not the exclusive mode of proof that could be used. Although he rejected the

---

65  *Criminal Code*, s. 667(5).
66  *Ibid.*, s. 667(3).
67  See *R. v. Gordon* (1972), 8 C.C.C. (2d) 132 (B.C.C.A.), where a certificate was rejected because it was unclear after a re-numbering of the Code which section was involved.
68  [1987] 2 S.C.R. 383 [*Albright*].

use of provincial evidence statutes as vehicles for admissibility,[69] common law methods of proof were available. He characterized the certificate as hearsay evidence. Without commenting on the possibility of a public documents exception, he concluded that *Gardiner*[70] provided that "irrespective of the hearsay rule, all credible and trustworthy evidence is admissible at a sentencing hearing."[71] It is important to note that while the Supreme Court upheld the use of the provincial document as proof, Lamer J. indicated that the "appellant did not dispute the fact of his convictions, but only the means by which they were to be proved." This curious comment may suggest that provincial certificates, although potentially admissible at common law, are not sufficient evidence if details of the record are disputed since the document by itself provides no identification linking it to the accused. The *Criminal Code* procedure makes identification a *sine qua non*. While *Albright* may appear to open some doors, a court should not accept a documentary record not encompassed by section 667(1) without proof linking it to the accused whenever a record is disputed. Using the *Code* procedure is the safer route.

# G. THE PRE-SENTENCE REPORT

Courts have long recognized the need to obtain background information about the offender especially when considering non-custodial sanctions. The development of the pre-sentence report (PSR) is closely linked to probation. In Canada, formal probation services having been introduced in Ontario in 1921,[72] the role has been given in most jurisdictions to probation officers. While sentencing information has been collected and presented to the courts for some time, the inclusion of an express power in the *Code* to order a PSR only occurred in 1969.[73] Prior to that time, some provincial probation statutes spoke to the issue of pre-sentence

---

69   Lamer J. followed the decision in R. v. *Marshall* (1960), [1961] S.C.R. 123, which limited the scope of s. 37 of the *Canada Evidence Act*, R.S.C. 1985, c. C-5 as a vehicle for permitting provincial legislation to change generally applicable admissibility rules for the criminal process.
70   Above note 2.
71   *Albright*, above note 68 at 391.
72   See the discussion of probation in Chapter 9, below.
73   See *Criminal Law Amendment Act*, 1968–69, S.C. 1968–69, c. 38, s. 75..

reports, but the *Code* was silent.[74] It was not until the 1996 amendments that the *Code* provided any details as to the required contents of a PSR.

Section 721(1) now empowers a court to order a PSR "for the purpose of assisting the court in imposing a sentence or in determining whether the accused should be discharged pursuant to section 730." In theory, a PSR is available in all cases except where the accused is a corporation or unless a province exercises authority under section 721(2) to promulgate regulations "respecting the types of offences for which a court may require a report." While there may be concerns about the expense and burden of preparing PSRs, it is unlikely that a province would attempt to exclude any particular offence for this provision given their general utility.

Section 721(3) now addresses the issue of content and requires that a PSR, "unless otherwise specified by the court," will contain information which deals with

- "the offender's age, maturity, character, behaviour, attitude, and willingness to make amends";
- the history of previous dispositions under the *Young Offenders Act* and of previous findings of guilt under this Act and any other Act of Parliament; and
- the history of any alternative measures used to deal with the offender, and the offender's response to those measures.

The *Criminal Code* also permits the judge to request other material in the PSR so long as the parties have had an opportunity to make submissions before the order is made.[75] While the *Code* structure ensures that a PSR will include relevant data, it does not address the converse question: what material ought not to be included in a PSR? There is a healthy body of appellate cases which have attempted to ensure that the PSR does its expected job in a fair manner without encroaching on the terrain of other participants.

There is judicial agreement that the PSR should not include any facts or commentary which relate to the offence or the offender's role in it. Facts about the offence intended to reduce its gravity or place blame on someone else should not be included in a PSR.[76] In *R. v. Rudyk*,[77] MacKeigan C.J.N.S. commented:

---

74  In *R. v. Benson* (1951), 100 C.C.C. 247 (B.C.C.A.), the court in discussing the role of a PSR quoted from s. 4 of the *Probation Act*, R.S.B.C. 1948, c. 268, which provided a framework for the PSR.
75  *Criminal Code*, s. 721(4).
76  See *Urbanovitch*, above note 1.
77  (1978), 1 C.R. (3d) S-26 at S-31 (N.S.C.A.).

I would here urge that a pre-sentence report be confined to its very necessary and salutary role of portraying the background, character and circumstances of the person convicted. It should not, however, contain the investigator's impressions of the facts relating to the offence charged, whether based on information received from the accused, the police or other witnesses, and whether favourable or unfavourable to the accused. And if the report contains such information the trial judge should disregard it in considering sentence.[78]

A PSR can include the spectrum of personal information which may be relevant to sentencing including family, education, employment, community involvement, and health, but does not extend to information about unproven offences or previous acts of misconduct.[79] Although the consequences of an offence are relevant, they should not generally be discussed in a PSR. Courts have held that it is inappropriate for a PSR to include information from a victim about injuries suffered and attitudes towards the offender.[80]

It has long been recognized that a fair hearing includes giving the offender an opportunity to challenge adverse material. In the early days of PSR development, Sloan C.J.B.C. stated:

. . . a convicted man ought to be informed of the substance of a Probation Officer's report, insofar as it is detrimental to him, so that he may have an opportunity to agree therewith or explain or deny it if he chooses so to do.

If the report contains prejudicial observations which the Court considers relevant and likely to influence his sentence and this material is denied by the prisoner then proof of it, if required, should be given in open Court when its accuracy may be tested by cross-examination. Alternatively, if the Court does not consider it of sufficient importance to justify formal proof then such matters should be ignored as factors influencing sentence.[81]

To ensure fairness, section 721(5) of the *Criminal Code* requires that a copy of the PSR be given "as soon as practicable after filing" to the prosecutor, and either to the offender or the offender's counsel "as directed by the court." Other than the case of an unrepresented accused, most

---

78   *Ibid.*
79   See *R. v. Arsenault* (1981), 24 C.R. (3d) 269 (P.E.I. S.C.).
80   *Ibid.* While injuries are usually relevant, they are adduced in a different manner. The Crown can adduce this material or it can be included in a VIS: see below at 8(I).
81   *Benson*, above note 74 at 256. See also *R. v. Dolbec* (1962), [1963] 2 C.C.C. 87 (B.C.C.A.).

documents will go to counsel and it is difficult to understand why the *Code* contains a discretion to order delivery either to the offender or counsel. Perhaps there may be situations where the author of the report is concerned about showing some of it to the offender. Counsel should always be reluctant to keep any material from her client since this is the only way to obtain effective instructions. Curiously, a 1999 amendment made the "as directed by the court" qualification applicable only to a PSR and not a victim impact statement (VIS).[82] This history further confounds the question of underlying purpose.

Section 721(4) empowers the judge to order any material not specifically addressed in section 721(3) to be included in a PSR so long as the judge has heard the view of the offender and the prosecutor on requesting the material. This could include issues about available resources. It could also relate to the local, historical, or personal factors encompassed by "the circumstances of aboriginal offenders" as used in section 718.2(e). The decision in *R. v. Gladue* has made it clear that it is the court's duty to inform itself if counsel has not done so. The PSR and sections 723(3) and (4) are the only vehicles which can apprise a court of relevant background factors and existing alternatives to incarceration.[83]

Not everything included in a PSR will meet with the approval of the parties. Certainly, extraneous factors ought to be excised. Some relevant factors will be the subject of a factual dispute. The PSR is mentioned in the general section dealing with resolving factual disputes. Section 724(3)(b) provides that the party wishing to rely on a fact has the burden of proving it, including a fact within a PSR. If it is an aggravating fact, then section 724(3)(e) requires the Crown to prove it beyond a reasonable doubt. However, if it is a fact which the offender wants to use, section 724(3)(d) seems to require the offender to prove it on a balance of probabilities. As discussed above, there may be an issue about whether this reverse onus conforms with principles of fundamental justice. If it is constitutional, and requires an offender to prove a challenged fact, this can likely be done by calling the probation officer. Even though the testimony will be hearsay, the Supreme Court has confirmed the admissibility of hearsay evidence on a sentencing

---

82   Previously, s. 722.1 (enacted by S.C. 1995, c. 22, s. 6) required the prompt delivery of both PSR and VIS. The "as directed by the court" qualification applied to both kinds of reports. When the provisions dealing with VIS were amended in 1999, the former s. 722.1 was split. The remaining provision dealing with VIS alone does not include the "as directed by the court": see s. 722.1 as am. by *An Act to amend the Criminal Code (victims of crime) and another Act in consequence*, S.C. 1999, c. 25, s. 18.

83   See *Gladue*, above note 10. See also the discussion of judicial notice, below, at 8(K).

hearing so long as it is credible and trustworthy.[84] Assume that a PSR indicates that an offender has a good employment record and the Crown disputes this. Surely, the testimony of a probation officer indicating conversations about the offender with employers X, Y, and Z should, in the absence of contradictory evidence, satisfy the burden without requiring the attendance of the employers. Similarly, confirming letters from the employers should be satisfactory.

## H. THE OFFENDER'S RIGHT TO SPEAK

Before the 1996 amendments, the offender's right to place his or her position before the sentencing judge was ensured by two different routes. First, the Supreme Court confirmed that the imposition of a sentence without hearing from the offender was a denial of the right to a fair hearing protected by the Canadian *Bill of Rights*.[85] Secondly, although buried in the part dealing with jury trials, the *Criminal Code* provided that the judge "shall ask the accused whether he has anything to say before sentence is passed upon him."[86] This mandatory provision was followed by the qualification that an omission did not "affect the validity of the proceedings." In the post-*Charter* era, the New Brunswick Court of Appeal examined a situation where, after a long trial, the judge refused to give the offender another opportunity to air his views and did not permit a speech before the imposition of sentence.[87] It reached three conclusions about section 668:

> First of all, the earlier trial process is in no way invalidated; secondly, the saving provision of the section applies to inadvertent acts of the trial judge; and thirdly, any deliberate act of denial of a codified right relating to imprisonment is an infringement of the accused's constitutional right to liberty under section 7 and should bear consequences in the sentencing process.[88]

---

84   See *Gardiner*, above note 2.

85   See *R. v. Lowry* (1972), [1974] S.C.R. 195. See also *R. v. Schofield* (1976), 36 C.R.N.S. 135 (N.B. S.C.(A.D.)).

86   Section 668. The antecedent provision in the *Criminal Code, 1892* (Can.), 55-56 Vict., c. 29 was s. 733(1), which differed only slightly by using the phrase "shall ask him whether he has anything to say why sentence should not be passed upon him according to law."

87   See *R. v. Dennison* (1990), 80 C.C.C. (3d) 78 (N.B.C.A.) [*Dennison*].

88   *Ibid.* at 84.

As a result, the majority reduced an otherwise fit sentence of twelve years to nine years to reflect the *Charter* breach.[89]

The 1996 amendments ensured that the offender's position would be canvassed, and also preserved the right to speak. The imposition of sentence is not an arbitrary act but must follow "proceedings to determine the appropriate sentence."[90] A proceeding means a hearing and a hearing must be fair. Section 723(1) requires the judge to "give the prosecutor and the offender an opportunity to make submissions with respect to any facts relevant to the sentence to be imposed." Clearly, this cannot be restricted to facts but must include a submission on the implications of the facts for an appropriate disposition. Moreover, section 726 provides:

> Before determining the sentence to be imposed, the court shall ask whether the offender, if present, has anything to say.

This is different from its predecessor in two important ways. First, the right arises before determination of the sentence and not simply the passing of sentence. More importantly, it is not accompanied by the qualification which would save an omission from invalidating the process. Referring to the "exigencies of busy courts," commentators have suggested that, notwithstanding section 726, it is rare that offenders are given an opportunity to speak unless they are appearing without counsel.[91] Since section 726 is cast in mandatory language, it is necessary to consider the consequences of a failure to offer the offender an opportunity to speak, especially when another provision also seems to ensure that the sentencer hears from the offender before determining the sentence.

The roots of section 726 can be traced back to the ancient right of allocution, which entitled the offender to claim mercy personally from the sentencer before sentence was pronounced.[92] For example, execution could be avoided in a capital offence by claiming benefit of clergy. While allocution arose during a period when an accused did not have an

---

89  Whether a reduction of sentence is an available response to a *Charter* violation is a controversial issue: see *R. v. Glykis* (1995), 41 C.R. (4th) 310 (Ont. C.A.); and A. Manson, "*Charter* Violations in Mitigation of Sentence" (1995), 41 C.R. (4th) 318.

90  *Criminal Code*, s. 720.

91  See J.V. Roberts & D.P. Cole, "Introduction to Sentencing and Parole" in J.V. Roberts & D.P. Cole, eds., *Making Sense of Sentencing* (Toronto: University of Toronto Press, 1999) 3 at 15.

92  See P.W. Barrett, "Allocution" (1944) 9 Mo. L. Rev. 115 & 232. Barrett notes that the major historical authority is not a judicial pronouncement but Blackstone's *Commentaries*: see Sir W. Blackstone, *Commentaries on the Laws of England* (Oxford: Clarendon Press, 1765). He suggests, at 116, that Blackstone was merely stating "what was then the prevailing custom and practice."

opportunity to give evidence, its role has been continued in modern times. In *Green v. United States*,[93] a man charged with bank robbery was about to be sentenced when the judge asked, "Did you want to say something?" Counsel then proceeded to make a lengthy sentencing submission. After receiving a twenty-year sentence, the offender appealed arguing that a mandatory rule required the judge to ask him personally whether he had anything to say before sentence was passed. In the United States Supreme Court, the justices were split over the ambiguity of the situation and whether the judge had invited a personal submission which was waived by the offender in lieu of a submission by counsel. However, the justices were unanimously in support of the right of the offender to speak in addition to a submission by counsel. Frankfurter J. said:

> We are not unmindful of the relevant major changes that have evolved in criminal procedure since the seventeenth century — the sharp decrease in the number of crimes which were punishable by death, the right of the defendant to testify on his own behalf, and the right to counsel. But we see no reason why a procedural rule should be limited to the circumstances under which it arose if reasons for the right it protects remain. None of these modern innovations lessens the need for the defendant, personally, to have the opportunity to present to the court his plea in mitigation. The most persuasive counsel may not be able to speak for a defendant as the defendant might, with halting eloquence, speak for himself.[94]

The issue of allocution has, in the United States, returned recently to its original context — the death penalty. The current issue is whether a convicted person in a death penalty case has the right to make an unsworn address to the jury during the penalty phase without cross-examination. A number of circuits have held that allocution is a constitutional right protected by the right to due process.[95] While the issue has not been addressed directly by the United States Supreme Court, there have been decisions in which a right of allocution has been assumed[96] or mentioned without criticism.[97]

---

93   365 U.S. 301 (1961).

94   *Ibid.* at 304.

95   See *Boardman v. Estelle* (1992), 957 F.2d 1523 (9th Cir. 1992); *Ashe v. North Carolina*, 586 F.2d 334 (4th Cir. 1978); *United States v. Moree*, 928 F.2d 654 (5th Cir. 1991). I thank Jeremy Goldman of Yale Law School for these and the following American authorities.

96   See *McGautha v. California*, 402 U.S. 183 (1971).

97   See *Hill v. United States*, 368 U.S. 424 at 429 (1962).

Recognizing the importance of allocution, what is the consequence of a failure to offer the offender the right to speak? Clearly, a refusal of a request to speak or a deliberate denial is grounds for a review of the sentence. Prior to 1996, an inadvertent omission would not invalidate the sentencing.[98] Assuming that an offender represented by counsel has placed his or her position on sentence before the court, and has been afforded a fair opportunity to do so, there is no reason why an inadvertent omission should undermine the sentence. However, a denial of the right to speak, once requested, is a different matter. In the American death penalty cases, where the right to allocution is recognized, a prisoner cannot be refused the opportunity to speak personally to the sentencer to plead for leniency. Section 726 establishes the continuity of that right in Canada: an offender who voices a desire to speak cannot be refused. Since most offenders would not be aware of an historic right to speak to the sentencer, and given the mandatory language in the *Code*, the better practice is to ensure that every offender is offered the opportunity.

While section 726, consistent with the right of allocution, enables an offender to speak personally to the sentencer, it does not contemplate giving unsworn factual evidence. That is a separate matter. Disputes over facts should be resolved by reference to the appropriate burden of proof, and a hearing, if necessary. The problem of confusing the two processes was apparent in *R. v. Izzard*,[99] a Crown sentence appeal arising from an armed robbery by three men. At the sentencing hearing of one offender, after submissions from counsel, the judge asked whether the offender had anything to say. The offender indicated that he did not know that his accomplice had a knife. The Crown argued that this information should be given under oath and be subject to cross-examination. Instead, the judge continued his conversation with the offender and sentenced him to one year imprisonment to be followed by two years probation. On appeal, Glube C.J.N.S. noted that the comments about the knife seemed to be important to the judge. They had not been raised by counsel and, once questioned by the Crown, should not have been relied upon unless adduced in accordance with ordinary procedure. However, the offender's remarks about his plans for the future and his support were considered appropriate. Finding that the sentence did not adequately reflect the objectives of deterrence, denunciation, and promoting a sense of responsibility in the offender, the sentence was varied to two years imprisonment with

98   See *Dennison*, above note 87 ; and s. 668 of the 1985 *Criminal Code*.
99   (1999), 175 N.S.R. (2d) 288 (C.A.).

two years probation. As far as section 726 is concerned, the *Izzard* case indicates the need to distinguish between the facts of the offence which, if disputed, are governed by section 724(3), and personal comments by the offender that relate to his or her character and situation that may support leniency.

# I.   VICTIMS AND VICTIM IMPACT STATEMENTS

The role of victims in the sentencing process has changed dramatically over the past two decades. While the issue of harm caused by an offence has always been a relevant factor, until very recently information about consequences to victims was under the control of Crown counsel. Attempts by victims to obtain standing at sentencing hearings were rebuffed by presiding judges who took the traditional view that the Crown represented the public interest, including the interests of the victims.[100] Concerns about how victims are treated by the criminal justice process have grown into a political lobby with far-reaching interests and vocal advocates.[101] For sentencing purposes, they have produced a statutory form of recognition at the sentencing hearing by carving out a role for "victim impact statements" (VIS).[102]

Section 722(1) requires a sentencing court to consider a statement from a victim "describing the harm done to, or loss suffered by, the victim arising from the commission of the offence." Where the offence results in death or incapacity, a statement can be obtained from the spouse, any relative, or someone who has legal or de facto custody or the responsibility to care for the incapacitated victim or a dependent.[103] Other than cases of death or incapacity, a victim is defined as "a person to whom harm was done or who suffered physical or emotional loss as a result of the commission of the offence."[104] This definition was amended in 1999 to change "the person" to "a person." The use of the definite article in the earlier version had persuaded the New Brunswick Court of Appeal that the original definition restricted the applicability

---

100   See *R. v. Antler* (1982), 69 C.C.C. (2d) 480 (B.C. S.C.); and *R. v. Robinson* (1983), 38 C.R. (3d) 255 (Ont. H.C.).

101   See K. Roach, *Due Process and Victims' Rights: The New Law and Politics of Criminal Justice* (Toronto: University of Toronto Press, 1999), especially at 278–309.

102   Although amended since, the VIS provisions were first enacted in 1988: see R.S.C. 1985, 4th Supp., c. 23, s. 7.

103   *Criminal Code*, s. 722(4)(b).

104   *Ibid.*, s. 722(4)(a).

of the provision to a single victim.[105] Accordingly, the sentencing court was precluded from considering the VIS from the estranged wife and child of the offender who were present when he assaulted her new companion. By replacing "the" with "a," Parliament has indicated that the set of victims may be larger than just the person who was the immediate focus of an assault.

Other than the requirement in section 722(1) that the statement should describe "the harm done" or "loss suffered," the only other details about the VIS are contained in section 722(2) which provides that it must be in writing and "in accordance with the procedures established by a program designated for that purpose" by the province. This suggests that every province and territory would prescribe a form, which would be produced and developed by a program established to deal with this and any other ancillary procedures. In Ontario, rather than prescribing a form by regulation, a program has been designated by regulation;[106] this program has developed a form and an information guide.[107]

In R. v. Gabriel, numerous VIS were filed and two oral submissions received in the course of sentencing an accused for criminal negligence causing death. The scope and variety of the VIS caused Hill J. to consider the issues of relevance, content, and a discretion to permit oral rather than written submissions. He began by commenting:

> Without, in any fashion, diminishing the significant contribution of victim impact statements to providing victims a voice in the criminal process, it must be remembered that a criminal trial, including the sentencing phase, is not a tripartite proceeding. A convicted offender has committed a crime — an act against society as a whole. It is the public interest, not a private interest, which is to be served in sentencing.[108]

Recognizing that the VIS "should not be structured so as to foster or encourage any element of personal revenge," he concluded that VIS can only contain relevant information about harm and loss. They should not include criticisms of the offender, statements about the

---

105   See R. v. Curtis (1992), 69 C.C.C. (3d) 385 (N.B.C.A.).

106   O.C. 424/94 (issued 9 March 1994) provides that the "Ministry of the attorney general create and administer a program to establish forms and procedures respecting victim impact statements for the purpose of s. 735 [now s. 722] of the Criminal Code" and that this program be designated for the purpose of s. 735(1.2) [now s. 722(2)].

107   See the appendix to R. v. Gabriel (1999), 26 C.R. (5th) 364 at 382–89 (Ont. S.C.) [Gabriel].

108   Ibid. at 374.

facts of the case, or recommended punishments.[109] Clearly, the scope of VIS must be restricted to personal statements of harm and loss.

In *Gabriel*, Hill J. also addressed the issue of oral VIS. His remarks suggest that he was contemplating only permitting a victim to read a prepared and vetted VIS and not an opportunity to stand up and to extemporize. He concluded that a sentencing judge has a discretion to permit an oral VIS but that caution is required to ensure that the victim, while reading his or her statement, does not "improvis[e] beyond the four corners of the statement," or descend into accusation or invective towards the offender which might destabilize the courtroom. Although this is sage advice for a judge faced with a request to present a VIS orally, the 1999 amendments may have changed this situation.

The 1999 amendments ensure that victims will have a greater opportunity to participate in the sentencing process. Section 722.2 provides:

(1) As soon as practicable after a finding of guilt and in any event before imposing sentence, the court shall inquire of the prosecutor or a victim of the offence, or any person representing a victim of the offence, whether the victim or victims have been advised of the opportunity to prepare a statement referred to in subsection 722(1).

(2) On application of the prosecutor or a victim or on its own motion, the court may adjourn the proceedings to permit the victim to prepare a statement referred to in subsection 722(1) or to present evidence in accordance with subsection 722(3), if the court is satisfied that the adjournment would not interfere with the proper administration of justice.

In the past, Crown counsel played the determinative role in whether to put a VIS forward. This provision imposes a duty on the judge to inquire about whether there has been advice about, and an opportunity for, the preparation of VIS. At this stage, either the prosecutor or the victim can seek an adjournment to prepare a VIS. While this does not give the victim standing, it suggests that a VIS can be put before the court regardless of the Crown's view. Still, the court would have to be satisfied that the author is a victim within the statutory definition and that the statement meets the requirements of relevance. As with all material of an evidentiary nature, there is also an over-riding judicial discretion to ensure that the probative value exceeds any prejudice.

---

109  See *R. v. Coelho* (1995), 41 C.R. (4th) 324 (B.C.S.C.), where a father of the victim was denied an opportunity to make a submission about the length of sentence.

The 1999 amendments also raise a question about Hill J.'s analysis of the discretion to permit an oral submission. Now, section 722(2.1) provides:

> The court shall, on the request of a victim, permit the victim to read a statement prepared and filed in accordance with subsection (2), or to present the statement in any other manner that the court considers appropriate.[110]

This new provision must be read in context. First, although it uses the phrase "on the request of the victim," nothing has changed to give a victim standing in general at the sentencing hearing. Accordingly, this provision is not triggered until and unless there has been a decision to prepare and file a VIS either by the Crown or after the section 722.2(1) inquiry. This will result in a written document which must be vetted to guarantee relevance and excise anything that is extraneous and prejudicial before it can be read into the record.[111] Section 722(2.1) enables the victim to ask that the VIS be given orally but surely the judge retains discretion to permit or disallow an oral submission. The judge must maintain control of the process and cannot abdicate a decision which, as noted by Hill J., can have both fairness and security concerns. It is not uncommon, and should not be surprising, that a VIS contains harsh and angry words.[112] The judge must have the residual discretion[113] to decide whether a submission can be given orally and, if so, must ensure that the written VIS contains only relevant material and must advise the victim that it cannot be amplified. The argument that a judge must accede to a victim's request to make an oral submission is untenable and is a strained reading of the new section 722(2.1) which gives the judge two options: permit an oral submission, or permit the VIS to be presented in another way.

---

110  An Act to amend the Criminal Code (victims of crime) and another Act in consequence, S.C. 1999, c. 25, s.17(1).

111  The VIS is filed with the court and copies are delivered to the counsel: see s. 722.1. Any issue of relevance or inappropriate language is dealt with before the VIS is adduced into the record.

112  See the appendices to R. v. K.L., [1999] O.J. No. 5085 (Sup. Ct.) (QL) on a dangerous offender application. Appendix B contains the written VIS and the transcript of an oral submission. Note that most of the oral submission is anger and invective, and statements about the facts of the case which would fail the test of relevance in Gabriel.

113  See Baron v. Canada, [1993] 1 S.C.R. 416 at 435–46 (residual discretion).

In practice, it appears that VIS, once vetted for relevance, are rarely challenged. Still, there must be a vehicle for resolving a challenge that is both fair and consistent with the statutory framework. The question of challenging a VIS is not separately addressed in the *Criminal Code*. Although this suggests that a factual dispute over a VIS should be resolved in the ordinary way, section 724(3) makes specific mention of pre-sentence reports but not VIS. Moreover, the major difficulty with applying section 724(3) to a VIS is that it suggests that the Crown would have the burden of proving a disputed element beyond a reasonable doubt. This would, in most cases, require calling the victim. One of the reasons for permitting written VIS is to place a description of harm and loss before the court without having to call the victim to testify. This would be undermined if an offender could force a victim into the witness stand simply by saying "I dispute this." Perhaps the proper resolution of this dilemma of how to protect both the interest of the offender and the victim is to return to the idea of an evidentiary burden. An evidentiary burden means that an offender must be able to point to some evidence in the case, whether called by the offender or not, to justify going forward with the issue. At the VIS stage, an evidentiary burden would be satisfied if any material or evidence, including the contents of the VIS, when read within the factual context of the case as whole, cast doubt on the impugned assertion. On the other hand, a specious or empty challenge without factual support should not require the Crown to prove the allegation of harm or loss.

## J. PSYCHIATRIC, PSYCHOLOGICAL, AND MEDICAL REPORTS

An offender will always be permitted to adduce expert opinions from psychiatrists, psychologists, physicians, and other experts, which address relevant concerns like the presence or absence of mental disorder or other conditions which affect behaviour and decision making. Subject to challenge and a requirement of more formal proof, these reports can usually be presented in written form as credible and trustworthy hearsay. Occasions will arise, however, when it is the Crown that wants to adduce some psychiatric material which may relate to an issue of future risk. Here, the issue of admissibility becomes murky. If psychiatric material exists, the Crown can attempt to obtain and adduce it. Depending on the nature of the material, who possesses it, and how it was generated, there may be issues of privilege[114] or statutory protection.[115] A different issue arises when the Crown wants the court to order a psychiatric assessment to obtain material that does not already exist.

## 1) Admissibility of Crown Psychiatric Assessments

Before the mental disorder provisions were amended in 1991,[116] the *Criminal Code* contained provisions which permitted remands for psychiatric assessments. While the resulting reports often canvassed all medico-legal issues including fitness, insanity, and disposition, the empowering sections were actually directed solely to the issue of fitness.[117] Notwithstanding the compelled nature of these assessments, a majority of the Supreme Court held that the resulting reports could be admitted at a sentencing proceeding, including a dangerous offender application.[118]

The 1991 amendments dealt in a thoughtful and comprehensive way with the need for psychiatric assessments when a mental disorder issue was present. Section 672.11 authorizes an assessment order whenever there are reasonable grounds to believe that such evidence is necessary to determine an issue of fitness, a section 16 mental disorder, or a disposition following one of those findings. It does not permit a compelled psychiatric assessment for the purposes of sentencing following

---

114  In *R. v. Gruenke*, [1991] 3 S.C.R. 263, the Supreme Court recognized the possibility of a privilege being afforded to material on a case-by case basis if four criteria were met: (1) the material originated in confidence; (2) condfidentiality is essential to the relationship that generated the material; (3) the relationship is one which the community "sedulously" fosters; and (4) the harm that would result from disclosure would be greater than the benefit of disclosure. One can assume that, in certain circumstances, this might apply, for example, to material from a psychiatrist who has a treatment relationship with an offender.

115  See *Criminal Code*, s. 672.21(3), discussed below, which permits use of "protected statements" only for listed purposes. Sentencing does not appear to be one of them, assuming that "disposition" in s. 672.21(3)(b) means a disposition under s. 672.54.

116  See *An Act to amend the Criminal Code (mental disorder) and to amend the National Defence Act and the Young Offenders Act in consequence thereof*, S.C. 1991, c. 43, s. 4, which repealed pre-existing provisions and replaced them with the current regime in ss. 672.1–672.95.

117  See A. Manson, "Ordering Psychiatric Examinations" (1986), 53 C.R. (3d) 387.

118  See *Jones*, above note 28, Gonthier J. for a five-person majority; Lamer C.J.C., Cory, Sopinka, and Major JJ. dissenting.

a conviction.[119] However, the question arises whether a report from a properly authorized assessment intended for fitness or section 16 purposes can subsequently be used during the sentencing stage if the person is convicted. Section 672.21(2) provides that a "protected statement" cannot be used without the accused's consent in any proceeding except for specified purposes which do not include sentencing. A "protected statement" is defined as follows:

> . . . a statement made by the accused during the course and for the purposes of an assessment or treatment directed by a disposition, to the person specified in the assessment order or the disposition, or to anyone acting under that person's direction[120]

Accordingly, any statements by an offender during an assessment are protected and should not be admissible during the sentencing phase.

By extension, the opinions of experts based on the assessment are also not admissible for sentencing purposes without the offender's consent since these opinions would, at least in part, be based on protected statements. In R. v. D.K. an accused was charged with a number of sexual assaults.[121] He consented to an assessment under section 672.11. The assessment found him fit to stand trial but also concluded that he was a sexual sadist with a propensity for the infliction of suffering and humiliation. The accused entered a number of guilty pleas and, not surprisingly, the Crown wanted to use the assessment report or the psychiatrist's opinion evidence on the sentencing. Weekes J. concluded that the purpose behind the section 672.21 protection was to "create an opportunity for the open flow of information from the accused to the professionals performing the assessment." Accordingly, to maintain the integrity of the assessment process, the report was not admitted into evidence since it would "inevitably make reference to protected statements." Similarly, the results of phallometric testing conducted during the assessment were also excluded as "protected statements."[122] Consistent with the rulings in R. v. D.K., any opinions or findings arising, or based upon, a section 672.11 assessment should not be admissible at

---

119   See R. v. Snow (1992), 76 C.C.C. (3d) 43 (Ont. Gen. Div.). Although s. 672.11(e) appears to apply post-conviction, it only relates to a s. 747.1(1) treatment order, and that provision has never been proclaimed in force.

120   Criminal Code, s. 672.21(1).

121   [1999] O.J. No. 5063, Weekes J. (Ont. S.C.) (QL).

122   See R. v. D.K. (No. 2), [2000] O.J. No. 8 (Ont. S.C.) (QL).

the sentencing stage without consent. An opinion which was formulated before the 1991 amendments, or which can be isolated from protected statements, can be admissible for sentencing purposes subject to the offender's right to dispute it.

## 2) Using *Mental Health Act* Powers to Remand for Assessment

While it is clear that a section 672.11 assessment cannot be ordered to generate material for sentencing purposes,[123] in some cases resort has been made to provincial mental health legislation to provide a vehicle to fill this arguable gap. In R. v. *Lenart*,[124] prior to sentencing convictions for arson and dangerous driving, the trial judge ordered a thirty-day remand to a psychiatric facility to obtain an assessment. This was done over the objections of defence counsel and on the apparent authority of sections 21 and 22 of the *Mental Health Act*.[125] With reference to the subsequent psychiatric report that diagnosed the offender as having a "personality disorder with anti-social features," the judge sentenced the offender to terms of eighteen months and six months consecutive for a total of two years. On appeal against sentence, the Court of Appeal entertained a constitutional challenge based on a "distribution of legislative powers" argument but did not hear a section 7 argument since it had not been raised below.[126] The majority[127] upheld the application of the *Mental Health Act* powers to the sentencing stage of the criminal process concluding that the pith and substance of the legislation was mental health, a matter within provincial competence; it only touched on federal matters and did not conflict with any federal provisions. In dissent, Goudge J.A. took a very different view even to the extent of doubting whether, on their face, sections 21 and 22 could

---

123   This was confirmed by Finlayson J.A. for the majority in R. v. *Lenart* (1998), 123 C.C.C. (3d) 353 (Ont. C.A.) [*Lenart*].

124   *Ibid.*

125   R.S.O. 1990, c. M.7.

126   Relying on R. v. *Ryan* (1992), 12 C.R. (4th) 173 (Ont. C.A.). Clearly, the s. 7 *Charter* argument was based on the protections against self-incrimination embodied in s. 7. One can also conceive of an argument under s. 9 that the detention, unrelated to the purposes of the *Mental Health Act*, is arbitrary even if it is justifiable under a division of powers analysis.

127   Finlayson J.A. with Abella J.A. concurring.

apply to the situation of a convicted person who is in custody.[128] With respect to the divisions of powers issue, he held the provisions of the *Mental Health Act* should be read down to prevent unconstitutional intrusion into the federal sphere of sentencing:

> It seems to me that the doctrine of interjurisdictional immunity has become unshakably imbedded in our jurisprudence. Moreover, it is a valuable judicial tool in the increasingly complex and sophisticated world of modern federalism. Clearly a valid provincial law can affect a federal subject but only up to the point that, in the language of Beetz J., the application of that provincial law would bear upon the federal subject in what makes it specifically of federal jurisdiction. If the proposed application of the provincial law would affect a signature dimension of the federal subject, that is, if it affects the core of that subject, then the provincial law must be read down to exclude that application.
>
> Finlayson J.A. would limit the application of the doctrine to provincial legislation that is prohibitive. He would not extend it to provincial legislation that is permissive. With respect, I disagree with this limitation. . . .[129]

His disagreement was based on the recognition of how the psychiatric material would relate to the criminal process and thereby intrude into federal jurisdiction. First, the material generated by the assessment would likely always be used in the subsequent sentencing and would be central to that function. Second, the process employed to obtain the material was directly invasive and diminished the liberty of the offender. While the majority had referred to the absence of a reference to sentencing in section 672.11 as a gap that could usefully be filled by the *Mental Health Act* provisions, Goudge J.A. found the conspicuous absence of sentencing to reflect an express decision about the extent of intrusions which Parliament would countenance.

Given the fact that the entire section 672 represented a comprehensive overhaul of the way in which the criminal process deals with mental disorder issues, including psychiatric assessments and remands, Goudge J.A. must be right that the absence of sentencing

---

128 Goudge J.A. notes that s. 21 of the *Mental Health Act* contemplates individuals, including a convicted person who is out of custody, and authorizes an order requiring attendance at a psychiatric facilty for an assessment. Section 22 applies to someone in custody charged with an offence and permits a remand to a psychiatric facility for an assessment. Neither speaks to a person who has already been convicted and is in custody.

129 *Lenart*, above note 123 at 382.

purposes in section 672.11 is significant and cannot be treated as if it were an oversight. To permit reliance on the *Mental Health Act* powers is to permit provincial legislation to subvert the federal approach to an issue within its sphere of competence. Unfortunately, it appears that the decision in *Lenart* was not appealed to the Supreme Court of Canada. For Ontario, this leaves a questionable precedent, one which reflects a pragmatic concern to provide the sentencing judge with psychiatric material when the accused does not consent and the *Criminal Code* does not permit it. However, it must be remembered that the *Lenart* decision does not address *Charter* arguments which may present other opportunities to insulate an offender from compulsory psychiatric assessment for sentencing purposes.

# K. JUDICIAL NOTICE AND SENTENCING

In *R. v. Gladue*,[130] the Supreme Court explained the sentencing judge's duty under section 718.2(e) in relation to aboriginal persons. Clearly, it is necessary for judges to carry out the sentencing function informed by relevant background information as it relates to aboriginal people in general and the offender in particular. Speaking of the problem of over-incarceration and both the history and residue of systemic discrimination, the Court said:

> How then is the consideration of s.718.2(e) to proceed in the daily functioning of the courts? The manner in which the sentencing judge will carry out his or her statutory duty may vary from case to case. In all instances it will be necessary for the judge to take judicial notice of the systemic or background factors and the approach to sentencing which is relevant to aboriginal offenders.[131]

The usual evidentiary rule for judicial notice involves a fact which is either so notoriously known and beyond dispute, or so easily provable by readily accessible sources, that the court can dispense with formal proof.[132] There is, however, some support for taking notice of "social framework facts" in the joint decision of L'Heureux-Dubé and McLachlin JJ. in *R. v. S.(R.D.).*[133] The Supreme Court has confirmed this function

---

130   Above note 10.
131   *Ibid.* at 731–32.
132   See D. Paciocco & L. Stuesser, *The Law of Evidence*, 2d ed. (Toronto: Irwin Law, 1999) at 285–88.
133   [1997] 3 S.C.R. 484 505–9.

in relation to the situation of aboriginal persons for sentencing purposes but it has also outlined the current and historical situation so that the essence of what can be judicially noticed has been, to a great extent, particularized in *Gladue* itself. There may well be other situations in different parts of the country where social framework may bear heavily on sentencing issues. Perhaps there will be more scope for the use of judicial notice. If the facts are controversial, however, this is not the right vehicle to deal with them; it would be preferable if sentencing judges used the new powers in sections 723(3) and (4) to determine the relevant background information.

Another situation where it may be tempting to contemplate judicial notice is in relation to the issue of prevalence of a particular crime in a community. This can have relevance to sentencing although there is a controversy about the legitimate limits of exemplary sentencing. Judges must, if they are concerned about the issue of prevalence, ensure that they act only on proven facts. Even when evidence is adduced from police authorities, courts have placed stringent requirements on the quality of statistical summaries before they will take them into account.[134] More to the point, courts have directed sentencing judges not to make assumptions about prevalence from their own day-to-day experience.[135] There are too many unknown factors that go into the make-up of the dockets to derive any valuable evidence from the number of cases that seem to come forward. The comments in *Gladue* about judicial notice should not be taken out of context to expand in general terms the sentencing judges' ability to dispense with proof.

## L.  JOINT SUBMISSIONS

Plea negotiations can result in a mutual position as to the appropriate sentence, or at least some aspect of the sentence. This is known as a joint submission. A trial judge is not bound by a joint submission but it must be given serious consideration.[136] While some may suggest that a trial judge can depart from a joint submission simply because she disagrees with it, a tougher standard was offered by the Martin Commit-

---

134   Compare *R. v. Johnas* (1982), 2 C.C.C. (3d) 490 at 492–93 (Alta. C.A.) with *R. v. Petrovic* (1984), 47 O.R. (2d) 97 at 109–10 (C.A.).

135   *R. v. Priest* (1996), 110 C.C.C. (3d) 289 at 279–80, Rosenberg J.A. (Ont. C.A.).

136   See *R. v. Rubenstein* (1987), 41 C.C.C. (3d) 91 (Ont. C.A.).

tee.[137] It recognized that the joint submission is not binding but is entitled to "great weight" in order to bring some certainty to resolution discussions. It suggested that the proper test for justifying a departure is whether the proposed sentence brings the administration of justice into disrepute or is otherwise contrary to the public interest.[138] One can add to this the proviso that the sentence does not constitute an error in principle. Regardless of the nature of the negotiations that produced the joint submission, sentencing is done in open court and the record should contain sufficient information to support the sentence. Given the general acceptance of the Martin Committee test, the joint submission should usually be followed. When a judge decides not to do so, the record should clearly indicate the basis for the departure. This is especially true when the sentence imposed is harsher than that submitted by the parties who, it can be assumed, know more about the case than the sentencing judge. Even when there is no joint submission, some courts have taken the position that the judge should not impose a harsher sentence than that submitted by the Crown without a "valid and compelling reason."[139]

## M. LENGTHY ADJOURNMENTS OF THE SENTENCING HEARING

In many cases, sentencing will follow immediately upon the entry of a conviction or a finding of guilt. In other situations, an adjournment will be required to enable counsel to prepare their sentencing positions. Section 720 of the *Criminal Code* now provides that the court "shall, as soon as practicable after an offender has been found guilty, conduct proceedings to determine the appropriate sentence to be imposed." A substantial number of authorities have also denounced lengthy delays in sentencing. The traditional view has been that the sentencing should respond to the offence and the circumstances of the offender and that it is inappropriate to use a lengthy adjournment as a

---

137   Ontario, Attorney General, *Report of the Attorney General's Advisory Committee on Charge Screening, Disclosure and Resolutions Discussions* (Toronto: The Committee, 1993) (Chair: G.A. Martin).

138   *Ibid.* at 16, recommendation 58.

139   *R. v. Winn* (1995), 43 C.R. (4th) 71 (Ont. Prov. Div.).

threat to induce proper behaviour.[140] Most of these decisions arose in situations where the sentencing judge had used the threat of the future sentence to coerce good behaviour pending the imposition of that sentence. By this method, an offender could be controlled for periods longer than warranted by the offence. Accordingly, the rejection of lengthy delays was premised, quite appropriately, on concerns about the unfairness and uncertainty that can flow from delay.

In the modern context, however, a new issue has arisen. Many offenders come to court with long-term drug and alcohol addictions, or other personal problems, which contribute significantly to their criminality. As well, some offenders come from communities that have developed special community-based or restorative justice responses to local offences. The particular offence facing the sentencing judge may point to custody, but most observers would agree that a non-custodial alternative that successfully re-integrates the offender as a healthy member of the community would be preferable[141] if the offender is sincerely committed to reformation. Recently, having heard from an aboriginal sentencing circle regarding an offender who exhibited serious alcohol abuse problems, a judge considered that a lengthy adjournment for rehabilitative purposes was permissible because of the relevance of the problem to future conduct and the impossibility of assessing treatment sincerity beforehand.[142] Without referring to this decision, the Saskatchewan Court of Appeal has rejected the power to postpone sentence. In a controversial decision, it heard a Crown appeal in a case involving a sentencing circle which recommended banishment to a remote island.[143] The judge had accepted the circle's recommendation but, rather than imposing a final sentence, adjourned the matter for one year and gave effect to the recommendation by altering the bail conditions. The court allowed the Crown appeal holding that it was an error to delay sentencing in this way.

These cases involve what is sometimes known as "therapeutic" adjournments. The terms of the offender's release are varied to include

---

140  See *R. v. Fuller*, [1969] 3 C.C.C. 348 (Man. C.A.). See also G. Renaud, "*R. v. Fuller*: Time to Brush Aside the Rule Prohibiting Therapeutic Remands?" (1993) 35 Crim. L.Q. 91 & 156. There is some pre-twentieth century authority for the practice of "respite," whereby at common law judgment or sentencing could be postponed to a future date: see *Keen* v. *The Queen* (1847), 116 E.R. 352, Cox C.C. 340 (Q.B.).

141  See, for example, *R. v. Preston* (1990), 79 C.R. (3d) 61 (B.C.C.A.).

142  See *R. v. N.(D.)* (1993), 27 C.R. (4th) 114 (Y. Terr. Ct.).

143  See *R. v. T.(W.B.)* (1995), 104 C.C.C. (3d) 346 (Sask. C.A.).

the recommended attendance or participation and the case postponed until some solid information can be provided about the success or failure of the approach. These lengthy adjournments seem, on quick analysis, to violate section 720 and run in the face of appellate authority. However, if they are granted on consent for the benefit of the offender, they do not implicate the concerns about coercion, unfairness, and uncertainty that underlie most of the older authorities. Especially when dealing with offenders in areas where constructive resources exist, judges should be encouraged to be creative. Section 720 is part of the 1996 amendments, which include a new interest in non-custodial sentences:[144] it should not be applied in a manner that makes it an obstacle to constructive sentencing. Certainly, this is a strong argument when the offender is an aboriginal person and section 718.2(e) applies.[145] There is no reason why it should not be an acceptable approach for all offenders when resources are available and there is some prospect that a sincere and timely effort may produce significant change.

## FURTHER READINGS

GREEN, R.G., *Justice in Aboriginal Communities: Sentencing Alternatives* (Saskatoon: Purich Publishing, 1998)

RENAUD, G., "*R. v. Fuller*: Time to Brush Aside the Rule Prohibiting Therapeutic Remands" (1993) 35 Crim. L.Q.

ROACH, K., *Due Process and Victims' Rights: The New Law and Politics of Criminal Justice* (Toronto: University of Toronto Press, 1999)

---

144   See the discussion of *Gladue*, above note 10, and in Chapter at 4(D)(4).
145   See *Gladue*, *ibid*.

# CHAPTER 9

# SENTENCING OPTIONS

## A. INTRODUCTION

Over the past thirty-odd years, a number of important studies have influenced thinking about sentencing options but the most significant work has been done by the Ouimet Committee,[1] the Law Reform Commission of Canada,[2] and the Canadian Sentencing Commission.[3] Common to all these groups was the acceptance of the principle of restraint, especially as it relates to imprisonment and the need for more non-custodial options. Since the Ouimet Report in 1969, Parliament has added some new alternatives to the sentencing matrix: discharges, intermittent sentences, and conditional sentences. During the same period, judges have been creative in their use of probation orders to embrace new ideas like community service orders and, in some jurisdictions, electronic monitoring. The following discussion canvasses all available

---

1   See Report of the Canadian Committee on Corrections, *Toward Unity: Criminal Justice and Corrections* (Ottawa: Queen's Printer, 1969) (Chair: R. Ouimet) [*Ouimet Report*].
2   See Law Reform Commission of Canada, *A Report on Dispositions and Sentences in the Criminal Process: Guidelines* (Ottawa: The Commission, 1976) [*Law Reform Commission Report*].
3   Canadian Sentencing Commission, *Sentencing Reform: A Canadian Approach* (Ottawa: Supply and Services Canada, 1987) (Chair: J.R. Omer Archambault) [*Report of the Canadian Sentencing Commission*].

sentencing options, from the least intrusive to imprisonment, the harshest penalty available in Canada. How a sanction relates to the objectives of sentencing in section 718 of the *Criminal Code* can be determined by asking whether it is punitive, incapacitative, rehabilitative, or reparative in nature. The goal of this chapter is not to provide a criminological or penological critique of the various options; it is simply to explain the pre-conditions, principles, and technical consequences of each available sanction.

# B. DIVERSION

By definition, diversion is not a sentencing option since it involves removing someone from the criminal process to another forum where they are not convicted or found guilty, and are not sentenced. They are, however, usually required to take responsibility for their actions and expected to do something in response. The idea of diverting people from the criminal process is not new. Police have been doing it for years in various forms, the warning being the most rudimentary one. To a lesser extent, prosecutors have been instruments of diversion when they have withdrawn charges because the conduct does not seem to warrant a criminal sanction or the small degree of damage done has been repaired.

More recently, communities have become involved in voluntary diversion programs where, in a stipulated set of circumstances, the offender is directed to the diversion project. Then, an appropriate disposition like an apology, community service, or reparative gesture is proposed. If performed, the police or prosecutors are informed and the charge is subsequently withdrawn. If not performed, the matter may be returned to court. Another example occurs when people appear to have psychiatric problems and, instead of a criminal charge, the resources of the mental health system are invoked.

The *Young Offenders Act* included a specific procedure for diversion which was known as "alternative measures."[4] With identical wording, "alternative measures" for adults was added to the *Criminal Code* in 1996 through the enactment of section 717. This provision contains a number of significant features. The offender must be given an opportunity to consult counsel, must admit responsibility, and must consent to participation.[5] As well, the prosecutor must have "sufficient evidence

---

4   *Young Offenders Act*, R.S.C. 1985, c. Y-1, s. 4.
5   *Criminal Code*, s. 717(1)(c), (d), & (e).

to proceed with the prosecution of the offence."[6] In other words, diversion should not be used if the appropriate prosecutorial response is to withdraw the charge because there is no likelihood of conviction. Another feature of section 717, translated from the *Young Offenders Act*, is that the prosecutor is the gatekeeper: that is, the judge cannot order the invocation of alternative measures — it must either be commenced, or at the very least endorsed, by the Crown. As well, section 717(1)(a) refers to "a program of alternative measures authorized by the Attorney General or the Attorney General's delegate" which adds a layer of bureaucracy that may discourage local initiatives. Given that the decision to use alternative measures rests with the Crown, who should know local resources, the need for program approval seems superfluous.

# C. ABSOLUTE AND CONDITIONAL DISCHARGES

## 1) Discharges and the Ouimet Committee

The 1969 report of the Ouimet Committee on Corrections expressed concern about the "handicaps that accompany a criminal record" and recommended that courts have the power, after considering the "nature of the charge and the character of the accused" to decide not to record a conviction after a finding of guilt.[7] In the Committee's view, the offender would either be discharged absolutely or subject to conditions, and an absolute discharge would have the same effect as an acquittal.[8] If conditions were attached, they would include the requirement to "keep the peace and be of good behaviour" and, if ordered, could also include probation supervision. If the offender violated a condition, he or she could be returned to court where a conviction could be entered and a sentence imposed. Although a first offender who had committed a minor offence was used as an example of someone worthy of a discharge, this was not offered as a pre-condition. The only criterion specifically recommended by Ouimet was that the person had not previously been given a discharge. Most of these recommendations found their way into the new legislation.

6   *Ibid.*, s. 717(1)(f).
7   *Ouimet Report*, above note 1 at 194–95.
8   *Ibid.* at 194.

## 2) The *Criminal Code* Provisions

Enacted in 1972, the discharge provisions gave courts the power to relieve against both the fact and stigma of a criminal conviction.[9] Now, an offender, other than a corporation, may be granted an absolute or conditional discharge which means that, notwithstanding a finding of guilt, the offender is "deemed not to have been convicted."[10] Even if a judge jumps the gun and orally registers a conviction immediately upon accepting a guilty plea, hearing a verdict, or reaching a finding of guilt, this does not prevent entertaining a discharge application.[11] In any case where there is a finding of guilt and a discharge, the offender can still appeal the finding of guilt if they believe that it was reached in error.[12] At the same time, a finding of guilt stands as a bar to a subsequent prosecution.[13]

If a person is discharged with conditions, those are controlled by a probation order under section 731(2). During the currency of that order, if the person is convicted of another offence, including the offence of breaching the probation order, he or she may be brought back to court on the original charge, at which time a conviction can be entered and a sentence imposed.[14]

The only offences excluded from the discharge provisions are those requiring a minimum penalty or those punishable by life or fourteen years imprisonment.[15] There are no strict pre-requisites except that a discharge must be in the offender's best interests and not contrary to

9   See *Criminal Law Amendment Act, 1972*, S.C. 1972, c. 13, s. 57. It has been suggested that the impetus for the 1972 amendments, in addition to the Ouimet recommendation, was the concern about the large number of young people convicted for marijuana possession who could be prejudiced in the future because of the employment, travel or immigration implications of a conviction: see A. Edgar, "Sentencing Options in Canada" in J.V. Roberts & D.P. Cole, eds., *Making Sense of Sentencing* (Toronto: University of Toronto Press, 1999) 112 at 119.

10  *Criminal Code*, s. 730(3).

11  See *R. v. Sampson* (1975), 23 C.C.C. (2d) 65 (Ont. C.A.) [*Sampson*].

12  *Criminal Code*, s. 730(3)(a).

13  Section 730(3)(c), *ibid.*, ensures that the offender can plead "autrefois convict" to a subsequent charge for the same offence.

14  *Ibid.*, s. 730(4). This power may be exercised "in addition to or in lieu" of the power in s. 732.2(5)(e) which, in the case of a conditional discharge, enables the prosecutor to apply to have a probation condition changed or the term of the probation extended for not more than one year.

15  This re-condition refers to the offence for which the sentence is being considered, not the offence which generated the prosecution. So, if a person was convicted of an included offence punishable by less than fourteen years imprisonment, a discharge would be available regardless of the maximum punishment for the larger offence: see *Sampson*, above note 11.

the public interest.[16] While one would assume that a discharge would always be beneficial to the offender, this has been interpreted as requiring a finding that the case presents no concern about individual deterrence and the offender appears to be a person of "good character." In other words, "it is not necessary to enter a conviction against him in order to deter him from future offences or to rehabilitate him."[17] It is not even a pre-condition that the offender not have received a discharge before, although a previous discharge may say something about the offender's character which suggests a need for individual deterrence.[18]

It is an error to exclude an individual from consideration simply because he or she is not young.[19] A common reason for requesting a discharge is the desire to avoid specific consequences of a conviction, often relating to immigration status, professional qualification, or other employment issues. However, the fact that a conviction would not present immediate negative consequences to the offender is no reason to deny a discharge;[20] implicitly, the benefit to the individual is the ability to go through life without the stamp of a conviction. The major issue is whether a discharge somehow prejudices the public interest.

## 3)  Discharges and the Public Interest

The role of the public interest is difficult to define. It is not framed in the restrictive terms of public safety or danger but in the larger language of "the public interest" which conjures up concerns beyond the individual offender. Early cases focused on the issue of general deterrence,[21] but more recent decisions have canvassed issues that relate to the institutional role of the sentencing process. Still, the genesis for the discharge sanction was the concern that the negative consequences of a conviction, whether immediate or potential, would outweigh any value to be gained from the formal stigmatization of the offender as a convicted person. Accordingly, it should be the individual consequence which is eval-

---

16   *Criminal Code*, s. 730(1).

17   See *R. v. Fallofield* (1973), 13 C.C.C. (2d) 450 at 454–55 (B.C.C.A.). See also *R. v. Sanchez-Pino* (1973), 11 C.C.C. (2d) 53 at 58–60 (Ont. C.A.).

18   See *R. v. Elsharawy* (1997), 119 C.C.C. (3d) 565 at 569 (Nfld. C.A.) [*Elsharawy*]; and *R. v. Stuckless*, [1999] N.S.J. No. 352 (S.C.). Both cases consider *R. v. Tan* (1974), 22 C.C.C. (2d) 184 (B.C.C.A.) and conclude that it does not stand for the proposition that a person cannot receive a second discharge.

19   See *R. v. Culley* (1977), 36 C.C.C. (2d) 433 (Ont. C.A.).

20   See *R. v. Myers* (1977), 37 C.C.C. (2d) 182 (Ont. C.A.).

21   See *Fallofield*, above note 17 at 455.

uated in the circumstances of the offence. There is no need to show that the public interest would be promoted or enhanced by a discharge. The test is simply whether permitting the offender to avoid the stigma of a conviction undermines the public interest in some definable way.

In *R. v. Bram*,[22] a fifty-eight-year-old "skip tracer" was convicted of offering money to employees of a telephone company to provide confidential information. He was a holocaust survivor who was described as an "upright citizen." For a time at least, he did not appreciate that what he was doing was an offence. The trial judge gave him an absolute discharge and the Crown appealed. Relying on an earlier decision,[23] the court started its analysis with the proposition that "an absolute discharge should be used sparingly in the interests of preserving the general deterrence principle of criminal sentencing." However, it added that discharges are not to be restricted to cases of "trivial or unintentional offences." While the seriousness of the offence is relevant, it is not determinative.[24] The Alberta Court of Appeal upheld the absolute discharge on the basis that the offence was not prevalent, the offender received little benefit from it, and there was confidence he would not re-offend. While the court's focus was primarily on the issues of deterrence, it added the observation that it did not appear that "the public interest requires that persons dealing with him in the future be able to determine that the offence was committed."

It is easy to understand the rationale for a discharge in the abstract. Situations will arise, especially for young first offenders, where the lifelong stigma and potential adverse consequences of a conviction are not warranted by the conduct in question. However, other cases move beyond the abstract and present real and immediate consequences which will flow directly from a criminal conviction.

### a) Public Interest vs. Immigration Status
Courts commonly hear the argument that an individual's immigration status may be affected by a conviction. Certainly, there is an inadmissible

---

22  (1982), 30 C.R. (3d) 398 (Alta. C.A.) [*Bram*].

23  *R. v. MacFarlane* (1976), 55 A.R. 222 (C.A.).

24  See, for example, *R. v. Prestone* (1998), 47 M.V.R. (3d) 130, Barnett, T.C.J. (Y. Terr. Ct.) (dangerous driving). See also *R. v. Kilukishak*, [1989] N.W.T.J. No. 86, De Weerdt J. (S.C.) (QL), dismissing a Crown appeal against an absolute discharge in a case of spousal assault involving a young accused who had reconciled with his wife. De Weerdt J. spoke of the public interest in encouragaing the healing of family conflict, notwithstanding concerns about the prevalence of the offence.

class defined by conviction for certain offences.[25] There is also the concern that anyone awaiting determination of immigration status may be prejudiced by the fact of a criminal conviction even if it does not move the individual into an inadmissible category. Courts have considered the relation between immigration status and discharges and have generally held that the negative consequence does not, by itself, justify a discharge.[26] In R. v. *Shokohi-Manesh*,[27] the offender was found guilty of possessing a stolen cellular phone. The offender claimed he had found the phone. The judge concluded that he had converted it to his own use after finding it outside a restaurant. The Crown opposed a discharge because of the value of the item. The judge rejected a discharge. He convicted and suspended sentence for two years with a standard probation order. The Court of Appeal was advised that the conviction presented a bar to the offender's claim for refugee status in Canada. Noting that he was a first offender, Taylor J.A. said:

> Clearly, the granting of a discharge will not in itself ensure that the appellant's application before the immigration authorities will in fact be approved. But I think the fact that here a refusal of a discharge would absolutely bar him from consideration for refugee status admission is a consideration that, in this particular case, can properly be given weight without offending the public interest.[28]

Noting his age, good employment record, and remorse, the court allowed the appeal and entered an absolute discharge.

### b)  Public Interest vs. Employment Consequences

Another common claim is based on employment consequences. In R. v. *Burke*,[29] the appellant was one of a number of Christian Brothers who had been prosecuted for various offences of abuse against boys residing at the Mount Cashel Orphanage. After a successful appeal to the Supreme Court on more serious matters, he remained convicted of assault causing bodily harm consisting of beating a nine-year-old on the buttocks with a plastic belt. He sought a discharge so that he could return to teaching. He had left Mount Cashel and Newfoundland in 1981, but

---

25   See s. 19(1)(c) of the *Immigration Act*, R.S.C. 1985, c. I-2, which makes inadmissible the class of persons who have been convicted in Canada of an offence punishable by a maximum of ten years imprisonment.

26   See R. v. *Melo* (1975), 26 C.C.C. (2d) 510 (Ont. C.A.).

27   (1992), 69 C.C.C. (3d) 286 (B.C.C.A.).

28   *Ibid.* at 288.

29   (1996), 108 C.C.C. (3d) 360 (Nfld. C.A.) [*Burke*].

had been the subject of media scrutiny and public denunciation for a number of years along with other former employees at Mount Cashel. The court received a large number of letters of support from former students, co-workers, and others attesting to his integrity and dedication as a teacher. Remarking that there was no need for individual deterrence, the court concluded that "it would obviously be in the public interest for a person of his calibre to return to the teaching profession."[30] In setting aside the conviction and replacing it with an absolute discharge, the court noted that its ruling should not be perceived as a minimization of the seriousness of the offence committed by the offender, but rather a function of his suitability for the sanction given its "intent and meaning."[31] The court also noted the "severe repercussions" already suffered by the offender, likely referring to the public condemnation, which also satisfied the need for denunciation. This suggests that a discharge is available even in serious cases so long as the function of denunciation has been satisfied and there is ample support for a personal claim that a conviction will produce additional consequences not justifed in the circumstances.

Difficult considerations apply when the accused is a police officer. While a finding of guilt may produce professional consequences, a conviction may be a career-ending event. Courts have expressed concern about the need to assure members of the public that they can expect law enforcement officers to respect the law.[32] As a result, in most cases where the offence is an assault on a prisoner in custody or under arrest, discharges are not commonly granted.[33]

c)  The Need to Denounce: Sports Cases
Recently, a number of cases involving assaults in sports have been decided. In *R. v. Aussem*, a conditional discharge was denied to a twenty-two-year-old hockey player convicted of assault with a weapon for striking another player with a stick.[34] The judge concluded that a discharge would be contrary to the public interest since it would "tend to diminish the serious nature of these assaults, thereby sending an incorrect message to the players, officials, and spectators." This reflects a concern that a response to the offender's personal claim of potential adverse consequences will be viewed as leniency that would detract

---

30  *Ibid.* at 363.
31  *Ibid.* at 364.
32  See *R. v. Bottrell (No. 2)* (1981), 62 C.C.C. (2d) 45 (B.C.C.A.).
33  See *Bottrell (No. 2), ibid.*; and *R. v. Griffin* (1975), 23 C.C.C. (2d) 11 (P.E.I. C.A.).
34  [1997] O.J. No. 5582 (Prov. Div.) (QL).

216 THE LAW OF SENTENCING

from the need to denounce the offence. Here, the central issue is the need to ensure recognition of the conduct as a criminal offence. Similar conclusions have been reached in cases where parents supporting their children at sporting events had turned arguments with officials into assaults. Again, the need for denunciation in the sense of underscoring the criminal nature of the conduct has persuaded trial judges not to grant discharges to mature offenders with no previous record.[35]

### d) Conclusion

A useful summary of the relevant considerations under the "not contrary to the public interest" aspect can be found in R. v. *Waters* where an accused was convicted of mischief and fined $450.[36] He was a Greenpeace activist who had tresspassed and committed the offence of hanging a banner citing the dangers of uranium mining. On appeal, Wedge J. considered the prospect of a discharge and the public interest. In substituting a conditional discharge for the conviction and fine, she said:

> The second condition precedent is that a discharge would not be against the public interest. This condition involves a consideration of the principle of general deterrence. In determining whether a particular sentence is necessary to deter others who would act in like manner, I must take note of the gravity of the offence, its incidence in the community, public attitude towards it and public confidence in the effective enforcement of the criminal law. The interest of the public must be given due weight, but does not preclude the use of the discharge provisions.[37]

This succinct explanation of the relevant considerations was recently adopted and applied by the Newfoundland Court of Appeal.[38]

Of course, the genesis of the discharge option is to provide a way to avoid the stigma of a criminal conviction in appropriate cases. Accordingly, where the individual circumstances indicate an inordinate penalty because of a certain or likely adverse consequence, the sentencing court should be prepared to contemplate a discharge even if the offence on its

---

35  See R. v. Bebis, [1989] O.J. No. 1620 (Dist. Ct.) (QL); and R. v. *Musselman*, [1999] O.J. No. 4666 (Sup. Ct.) (QL). Obviously, the recent case of Marty McSorley, a professional hockey player who received a conditional discharge for assaulting an opponent with a hockey stick, stands in contrast to the cases discussed above. See G.V. Krainetz, "Crime, No Punishment," *Globe and Mail*, October 9, 2000.

36  (1990), 54 C.C.C. (3d) 40 (Sask. Q.B).

37  *Ibid.* at 47.

38  See *Elsharawy*, above note 18 at 567.

face may suggest some reason to consider general deterrence or denunciation; sometimes, the denunciation can be achieved in other ways.[39]

In other cases, the inordinate penalty, especially after taking into account the consequences of a public trial and finding of guilt, may be sufficient to sustain a discharge even for a more serious offence.[40] Given the importance of employment to social integration, when a criminal conviction would disentitle the offender from continuing an occupation, or pursuing one for which some commitment has been shown, courts should be careful not to overstate the public interest in a conviction. Of course, the argument for a discharge is diminished if there is a link between the conduct which produced the offence and the occupation or employment in issue.[41] Similarly, when considering a claim based on immigration status, the key issue is whether the collateral effect of denying the opportunity to live in Canada would be an inordinate penalty. The level of culpability is an important ingredient, determined both by the gravity of the offence and the offender's level of participation. While the criminal courts should not be treating offences with impunity, neither should they be the moral guardians of Canada's immigration policy. For a discharge, the issue is always whether the offence committed by this offender warrants the stigma and consequences of a conviction.

## 4) The Effect of a Discharge

It is commonly assumed that a discharge does not produce a criminal record. More accurately, it does not produce a record of a criminal conviction. The Ouimet Committee had argued that a discharge should be tantamount to an acquittal. (In Canadian law, we do not distinguish between kinds of acquittals; all stand for innocence regardless of how they were achieved.)[42] However, while section 730(3) says that an offender is "deemed not to have been convicted of the offence," it does not treat the discharge as tantamount to an acquittal since the finding of guilt is not expunged. In fact, there is a record of the discharge.[43] Accordingly, when questioned about previous involvement with the criminal justice system, some care should be taken before answering. A person who has been

---

39   See *Burke*, above note 29.
40   This is especially appropriate if there are factors which mitigate moral culpability: see *R. v. Bowden*, [1999] O.J. No. 142 (C.A.).
41   See the discussion of "collateral or indirect consequences" in Chapter 7, above, at 7(B)(7).
42   See *Grdic v. R.*, [1985] 1 S.C.R. 810 [*Grdic*].
43   See note 44, below.

granted a discharge can honestly respond "no" if asked whether he or she has a previous conviction or even a criminal record. However, if the question is whether they have ever been found guilty then the situation is different. A truthful answer would be: "Yes, but I was given a discharge." Moreover, there is the pardon issue. Until 1992, people who had been granted discharges had to apply for pardons but now the record of a discharge is automatically purged from the system. This suggests that when a record of a discharge is no longer accessible, the effect is tantamount to receiving a pardon. Prior to expungement, one would have to acknowledge the finding of guilt for which a record would exist.

These distinctions are not trivial nor are they simply semantic. Permitting questions about discharges for employment or professional purposes undercuts the conceptual premise for the discharge. Potential consequences while travelling abroad are also serious. It would have been preferable if Parliament had followed Ouimet and treated a discharge as tantamount to an acquittal, even if it qualified the status by allowing its disclosure during a subsequent sentencing for a limited period of time.

The *Criminal Records Act*[44] deals expressly with the discharge record and provides limits on disclosure:

> 6.1(1) No record of a discharge under section 730 of the Criminal Code that is in the custody of the Commissioner or of any department or agency of the Government of Canada shall be disclosed to any person, nor shall the existence of the record or the fact of the discharge be disclosed to any person, without the prior approval of the Minister, if
>
> (a)  more than one year has elapsed since the offender was discharged absolutely; or
>
> (b)  more than three years have elapsed since the offender was discharged on the conditions prescribed in a probation order.
>
> (2) The Commissioner shall remove all references to a discharge under section 730 of the Criminal Code from the automated criminal conviction records retrieval system maintained by the Royal Canadian Mounted Police on the expiration of the relevant period referred to in subsection (1).

Accordingly, a discharge record cannot be disclosed one year after an absolute discharge and three years after the expiry of the conditions attached to a conditional discharge without Ministerial approval. If a local

---

44   R.S.C. 1985, c. C-47, as amended by S.C. 1992, c. 22, ss. 1–10.

prosecutor wanted to indicate to a sentencing court that a discharge ought not to be considered because the offender had previously received one, this submission could not be made after the expiry of the relevant period without the consent of the Solicitor General of Canada. While it may be argued that dicta in *R. v. Elsharawy*[45] suggests that the behaviour which generated the earlier prosecution will always be relevant even if the finding cannot be proven, the circumstances in that case did not address whether the *Criminal Records Act* precludes disclosure absolutely.[46]

# D. PROBATION

## 1) A Brief History of Probation

The origins of probation[47] can be traced to American and English roots in the first half of the nineteenth century. In England, Matthew Davenport Hill was a Recorder in Birmingham from 1839 to 1865. He began the practice of releasing young offenders into the guardianship of local citizens. A "confidential officer" was used to follow cases and report on their success or failure. In 1876, the Church of England Temperance Society appointed a missionary to work in the Southwark Police Court. His job was to offer aid to alcoholic offenders. Soon, the number of missionaries in courts increased dramatically. The practice developed of offering the supervision of a missionary after a finding of guilt for certain offences in the place of a sentence. This was formalized in legislation in 1887.[48] In 1907, the *Probation of Offenders Act*[49] was enacted,

---

45 Above note 18.
46 *Ibid.* at 568–69. The issue in this case was whether the previous finding meant that the offender was not a first offender even though the previous finding related to a subsequent offence.
47 See R. Harris, "Probation Round the World: Origins and Development" in K. Hamai et al., eds., *Probation Round the World: A Comparative Study* (London: Routledge, 1995) 25.
48 For a discussion of the genesis and terms of the *Probation of First Offenders Act, 1887* (U.K.), 50 & 51 Vict., c. 25, see L. Radzinowicz & R. Hood, *The Emergence of Penal Policy in Victorian and Edwardian England*, vol. 5 of *A History of English Criminal Law and Its Administration from 1750* (London: Stevens & Sons, 1986) at 635–39.
49 *An Act to permit the Release on Probation of Offenders in certain cases, and for other matters incidental thereto, 1907* (U.K.) 7 Edw. 7, c. 17. See the discussion in Radzinowicz & Hood, above note 48 at 642–47. See also G. Mair, "Community Penalties and the Probation Service" in M. Maguire, R. Morgan, & R. Reiner, eds., *The Oxford Handbook of Criminology*, 2d ed. (Oxford: Clarendon Press, 1997) 1195 at 1199.

which formally authorized a probation order, distinct from binding over, to be used in lieu of sentencing. The offender would be supervised for a period of time by an officer who would serve the sometimes contradictory role of both advisor and monitor. While the system anticipated the continued use of volunteers, the regular officers were to be paid a salary and not a per capita fee.

In the United States, a Boston shoemaker named John Augustus played a similar initiating role. He began visiting courts in 1841 concerned to provide help to alcoholic offenders. He would approach the court before trial and ask that offenders be bailed to his care. Subsequently, he would attend court with his charges to explain their progress and, if successful, a nominal sentence would be imposed. He expanded his efforts beyond alcoholics and historical accounts suggest that over a ten-year period he assisted over one thousand offenders.[50] In 1878, Massachusetts led the country by passing a probation statute which acknowledged the practice and gave institutional authority to what was referred to as reform without punishment. As in England, the efforts of volunteers provided the impetus for the addition of a non-punitive tool for responding to some groups of offenders.

Probation in Canada has followed the path of English developments, with an early form of probation accompanying the suspension of passing of sentence.[51] This is different from the mechanism of suspending the execution of a specific sentence already imposed.[52] In jurisdictions which suspend the execution of a sentence,[53] failure to abide by specified conditions can trigger the original sentence. If the passing of sentence has been suspended, then the remedy is to return the offender to court to have a fit sentence imposed. Section 971 of the *Criminal Code, 1892*, repeating the earlier provision borrowed from the English statute of 1887,[54] provided for a form of probation for first offenders. After a conviction for an offence punishable by not more than two years imprisonment, the court, taking into account the youth, character, and antecedents of the offender, and the "trivial nature of the

---

50   By 1858, 1946 persons had been bailed into Augustus' care: see Harris, above note 47 at 28–29.

51   See *An Act to permit the Conditional Release of First Offenders in Certain Cases, 1889* (Can.), 52 Vict., c. 44, s. 2.

52   Canadian courts have held that it is wrong for a judge to indicate a fixed term and then suspend the passing of sentence: see *R. v. Sangster* (1973), 21 C.R.N.S. 339 (Que. C.A.).

53   This is often the approach in civil law systems.

54   First enacted in Canada in 1889 by *An Act to permit the Conditional Release of First Offenders in Certain Cases, 1889* (Can.), 52 Vict., c. 44, s. 2.

offence," could order that he be released on recognizance with or without sureties. The statutory test in section 971 asked the question whether it was "expedient that the offender be released on probation of good conduct." The term of the recognizance was in the court's discretion and the only available conditions were to "keep the peace and be of good behaviour," and return to court when required. A related provison restricted this power to cases where either the offender or the surety had a "fixed place of abode or occupation" within the jurisdiction.[55] If the offender breached a term of the recognizance during its currency, he could be returned to court to be sentenced on the original charge.[56] While the potential duration of a recognizance was controversial, its length was capped at two years in the 1955 *Code* revision.[57]

While the provision discussed above is the predecessor to the current form of probation attached to a suspended sentence, the *Criminal Code, 1892,* also contained a statutory form of the common law power to "bind over" by recognizance, which could be attached to another sanction. Section 958 of the *Criminal Code, 1892,* empowered a sentencing judge "in addition to any sentence imposed," other than death, to enter into his own recognizances, or to give security to bind an offender over to

> . . . keep the peace, and be of good behaviour for any term not exceeding two years, and that such person in default shall be imprisoned for not more than one year after the expiry of his imprisonment under his sentence. . . .

The default referred to was the failure to enter into the recognizance or to post security, not a breach of condition after entering into the recognizance. As with the suspended sentence, the potential length of these recognizances was set by the 1955 *Code* revision at two years.[58]

During the twentieth century, a number of noteworthy developments occurred, the most important of which was the move from volunteers to professional probation officers. By legislation, Ontario and British Columbia set up formal probation functions as part of the civil service in 1922 and 1946 respectively.[59] Secondly, the Ouimet Committee

---

55  *Criminal Code, 1892*, above note 54 , s. 972.

56  *Ibid.*, s. 973.

57  See *Criminal Code*, S.C. 1953-54, c. 51, s. 638(2).

58  *Ibid.*, s. 637(1).

59  See Harris, above note 47 at 36. See also the discussion of the development of probation in Canada, *Report of the Royal Commission to Investigate the Penal System of Canada* (Ottawa: King's Printer, 1938) at 226–31 (Chair: J. Archambault), commonly known as the Archambault Report.

recommended abandoning the anachronistic recognizance with all the historical baggage it carried in favour of a distinct probation order lasting up to three years with mandatory and optional conditions.[60] Supervision would always be a condition of probation. While these recommendations were subsequently adopted, the Committee's argument that the power to add probation to a sentence of imprisonment should be repealed, since this kind of extended control was already within the parole function, has not been carried into effect. Other curious and anomalous developments were, from time to time, enacted and then repealed.[61]

## 2) Eligibility for Probation

While there have been many restrictions on eligibility in the past, the current regime is quite flexible. Aside from a conditional discharge,[62] there are three routes to probation.

First, the passing of sentence may be suspended and the offender placed on probation pursuant to section 731(1)(a) which provides:

> Where a person is convicted of an offence, a court may, having regard to the age and character of the offender, the nature of the offence and the circumstances surrounding its commission,
> (a) if no minimum punishment is prescribed by law, suspend the passing of sentence and direct that the offender be released on the conditions prescribed in a probation order;

Looking at the underlying offence, the only restriction on a suspended sentence is that the offence does not carry a minimum penalty. The applicable maximum is, at least in theory, irrelevant.[63] In terms of the offender, while the court should take into account "age and character," there is no "first offender" requirement. The suspended sentence with

---

60   See *Ouimet Report*, above note 1 at 295, 300–302.
61   For example, a requirement had been inserted that a suspended sentence for an offence punishable by more than two years imprisonment required the consent of Crown counsel. Another provision permitted a court to order an offender to pay costs when placed on probation. Both these requirements are inconsistent with any sound theoretical approach to probation. They were both repealed by the 1955 *Criminal Code* revision.
62   See *Criminal Code*, ss. 730(1), 731(2).
63   It can extend to offences for which the maximum sentence is life imprisonment. For example, there have been suspended sentences in manslaughter cases, although uncommon: see, for example, *R. v. Millar* (1994), 31 C.R. (4th) 315 (Ont. Gen. Div.).

probation under section 731(1)(a) must stand alone, and the sentencing judge cannot add a fine to it.[64]

The second kind of probation order is covered by section 731(1)(b) which provides that a probation order can be imposed "in addition to fining or sentencing the offender to imprisonment for a term not exceeding two years." This includes two major restrictions. First, a probation order can be imposed in addition to one of the other sanctions, fine or imprisonment, but not both. Second, the underlying term of imprisonment cannot be more than two years. The two-year limitation on imprisonment has been subject to extensive judicial interpretation. Perhaps reflecting the Ouimet concern that adding probation onto imprisonment was unsound, courts have interperted the phrase "for a term not exceeding two years" to render probation illegal when attached to terms which, in the aggregate, add up to more than two years. The intention attributed to Parliament was that the utility of community-based probation was limited to persons who had served terms of no more than two years. Prisoners released from longer sentences would be subject to supervision by federal parole officers. As a result of this analysis, it is the length of incarceration that is important and not how it was constructed. This means that probation cannot be added to sentences which individually are less than two years but, when added together, require the offender to serve an aggregate term that exceeds two years.[65] The same result occurs if part of the underlying term is a parole or statutory release remanet that must be served due to revocation.[66] Even if a consecutive sentence is imposed after, and separate from, an earlier probation order, if the total term to be served exceeds two years, then the probation order attached to the earlier sentence is rendered illegal and has no effect.[67] Accordingly, an offender would no longer be required to comply with probation terms and could not be prosecuted for non-compliance after that date. Of

---

64   See *R. v. St. James* (1981), 20 C.R. (3d) 389 (Que. C.A); *R. v. Kelly* (1995), 104 C.C.C. (3d) 95 (Nfld. C.A.); and *R. v. Polywjanyj* (1982), 1 C.C.C. (3d) 161 (Ont. C.A.), where the thirty-day suspended sentence was deleted leaving the $650 fine.

65   See *R. v. Young* (1980), 27 C.R. (3d) 85 at 90 (B.C.C.A.) [*Young*], where Lambert J.A. said that it was "contrary to the intent of the Code and to the intent of Parliament" to permit the imposition of a "period of probation following consecutive sentences which total more than two years, even if none of those sentences is in itself longer than two years."

66   See *R. v. Currie* (1982), 65 C.C.C. (2d) 415 (Ont. C.A.) [*Currie*].

67   See *R. v. Miller* (1987), 36 C.C.C. (3d) 100 (Ont. C.A.) [*Miller*].

course, an allegation of breach prior to the imposition of the consecutive sentence could be prosecuted since the order was lawful and effective up to that time.

The third kind of probation order is authorized by section 732(1)(b) which governs intermittent sentences.[68] During the non-custodial periods between the specifed times when the person is in custody serving a sentence intermittently, the person must be on probation and must conform with the terms of a probation order. These orders are integrated with the intermittent sentence and its purpose. They are often constructed with a view to ensuring an orderly and sober attendance at the local jail by, for example, authorizing a breathalyzer test. Since 1996, the new language of section 732(1)(b) makes it clear that probation can extend beyond the custodial sentence. In any case where this is intended, the optional conditions should clearly indicate the part or parts of the sentence to which they apply.

## 3) The Commencement and Duration of a Probation Order

A probation order under section 731(1)(a) is part of a suspended sentence and usually commences when it is imposed.[69] Its commencement cannot be postponed by making it consecutive to another probation order.[70] However, if the order is made under section 731(1)(b) and is attached to a sentence of imprisonment, or the offender is already subject to a term of imprisonment of less than two years, the period of probation commences after the sentence of imprisonment.[71] Similarly, if the offender is, at the time the probation order is made, subject to a conditional sentence, the probation order commences at the expiration of the conditional sentence.[72]

Until the 1996 amendments, there was a serious question about the commencement of a probation order that followed a sentence of imprisonment. If the underlying sentence was the maximum sentence of two years, it would be served in a penitentiary and the offender

---

68 See the discussion of intermittent sentences, below, at 9(H).
69 See *Criminal Code*, s. 732.2(1)(a). If at the time of sentencing the offender is serving a term of imprisonment previously imposed, the judge can suspend sentence under s. 731(1)(a); the period of probation would not commence until the offender is released from that term of imprisonment: see s. 732.2(1)(b).
70 See *R. v. Hunt* (1982), 2 C.C.C. (3d) 126 (N.S. S.C. (A.D.)).
71 See *Criminal Code*, s. 732.2(1)(b). See also the discussion below about the evolution of the current provision which now clarifies when the probation order begins given the variety of situations that may arise.
72 *Ibid.*, s. 732.2(1)(c).

would either be released on parole or on statutory release after serving two-thirds of the sentence.[73] In either case, the prisoner would be subject to conditions and the potential return to penitentiary confinement for a breach. If, however, the offender was serving a provincial sentence of less than two years, she could be released on parole with conditions or by reason of remission at approximately two-thirds of the sentence. In the latter situation, since provinces do not exercise supervisory authority over remission-based release, the prisoner was not subject to conditions or re-incarceration.

This raised a number of questions and potentially anomalous results. The *Criminal Code* merely provided that the probation would commence upon expiry of the sentence. If the probation period commenced upon release from custody, it would overlap with conditional release supervision for federal prisoners. Would the prisoner be bound by both supervisory regimes and subject to both sets of consequences? If probation commenced at warrant expiry, there would be a hiatus in supervision for provincial prisoners equal to the amount of remission they had earned pending the commencement of probation supervision. To avoid this hiatus, the Manitoba Court of Appeal interpreted the expiry of the sentence to mean the expiry of the custodial portion.[74] Of course, this meant that probation supervision for federal prisoners would run concurrently with any conditional release to which the prisoner was subject.

The 1996 *Code* amendments clarified this issue. Section 732.2(1)(b) now provides that a probation order commences "as soon as the offender is released from prison or, if released from prison on conditional release, at the expiration of the sentence of imprisonment." Accordingly, there is no overlap of supervision. If the offender is subject to conditional release, either parole or statutory release, then the probation order does not come into effect until the warrant expiry date. If the prisoner is released from a provincial sentence by reason of remission and is not subject to conditional release, the probation order commences upon release.

If a person on probation is subsequently incarcerated either in default of payment of a fine or because of a new sentence of imprisonment, the probation term continues to run except that compliance with some conditions may be impossible, and thus unenforceable, during that period.[75] If, however, the new sentence of imprisonment is longer

---

73   Assuming the prisoner would not be detained and kept until warrant expiry: see
      *Corrections and Conditional Release Act*, S.C. 1992, c. 20, 129–32.

74   See *R. v. Constant* (1978), 40 C.C.C. (2d) 329 (Man. C.A.) [*Constant*].

75   See *Criminal Code*, s. 732.2(2).

than two years, or merges with an unexpired element[76] such that the aggregate is longer than two years, the period of probation ought to be considered illegal and of no effect. This would be the result of the application of the various appellate court rulings which limited probation as an additional sanction to imprisonment terms of two years or less.[77]

The probation order must specify "the period for which it is to remain in force."[78] Section 732.2(2)(b) provides that "no probation order shall continue in force for more than three years after the date on which the order came into force."

Accordingly, following the Ouimet recommendation, three years is the maximum duration of a probation order. This can, however, be extended for a year if the probation order is part of a suspended sentence and the offender commits another offence.[79] The three-year cap also applies to a probation order made in conjunction with an intermittent sentence under section 732(1)(b) that was intended to run beyond the custodial period. That kind of order would commence whenever imposed[80] and could run after the end of the intermittent sentence but could not extend for more than three years from the date of imposition. This must be a continuous period from the date of imposition which includes days of custody. Any other interpretation is unsupported by the *Code* and would produce an accounting nightmare to determine when the stipulated probation order would terminate.

## 4) Available Probation Conditions

Aside from the residual category in section 732.1(3)(h) which is drafted in broad general terms, the conditions which potentially can be included in a probation order are set out fairly precisely in the *Code*. The mandatory conditions, which must be included in every order, are found in section 732.1(2):

(a)  keep the peace and be of good behaviour;
(b)  appear before the court when required to do so by the court; and

---

76  By reason of parole or statutory release revocation.
77  See *Young*, above note 65 ; *Currie*, above note 66; and *Miller*, above note 67.
78  As required by *Criminal Code*, s. 732.1(4) and Form 46.
79  See *ibid.*, s. 732.2(5)(e) regarding the ability to revoke a suspended sentence or add up to one year on to the period of probation. See also the discussion, below, at 9(D)(6). The fact that this potentially authorizes a period of probation of longer than three years was first drawn to my attention by Judge C.C. Barnett's article, "Probation Orders Under the Criminal Code" (1977), 38 C.R.N.S. 165 at 211–13.
80  See *Criminal Code*, s. 732.2(1)(a).

(c) notify the court or the probation officer in advance of any change of name or address, and promptly notify the court or the probation officer of any change of employment or occupation.

The range of optional conditions which, at the court's discretion, may be added to a probation order are in section 732.1(3):

(a) report to a probation officer
    (i) within two working days, or such longer period as the court directs, after the making of the probation order, and
    (ii) thereafter, when required by the probation officer and in the manner directed by the probation officer;
(b) remain within the jurisdiction of the court unless written permission to go outside that jurisdiction is obtained from the court or the probation officer;
(c) abstain from
    (i) the consumption of alcohol or other intoxicating substances, or
    (ii) the consumption of drugs except in accordance with a medical prescription;
(d) abstain from owning, possessing or carrying a weapon;
(e) provide for the support or care of dependants;
(f) perform up to 240 hours of community service over a period not exceeding eighteen months;
(g) if the offender agrees, and subject to the program director's acceptance of the offender, participate actively in a treatment program approved by the province;
(g.1) where the lieutenant governor in council of the province in which the probation order is made has established a program for curative treatment in relation to the consumption of alcohol or drugs, attend at a treatment facility, designated by the lieutenant governor in council of the province, for assessment and curative treatment in relation to the consumption by the offender of alcohol or drugs that is recommended pursuant to the program;[81]
(g.2) where the lieutenant governor in council of the province in which the probation order is made has established a program governing the use of an alcohol ignition interlock device by an offender and if the offender agrees to participate in the program, comply with the program;[82] and

---

81  Added by *An Act to amend the Criminal Code (impaired driving and related matters)*, S.C. 1999, c. 32, s. 6, in force 1 July 1999 (S.I./99-73).
82  *Ibid.*

(h) comply with such other reasonable conditions as the court considers desirable, subject to any regulations made under subsection 738(2), for protecting society and for facilitating the offender's successful reintegration into the community.

The nature of probation provides a context which limits both the scope and availability of certain conditions. Many courts have suggested that probation orders should be geared to personal rehabilitation and should not include conditions which are purely punitive. As is discussed below, decisions dealing with the scope of the residual category provide the greatest support for this approach, starting with some decisions of Martin J.A. of the Ontario Court of Appeal who had been a member of the Ouimet Committee and obviously shared its views on probation. Following through with this view of the nature of probation, section 732.1(3)(c) appears to provide clear authority for prohibitions against the consumption of alcohol or drugs, but such conditions should only be applied when there is a link between the use of alcohol or drugs and the offence.[83]

The definition of the residual category in section 723.1(3)(h) was revised in 1996. It may be open to argue that this change broadens the potential scope of the residual category; whether it has changed the nature of probation, and the inherent limits of other conditions, is questionable. The 1996 amendments also expressly authorized community service as part of a probation order although they have been used and judicially supported[84] since the 1970s. Given the anticipated restorative nature of community service, if Parliament wanted to expand probation to encompass punitive orders, would it have chosen to incorporate community service into probation rather than making it a free-standing sanction?

The optional conditions can be varied at any time during the period of probation on application by "the offender, the probation officer or the prosecutor."[85] The court that made the probation order may, after hearing from the "offender and one or both of the probation officer and the prosecutor," vary any of the optional conditions based on "a change in the circumstances;"[86] relieve the offender from compliance, either absolutely or on terms;[87] or decrease the period of the

---

83  See *R. v. Caja* (1977), 36 C.C.C. (2d) 401 (Ont. C.A.) [*Caja*].
84  See *R. v. Shaw* (1977), 36 C.R.N.S. 358 (Ont. C.A.).
85  See *Criminal Code*, s. 732.2(3).
86  *Ibid.*, s. 732.2(3)(a).
87  *Ibid.*, s. 732.2(3)(b).

entire probation order.[88] It is an interesting question whether the court must be the same judge who made the initial probation order. In the case of applications to revoke or vary under section 732.2(5) following a conviction, courts have held that the application must be heard by the original court.[89] The argument in favour of returning to the same judge is even stronger when the object is a variation.

There are two limits on the variation power worthy of note. First, the *Criminal Code* is silent as to whether a judge can vary of her own motion. In some jurisdictions it is common to structure a series of probation reviews by using the power in section 732.1(2)(b) to require re-attendance in court. While this is a useful tool to supervise one's orders, section 732.2(3) authorizes the prosecutor, the offender, or a probation officer to apply for a variation. It is silent on whether a court can vary of its own motion. This can be significant given that some trial courts have inherent jurisdiction and others are pure creatures of statute. However, even creatures of statute must have the ability to maintain their own process. Ensuring the integrity of their orders is arguably part of this power so long as the variation cannot be characterized as an increase in the burden of the original sentence. Secondly, it should be noted that an application to vary cannot lead to a revocation of a suspended sentence. Regardless of a judge's second thoughts, this can only be triggered by the process in section 732.2(5), discussed below.[90]

### a) "Keep the Peace and Be of Good Behaviour"

While the "peace" and "behaviour" references seem to denote two distinct elements, their scope has been the subject of considerable attention. In *R. v. Stone*, it was held that keeping the peace referred to disruptions of the public order but the good behaviour obligation extended to lawful conduct and encompassed the duty to meet the "standard of conduct expected of all law-abiding and decent citizens."[91] More recently, the issue was canvassed by the Newfoundland Court of Appeal in *R. v. R.(D.)*, a young offender's case.[92] The Crown alleged that the offender had breached the "keep the peace and be of good behaviour" condition

---

88   *Ibid.*, s. 732.2(3)(c).
89   See *R. v. Graham* (1975), 27 C.C.C. (2d) 475 (Ont. C.A.) [*Graham*], which held that only when the original judge is unable to act or the jurisdiction over the order has been transferred does another judge have jurisdiction to deal with the suspended sentence.
90   See *R. v. Lake* (1986), 27 C.C.C. (3d) 305 (N.S. S.C. (A.D.)).
91   (1985), 22 C.C.C. (3d) 249 at 256, Steele J. (Nfld. S.C.).
92   (1999), 27 C.R. (5th) 366 (Nfld. C.A.) [*R.(D.)*].

230 THE LAW OF SENTENCING

of a probation order by running away from a group home. Residence was not a specific condition of the probation order. For the court, Green J.A. disagreed with the earlier decision in *Stone*. Although he concluded that the concept of "good behaviour" is broader in scope than "keeping the peace," he held that any actionable non-compliance must involve a breach of the law. In addition to his historical analysis,[93] the principle of legality and the importance of notice were central to this conclusion:

> . . . the principle that a person is entitled to know in advance whether his or her specific conduct is illegal before engaging in the activity that leads to his or her being charged with an offence (here, breach of probation) is a strong argument for limiting the content of the obligation to be of good behaviour to an obligation to comply with existing laws or orders. A person is deemed to know the law and, hence, holding a probationer accountable for breach of the obligation of good behaviour on the basis of breach of a statutory provision or an order specifically applicable to him or her does not offend the principle in question.[94]

While Green J.A. includes "quasi-criminal or regulatory" offences within the potential reach of the probation obligation, it is unclear whether a breach of a municipal by-law would also qualify. His concerns about notice and precision, combined with his appropriate reluctance to expand the grasp of the criminal law, suggest that a by-law infraction is not encompassed by the "good behaviour" duty. A probationer's parking problems should not end up in criminal court. On the other hand, a refusal to comply with a lawful order made under a municipal by-law might be different.

### b) Reporting to a Probation Officer

The obligation to report is not a mandatory requirement, but if the judge wants some form of probation supervision, regardless of whether it is tightly crafted or loose, there must be a requirement in the order that the offender report. The order must indicate when the offender should report for the first time, which must be "within two working days, or such longer

---

93 When looking for authority that describes the potential scope of probation conditions, Green J.A. wrongly quoted at 375 from the decision of Martin J.A. in *R. v. Ziatas* (1973), 13 C.C.C. (2d) 287 (Ont. C.A.) [*Ziatas*]. Those remarks did not relate to the scope of probation conditions in general but rather were a paraphrase of the residual category as it was framed at the time. See the discussion of the residual category, below, at 9(D)(4)(d).

94 *R.(D.)*, above note 92 at 385.

period as the court directs."[95] After the initial meeting, the decision about when the offender must report is delegated to the probation officer. Since this kind of delegation must only be administrative in nature,[96] if a judge wants to impose an intensive form of probation requiring regular meetings at precise and short intervals, this should probably be effected through the residual category, section 732.1(3)(h), with a clear order, rather than delegating the function to the probation officer.

## c) Treatment Orders

Section 732.1(3)(g) now provides that a probation order can require an offender to "participate actively in a treatment program" so long as the offender agrees, is accepted into the program, and the program is approved by the province. The last qualification, approval by the province, seems to be ignored so long as someone involved in the treatment program is provincially qualified or licensed. The offender's agreement is consistent with the rehabilitative and non-punitive nature of probation. It is also likely a function of some judicial concerns about compelling certain kinds of treatment, especially involving medication.

In *R. v. Rogers*,[97] the offender had been convicted of possessing a dangerous weapon. He had been carrying a knife on the street, poking at people, but without actual contact. The offender was a chronic schizophrenic who was off his medication and had a history of medical noncompliance. The trial judge sentenced him to one day imprisonment and placed him on probation for fifteen months. One of the conditions was that he report to a multi-disciplinary community agency known as the "Inter Ministerial Project" and take whatever psychiatric assessment or treatment it recommended. Pending the appeal, the offender was under the care of a private physician and was taking his prescribed medication. On appeal, it was argued that a probation order compelling psychiatric treatment violated section 7 of the *Charter*. Anderson J.A. held:

> In my opinion, a probation order which compels an accused person to take psychiatric treatment or medication is an unreasonable restraint upon the liberty and security of the accused person. It is contrary to the fundamental principles of justice and, save in exceptional circumstances, cannot be saved by s. 1 of the *Charter*. Exceptional circumstances are not present here.[98]

---

95 See *Criminal Code*, s. 732.1(3)(a)(i).

96 See *R. v. McNamara* (1982), 66 C.C.C. (2d) 24 (Ont. C.A.); *R. v. Sterner* (1982), 60 C.C.C. (2d) 68 (Sask. C.A.), aff'd [1982] 1 S.C.R. 173.

97 (1990), 61 C.C.C. (3d) 481 (B.C.C.A.) [*Rogers*].

98 *Rogers, ibid.* at 488.

The "protection of the public" argument was insufficient to justify using probation, an essentially rehabilitative sanction, to compel treatment and medication. He added that if, in another case, the risk to society is so great, then probation will be the wrong sanction. This does not stop a probation order from seeking to protect the public, short of compelling treatment. Accordingly, the conditions were amended to impose an obligation on the offender to take reasonable steps to maintain himself so that his chronic schizophrenia will not cause him to behave in a manner dangerous to himself or others. Another condition required him to attend at the Inter Ministerial Project but only to take treatment or medication if he consented. If he did not consent, or withdrew his consent, he was required to attend forthwith upon his probation officer who could assess whether he was in breach of the principal condition. On first reading, this may sound subversive or even disingenuous but it is consistent with the view that only a pressing and immediate danger can justify compulsory treatment by the state. If the offender appears to the probation officer to be dangerous, then the probation officer could either invoke the civil mental health processes on the basis that the offender was an imminent danger to others or commence a breach proceeding which would allow for arrest. Given the offender's history, avoiding the criminal process would be a preferable response.

Subsequently, a similar conclusion was reached by the Saskatchewan Court of Appeal in R. v. Kieling,[99] where the offender was obsessed with the singer Anne Murray and was convicted on four counts of breach of probation for failing to comply with a term that he not telephone her. The trial judge fined him a total of $2000 and placed him on probation. He appealed the conviction and sentence to the Queen's Bench; the Crown also appealed the sentence. That court substituted a sentence of sixty days followed by probation, including a condition that he report to a psychiatrist and accept whatever treatment may be recommended. On a further appeal, Court of Appeal recognized the decision in Rogers but reached its decision on non-Charter grounds. It struck out the psychiatric treatment condition on the basis that none of the specific conditions nor the residual category authorized compelling someone to be the subject of forced medication.

The appellate judge in R. v. Laycock[100] was faced with a woman who had been convicted of causing a disturbance and assaulting a police officer. She suffered from bipolar affective disorder and experienced

99   (1991), 64 C.C.C. (3d) 124 (Sask. C.A.).
100   (1995), 133 Sask. R. 69 (Q.B.).

psychotic moods. The trial judge placed her on probation with a condition that she "participate in a program of psychiatric counselling and/ or treatment as directed by a psychiatrist including prescribed medication." Relying on the authority of both *Rogers* and *Kieling*,[101] he concluded that there was no authority to order that she submit to psychiatric treatment. However, since she was not opposed to the condition, he left it in. Hence, we have a judicial recognition of exactly the situation which section 732.1(3)(g) now provides.

Not all appellate courts have expressed concern about compelling psychiatric treatment and medication. In *R. v. Hynes*,[102] the appellant had been convicted of mischief for throwing rocks at his neighbour's house. He had a lengthy record and was drunk at the time. More significantly, he was a paranoid schizophrenic who had stopped taking his medication. The trial judge sentenced him to two years in the penitentiary, which resulted in his transfer from Newfoundland to Kingston Penitentiary. In reviewing the sentence, the court remarked, without offering any authority or discussion, that there "is no way that the court can mandate medical treatment while a prisoner is in custody although it may be made a condition of probation."[103] Ultimately, the court reduced the sentence to one year, to be followed by a three-year probation order which included the condition that he abide by "conditions set up by adult corrections for taking and ensuring that he take all medically prescribed" drugs.

### d) The Residual Category
For many years, the residual category was cast in terms of securing good conduct and preventing repetition, the language which now applies to the residual category for conditional sentences.[104] A number of appellate court decisions interpreted the earlier provision with close regard to the context of probation and its premises, which is not surprising given that some of the first decisions were written or supported by Martin J.A., a prominent member of the Ouimet Committee which had supported a large role for probation as a sentencing tool.[105] As a result, it was generally considered that conditions that were solely

---

101   As well as an earlier case, *R. v. Soonias* (1981), 12 Sask. R. 296, Gerein J. (Q.B.).

102   (1991), 64 C.C.C. (3d) 421 (Nfld. C.A.).

103   *Ibid.* at 428.

104   See *Criminal Code*, s. 742.3(2)(f). Also see the discussion of the residual category in A. Manson, "Conditional Sentences and House Arrest" (1998), 19 C.R. (5th) 353 at 354–57 ["Conditional Sentences and House Arrest"].

105   See *Ziatas*, above note 93; and *Caja*, above note 83.

punitive should not be included. The scope of the residual category was rehabilitative. Consequently, prohibitions could only be crafted if they related to a factor that was relevant to the offence. For example, an alcohol or drug condition was reasonable only if there was an indication that alcohol or drug abuse played a role in the offence.[106] Similarly, a prohibition against driving for purely punitive purposes was also not acceptable.

Since 1996, the residual category for probation in section 732.1(3)(h) reads:

> such other reasonable conditions as the court considers desirable . . . for protecting society and for facilitating the offender's successful reintegration into the community.

This language is more clearly consistent with the rehabilitative purpose of probation although it uses the phrase "for protecting society." In *R. v. Proulx*,[107] in the course of distinguishing probation from conditional sentences, Lamer C.J.C. scrutinized the current probation residual category. He concluded that the reason for the change was to "make clear the rehabilitative purpose of probation"[108] and to distinguish the scope of the residual categories for probation, and conditional sentences.

#### i) Banishment

Two specific questions raised by the issue of banishment, fall under the residual category. First, can a probation order exclude someone entirely from a community? And second, can a probation order exclude an offender from a geographical portion of the community? Both have recently generated controversy.

In *R. v. Taylor*,[109] the offender was convicted of sexual assault, uttering a death threat, and assault in respect of offences committed upon his spouse. He was a twenty-eight-year-old member of the Lac La Ronge Indian Band. He and the victim had lived together for over two years and had a child. They had separated a few weeks before the offences were committed. Notwithstanding the objections of Crown counsel, the trial judge decided to hold a sentencing circle.[110] The circle

---

106   There is now a specific provision in the *Criminal Code*, s. 732.1(3)(c), that deals with the consumption of alcohol or drugs.

107   [2000] 1 S.C.R. 61 [*Proulx*] See the discussion below at 9(J)(1).

108   *Ibid.* at 88.

109   (1997), 122 C.C.C. (3d) 376 (Sask. C.A.) [*Taylor*].

110   The trial judge had had experience with the type of circle used by the Piegan (Blackfoot) people but the Lac La Ronge Band were Cree.

comprised twenty-six people including the judge, both counsel, the offender and his father, mother, and sister, three elders, a court worker, and various other members of the community. It sat for two days. The victim was not consulted about whether to hold a circle but she participated on both days. The attitude of the circle was divided. One group in the circle was concerned about denunciation and incapacitation while the other faction expresssed frustration with the failure of incarceration. It was then suggested that they should consider banishment or isolation on a remote island.

The circle ultimately recommended one year of isolation and Crown counsel suggested adding three years probation to it. Everyone agreed that a psychological assessment was necessary to ensure that Mr. Taylor could cope with isolation. The judge accepted the recommendation but decided, instead of sentencing the offender, to adjourn the sentencing for a year and amend the judicial interim release terms, requiring him to remain isolated at a remote location. The Crown appealed and the Court of Appeal remitted the case back to the judge to impose a sentence. After a sentencing hearing, and taking into account the nine months of presentence custody and the six months already spent in isolation, the judge imposed a sentence of ninety days imprisonment and three years probation including a condition that the offender spend an additional six months in isolation. There were also conditions that he take anger management and sexual abuse assessment counselling after the period of isolation. The Crown appealed arguing that greater deterrence and public protection were required. Central to the case was the existence of a legal power to order isolation or banishment.

Bayda C.J.S. for the majority noted that if banishment or isolation was a permissible condition of probation, it had to be authorized by the residual category applicable at the time.[111] The scope of this category, however, had to be determined in light of the general nature of a probation order, which he described as seeking

> . . . to secure "the good conduct" of the offender and to deter him from committing other offences. It does not particularly seek to reflect the seriousness of the offence or the offender's degree of culpability. Nor does it particularly seek to fill the need for denunciation of the offence or the general deterrence of others to commit the same or other offences. Depending upon the specific conditions of the order there may well be a punitive aspect to a probation order but punishment is

---

111   Note the discussion, above, at 9(D)(4)(d), about the 1996 change to the residual category.

not the dominant or an inherent purpose. It is perhaps not even a secondary purpose but is more in the nature of a consequence of an offender's compliance with one or more of the specific conditions. . . .[112]

Recognizing that probation is an individualized sanction intended to "influence the future of the offender," Bayda C.J.S. had to determine whether isolation was designed to punish or promote good conduct. A brief historical analysis revealed that for First Nations people, banishment played various roles, and ranged from complete to partial exclusion. He considered the comments made in the sentencing circle and concluded that the isolation proposed for Mr. Taylor was "an individualized measure having as its central purpose the influencing of the offender's future behaviour" and not a punitive measure intended to denounce and punish.[113] Accordingly, he concluded that a sentencing court did have, under the rubric of probation; the power to isolate an individual. However, it is only appropriate if it is a reasonable condition in the circumstances as part of an overall fit sentence. Later in his careful judgment, Bayda C.J.S. found the ninety-day sentence followed by probation with banishment to be a fit sentence. It was partly retributive and partly restorative, and responded appropriately to the applicable principles of denunciation and parity. It also served the newly entrenched objective in section 718(f) of promoting a "sense of responsibility in offenders, and acknowledgment of the harm done to victims and to the community." The Crown appeal was dismissed.[114]

A different kind of banishment was at issue in *R. v. Reid*.[115] The accused was convicted of possession of marijuana for the purposes of trafficking, and failure to appear in court. The Crown argued that a fit sentence would be thirty days incarceration followed by a one-year probation order that prohibited the offender from entering a part of the downtown core described as the "red zone" — the part of Victoria in which, the police argued, drug trafficking was concentrated. The Crown took the position that every person charged with trafficking or possession for the purposes of trafficking in the "red zone" should be banned from entering it. The offender argued that the prohibition would violate his *Charter* right of freedom of association under section

---

112  *Taylor*, above note 109 at 394.

113  *Ibid.* at 397.

114  Cameron J.A. would have substituted a term of imprisonment of two years less a day, after applying appropriate credits to the four years that was, in his view, fit: *ibid.* at 441.

115  [1999] B.C.J. No. 1603, Gove P.C.J (Prov. Ct.) (QL).

2(b), his mobility rights under section 6, his right to liberty under section 7, his equality rights under section 15, and his right not to be subjected to cruel and unusual punishment under section 12.

After hearing substantial evidence on the utility of banning people from this area, Gove P.C.J. concluded that many of the offenders who had been banned previously were poor, often addicted to drugs, and in need of services that were "almost exclusively available" within this area.[116] With respect to the various *Charter* claims, the judge was concerned about imposing a prohibition on all members of a class automatically and without regard to its consequences to the particular offender. Without analysing the various *Charter* claims, he concluded succinctly:

> . . . to impose the "red zone" on Reid based solely on the type of offence for which he is convicted and not based on his unique circumstances, would be, for me to act arbitrarily and such arbitrariness would be in violation of his constitutionally guaranteed rights. That is not to say that a condition of an area restriction, including the Victoria "red zone" is, of itself, unconstitutional and violates an individual's rights under the *Charter*.[117]

He accepted that probation could include orders to stay away from a victim, which might include a precise geographical definition. Similarly, especially with youthful offenders, it may be appropriate to order that someone stay away from specific adults or places where certain adults congregated. These represented specifically tailored prohibitions for rehabilitative purposes. Cases where banishment had been found to be inappropriate or illegal consisted largely of situations where the objective was purely punitive or to rid the community of a perceived nuisance.[118] Ultimately, he concluded that it was wrong to issue a prohibition solely to deter others or without evidence of particular circumstances that would justify it. He imposed a suspended sentence with probation for eight months with the conditions that the offender perfom twenty-five hours of community service and attend school or seek and maintain employment.

### ii) *Electronic Monitoring and Home Confinement*
Also falling under the residual category is electronic monitoring, one of the new technologies of sentencing where a device fastened to an

---

116   *Ibid.* at para. 50.
117   *Ibid.* at para. 63.
118   *Ibid.* at paras. 73–80, including an extensive quotation from Bayda C.J.S. in *R. v. Malboeuf* (1982), 68 C.C.C. (2d) 544 (Sask. C.A.).

offender permits authorities to determine the offender's whereabouts. It can be an important feature of home confinement, or house arrest as it is commonly called. It can also be used as an aspect of other conditions intended to monitor and control an offender's mobility or contact with the community. Some provinces, especially Saskatchewan and British Columbia, have embraced this new technology, while others have been more reluctant.[119] Neither home confinement nor electronic monitoring are specifically authorized by the *Code*. Authority for them must lie within either the residual category for probation, or conditional sentences, or both.

R. v. M.(D.E.S.)[120] involved sexual offences which occurred a number of years before between a brother and sister. The wrongful sexual activity began when both were children. A complaint to police was made years later after a family dispute. The brother was charged only with offences committed by him after he became an adult. He was sentenced to forty-five days imprisonment, to be served intermittently, followed by two years probation. The Crown appealed seeking a longer term of incarceration. The British Columbia Court of Appeal observed that the offences, rape and sexual intercourse with a person under the age of fourteen, would ordinarily warrant a sentence of two years less a day. However, it was concerned with the impact that this would have on the offender's family unit and his apparent rehabilitation. Accordingly, it maintained the forty-five-day intermittent sentence but added a home confinement requirement to the probation order. It concluded that this was permitted under the residual category since it was intended to "maintain rehabilitation" which was consistent with the rehabilitative goal of probation.

While the decision in *R. v. M.(D.E.S.)* about maintaining rehabilitation may have been a bit of linguistic subterfuge since the court seemed to be saying that the offence required a greater restriction of liberty, the scope of the residual category appears to be broad enough to cover electronic monitoring. Other appellate courts have not questioned it. The Saskatchewan Court of Appeal dealt directly with this issue in *R. v. McLeod*.[121] The offender, with a long criminal record, was charged with unlawfully trafficking in a prescription drug and breach of probation. The trial judge had imposed a suspended sentence with two years probation and electronic monitoring for the first six months. The Crown

---

119   See the discussion of *R. v. Frittaion* (1997), 10 C.R. (5th) 394 (Ont. Gen. Div.) in Chapter 8, at 8(B), for an example of Ontario's reluctance.

120   (1993), 80 C.C.C. (3d) 371 (B.C.C.A.).

121   (1993), 81 C.C.C. (3d) 83 (Sask. C.A.).

appealed, seeking a six-month custodial sentence. In the course of well-developed reasons, Vancise J.A. dismissed the appeal and presented a lengthy discussion of electronic monitoring, which neither party challenged on constitutional grounds. He accepted its legitimacy as an aspect of intensive probation, and approved its utility to

> . . . reduce the number of persons who are imprisoned, to facilitate their rehabilitation, and, at the same time, afford protection to the public by keeping those persons who are partially at liberty under surveillance.[122]

He concluded that there are "a wide range of offenders who commit non-violent crimes who are eligible for consideration of this sanction."[123]

Clearly, electronic monitoring, especially when combined with intensive probation supervision and conditions dealing with drugs or alcohol abstention, can be a useful adjunct to the sanction of probation even though the language of the residual category has been changed. Where there is no presumption of incarceration and the goal is a purely rehabilitative one, electronic monitoring can be considered as an adjunct to probation. Where custody of less than two years is suggested by the offence and a conditional sentence is being considered, the desire to restrict liberty as a punitive measure may be achieved through using electronic monitoring as an aspect of the conditional sentence.[124]

## 5) Extra-territorial Effect

Judges have power to act within their territorial jurisdiction, but criminal law orders are emanations of federal law and have federal scope. The interesting question thus arises whether a Canadian probation order covers the offender's conduct if he or she leaves Canada temporarily. *R. v. Greco*[125] involved a man who assaulted his girlfriend while

---

122  *Ibid.* at 99.
123  *Ibid.* at 102. See also *R. v. R.(W.S.)* (1995), 128 Sask. R. 158 (C.A.) (C.A.), in which another panel of the same court set aside a sentence of probation with electronic monitoring in a sexual assault case and substituted a sentence of 2 1\2 years imprisonment.
124  See *R. v. Gagnon* (1998), 130 C.C.C. (3d) 194, Fish J.A. (Que. C.A.) [*Gagnon*]; *R. v. Sidhu* (1998), 129 C.C.C. (3d) 26 (B.C.C.A.) [*Sidhu*]; and "Conditional Sentences and House Arrest," above note 104. In *Proulx*, above note 107, Lamer C.J.C. stated that house arrest should be the norm for conditional sentences. He did not specifically mention electronic monitoring but this is implicit given his general approval of *Gagnon*.
125  (1999), 26 C.R. (5th) 45 (Ont. C.J.).

on vacation in Cuba. At the time he was on probation for an unrelated matter. As a result, he was subject to the stricture that he keep the peace and be of good behaviour. A charge was laid under section 733.1 and the accused argued that a Canadian court had no jurisdiction to hear a prosecution in relation to conduct that occurred exclusively outside the country. Lampkin J. held that a probation order is an *in personam* order which follows the probationer everywhere even if it is only enforceable in Canada. Once the probation order is proven, the Canadian court had jurisdiction even if the factual allegation related to conduct committed outside the country.[126] While a Cuban court could have prosecuted the assault, it could not have dealt with the Canadian offence of breach of probation. Accordingly, Lampkin J.'s conclusion presents no affront to concerns about international comity.[127]

## 6) The Consequences of Breaching Probation Conditions

If it appears that a person on probation has not complied with a term of the probation, a number of options are available. Depending on the nature of the breach, the supervising probation officer may decide that no action needs to be taken. Alternatively, the matter may suggest a variation in the conditions of probation. This could arise because the incident discloses an impracticality which makes the condition unfair. Conversely, the supervising officer may conclude that the breach requires a response to make a point about the importance of compliance but that this message can be conveyed by making the probation conditions more onerous. Section 732.2(3) permits the probation officer[128] to apply to the court that made the probation order for a variation. On such an application, the period of probation cannot be increased.

### a) What May Constitute a Breach?

Probably the most common response to a probation breach is a prosecution for non-compliance. The creation of breach of probation as a separate offence was opposed by the Ouimet Committee. Consistent with its view that probation should not be attached to a term of imprisonment but used only after a suspension of sentence, the Committee argued that the sanctions for non-compliance should be either a varia-

---

126   *Ibid.* at 55–56, relying on *R. v. Libman*, [1985] 2 S.C.R. 178.

127   See D. King, "Jurisdiction for Offences Committed Outside Canada" (1999), 26 C.R. (5th) 58 at 60.

128   Or the prosecutor or the offender. See the discussion of variations, above, at 9(D)(4).

tion of the order or a revocation of the suspension followed by the imposition of an appropriate sentence.[129] Certainly, there is an attractive conceptual consistency about the Ouimet Committee's approach to probation which is not apparent in a scheme that responds to a sentencing mistake by creating a new offence.

An offence of probation breach was enacted, however.[130] It was recently amended[131] to lower the requisite fault standard.[132] Section 733.1(1) now provides that an "offender who is bound by a probation order and who, without reasonable excuse, fails or refuses to comply with that order is guilty" of a hybrid offence punishable by up to two years imprisonment on indictment or up to eighteen months by way of summary conviction. The previous provision premised responsibility on wilful non-compliance. For the Supreme Court, Wilson J. in *R. v. Docherty* interpreted that offence as requiring subjective awareness that the conduct would breach the probation. While knowledge of unlawfulness is usually no defence, an honest belief that one's conduct was not unlawful could result in a conviction for an underlying offence but an acquittal on the probation breach prosecution. Accordingly, the accused's belief that he could sit drunk in his car without committing an offence did not, in the circumstances, provide a defence to impaired "care or control," but it did exonerate him on the probation breach charge because he lacked the subjective awareness or intention to wilfully violate the "keep the peace and be of good behaviour" requirement. As of 1996, the word "wilfully" has been removed but this does not necessarily displace the logic of *Docherty*.[133] The element of "without reasonable excuse" will likely be read as placing an evidentiary burden on the offender to adduce some evidence or point to something in the Crown's case that gives an air of reality to the defence.[134]

---

129   See *Ouimet Report*, above note 1 at 302.

130   See *Criminal Law Amendment Act, 1968-69*, S.C. 1968-69, c. 38, s. 75.

131   See *An Act to amend the Criminal Code (sentencing) and other Acts in consequence thereof*, S.C. 1995, c. 22, s. 6.

132   Perhaps as a response to the high threshold articulated in *R. v. Docherty*, [1989] 2 S.C.R. 941, discussed below. Certainly, the removal of "wilfully" ensures that the offence can be committed recklessly: see *R. v. Buzzanga and Durocher* (1979) 49 C.C.C. (2d) 369 (Ont. C.A.).

133   *Ibid.* Although the removal of "wilfully" brings recklessness into play, one can still argue that a belief in legality or justification precludes a finding of probation breach.

134   If Lampkin, J. in *R. v. Greco* (1999), 141 C.C.C. (3d) 36 (Ont. Ct. of Justice) at 48 he suggests that the new provision creates a persuasive burden. If that is what Parliament intended it will likely run afoul of s. 11 (d) of the *Charter*: see *R. v. Laba*, [1996] 3 S.C.R. 965; *R. v. Curtis* (1998), 123 C.C.C. (3d) 178 (Ont. C.A.).

Given the breadth of conditions, both optional and mandatory, which may be included in a probation order, the scope of the conduct which can generate a breach prosecution is truly infinite. A failure or refusal to perform a condition can be sufficient but the issue can become a debate about the actual probation obligation. Conditions which are vaguely drawn may present a problem for a prosecutor. With the deletion of the word "wilfully," a breach prosecution requires proof of intention or recklessness. Of course, inferences can be drawn from proven facts so that if the offender is required to report every Wednesday to her probation officer, the testimony of her officer that a Wednesday passed with no visit would be sufficient to require evidence of "reasonable excuse." However, the situation would be different if the condition only required the offender to "see an employment counsellor." This is much too vague to be enforceable. Upon questioning the offender about whether he had seen a counsellor, the answer might be: "No; maybe I'll go next week." Without a clearer obligation, this does not constitute either a failure or a refusal.

### b) Breach of an Illegal Condition or Order

Situations may arise where there is an argument that a condition or the entire probation order is illegal. While these issues can be resolved by way of appeal or certiorari in the case of summary convictions, can an offender use a defect as a defence to a charge of breach of probation in the absence of a step to rectify or nullify the order? There is a line of procedural defect cases[135] where the failure to comply with a mandatory duty prescribed in relation to a probation order provides a defence. In these cases, the duty usually involves service or confirmation of the probation such that a failure may raise an issue of notice. Accordingly, the orders are considered to be unenforceable but not a nullity.[136] In *R. v. Trabulsey*,[137] Watt J. allowed a Crown appeal from a dismissal of a breach of probation charge in a situation where the offender had filed a Notice of Appeal in respect of the original order. He concluded that an order stands until set aside and the filing of a Notice of Appeal did not constitute a stay. Although he was not dealing with the effect of an inherent defect, the decision reflects the traditional view which usually prevents collateral attacks.

---

135   See *R. v. Piche* (1976), 31 C.C.C. (2d) 150 (Ont. C.A.); *R. v. Bara* (1981), 58 C.C.C. (2d) 243 (B.C.C.A.); and *R. v. Scott* (1980), 56 C.C.C. (2d) 111 (Alta. C.A.).

136   See *Bara, ibid.* at 252.

137   (1993), 84 C.C.C. (3d) 240 (Ont. Gen. Div.).

If an order can be characterized as a nullity, however, then it ought to be unenforceable. A probation order attached to a sentence greater than two years would be a nullity. This is not a case in which there is any doubt about the propriety of the order. It represents a clear excess of jurisdiction on the part of the sentencing judge and cannot subject an offender to penalties for non-compliance.

Where the addition of a subsequent sentence invalidates a previously imposed order,[138] can this be considered a nullity? The answer may lie in the way the *Criminal Code* deals with the commencement of a probation order. Section 732.2(1) explains when a probation order "comes into force." That language is significant: it provides that an order attached to a term of imprisonment is not simply postponed, but has no "force" until a future date. Accordingly, an event such as a subsequent sentence which extends the term of imprisonment beyond two years must necessarily occur before the period of probation "comes into force." If it occurred after, then section 732.2(2)(a) would apply and the probation period would run concurrently. Thus, an invalidation before the order "comes into force" should be considered a nullity. Moreover, given the general level of misunderstanding about the complexity of some of these sentencing provisions, it would be unfair to say that the offender who has good legal advice can appeal and free herself easily from the probation constraint, probably on consent, but that everyone else is expected to comply with an illegal order.

## c) Revocation

Although rarely used, when an offender is convicted of another offence including breach of probation under section 733.1, the prosecution can, if the offender was the subject of a suspended sentence, apply to "the court that made the probation order" for a hearing at which the court can consider whether to revoke the suspended sentence and impose "any sentence that could have been imposed" at the time the passing of sentence was suspended.[139] Revocation only applies to suspended sentences. For other probationers, the prosecutor may apply to change the probation conditions, or extend the period of probation by up to one year.[140] It has been questioned whether the phrase "the court that made the probation order" means that only the original sentencing judge can entertain these applications. This limit would provide some measure of consistency, in the sense that the person who opted for the

---

138  See *Miller*, above note 67.
139  See *Criminal Code*, s. 732.2(5)(d).
140  *Ibid.*, s. 732.2(5)(e).

sanction should have the opportunity to consider whether subsequent misconduct is sufficient to warrant a change, small or substantial. The Ontario Court of Appeal accepted this rationale[141] and has held that the application must go to the same judge who made the original order unless there has been a transfer of jurisdiction[142] or there is evidence that the original judge is incapable of hearing or proceeding with the application. Interestingly, it has also been held that when the probation order is imposed by a panel of an appellate court, it is not necessary that an application to revoke or vary be brought before the same panel.[143]

There are very few examples of judicial consideration of the revocation function. While section 732.2(5) makes it clear that the prosecutor must make the application, and that the court must hear from both the prosecutor and the offender, there is no other structure to the process. In a case where an offender in custody on other matters was simply brought to court without notice and without an opportunity to consult counsel, Dubin J.A. held, in a pre-*Charter* case:

> Although the present Criminal Code does not require the formalities of an information and is silent as to procedure, I am satisfied that the basic principles of natural justice must prevail; one of which principles relevant here is that no man shall be condemned unless he has been given prior notice of the allegations against him and a fair opportunity to make full answer and defence.[144]

Notice should indicate to the offender both the basis for the section 732.2(5) hearing and the remedy which the prosecutor is seeking. Otherwise, the offender is handicapped in making informed choices, especially about whether to retain counsel. A failure to provide adequate notice will result in an unfair hearing and will be sufficient grounds for appellate intervention.[145]

Certainly it is clear that if the decision is to revoke, the sanction must be chosen on the basis of what would have been appropriate at the time of the original sentencing, with the added qualification that probation has been rejected. This does not necessarily mean a custodial sanction. If the offender has means, a fine or combination of fine and restitution can be considered. If custody appears to be the appropriate

---

141  See *Graham*, above note 89.
142  See *Criminal Code*, s. 733.
143  See *Alberta (A.G.) v. H.* (1983), 6 C.C.C. (3d) 382 (Alta. C.A.).
144  *R. v. Tuckey* (1977), 34 C.C.C. (2d) 572 (Ont. C.A.).
145  Section 673 of the *Criminal Code* defines "sentence" for the purpose of an appeal as including a disposition made under s. 732.2(5).

sanction, its duration ought not to be extended in light of conduct subsequent to the original sentencing. Similarly, a custodial sentence cannot be made consecutive to a sentence imposed after the date the passage of sentence was originally suspended.[146]

# E. FINES

The power to order a monetary penalty is an ancient sanction. A fine is defined as including a "pecuniary penalty or other sum of money, but does not include restitution."[147] Regardless of its amount, the public considers it to be a form of leniency.[148] Clearly, this is a function of the generally held attitude that imprisonment is the anchor of the sentencing system and anything less has no punitive element. This unfortunate view adds self-perpetuating momentum to its premise and discourages imaginative sentencing. Recent changes, especially the assertion of restraint in sections 718(c) and 718.2(d) and (e), the interest in promoting "a sense of responsibility" in section 718(f), and the specific amendments to the fine provisions, may result in greater use of fines and other monetary sanctions as an appropriate means of responding to offenders and offences.

The 1996 amendments made substantial progress in modernizing the use of the fine, which had been encumbered by anachronistic and unfair qualifications. From before the *Criminal Code, 1892*,[149] until 1996, it was impossible to impose a fine for an offence punishable by more than five years imprisonment except in conjunction with a term of imprisonment. This led to the public charade of a fine levied in addition to a single day of imprisonment to avoid the *Code* restriction. Now, a sentencing court is free to impose a fine by itself or in addition to any other sanction unless the offence carries a minimum term of imprisonment, in which case a fine can only be imposed in addition to that minimum term.[150]

A more important aspect of the 1996 amendments is the attention directed to an offender's means, both in relation to the imposition of the fine in the first place and also to the possibility of imprisonment in

---

146  See *R. v. Clermont* (1986), 30 C.C.C. (3d) 571 (Que. C.A.), aff'd [1988] 2 S.C.R. 171; and *R. v. Oakes* (1977), 37 C.C.C. (2d) 84 (Ont. C.A.).
147  See *Criminal Code*, s. 716.
148  See A.N. Doob & V. Marinos, "Reconceptualizing Punishment: Understanding the Limitations on the Use of Intermediate Punishments" (1995) 2 U. Chi. Roundtable 413.
149  See *An Act respecting Punishments, Pardons and the Commutation of Sentences*, R.S.C. 1886, c. 181, s. 31, subsequently enacted as s. 958 of the *Criminal Code, 1892*, above note 54.
150  *Criminal Code*, s. 734(1).

default of payment. Before 1996, it was not rare to see excessive fines imposed without any inquiry into the offender's means, sometimes even in the face of an offender's inability to pay, even though appellate courts had held that a fine should only be imposed if it was "within the offender's ability to pay."[151] Imprisonment in default was often the result.

In its 1987 report, the Canadian Sentencing Commission observed that the portion of the 1983 prison populations in British Columbia, Ontario, and Quebec made up of fine defaulters was 14 percent, 32 percent, and 48 percent respectively.[152] The system did not seem to comprehend that, for many people, poverty had become a basis for imprisonment and our jails were filled with people serving default terms for non-payment of fines. As a result of the entrenchment of the *Charter*, courts started to hear claims of section 7 violations in relation to the process of incarceration for non-payment without any inquiry into the circumstances.[153]

The 1996 amendments made a means inquiry a condition precedent to the imposition of a fine in most cases. Section 734(2) now provides:

> Except when the punishment for an offence includes a minimum fine or a fine is imposed in lieu of a forfeiture order, a court may fine an offender under this section only if the court is satisfied that the offender is able to pay the fine or discharge it under s. 736.

There are some statutory minimum fines and, when there is no form of exemption expressly available, a fine can mean imprisonment in default. Not every jurisdiction has an approved fine option program established under section 736. Accordingly, these are open to challenge on section 12 *Charter* grounds. One would need to demonstrate that a minimum fine is a grossly disproportionate sanction[154] taking into consideration the circumstances of the offence and the offender.

---

151   See *R. v. Snider* (1977), 37 C.C.C. (2d) 189 at 190 (Ont. C.A.).

152   See *Report of the Canadian Sentencing Commission*, above note 3 at 381.

153   See, for example, *R. v. Deeb* (1986), 28 C.C.C. (3d) 257 (Ont. Prov. Ct. (Crim. Div.)); and *R. v. Hebb* (1989), 47 C.C.C. (3d) 193 (N.S. S.C. (T.D.)).

154   In *R. v. Piscione* (1997), 12 C.R. (5th) 131 (Ont. Prov. Ct.), Bigelow J. held that the minimum $1000 per count fines under s. 238(1) of the *Income Tax Act*, R.S.C. 1985 (5th Supp.), c. 1, violated s. 12 of the *Charter* and he sentenced the impecunious offender to probation with community service. On the other hand, both the Quebec Court of Appeal and the Prince Edward Island Supreme Court, Appeal Division, have rejected the argument that the formula for the mandatory minimum fine under s. 240(1) of the *Excise Act*, R.S.C. 1985, c. E-14 (as am. by S.C. 1994, c. 29, s. 15) violates s. 12 of the *Charter*: see *R. v. Zachary* (1996), 3 C.R. (5th) 96 (Que. C.A.); and *R. v. MacFarlane* (1997), 121 C.C.C. (3d) 211 (P.E.I. S.C.(A.D.)).

# 1)  The Process of Imposing a Fine

The *Criminal Code* expressses no limit on the size of a fine but the quantum must be proportionate to the harm done and the degree of culpability, adjusted to accommodate the ability to pay. Ability to pay does not mean immediate ability; fines can be extended over lengthy periods of time with clear requirements stipulating when payments are to be made.[155] In addition, the fine, or part of it, can be paid out of any money seized from the offender upon arrest if there is no one else claiming ownership of the funds.[156]

Two mandatory requirements will, if followed, enhance the utility of fines by reducing the misunderstandings that can lead to defaults. Section 734.1 requires the court to make an order that "clearly sets out" the following:

(a)  the amount of the fine;
(b)  the manner in which the fine is to be paid;
(c)  the time or times by which the fine, or any portion thereof, must be paid; and
(d)  such other terms respecting the payment of the fine as the court deems appropriate.

This is followed by the requirement that a copy of the order be given to the offender along with an explanation of its terms, available fine option programs, and how to apply to amend the terms of the order.[157] It is critical that the offender know that the power to vary in section 734.3 includes the power to extend the time for payment, and that an application can be made without enormous difficulty. While there have been arguments in relation to other sanctions about whether the word "court" means the judge personally, section 734.2, because it includes the delivery of a copy of the order,[158] seems to contemplate a delegated administrative function which would also include the giving of the necessary explanations. However, the purpose is clear, and the court must take "reasonable measures" to ensure that the offender under-stands the order and the other relevant aspects of the fine process.[159] Since section 734.1 prescribes what the order must contain, these must

---

155   See *Criminal Code*, s. 734.1(c).
156   *Ibid.*, s. 734(6).
157   *Ibid.*, s. 734.2.
158   *Ibid.*, s. 734.2(a)(i).
159   *Ibid.*, s. 734.2(b).

be read in open court and it would be prudent to add an explanation of them along with the added factors mentioned in section 734.2.

## 2) The Consequences of Default of Payment

While section 734.1(c) requires the judge to stipulate when "the fine, or any portion thereof, must be paid," the definition of default refers only to the point when "the fine has not been paid in full."[160] This suggests that if the original order provided for a sequence of payments, default does not occur when a payment is missed but only when the last date in the sequence is reached and the fine has not been paid in full.

The Crown has a number of new options available to pursue an offender in default. Since the proceeds of most fines belong to Her Majesty in right of the province in which the fine was imposed,[161] a default can result in a refusal to issue or renew any provincial licenses, permits, or similar authorizations. This should become an easy way to collect unpaid fines. In similar recognition of the fine as a monetary obligation owed, the attorney general of the province, or in rare situations the attorney general of Canada,[162] can file the order as a civil judgment in any civil court in Canada that has the requisite monetary jurisdiction. Then, the Crown can proceed to execution.[163]

## 3) Imprisonment in Default of Payment of a Fine

There is a clear historical link between fines and imprisonment. Initially, the fine, coming from the Latin word "finis" meaning "end," was a payment that ended a period of imprisonment for an unpaid debt or lower-order offence. In the modern era where a fine became an alternative, although sometimes an adjunct, to imprisonment, it is not surprising that non-payment could produce a period of incarceration.

Prior to the 1996 amendments, a judge ordering a fine could include a stipulated period of custody in default of payment. While a

---

160  *Ibid.*, s. 734(3). See also s. 734.7(1)(a), which provides that a warrant of committal in default cannot be issued "until the expiration of the time allowed for payment of the fine in full."

161  *Ibid.*, s. 734.4.

162  Those situations defined in s. 734.4(2), where the proceeds of the fine go to Her Majesty in right of Canada. These are where the fine arises from a breach of a revenue law, a breach of duty by an officer or employee of the Government of Canada, or proceedings instituted by the Government of Canada where it bears the costs of prosecution.

163  *Ibid.*, s. 734.6.

default period may have been automatic for some judges, it was in theory discretionary. The Law Reform Commission argued in 1976 that incarceration for default should be limited to cases of wilful non-payment and only authorized after a hearing.[164] The Sentencing Commission echoed these arguments in 1987 and developed a fine default model that moved through six stages, including the attachment of wages and alternative work programs, with imprisonment only as a last resort.[165] The Commission's model also included a formula for translating a sum of monetary default into a period of incarceration using per diem rates. Different rates would apply to different portions of the fine. For example, a $100 fine might result in five days incarceration but an additional $100 would only require an additional four days for a total period of nine days incarceration. In many ways, the 1996 amendments incorporated the Commission's general approach although not all of its details, including the differential formula.

Section 734(5) now provides a formula for calcualting default time and section 734(4) indicates that this pre-determined amount of time "shall be deemed to be imposed in default of payment of the fine." There is an argument that this deeming effect ensures that a default period, if imposed, is standardized, but that there is still residual discretion for a judge to order expressly that no default time be added.[166] In any event, the formula in section 734(5) is premised on dividing the unpaid fine and related costs by the applicable minimum wage for an eight-hour workday. That is, the default period is a fraction "rounded down to the nearest whole number" where the numerator is the unpaid fine and the cost of conveying the offender to prison, and the denominator is eight times the provincial or territorial minimum wage. For example, if the unpaid fine is $1900, the cost of conveyance is $100, and the minimum wage is $8 per hour, the period of incarceration in default would be thirty-one days $\left(\frac{2000}{8\times8}\right)= 31.2$. The number of days cannot exceed the maximum applicable term of imprisonment.

A more important change is the process which must be followed before a warrant of committal in default of payment can issue. There cannot be a warrant unless the court is satisfied both that the civil

164  See *Law Reform Commission Report*, above note 2 at 65.
165  See *Report of the Canadian Sentencing Commission*, above note 3 at 382–87.
166  See the discussion in *Baron v. Canada*, [1993] 1 S.C.R. 416 about the potential implications of removing residual discretion. That was a search warrant case involving s. 8 of the *Charter* but a similar argument can be made about s. 7 and its balancing obligations especially when liberty is in issue.

mechanisms in sections 734.5 and 734.6 are not "appropriate in the circumstances" and that the offender has "without reasonable excuse" refused to pay the fine. Since section 734.7(3) incorporates the powers in other parts of the *Criminal Code* to compel the court appearance of an offender, this is consistent with a requirement that the warrant cannot issue without a hearing into the matters set out in section 734.7(1). Although a warrant for committal in default must include the default period as calculated pursuant to section 734(5), a partial payment of the fine reduces the period of imprisonment on a pro-rated basis.[167]

## 4)   Victim Fine Surcharge

While attention has been drawn to the the interests of victims within the criminal justice system, Parliament has created a way to fund services for victims through the victim fine surcharge. In the absence of a claim of hardship, whenever a court convicts or discharges an offender after a finding of guilty, it must impose a victim fine surcharge in addition to any other punishment. Section 737(1) provides that the amount can be up to 15 percent of a fine, or $10,000 where there is no fine imposed, or such lesser amount prescribed by regulation as a maximum amount. The only reason for not ordering payment of the surcharge is "undue hardship to the offender" or the offender's dependants.[168] If no surcharge is imposed the court must give reasons and enter them in the record of the proceedings.[169]

In *R. v. Crowell*, the constitutionality of the surcharge was challenged on the argument that this almost compulsory levy is a form of taxation not properly within Parliament's criminal law power.[170] The Nova Scotia Court of Appeal rejected this argument relying on a number of restitution cases.[171] It concluded that the victim fine surcharge was a "unique penalty," akin to restitution, which is not a true tax and not a true fine. It held that section 737 is a valid exercise of the federal criminal law-making power. As well as raising funds, the victim fine surcharge is an "expression of public reprobation."

---

167   See *Criminal Code*, s. 734.8.

168   *Ibid.*, s. 737(5).

169   *Ibid.*, s. 737(6).

170   (1992), 76 C.C.C. (3d) 413 (N.S. S.C. (A.D.)).

171   Principally, *R. v. Zelensky*, [1978] 2 S.C.R. 940 [*Zelensky*].

# F.  RESTITUTION

The statement of purpose and list of objectives in section 718 encourage the use of sanctions which attempt to compensate loss or repair damage.[172] Although a probation order which has a restorative element may be crafted,[173] the only *Criminal Code* provision which bears directly on individual compensation is section 738, which provides for a free-standing restitution order.[174] In the 1978 case of *R. v. Zelensky*,[175] the Supreme Court considered the constitutionality of another restitutionary remedy, since repealed, called a compensation order. Laskin C.J.C. traced the history of restitutionary mechanisms in the *Code* and found them to be a constitutional exercise of the criminal law power. He added that they should be used with restraint and caution. Specifically, he observed that the sentencing process should not encroach on civil dispute resolution which lies within the sphere of provincial legislative competence. Accordingly, it is not appropriate to seek a restitutionary order when there are serious legal or factual issues bearing on entitlement or amounts. These issues belong within the realm of civil litigation.

Prior to 1996, a number of cases considered the nature and extent of loss or damage which might be addressed by restitution. Section 738 now provides for restitution as a response to three kinds of loss:

(a)  Damage to, or loss of or destruction to, property as a result of an offence, attempted offence or arrest;

(b)  pecuniary damages including loss of income incurred by reasons of bodily harm which resulted from an offence, attempted offence or arrest;

(c)  expenses incurred as a result of moving out of the offender's household in cases of bodily harm caused or threatened to a spouse or child of the offender.

In all cases, the availability of a restitution order is qualified by the phrase "where the amount is readily ascertainable." This is consistent with the constitutional caution offered by Laskin C.J.C. in *Zelensky*. Similarly, the language of section 738 ensures that there can be no

---

172   See specifically *Criminal Code*, ss. 718(e), (f).
173   Either as community service under s. 732.1(3)(f), *ibid.*, or under the residual category in s. 732.1(3)(h).
174   This was added in the 1996 amendments to replace the repealed pre-existing scheme which allowed for restitution as part of a probation order and also provided another sanction known as a compensation order.
175   Above note 171.

restitution for pain and suffering, usually encompassed by the civil term "general damages." Again, this is a function of the *Zelensky* ruling. Legal fees and disbursements incurred to recover a loss are not to be included in a restitution order.[176] However, there is no requirement that the judge be satisfied about an ability to pay.

## 1) Ability to Pay

Cases dealing with the predecessor sanction, a compensation order, had held that there was no "ability to pay" threshold.[177] Given that the nature of the order is compensatory rather than punitive, and that there is no possibility of imprisonment in default, one might argue that restitution can be distinguished from a fine, where the judge must be satisfied about means to pay. More recent cases, however, have disagreed.

In *R. v. Siemens*, the Manitoba Court of Appeal struck out a restitution order of $59,000 imposed on a twenty-two-year-old facing a lengthy term of imprisonment.[178] It held that ability to pay is relevant because of the way in which a restitution order can affect future rehabilitation. Accordingly, a long prison sentence, in the absence of current financial ability, makes restitution futile. The court also held that, after considering ability to pay and potential impact on the chance for successful rehabilitation,[179] a restitution order could be made for part of an ascertained loss.[180] As well as ability to pay, the court expressed concern about the involvement of victims and multiple accused. Given the discretionary nature of the decision to order restitution, the court offered some additional guidance:

> (1) Where there is a plea bargain, and restitution is not part of it, the court should be slow to make an order of restitution unless it is for a very modest sum.

---

176   See *R. v. Devgan* (1999), 26 C.R. (5th) 307 (Ont. C.A.), leave to appeal to S.C.C. refused [1999] S.C.C.A. No. 518 (QL). While this case dealt with a compensation order imposed prior to the enactment in force of the 1996 amendments, its reasoning has been held to be applicable to the current provisions: see *R. v. Biegus* (1999), 141 C.C.C. (3d) 245 (C.A.) [*Biegus*].

177   See *R. v. Scherer* (1984), 16 C.C.C. (3d) 30 (Ont. C.A.). See also the dissent of Rowles J.A. in *R. v. Deen* (1997), 120 C.C.C. (3d) 482 at 499 (B.C.C.A.).

178   (1999), 136 C.C.C. (3d) 353 (Man. C.A.) [*Siemens*].

179   On the same point, the Ontario Court of Appeal, noting that a restitution order survives bankruptcy, has also held that this factor must be considered before making a restitution order since the continuing obligation can be an obstacle to rehabilitation: see *Biegus*, above note 176.

180   Relying on *R. v. Ali* (1987), 98 B.C.A.C. 239 (C.A.).

(2) Even in a case where the discretion of the sentencing judge is not constrained by a joint recommendation, an order of restitution must not be made as a mechanical afterthought to an incarceratory sentence.

(3) The fact that there were multiple participants in the crimes, as there were in these break and enters, is a factor which militates against a restitution order enforceable against one accused, but not against the others.[181]

As a result, the restitution order was set aside.

This decision supports the prevailing view that the criminal sanction of restitution can be useful but its imposition requires a consideration of the offender's circumstances and whether such an order will be an obstacle to rehabilitation. It further suggests that, when there are civil issues of liability or apportionment, these are better left to the civil litigation process. However, a criminal court has the power to order partial restitution. This could be used to apportion restitution amongst a group of co-accused so long as the division is done roughly by number without regard to civil issues of contribution, indemnity, or joint and several liability. Once there are any complications of a civil nature, the appropriateness of a restitution order diminishes quickly.

## 2) Who Raises the Issue?

Unlike the earlier compensation provision, there is now no need for an application by an aggrieved party. Instead, the issue of restitution can be raised either by the Crown or by the judge. In a case where fine, forfeiture, and restitution are all relevant and possible consequences, priority must be given to restitution which goes directly to a victim and not into the state's coffers.[182]

## 3) Enforcement

Enforcement of a restitution order seems simple at first glance but, on closer inspection, raises a number of questions. First, a restitution order can be paid out of money seized from the offender upon arrest unless there are disputes about entitlement.[183]

---

181 *Siemens*, above note 178 at 357.
182 See *Criminal Code*, s. 740.
183 *Ibid.*, s. 741(2).

Secondly, a restitution order can be filed in any civil court which has monetary jurisdiction and will be enforceable against the offender as if it were a judgment of that court in civil proceedings.[184] Conversely, a restitution order in an individual's favour does not affect his or her ability to seek a civil remedy, although obviously there can be no double recovery of damages.[185] As well, a previous civil judgment does not remove the sentencing judge's ability to consider restitution, although any amounts ordered in other proceedings should be taken into account.[186]

## 4)  Payment Schedules

The issue of whether payments can be ordered to be made on a scheduled basis is a difficult one. Section 738 simply allows the court to order an offender to make restitution by paying an authorized amount to another person; it is silent on how the order to pay can be structured. Section 741(1), which deals with enforcement by the civil process, can be triggered when a restitution order "is not paid forthwith." Moreover, it provides that judgment is entered in the amount of the restitution order rather than the balance owing. This suggests that payments cannot be apportioned and staggered over time.

Under the earlier regime, a restitution order could be part of a probation order. Much to the frustration of probation officers, who complained about being debt collectors, one often saw restitution orders with payment schedules included in probation orders. This express power has been removed from the probation provisions, which also suggests that there may be no power to stagger payments. However, section 738(2) empowers a province to pass regulations "precluding the inclusion of provisions on enforcement of restitution orders as an optional condition of a probation order or of a conditional sentence order." On its face, this implies that in the absence of a provincial regulation payments may be ordered over time according to a prescribed schedule as part of a probation condition under section 732.1(3)(h). While this may appear to be a sensible interpretation which gives flexibility to the court's power to facilitate restitution,[187] it is a dangerous one in that it expands the net of sanctions beyond what Parliament intended. It does

---

184   *Ibid.*, s. 741(1).

185   *Ibid.*, s. 741.2. This is a direct codification of the British Columbia Court of Appeal decision in *London Life Insurance Co. v. Zavitz* (1992), 12 C.R. (4th) 267 (B.C.C.A.).

186   See *Devgan*, above note 176.

187   See *R. v. Brown* (1999), 130 B.C.A.C. 250 (C.A.) [*Brown*], discussed below.

this by setting someone up for a breach of probation charge when there is no comparable sanction for breach of a restitution order. The remedy for a failure to comply with a restitution order is resort to the civil process, where issues like schedules for payment can be addressed.

In *R. v. Brown*,[188] the offender was convicted of fraud and sentenced to a conditional sentence of two years less a day followed by three years probation. The sentencing judge added, without specific reference to any *Code* provision, that "he is to pay restitution" amounting to 20 percent of each victim's loss repayable at the rate of one-fifth each year throughout the sentence. On appeal, the British Columbia Court of Appeal did not delete the restitution order or the repayment provisions. It held that a separate section 738 order should have been made in respect of each victim so that each one could decide whether to take civil enforcement steps. Ryan J.A. commented that the repayment process could be the subject of an application to the sentencing judge, on proper material, to vary the conditions. While not expressly addressed, it was implicit that use of the conditions of a conditional sentence or probation order to structure repayment was acceptable.

Whether the restitution order can itself contain a delayed payment date or a staggered payment scheme is another matter. In other words, can the restitution order provide a postponed date upon which the restitution is due, or even provide for instalment payments? If such powers exist, the arguments in support of them must be the court's ability to control its own process and to ensure the integrity of its own orders. This approach would ensure that no additional criminal liability could be created and, if it did not produce payment, would still leave the issue in the hands of the civil enforcement process. If a court is contemplating postponing payment, it must stipulate the default date when the full amount becomes payable. Similarly, if instalment payments are incorporated, the court should be careful to explain when, for civil enforcement purposes, default occurs. Still, the better answer might be to simply order restitution and leave the details of enforcement to a civil court.

# G. SPECIFIC PROHIBITIONS

The *Criminal Code* provides for specific prohibitions both as mandatory and discretionary responses to findings of guilt. The two most common forms are driving and weapons prohibitions. Section 446(5)

---

188   *Ibid.*

also provides the power to prohibit a person from "owning or having the custody or control of an animal or bird." This can only be triggered by an offence under section 446(1) which encompasses various examples of cruelty to, and neglect of, animals, including fighting or baiting.

## 1) Driving Prohibitions

Where an accused is convicted or discharged of an offence contrary to section 253 (impaired driving or "over eighty" or section 254(5) (refusing to comply with a demand), mandatory driving prohibitions imposed by section 259(1) apply in addition to any other sanction. They apply regardless of any applicable provincial or territorial driving license suspension that may follow conviction. The periods of prohibition are as follows:

- first offence: minimum of three months and maximum of three years
- second offence: minimum of six months and maximum of three years
- subsequent offence: minimum of one year and maximum of three years

For offences under sections 220, 221, 236, 249, 250, 252, and 255(2) or (3) committed "by means of a motor vehicle" or other conveyance, the judge may impose a driving prohibition, the potential length of which is determined by the maximum allowable sentence of imprisonment. If the offence is punishable by life imprisonment, the prohibition can be of any duration. For offences subject to imprisonment between five years and life, the prohibition can go up to ten years. The other offences carry maximum discretionary driving prohibitions of three years commencing after any sentence of imprisonment imposed for the offence. An individual who drives during a period of disqualification commits another offence.[189]

Sections 259(1) and (2)(c) extend the available prohibition by including the phrase "plus any period to which the offender is sentenced." This is not a postponement of the period of prohibition, but rather an increase in the length of the potential prohibition when a period of imprisonment is imposed. In R. v. Laycock, dealing with a predecessor provision, the Ontario Court of Appeal concluded that the prohibition commenced immediately and could not be postponed until after a term of imprisonment.[190] While the statutory language has changed, some of the court's concerns are still present. For example, if

189   See *Criminal Code*, s. 259(4). Disqualification includes any of the above driving prohibitions or a disqualification from driving or operating a vehicle under provincial, territorial, or federal law: see s. 259(5).
190   (1989), 51 C.C.C. (3d) 65 (Ont. C.A.).

the current phrase was interpreted to postpone the prohibition until after the custodial term, what about temporary absence passes, periods of parole, or day parole? The better interpretation is to read the phrase "plus any period to which the offender is sentenced to imprisonment" as an increase in the available prohibition rather than a postponement.

While appellate decisions[191] discussing the relevant principles are uncommon, it is clear that extensive prohibitions will be considered in light of the gravity of the offence, especially the nature of the driving, the degree of impairment, the consequences in terms of injury or death, and the existence of a previous driving record.[192]

An example of the interplay of factors is *R. v. Bowler* where a twenty-year-old was convicted of dangerous driving causing bodily harm.[193] He had a previous conviction for dangerous driving and a lengthy record for driving violations. However, he suffered from a learning disability and had only attained a Grade three education. The driving involved racing on a public highway. The offender had been convicted of speeding while on bail for the instant offence. Hill J. concluded that he had shown "contempt for the rules and regulations of the roadway and abuse of the privilege of driving." He sentenced him to twelve months imprisonment and imposed a two-and-a-half year driving prohibition. Clearly, the custodial sentence was uppermost in the judge's mind.

By way of contrast, *R. v. Iafrate* involved a more mature offender who was sentenced to a short term of imprisonment followed by a ten-year driving prohibition.[194] The Ontario Court of Appeal gave mitigating effect to a voluntary abstention of driving from the time of the offence to the sentencing, and reduced the prohibition to eight years. In *R. v. Maccarone*,[195] a man convicted of dangerous driving causing death was sentenced to three years imprisonment and a ten-year driving prohibition. The offender had no previous criminal convictions but was driving while suspended at the time of the offence. Although not found to be impaired, he had been drinking. On appeal, the driving prohibition was reduced to five years in light of his rehabilitative

---

191  A driving prohibition under s. 259(1) or (2) of the *Criminal Code* can be reviewed on a sentence appeal either by itself or in conjunction with other elements of the sentence since it is included in the definition of "sentence" in s. 673.

192  Including provincial driving infractions: see *R. v. Maccarone* (1999), 42 M.V.R. (3d) 154 (Ont. C.A.) [*Maccarone*].

193  [1999] O.J. No. 2280 (Sup. Ct.) (QL).

194  [1999] O.J. No. 1789 (C.A.) (QL).

195  Above note 192.

progress in dealing with his alcohol problems. In dissent, Finlayson J.A. noted that the National Parole Board had jurisdiction under section 109 of the *Corrections and Conditional Release Act* to reduce a period of prohibition after five years of it had elapsed. He suggested that this was the appropriate response to the offender's concerns about the lengthy prohibition.

## 2)  Firearms and Weapons Prohibitions

Section 109(1) of the *Criminal Code* provides for a far-reaching mandatory prohibition which applies when an offender is convicted of

(1)  an indictable offence punishable by imprisonment for ten years or more which involves bodily harm or the threat of bodily harm;

(2)  various weapons offences or criminal harassment;[196]

(3)  importing or producing drugs;[197] and

(4)  offences involving a firearm, cross-bow, or prohibited or restricted weapon where the offender is already subject to a prohibition.

For first offences, the prohibition lasts for ten years in respect of the possession of a firearm, cross-bow, restricted weapon, ammunition or explosive, and for life with respect to prohibited firearms, restricted firearms, prohibited weapons, prohibited devices and prohibited ammunition.[198] For subsequent offences, the prohibitions are all for life.[199]

The mandatory nature of the predecessor prohibition generated a lot of litigation over the issue of constitutional exemptions in situations where the impact of the prohibition was inordinately severe. For example, the Yukon Territorial Court of Appeal permitted a constitutional exemption in *R. v. Chief* where the offender was a subsistence hunter.[200] It was accepted that the penalty was grossly disproportionate to the offender's culpability and, in his situation, would produce a cruel and unusual punishment. While the prohibition was, in general, constitutionally valid, the offender was entitled to an exemption from

---

196   See *Criminal Code*, s. 109(1)(b), which includes offences under ss. 85(1), 85(2), 95(1), 99(1), 100(1), 102(1), 103(1), & 264 (criminal harassment).

197   *Ibid.*, s. 109(1)(c), which includes offences under ss. 6(1), 6(2), 7(1), & 7(2) of the *Controlled Drugs and Substances Act*, S.C. 1996, c. 19.

198   See *Criminal Code*, s. 109(2). For the definitions of prohibited firearm, prohibited weapon, restricted firearm, restricted weapon, prohibited device, and prohibited ammunition, see s. 84.

199   *Ibid.*, s. 109(3).

200   (1989), 51 C.C.C. (3d) 265 (Y.C.A.).

its applicability. Subsequently, in *R. v. Kelly*, a police officer argued that he was entitled to an exemption since he required a gun to continue working in the security field.[201] The Ontario Court of Appeal rejected this argument holding that the provision should either be struck down because it permitted a violation of section 12, or it should be applied. The constitutionality of the prohibition could be tested by using either the instant case or a "reasonable hypothetical"[202] circumstance, but if it passed muster, there should be no exemption. The Supreme Court has not yet ruled on the availability of this kind of constitutional exemption[203] but there are cases on the current docket which may resolve the issue.[204]

Parliament has recognized the need to provide some exemptive vehicle: section 113(1) permits the court that is imposing the section 109 prohibition or, if already imposed, a court that has jurisdiction to make such orders, to order a chief firearms officer to issue a license on specific terms and conditions if satisfied that

(a) the person needs a firearm or restricted weapon to hunt or trap in order to sustain the person or the person's family, or

(b) a prohibition order would constitute a virtual prohibition against employment in the only vocation open to the person.

The scope of section 113(1)(b) will require interpretation. It need not conform to the conclusions reached in earlier cases, when the issue was whether the prohibition produced a section 12 violation, but the idea of disproportionate consequences may be useful. The word "vocation" indicates a form of employment that involves commitment and training. Accordingly, it is not so much the question whether the offender can obtain employment but whether the prohibition will result in a loss of a discrete career. It remains to be seen whether the career must be the product of a long-term investment by the offender or whether a novice can also qualify. If the issue is one of disproportionality of

---

201   (1990), 59 C.C.C. (3d) 497 (Ont. C.A.).
202   As discussed in *R. v. Goltz*, [1991] 3 S.C.R. 485.
203   It was left open in *R. v. Sawyer*, [1992] 3 S.C.R. 809. The granting of exemptions during a period of suspension after a declaration of invalidity, as approved in *Corbière v. Canada (Minister of Indian and Northern Affairs)*, [1999] 2 S.C.R. 203, is a different matter.
204   See *R. v. Latimer* (1998), 131 C.C.C. (3d) 191 (Sask. C.A.), discussed below in Chapter 10, at 10(A)(3). The appeal to the Supreme Court of Canada was argued in June 2000 and judgment was reserved.

consequences, it is doubtful that one's purported ambitions, even if sincere, will be sufficient.

# H. INTERMITTENT SENTENCE

Following the recommendations of the Ouimet Committee, the *Criminal Code* was amended in 1972[205] to permit sentences of imprisonment of ninety days or less to be served intermittently. A number of technical issues arose in relation to intermittent sentences and their integration with probation and other sentences of imprisonment: the 1996 amendments have gone a long way to removing these obstacles. In their place, however, is a political controversy over the efficacy of the intermittent sentence.

Section 732(1) establishes discretion to order that a sentence of ninety days be served in segments, with a probation order in effect when the offender is not in custody. It provides:

> Where the court imposes a sentence of imprisonment of ninety days or less on an offender convicted of an offence, whether in default of payment of a fine or otherwise, the court may, having regard to the age and character of the offender, the nature of the offence and the circumstances surrounding its commission, and the availability of appropriate accommodation to ensure compliance with the sentence, order
>
> (a) that the sentence be served intermittently at such times as are specified in the order; and
>
> (b) that the offender comply with the conditions prescribed in a probation order when not in confinement during the period that the sentence is being served and, if the court so orders, on release from prison after completing the intermittent sentence.

The *Criminal Code* does not prescribe the potential bases for imposing an intermittent sentence but requires the judge to consider the age and character of the offender, and the circumstances of the offence. The usual reasons for an intermittent sentence are to avoid loss of employment or interruption of education, or to ensure continuity of care for children,[206] but the discretion is sufficiently broad to encompass other grounds. "Intermittent" means "from time to time" and an order under section 732 need not be for weekends but can be for whatever period is

---

205   *Criminal Law Amendment Act, 1972*, above note 130, s. 58.
206   See *R. v. Parisian* (1993), 81 C.C.C. (3d) 351 (Man. C.A.).

relevant to the basis for the intermittent sentence. For example, an offender who works from Friday to Tuesday can serve a sentence on Wednesdays and Thursdays. However, the times of arrival and departure must be clearly specified.[207] The limit is ninety days and cannot be extended by using consecutive sentences.[208]

With respect to integration with other sanctions, the 1996 amendments have confirmed that the period of probation can extend beyond the service of the custodial term. Since this extended period of probation is authorized by section 732(1)(b) and not section 731(1), the general probation provision, it should not be subject to the restrictions in section 731(1). Accordingly, even if the probation period extends beyond the custodial sentence, a fine can also be imposed.[209] The length of the probation period, if it extends beyond the custodial period, cannot be more than three years from the date of imposition.[210] Section 732(2) permits an offender to apply to have an intermittent sentence converted into a straight-time sentence. Section 732(3) provides that the unexpired portion of an intermittent sentence automatically becomes a straight-time sentence when the offender receives a subsequent sentence of imprisonment for another offence unless the judge who imposes the subsequent sentence specifically preserves it. Unless the subsequent sentence is very short, it would be a rare situation where there would still be some benefit to an intermittent sentence.[211]

Since its inception, there have been occasions when correctional authorities at both the local or provincial/territorial level have complained about the difficulties in accommodating individuals ordered to serve intermittent sentences. Occasionally, overcrowding at local facilities has produced reports that persons arriving to serve intermittent sentences were sent home on temporary absence passes because of a

---

207   It cannot be left to the offender to decide when she will serve the sentence: see *R. v. Downe* (1978), 44 C.C.C. (2d) 468 (P.E.I. S.C. in banco).

208   See *R. v. Fletcher* (1992), 2 C.C.C. (3d) 221 (Ont. C.A.), which held that the merger provisions of the *Parole Act*, R.S.C. 1970, c. P-2 added the two elements into a sentence greater than ninety days. See also *R. v. Aubin* (1992), 72 C.C.C. (3d) 189 (Que. C.A.).

209   See *R. v. Cartier* (1990), 57 C.C.C. (3d) 569 (Que. C.A.) which, although dealing with the earlier provision and the intervening probation period, applied the same analysis. It concluded that the general restriction that probation could be added to either a fine or imprisonment was only applicable to probation orders under s. 731(1), and not ones established under the intermittent sentence provision.

210   See the discussion under probation, above, at 9(D)(3).

211   Given that the usual reasons for imposing an intermittent sentence relate to avoiding unjustifiable disruption to important aspects of an offender's life.

lack of room. It is impossible to know whether accommodation problems are a result of the large numbers of intermittent sentences or a failure on the part of correctional authorities to properly plan for this kind of sentence. Regardless, the concern has added to the traditional considerations in section 732(1) the issue of "availability of appropriate accommodation to ensure compliance with the sentence." Clearly, this is intended to permit a judge to refuse an intermittent sentence because of accommodation concerns; however, it does not require it. Judges need not respond to unconfirmed third-hand reports of Friday night overcrowding, but may want to use the new powers under section 723(3) to order that evidence be adduced on the issue of accommodation and what steps have or have not been taken to implement intermittent sentences. While it would be unwise to craft sentences without regard to existing resources, it would be a fundamental error to permit correctional planning decisions to usurp the sentencing function by removing options from the matrix.

The perception of an accommodation problem has produced a lobby to repeal the intermittent sentence provisions. This would be unfortunate. They are widely used to preserve employment, educational programs, and even child care and custody arrangements.[212] The new conditional sentence discussed later in this chapter is not a substitute for the intermittent sentence since it cannot apply when there is a mandatory minimum penalty. It is likely that a large portion of intermittent sentences arise from the mandatory fourteen-day sentence for a second impaired driving offence and the minimum ninety-day sentence for a subsequent one.[213] When Parliament created an aggravated penalty range for driving offences it amended the minimum sentence of subsequent impaired offences by reducing it from three months to ninety days. The obvious reason was to permit intermittent sentences in appropriate cases. If intermittent sentences are removed from the *Code*, judges will have lost a useful sentencing tool. Moreover, the impact will be felt disproportionately by the working poor, single parents, and students.

---

212 In 1997–98, 13 percent of admissions to provincial/territorial institutions were intermittent sentences, ranging from a low of 3 percent in British Columbia to a high of 20 percent in Ontario: see M. Reed & J. Roberts, "Adult Correctional Services in Canada, 1997–98" *Juristat* 19:4 (April 1999) at 8. The low use rate in British Columbia is likely the result of an extensive electronic monitoring program which began in the late 1980s.
213 See *Criminal Code*, ss. 255(1)(a)(ii), (iii).

# I. IMPRISONMENT

Imprisonment is frequently used by Canadian courts as a response to crime. In 1998, there were, on average, 13,050 prisoners serving sentences in provincial or territorial institutions, and 13,756 prisoners in federal penitentiaries.[214] With the exception of the United States, one of the world leaders in imprisonment, Canada ranks ahead of most other western countries in terms of the percentage of its population that is incarcerated. In *R. v. Gladue*,[215] the Supreme Court focused on the over use of incarceration and interpreted the 1996 amendments as a direction to trial judges to use imprisonment as a sanction of last resort.

Section 718(c) could not be clearer: the sanction of confinement can be a just sanction only "where necessary." Combined with sections 718.2 (d) and (e), the principle of restraint is now entrenched. This means that the sentencing judge must consider all non-custodial sanctions before concluding that is reasonable in the circumstances to sentence an offender to imprisonment. Section 726.2 requires all judges to record the reasons for the sentence. It would be consistent with the principle of restraint if judges explained why non-custodial options were not reasonable in the circumstances.

If a sentence of imprisonment is considered necessary, courts should be sensitive to the offender's age and whether he or she has been imprisoned before. First sentences of imprisonment for youthful offenders should be concerned with individual deterrence and rehabilitation, taking into account the deterrent effect of the arrest, prosecution, and conviction.[216] As a result they should generally be at the low end of the range. Before moving to a lengthy sentence of imprisonment for any offender, the sentencing judge should consider whether the sentence is so long as to crush any prospects of rehabilitation, especially as a result of severing ties with supportive people. Of course, with crimes of violence, the gravity of the offence and a previous record can trump this consideration when protection becomes the overwhelming concern.

A sentence of imprisonment begins when it is imposed,[217] unless it is ordered to be served consecutively to another sentence. (A sentence

---

214  See Canadian Centre for Justice Statistics, *Corrections Key Indicator Report for Adults and Young Offenders* (Ottawa: Statistics Canada, 1999).
215  [1999] 1 S.C.R. 688 at 715–23 [*Gladue*].
216  See *R. v. McCormick* (1979), 47 C.C.C. (2d) 224 (Man. C.A.); and *R. v. Demeter* (1976), 32 C.C.C. (2d) 379 (Ont. C.A.).
217  *Criminal Code*, s. 719(1).

can be made consecutive to any other sentence imposed at the same time,[218] or to a sentence imposed earlier.)[219] A sentence of imprisonment of two years or more will be served in the penitentiary,[220] as will combined sentences with an aggregate length of two years or more.[221] A person already serving a sentence in a penitentiary who receives another sentence of imprisonment will also serve that in the penitentiary, regardless of its length.[222] An offender serving a provincial sentence who subsequently receives another sentence making the aggregate term two years or more will be transferred to the penitentiary.[223]

## J. CONDITIONAL SENTENCES OF IMPRISONMENT

This controversial option, enacted as part of the 1996 amendments, permits a judge to order that a term of imprisonment of less than two years be served in the community on conditions. The creation of the conditional sentence has influenced the Supreme Court's conclusion that the amendments represented a clear direction to judges to reduce the use of incarceration where reasonable alternatives existed. The first mention of a conditional sentence was in Bill C-19 in 1984, where it was included as a new form of suspended sentence.[224] Subsequently, it was not included in the 1990 Green Paper *Directions for Reform*[225] or Bill C-90 which died on the order paper in 1992.[226] These documents were criticized for not providing a new alternative to incarcera-

---

218   *Ibid.*, s. 718.3(4)(c). See the discussion of consecutive and concurrent sentences in Chapter 6, above.

219   Section 718(4)(a). The 1996 amendments made the sensible change of using the date of sentence as the relevant date and not the date of conviction as appeared in the predecessor provision: see discussion of *R. v. Paul*, [1982] 1 S.C.R. 621 in Chapter 6, above, at 6(B)(2).

220   *Criminal Code*, ss. 743.1(1)(a), (b).

221   *Ibid.*, s. 743.1(1)(c).

222   *Ibid.*, s. 743.1(2). This applies even if the penitentiary prisoner is out of custody on conditional release at the time of the conviction if the conditional release is not revoked: see *R. v. Dinardo* (1982), 67 C.C.C. (2d) 505 (Ont. C.A.).

223   *Criminal Code*, s. 743.1(5).

224   For an analysis of the history of the conditional sentence, see A. Manson, "Conditional Sentences: Courts of Appeal Debate the Principles" (1998), 15 C.R. (5th) 176 at 182–84.

225   Department of Justice, *Directions for Reform: Sentencing* (Ottawa: Supply and Services Canada, 1990).

226   Bill C-90, *An Act to amend the Criminal Code (sentencing) and other Acts in consequence thereof*, 3d Sess., 34th Parl., 1992 (1st Reading 23 June 1992).

tion as had been anticipated. The conditional sentence resurfaced in its current form, more or less, in Bill C-41. Section 742.1 now provides:

> Where a person is convicted of an offence, except an offence that is punishable by a minimum term of imprisonment, and the court
> (a) imposes a sentence or imprisonment of less than two years, and
> (b) is satisfied that serving the sentence in the commuity would not endanger the safety of the community and would be consistent with the fundamental purpose and principles of sentencing set out in sections 718 to 718.2
> the court may, for the purpose of supervising the offender's behaviour in the community, order that the offender serve the sentence in the community, subject to the offender's complying with the conditions of a conditional sentence order made under section 742.3.[227]

The enigma of the conditional sentence is apparent: when is a required sentence of imprisonment not required? Between 1996 and 1999, more than 42,000 conditional sentences were imposed.[228] Appellate courts struggled with a number of fundamental questions dealing with principles, methodology, duration, appropriate conditions, and even whether any offences were excluded from the regime. Many of these issues were resolved when the Supreme Court decided five conditional sentence cases on January 31, 2000.

## 1) The Supreme Court and Conditional Sentences

### a) R. v. Proulx
The lead decision in the conditional sentence package was rendered in the case of R. v. Proulx, which arose from convictions for dangerous driving causing death and causing bodily harm.[229] The offender had

---

227  One of the earliest decisions by an appellate court, R. v. Scidmore (1996), 112 C.C.C. (3d) 28 (Ont. C.A.), produced concern that there was no discretion to deny a conditional sentence if the sentence of imprisonment was less than two years and the offender did not represent a danger. This was effectively reversed in R. v. Pierce (1997), 114 C.C.C. (3d) 23 (Ont. C.A.). It led to a quick amendment, which added the phrase in s. 742.1(b) "and would be consistent with the fundamental purpose and principles of sentencing set out in sections 718 to 718.2": Criminal Law Improvement Act, 1996, S.C. 1997, c. 18, s. 107.1, in effect 2 May 1997.

228  See Department of Justice, Conditional Sentence Orders by Province and Territory, September 6, 1996 –September 30, 1999, Three Years of Data, Final Report, by C. La Prairie (Ottawa: Department of Justice, 1999). She calculated a total of 42,941 during the three-year period.

229  Above note 107.

been a licensed driver for seven weeks when, after consuming alcohol, he drove an unsound vehicle erratically on slippery roads. After about twenty minutes, he attempted to pass and struck an oncoming vehicle. One of his passengers was killed and the driver of the other car was seriously injured. The trial judge found that the offender would not endanger the community but rejected a conditional sentence on the basis that it would be inconsistent with the principles of general deterrence and denunciation. She sentenced him to eighteen months imprisonment. Subsequently, the Manitoba Court of Appeal[230] varied the sentence and turned it into a conditional sentence. All eight judges[231] who decided the case agreed that a conditional sentence was not appropriate and that the eighteen-month sentence should be restored.[232]

The court's decision, the last judgment written by Lamer C.J.C. before his retirement, represents a cautious attempt to carve out a role for conditional sentences which will provide trial judges with an alternative to both probation and custody. In a nutshell, whenever less intrusive non-custodial options are not reasonable, a conditional sentence should be used as a punitive alternative to incarceration unless the offence generates such a demand for denunciation and deterrence that only a custodial term will satisfy that demand. However, a detailed review is essential to appreciate how the judgment should affect future sentencing decisions.

Lamer C.J.C. commenced his analysis by returning to the larger question of the intent behind Bill C-41, which included the conditinal sentence provisions. Relying on the joint judgment of Cory and Iacobucci JJ. in *Gladue*, he observed that two of Parliament's "principal objectives" in enacting the legislation were "(i) reducing the use of prison as a sanction, and (ii) expanding the use of restorative justice principles in sentencing."[233] After discussing these goals, he examined the nature of the conditional sentence and held:

> The conditional sentence incorporates some elements of non-custodial measures and some others of incarceration. Because it is served in the community, it will generally be more effective than incarceration at achieving the restorative objectives of rehabilitation, reparations to the victim and community, and the promotion of a sense of

---

230   (1997), 121 C.C.C. (3d) 68 (Man. C.A.).
231   Cory J. did not participate in the decisions.
232   Since the conditional sentence had already been served, the Court stayed the eighteen-month term of incarceration.
233   *Proulx*, above note 107 at 78.

responsibility in the offender. However, it is also a punitive sanction capable of achieving the objectives of denunciation and deterrence. It is this punitive aspect that distinguishes the conditional sentence from probation. . . .[234]

Although the direct comparison with probation was inconclusive,[235] he held that Parliament intended the conditional sentence to be more punitive than probation since it is characterized as a "sentence of imprisonment"[236] and imprisonment is more punitive and restrictive of liberty than probation. He observed that conditional sentences should "generally include punitive conditions that are restrictive of the offender's liberty."[237] This means that conditions prescribing house arrest or strict curfews should be "the norm" and not the exception. If there is no reason for any punitive conditions then probation is likely the more appropriate sentence.

Clearly, the conditional sentence is situated on the range of sanctions between prison and probation. This, however, does not answer the methodological questions generated by the unusual language of section 742.1. With *Proulx*, a number of these controversies have been laid to rest. First, there is no "two step" requirement. The duration of a conditional sentence is not determined by the length of the custodial sentence which might be imposed, but is determined after it is decided to impose a conditional sentence, taking into account the types of conditions which may be appropriate. In other words, the judge who has concluded that the offence might warrant a sentence of imprisonment but not in the penitentiary range must then determine whether to impose a conditional sentence. The length of the sentence is then fitted to the sanction.

The choice may well be between a medium-range custodial term and a long conditional sentence. Lamer C.J.C. argued that this is necessary to preserve proportionality, since a conditional sentence is more

234  *Ibid.* at 82–83 (emphasis omitted).
235  He noted the differences in the mandatory conditions, the ability to order treatment in the *Criminal Code*, s. 742.3(2)(e), and the differences in the wording of the residual categories all of which support the conclusion that a conditional sentence is more punitive. Conversely, the penalty for breach of probation appears to be potentially greater than the penalty for breach of a conditional sentence which suggests that probation is a more serious sentence: *Proulx*, above note 107 at 83–85.
236  See the sub-heading before s. 742 of the *Criminal Code*. It reads "Conditional Sentence of Imprisonment." See also the language of s. 742.1(a): *Proulx*, above note 107 at 86.
237  *Ibid.* at 88.

lenient than imprisonment but meant to be more punitive than probation. He thus rejected the view that proportionality is maintained by
using the length of the custodial term in issue to determine the duration of the conditional sentence, thereby ensuring that, even if
breached, the period of state control will be commensurate. This argument, an emanation of Norval Morris' conception of desert which uses
proportionality as a brake and not an engine,[238] was rejected in *Proulx*.
While we can now anticipate longer conditional sentences, appellate
courts will need to develop a new scale of comparison to ensure that
the principles of restraint and parity apply to conditional sentences.

In determining whether to impose a conditional sentence or not, the
Supreme Court reached the important decision that no offence is presumptively excluded from the conditional sentence regime. Here, a number of parties had argued that such offences as sexual offences against
children, aggravated sexual assault, manslaughter, serious fraud or theft,
impaired or dangerous driving causing death or bodily harm, and trafficking in narcotics should never result in a conditional sentence. Asserting the need for sentencing to be an individualized process which relies
on judicial discretion, Lamer C.J.C. explained his conclusion:

> In my view, while the gravity of such offences is clearly relevant to
> determining whether a conditional sentence is appropriate in the cir-
> cumstances, it would be both unwise and unnecessary to establish
> judicially created presumptions that conditional sentences are inap-
> propriate for specific offences. Offence-specific presumptions intro-
> duce unwarranted rigidity in the determination of whether a condi-
> tional sentence is a just and appropriate sanction. Such presumptions
> do not accord with the principle of proportionality set out in s. 718.1
> and the value of individualization in sentencing, nor are they neces-
> sary to achieve the important objectives of uniformity and consis-
> tency in the use of conditional sentences.[239]

In the course of this part of the judgment, the Chief Justice drew an
important distinction between the gravity of the offence and the moral

---

238  See N. Morris, *The Future of Imprisonment* (Chicago: University of Chicago Press,
     1974) at 73–77. See also the debate between Julian Roberts and Andrew von
     Hirsch, on one side, and Allan Manson, on the other, in J.V. Roberts & A. von
     Hirsch, "Conditional Sentences of Imprisonment and the Fundamental Principle
     of Proportionality in Sentencing" (1998), 10 C.R. (5th) 222; and A. Manson, "A
     Brief Reply to Professors Roberts and von Hirsch" (1998), 10 C.R. (5th ) 232. In
     the end, Roberts and von Hirsch won.
239  *Proulx*, above note 107 at 106–7.

blameworthiness of the offender. He noted that the demand of proportionality is determined by reference both to the offence and the offender's "degree of responsibility," thereby militating against offence-based presumptions in either direction.

Section 742.1 requires the sentencing judge to be satisfied that "service in the community would not endanger the community." As the conditional sentence is constructed, Lamer C.J.C. held that preserving the safety of the community is a condition precedent to a conditional sentence. With respect to what endangerment means in this context, appellate courts had generated three possible interpretations: the risk posed by the particular offender of future personal injury offences; the risk of any criminal offences committed by the offender, including property offences; or a broader conception of risk that encompasses not only the offender but other potential offenders who may not be deterred as a result of leniency to the offender. The Supreme Court chose the middle approach. It agreed that only the risks posed by the offender should be considered but expanded the view of risk to include threats to property. This does not mean that any risk of re-offending, no matter how slight, should bar an individual from a conditional sentence. As he subsequently explained:

> Two factors must be taken into account in assessing the danger to a community posed by an offender: (i) the risk of the offender re-offending; and (ii) the gravity of the damage that could ensue in the event of re-offence.[240]

In other words, while the risk of any new offences must be considered, the risk of personal injury must be compared to the prospect of a property offence.

Moreover, future risk can be minimized by conditions as is evident from the language of section 742.3(2)(f) which speaks of conditions crafted to prevent a "repetition" of offences. Lamer C.J.C. used the example of drug addiction as a situation where the risk of new offences can be minimized by an appropriate treatment condition and supervision if the judge is satisfied that there is "a good chance of rehabilitation." Here it is important to note, as appellate courts have observed,[241] that hard-core drug addiction can be treated but success may involve a number of failures

---

240  R. v. Wells, [2000] 1 S.C.R. 207 at 222 [Wells].
241  See R. v. Hayman (1999), 135 C.C.C. (3d) 338 at 346–47, Rosenberg J.A. (Ont. C.A.); and R. v. Preston (1990), 79 C.R. (3d) 61 (B.C.C.A.). See also D.M. Tanovich, "A Breath of Fresh Air on the Incarceration Addiction in Drug Cases" (1999), 23 C.R. (5th) 242 at 251–53.

along the way. It is gratifying that the Supreme Court recognized that the conditional sentence can be a good vehicle for invoking and monitoring treatment for drug addiction, but courts have to recognize that a person can be committed to rehabilitation and still suffer setbacks. With drug addiction, courts must be tolerant and stay the course so long as there appears to be a real commitment to rehabilitation.

It has always been apparent that the conditional sentence is a discretionary tool, and that the hard issue goes back to the basic enigma: when is a custodial sentence both warranted and not warranted at the same time? The enigma is especially challenging when the offence is one of inherent gravity such as in *Proulx* and the other four cases considered at the same time. While the situation of the conditional sentence as a discrete, albeit unusual, sanction between prison and probation attempts to blunt the practical effect of the enigma, the discretionary decision remains difficult. Its importance is enhanced by the emphasis paid by the Supreme Court to deference. On this point, Lamer C.J.C. said:

> Several provisions of Part XXIII confirm that Parliament intended to confer a wide discretion upon the sentencing judge. As a general rule, ss. 718.3(1) and 718.3 (2) provide that the degree and kind of punishment to be imposed is left to the discretion of the sentencing judge. Moreover, the opening words of s. 718 specify that the sentencing judge must seek to achieve the fundamental purpose of sentencing "by imposing just sanctions that have *one or more* of the following objectives" (emphasis added). In the context of the conditional sentence, s. 742.1 provides that the judge "may" impose a conditional sentence and enjoys a wide discretion in the drafting of the appropriate conditions, pursuant to s. 742.3(2).
>
> Although an appellate court might entertain a different opinion as to what objectives should be pursued and the best way to do so, that difference will generally not constitute an error of law justifying interference. Further, minor errors in the sequence of application of s. 742.1 may not warrant intervention by appellate courts. Again, I stress that appellate courts should not second-guess sentencing judges unless the sentence imposed is demonstrably unfit.[242]

Deference will apply both to the findings, like the presence or absence of danger to the community, and to the ultimate exercise of discretion.

Notwithstanding the obvious complexity of the discretionary decision, the Supreme Court's analysis offered little help beyond reminding

---

242   *Proulx*, above note 107 at 124–25.

sentencing judges that it is fundamental to "consider which sentencing objectives figure most prominently in the factual circumstances"[243] of the case. If the case suggests a need to pursue both punitive and restorative objectives, then a conditional sentence will likely be the appropriate vehicle. Although a conditional sentence can promote denunciatory objectives, where "punitive objectives such as denunciation and deterrence are particularly pressing, such as cases in which there are aggravating circumstances, incarceration will generally be the preferable sanction."[244] At the end of the day, perhaps the most significant lesson for counsel and sentencing judges that flows from *Proulx* is the individualized nature of the process and the concomitant need to craft conditions which are realistic, practicable, and generally punitive. The conditions should promote the safety of the community which, by definition, includes enhancing the rehabilitative prospects of the offender.

### b) *Proulx*'s Four Companion Cases

While *Proulx* answered many of the outstanding controversies, its contribution as a clear direction to sentencing judges can be predicted by the various splits in the accompanying cases. While all eight judges agreed with the principles in *Proulx*, it was the only case that generated unanimity. In *R. v. Bunn*,[245] a case of "breach of trust" theft by a lawyer, the Supreme Court upheld the conditional sentence five to three. The fact that the offender was the sole caregiver for a disabled spouse was a significant factor militating against a custodial term.[246] In *R. v. L.F.W.*,[247] the judges split evenly on whether to uphold a conditional sentence for a man who, more than twenty-five years before, committed offences of indecent assault and gross indecency on a young girl who was between the ages of six and twelve. The offender apparently committed no other offences during the interim, had dealt successfully with an alcohol problem, and had a good work record.

---

243 *Ibid.* at 120.
244 *Ibid.*
245 [2000] 1 S.C.R. 183.
246 Regrettably, the majority also appeared concerned about the humiliation and loss of profession which resulted. Given that the breach of trust was professional in nature, the loss of his career should not have been characterized as mitigating. See the discussion of collateral and indirect consequences in Chapter 7, above. See also H.A. Kaiser, "*R. v. Bunn*: A Disconcerting Judicial Response to the Dishonest Lawyer" (2000), 30 C.R. (5th) 102.
247 [2000] 1 S.C.R. 132.

272 THE LAW OF SENTENCING

In *R. v. R.N.S.*,[248] all judges agreed that the nine-month sentence of imprisonment should be restored in a case of sexual assault and invitation to sexual touching committed on a step-daughter who was between the ages of five and eight. However, four judges[249] disagreed with the Chief Justice on his distinction between this case and *L.F.W.*, in which he supported a conditional sentence. The case of *R. v. R.(R.A.)*[250] involved a sexual assault conviction and two convictions for common assault committed at the workplace by an employer on an employee in her early twenties. L'Heureux-Dubé J. and five other judges allowed the appeal restoring the one-year term of imprisonment. In dissent, Lamer C.J.C. would have maintained the nine-month conditional with house arrest and sex offender treatment although he remarked that a lengthier conditional sentence would not have appeared so lenient. In the result, only *Bunn* and *L.F.W.* maintained their conditional sentences, and not without dissent.

In *Proulx* and its companion cases where the conditional sentence was set aside, the resulting terms of imprisonment were stayed due to prior completion of the conditional sentence. This luxury is not available to lower court judges who must sift throught the analysis in search of help. The Supreme Court has once again emphasized the principle of restraint and the need for an individualized response. Creativity in crafting conditions that respond to underlying problems, like drug addiction, may provide the best long-term protection to the community. A conditional sentence can have deterrent and denunciatory effect produced by restrictive conditions like house arrest. As well, there are situations where conditions can be used to convey an explicit denunciatory message. For example, although not a conditional sentence case, in *R. v. Hollinsky*[251] a young person convicted of impaired driving causing death was required to conduct speaking sessions at local high schools to explain the tragic consequences of impaired driving.

### c)  *R. v. Wells*: The Conditional Sentence and Aboriginal Offenders
A few weeks after releasing *Proulx*, the Supreme Court rendered its decision in *R. v. Wells*,[252] which involved a sentence of twenty months

---

248  [2000] 1 S.C.R. 149.
249  L'Heureux-Dubé, Gonthier, McLachlin, and Bastarache JJ. were the group of four who, in *L.F.W.*, were opposed to a conditional sentence.
250  [2000] 1 S.C.R. 163.
251  (1995), 103 C.C.C. (3d) 472 (Ont. C.A.), affirming the trial level decision of Nosanchuk P.C.J.
252  Above note 240.

imprisonment imposed on an aboriginal man convicted of sexual assault. He had assaulted a woman while she was asleep or unconscious. The offender had a favourable pre-sentence report and a record of two prior convictions for assault. The eighteen-year-old victim suffered vaginal abrasions but there was no evidence of penetration. She did not remember the event but was humiliated when she learned about it. Prior to the Supreme Court decision in *Gladue*[253] interpreting section 718.2(e) of the *Criminal Code*, both the trial judge and the Alberta Court of Appeal had rejected a conditional sentence. At both levels there was some evidence of efforts by the offender to deal with his alcohol problems.

For the Supreme Court, the case provided another opportunity to consider the role of conditional sentences in relation to offences requiring denunciation and deterrence, with the added dimension of section 718.2(e) and the "with particular attention to the circumstances of aboriginal offenders" qualification. After discussing *Proulx*, Iacobucci J. for a unanimous court commented on the general issue:

> Therefore, depending on the severity of the conditions imposed, a conditional sentence may be reasonable in circumstances where deterrence and denunciation are paramount considerations. Ultimately, however, the determination of the availability of a conditional sentence depends upon the sentencing judge's assessment of the specific circumstances of the case, including a consideration of the aggravating factors, the nature of the offence, the community context, and the availability of conditions which have the capacity to properly reflect society's condemnation.[254]

Commenting on section 718.2(e), he noted its remedial purpose focusing on the concept of restorative justice which requires attention to the needs of victims, the offender, and the community. By adding the reference to aboriginal offenders, Parliament has directed sentencing judges to address this historical social problem; but only to the extent that a remedy is available through the sentencing process. While section 718.2(e) may involve a different methodology for determining a fit sentence for aboriginal offenders, this does not necessarily "mandate" a different result.[255] Iacobucci J. noted that the scope of section 718.2(e), "as it applies to all offenders," requires the sentencing judge to adopt alternatives to incarceration when they are "reasonable in the circumstances."

---

253  Above note 215.
254  *Wells*, above note 240 at 226.
255  *Ibid.* at 229–30.

In this regard, there is no general rule that "the greatest weight is to be given to principles of restorative justice, and less weight accorded to goals such as denunciation and deterrence."[256] Looking at "particularly violent and serious offences," imprisonment will generally result as often for aboriginal offenders as non-aboriginal offenders.

However, Iacobucci J. cautioned, this does not mean that a category of offences is presumptively excluded from conditional sentences. The seriousness of the offence must be determined on a case-by-case basis. The Supreme Court unanimously upheld the sentence of twenty months imprisonment, concluding that the trial judge did not misconstrue the seriousness of the offence,[257] made no error in principle, did not overemphasize an appropriate factor, or fail to consider a relevant factor. This endorsement of the custodial term is consistent with the Court's response in *R. (R.A.)* and *R.N.S.* discussed above.

If one dissects *Wells*, the proper approach for considering a conditional sentence for an aboriginal offender involves the following sequential considerations:

1.  A preliminary consideration and exclusion of both a suspended sentence with probation and a penitentiary term of imprisonment as fit sentences;[258]
2.  Assessment of the seriousness of the particular offence with regard to its gravity, which necessarily includes the harm done, and the offender's degree of responsibility;[259]
3.  Judicial notice of the "systemic or background factors that have contributed to the difficulties faced by aboriginal people in both the criminal justice system, and throughout society at large";[260] and

---

256   *Ibid.* at 228.
257   Notwithstanding an apparent reliance on "starting point"guidelines which had been rejected by the Supreme Court in *R. v. McDonnell*, [1997] 1 S.C.R. 948: see *Wells, ibid.* at 231–32.
258   *Wells, ibid.* at 222–23.
259   *Ibid.* at 229–31. Whether an offence requires a penitentiary term is not always readily apparent, and is itself subject to restraint and the application of s. 718.2(e). In *R. v. Wood* (1999), 142 Man. R. (2d) 76 (C.A.), the court reversed a two year less a day conditonal sentence for sexual assault. The offender was an aboriginal person with no prior record, the court concluded that a fit sentence would have been four years given the violent nature of the rape, less credit for pre-sentence custody. The court accepted that his aboriginal background was relevant to determine what was fit but that the nature of the assault brought it outside the conditonal sentence range.
260   *Wells, ibid.* at 234.

4. An inquiry into the unique circumstances of the offender, including any evidence of community initiatives to use restorative justice principles in addressing particular social problems.[261]

While counsel and pre-sentence reports will be the primary source of information regarding the offender's circumstances, there is a positive duty on the sentencing judge to inform herself.[262]

A useful example of the utility of fully informing oneself is the decision of Smith J. in *R. v. L.L.J.*[263] The offender, a man with a serious alcohol problem and a veteran of the residential school experience, was convicted of sexual assault on his son's spouse. After hearing from community members about the offender, the victim, and their relationships with the community, Smith J. embarked on a literature review about the scope of the restorative justice principle in relation to aboriginal communities. She concluded that a restorative justice approach within the Cowichan community could benefit the offender, the victim, and the community. She imposed a conditional sentence of two years less a day with extensive conditions including abstinence from alcohol, alcohol treatment, and a continuing counselling relationship with a group of elders.

### d) Conditional Sentences and Sexual Assault

It is important to note that all the sexual assault cases considered in early 2000 by the Supreme Court would have resulted in a term of imprisonment, except *L.F.W.* which involved twenty-five-year old offences and split the Court four to four. Even the group who supported the twenty-one-month conditional sentence with restrictive conditions indicated that it was a close call, resulting primarily from deference to the trial judge rather than the inherent circumstances of the case. The Supreme Court has indicated that an offender convicted of sexual assault can receive a conditional sentence but it will be a difficult argument where there is a serious assault, abuse of vulnerable victims, or degrading acts. Certainly, the principles of denunciation and deterrence

---

261 *Ibid.* at 233, 234–35.
262 This may require resort to the new powers in the *Criminal Code*, ss. 723(3) & (4). See the discussion in Chapter 8, above, at 8(B).
263 [1999] B.C.J. No. 2016 (S.C.) (QL).

would require lengthy duration and restrictive conditions.[264] The age of the offences is relevant where the intervening period shows no repetition of offences and a serious effort to be of good character. Appellate courts have noted the need to consider the potential negative impact of incarceration when dealing with an offender who has treatment needs and positive rehabilitative prospects.[265]

## 2) Available Conditions

As with probation, the available conditions are divided into compulsory and optional categories. Many conditions are described in identical terms for both sanctions, but the differences are significant. First, two additional compulsory conditions must be included in every conditional sentence: the offender must report to a supervisor within two days or such longer period as the court directs and then when required by the supervisor,[266] and the offender cannot leave the jurisdiction without written permission from the court or supervisor.[267]

In the optional condition category, a major difference is the treatment condition. For probation, the offender must agree to treatment and must "participate actively if accepted by the program."[268] The consent requirement is obviously a response to cases like R. v. *Rogers* which expressed concern about the validity of probation orders requiring psychiatric treatment which might involve medication.[269] For conditional sentences, perhaps because of their implicit punitive character, a treatment order is not qualified by a consent requirement.[270]

---

264  See, for example, R. v. *Winters* (1999), 174 N.S.R. (2d) 83 (C.A.). The offender was a thirty-three-year-old single mother with no prior record. The victim was her friend's twelve-year-old son. The court deferred to the trial judge's conclusion about the conditional sentence including the finding of little risk to re-offend even though the offender continued to deny the offences, but found the conditions inadequate. It added a house arrest regime but did not require sex offender treatment in light of her denials. See also R. v. *C.(S.P.)* (1999), 175 N.S.R. (2d) 158 (C.A.), involving sexual assaults committed by a nineteen-year-old on his seven-year-old nephew.

265  See R. v. *Wismayer* (1997), 115 C.C.C. (3d) 18 (Ont. C.A.) (offender with obsessive/compulsive disorder); and R. v. *J.(D.J.)* (1998), 172 Sask. R. 182, Jackson J.A., Vancise J.A. concurring (C.A.) (learning disability).

266  See *Criminal Code*, s. 742.3(1)(c).

267  *Ibid.*, s. 742.3(1)(d).

268  *Ibid.*, s. 732.1(3)(g).

269  Above note 97. See the discussion, above, at 9(D)(4)(c).

270  Section 742.3(2)(e) of the *Criminal Code* merely says "attend a treatment program approved by the province."

The last distinction relates to the residual category which for conditional sentences is found in section 742.3(2)(f). Curiously, this provision is cast in identical language to that used as the residual category for probation prior to its revision by the 1996 amendments. This presents some confusion because that provision had been interpreted as insufficient to support  punitive probation conditions. However, that result was not so much a function of the language as it was the context of probation, which is not inherently punitive.[271] Consequently, section 742.3(2)(f) can provide a basis for reasonable conditions, which can be either restorative, rehabilitative, or punitive. Without doubt, this can include house arrest and, where available, electronic monitoring.[272]

Some guidance for the choice and crafting of conditions was offered by Lamer C.J.C. in *Proulx* where he said:

> In the event that a judge chooses to impose a conditional sentence, there are five compulsory conditions listed in s. 742.3(1) that must be imposed. The judge also has considerable discretion in imposing optional conditions pursuant to s. 742.3(2). There are a number of principles that should guide the judge in exercising this discretion. First, the conditions must ensure the safety of the community. Second, conditions must be tailored to fit the particular circumstances of the offender and the offence. The type of conditions imposed will be a function of the sentencing judge's creativity. However, conditions will prove fruitless if the offender is incapable of abiding by them, and will increase the probability that the offender will be incarcerated as a result of breaching them. Third, punitive conditions such as house arrest should be the norm, not the exception. Fourth, the conditions must be realistically enforceable. This requires a consideration of the available resources in the community in which the sentence is to be served.[273]

This was followed by a quotation from a paper delivered by Justice Mark Rosenberg, stressing the importance of conditions being enforceable without creating unacceptable burdens or "an intolerable intrusion

---

271 See "Conditional Sentences and House Arrest," above note 104. See also *Proulx*, above note 107 at 87–88.
272 See *Gagnon*, above note 124; *Sidhu*, above note 124; and "Conditional Sentences and House Arrest," above note 104. In *Proulx*, above note 107, Lamer C.J.C. stated that house arrest should be the norm for conditional sentences. He did not specifically mention electronic monitoring but this is implicit given his general approval of *Gagnon*.
273 *Proulx*, above note 107 at 121–22.

into the privacy of innocent persons."[274] Perhaps Justice Rosenberg was contemplating the kind of unreasonable burdens placed on an offender's family by the original conditions in *R. v. Waldner*,[275] where the majority ordered that the family had to move to a place at least ten miles from the residence of any child under fourteen, and had to pay for all psychological testing required by the sentence. These two conditions were subsequently deleted.[276] Judges must strive to ensure that conditions are clearly defined. They must be appropriate to the offender and must involve resources which are available and accessible. In other words, they must be practicable and inherently fair.

Once imposed, conditions can be varied upon application of the supervisor if a "change in circumstances makes a change to the optional conditions desirable."[277] The supervisor must give written notification of the proposed change and the reasons for it to the offender, the prosecutor, and the court.[278] The parties have seven days to request a hearing, or the court can order one of its own initiative.[279] If no hearing is required, the proposed change takes effect fourteen days after the court originally received notification of the proposed change.[280] The offender or the prosecutor can also seek a change to the optional conditions, but in these cases there must always be a hearing to consider the proposed variation.[281] If there is a hearing, it must be held within thirty days after the court received notification of the proposed change.[282] At the hearing the court can approve or refuse the proposed change, and can make any other changes to the optional conditions that it "deems appropriate."[283]

## 3) Blended Sentences

A "blended" sentence involves both incarceration and supervised time served in the community within the same sentence. This problematic concept has arisen in two separate contexts. First, can a single condi-

---

274   Justice M. Rosenberg, "Recent Developments in Sentencing" (National Judicial Institute, Education Seminar, 25–26 February 1998) [unpublished].
275   (1998), 15 C.R. (5th) 159 (Alta. C.A.). Berger J.A., who argued in favour of the conditional sentence, dissented from the two conditions.
276   *Ibid.*
277   *Criminal Code*, s. 742.4(1).
278   *Ibid.*
279   *Ibid.*, s. 742.4(2).
280   *Ibid.*, s. 742.4(4).
281   *Ibid.*, s. 742.4(5).
282   *Ibid.*, ss. 742.4(2), (5).
283   *Ibid.*, s. 742.4(3)(b).

tional sentence require that a part be served in custody and then, at a specified point, have the remainder served in the community? Surely this would constitute the judge as both the sentencer and the paroling authority, and is therefore inconsistent with section 742.1 which requires the judge, in qualifying situations, to choose between a sentence served in the community or in custody. This fixes the judge with an appropriate decision-making function, not one that involves predicting when in the future community service can be justified. Appellate courts have unanimously rejected this form of blended conditional sentence.[284] It has been laid to rest implicitly by *Proulx* which situated the conditional sentence between probation and imprisonment, and left no room for the self-contradictory model of a blended sanction.

The second manifestation of a "blended" sentence has not been answered by *Proulx* and its companions, at least not directly. This is the question of whether a judge can legitimately impose a conditional sentence in conjunction with a sentence of imprisonment. The issue can arise in two situations: (1) when the offender is already serving a sentence of imprisonment at the time of sentencing; or (2) when the offender is being sentenced for more than one offence, as was the case in *R. v. R.(R.A.)*.[285] The disposition ordered by the majority of the Supreme Court in that case, a custodial term of one year to be followed by a three-month conditional sentence for the common assaults, suggests that this kind of blended sentence is permissible. However, there was no argument on this issue and no discussion in the judgment. The general issue of integrating conditional sentences with other sentences involves a variety of inter-related questions. Its inherent complexity is reflected by the fact that section 718.3(5), apparently intended to deal with some of these issues, has never been proclaimed in force.

In *R. v. Alfred*, the offender was a physician convicted of numerous counts of indecent assault and sexual assault committed on male and female patients over an eighteen-year period.[286] The trial judge sentenced him to nine months imprisonment and a conditional sentence of two years less a day. Apparently, the trial judge believed that the conditional setence would be suspended by section 742.7 and would kick in after the custodial term. Treating the sentence as a thirty-three-

---

284  See *R. v. Fisher* (2000), 143 C.C.C. (3d) 413 (Ont. C.A.); *R. v. Kopf* (1997), 6 C.R. (5th) 305 (Que. C.A.); *R. v. Monkman* (1999), 132 C.C.C. (3d) 89 (Man. C.A.); *R. v. Wey* (1999), 244 A.R. 189 (C.A.); and *R. v. Hirtle* (1999), 136 C.C.C. (3d) 419 (N.S.C.A.).
285  [2000] 1 S.C.R. 163.
286  (1998), 122 C.C.C. (3d) 213 (Ont. C.A.).

month sentence with the first nine months served in custody, the court concluded that the total duration violated the intent and language of section 742.1(a), which limits conditional sentences to a term of less than two years. The court substituted a sixteen-month term of imprisonment to be served consecutively to the nine-month term.

From the start of the judgment it was clear that the court would not sustain a conditional sentence given the nature of the offences, the breach of trust, and the lengthy period over which they were committed. Nevertheless, the reasoning in *Alfred* suggests that a conditional sentence is intended as a substitute for a custodial term of no longer than two years and not as a way to increase the scope of a punitive sanction beyond that period. While this is a significant point, the case does not answer the question of blending a conditional sentence when the global length is less than two years. Moreover, the court did not consider the meaning of section 742.7 which purports to suspend a conditional sentence when a custodial sentence is subsequently imposed. Nor did it deal with whether a conditional sentence can ever be consecutive to another sentence.

In *R. v. Hill*,[287] the Nova Scotia Court of Appeal reviewed various sentences for narcotics offences. Facing four convictions, the trial judge imposed two custodial terms of three months concurrent and two fifteen-month concurrent sentences to be served in the community. Section 742.7(1) purports to suspend the running of a conditional sentence. Freeman J.A. observed that, in reference to the subsequent term of imprisonment, section 742.7 uses the phrase "whenever committed." Accordingly, it could be an offence that antedated the conditional sentence or was committed during the conditional sentence. In the latter example, the new offence would lead to a breach proceeding which, pursuant to section 742.6(9), could result in an order that the offender serve all of the unexpired conditional sentence in custody, or a specified part of it, with the conditional sentence resuming after. From this, Freeman J.A. deduced that "in some circumstances it is not illegal for an offender to be subject to a custodial sentence and a conditional sentence at the same time, the effect of the conditional sentence being suspended until the custodial sentence is served."[288] He concluded it was putting "too fine and technical a construction on what Parliament must have intended" if the scope of section 742.7 authorized subsequent sentences of imprisonment imposed on different days but not on the same day.

287   (1999), 140 C.C.C. (3d) 214 (N.S.C.A.).
288   *Ibid.* at 218.

This, however, ignores the fact that when sentences are imposed on the same day by the same judge, one can be assured that the same set of factors and principles are being applied, whether rightly or wrongly. Consequently, there may be a reason to distinguish between two sentences imposed by one judge and two sentences imposed by different judges. Freeman J.A. effectively applied this distinction when he examined the four sentences and concluded that the same considerations applied to all of them. Since they were all related to trafficking offences, if one demanded incarceration so did the others. Accordingly, he found that the trial judge had commited an error in principle and substituted a fifteen-month consecutive term for the fifteen-month conditional sentence.

This approach is based not on the technical requirements of sentencing but on a principled approach to conditional sentences when offences are sufficiently indistinguishable, compelling the same exercise of section 742.1 discretion. There is no problem with a conditional sentence and custodial sentence existing at the same time, but they should not be imposed at the same time if the sentencing considerations are indistinguishable.

Of course, the *Hill* conclusion does not apply if two convictions are distinguishable and raise different considerations like the sexual assault and common assaults in *R.CR.A.* In other words, if the sentencing analysis is based on different elements, it may be permissible to produce a custodial sentence for one offence and a conditional sentence for the other.[289] Another corollary of the *Hill* decision is that if section 742.7 automatically suspends a conditional sentence to resume after the completion of a subsequently imposed custodial sentence, there is nothing conceptually wrong with making a conditional sentence consecutive to a custodial sentence.

Where, however, is the power to postpone a conditional sentence? Section 719(1) provides that all sentences commence when imposed unless there is a provision which authorizes postponement. Here, this can only be sections 718.3(4)(a) and (c), the former dealing with sentences imposed at different times and the latter with sentences imposed at the same time for multiple convictions. These provisions use the

---

289 See *R. v. Hindes*, [2000] A.J. No. 808 (C.A.) [*Hindes*], where the Court found that the trial judge had erred in using the offender's post-offence conduct to aggravate the penalty for both offences, dangerous driving causing bodily harm and leaving the scene. It concluded, at para. 46, that a "blended sentence would be the appropriate sentence." Consequently, it allowed the appeal and substituted a six-month term of imprisonment for the dangerous driving offence and a consecutive twelve-month conditional sentence on the other count.

phrase "term of imprisonment" to describe both the earlier element and the consecutive element. A conditional sentence is described in the sub-heading preceding section 742 as a "conditional sentence of imprisonment." Moreover, section 742.1(a) makes the imposition of a "sentence of imprisonment of less than two years" an integral characteristic of a conditional sentence. Here, it is important to note that Lamer C.J.C. in *Proulx* remarked that a "conditional sentence is, at least notionally, a sentence of imprisonment."[290] Section 731(1)(b) which authorizes probation periods to be added to terms of imprisonment not exceeding two years uses both the phrase "sentencing the offender to imprisonment" and the word "term." Most appellate courts have concluded, or at least have accepted, that probation can be added onto a conditional sentence. If this can be done, it is only through the application of section 731(1). There appears to be no meaningful difference between a sentence of imprisonment and a term of imprisonment for these purposes, except that "term" may include more than one sentence. Accordingly, it would seem that a conditional sentence can be made consecutive to an already existing custodial sentence.

But when does a consecutive conditional sentence start? Section 732.2(1)(b) makes it clear when a probation order starts in relation to preceding sentences of imprisonment, taking into account conditional release, but there is no comparable provision dealing with conditional sentences. One answer is to use the date of release from custody as the commencement date, regardless of any overlap in supervision.[291] A different approach was taken in *R. v. Hindes*.[292] The Alberta Court of Appeal substituted a sentence of six months imprisonment on one count followed by a consecutive twelve-month conditional sentence for a separate but related offence. It ordered that the conditional sentence commence six months "after the date of commencement of the six month sentence," which means the warrant expiry date for that sentence. The court explained that there would be no hiatus in supervision caused by early release since, if released on parole, the offender would be subject to parole supervision. Unfortunately, the court did not contemplate early release by reason of remission. Since provinces do not exercise statutory release supervision, there will be a hiatus for the period of remission. It is curious that Parliament did not address this problem. Like the origi-

---

290   *Proulx*, above note 107 at 86.
291   See the discussion of *Constant*, above note 74 and accompanying text, referable to the probation situation before 1996 when there was no s. 732.2(1)(b) to provide a clear answer.
292   Above note 289.

nal breach provisions which desperately needed technical revision, this is another defect awaiting revision. The proper approach would be to replicate the effect of section 732.2(1)(b) which deals with the similar probation situation.

## 4) Breach of a Conditional Sentence

One of the early criticisms of the conditional sentence regime was that the breach provisions were inadequate. While they effected the offender's return to court to face a comparatively expeditious proceeding when a breach was alleged, there was no mechanism to stop the clock. In other words, the conditional sentence continued to run and could expire before any sanction for a breach was imposed. A series of substantial amendments which answered many of the criticims was enacted in 1999[293] to provide a more detailed scheme for dealing with breaches.

### a) The Breach Mechanism[294]

The first element of the breach mechanism is an expeditious proceeding. The hearing of a breach allegation must commence within thirty days of the offender's arrest[295] for the alleged breach with or without a warrant.[296] Once commenced, it can be adjourned for reasonable periods until the breach allegation is determined.[297] The breach allegation can be heard by any court with jurisdiction, either where the breach is alleged to have been committed or where the offender is arrested.[298] If the offender is arrested outside the province where the breach allegedly occurred, it can be heard there with the consent of the attorney general of the jurisdiction in which the breach was committed.[299] The conditional

---

293  See *An Act to amend the Criminal Code, the Controlled Drugs and Substances Act and the Corrections and Conditional Release Act*, S.C.1999, c. 5, s. 41.

294  For an excellent discussion of the breach mechanism, see C. Fleischaker, "The Breach Provisions of the Conditional Sentence . . . a.k.a. 'Expeditious Justice'" (2000). 43 Crim. L. Q. 305.

295  See *Criminal Code*, s. 742.6(3).

296  *Ibid.*, s. 742.6(1)(c), which provides that the proceeding is commenced, by the issuance of a warrant for the offender's arrest, the arrest without a warrant, or, if the offender is already in custody, an order compelling his appearance to answer the breach allegation: see s. 742.6(1)(d).

297  *Ibid.*, s. 742.6(3.3).

298  *Ibid.*, s. 742.6(3.1).

299  *Ibid.*, s. 742.6(3.2)(a). If the proceedings leading to the conditional sentence were instituted by the attorney general of Canada, then that is the person who must consent: see s. 742.6(3.2)(b).

284 THE LAW OF SENTENCING

sentence is suspended commencing with the issuance of a warrant, the arrest without a warrant, or, if the offender is otherwise in custody, the compelling of the offender's appearance to answer the breach allegation under section 742.6(1)(d).[300] The suspension continues until there is a determination whether a breach occurred or not.[301] The breach allegation "must be supported by a written report of the supervisor, which report must include, where appropriate, signed statements of witnesses."[302] That report is deemed to be admissible evidence at the hearing so long as the offender is given a copy and reasonable notice[303] but the offender can, with leave of the court, require the attendance of the supervisor or any witnesses who provided signed statements.[304]

The central provision of the breach mechanism is section 742.6(9), which provides:

> Where the court is satisfied, on a balance of probabilities, that the offender has without reasonable excuse, the proof of which lies on the offender, breached a condition of the conditional sentence order, the court may
>
> (a) take no action;
> (b) change the optional conditions;
> (c) suspend the conditional sentence order and direct
>
>     (i) that the offender serve in custody a portion of the unexpired sentence, and
>
>     (ii) that the conditional sentence order resume on the offender's release from custody, either with or without changes to the optional conditions; or
>
> (d) terminate the conditional sentence order and direct that the offender be committed to custody until the expiration of the sentence.

Given the ability to reach a decision without oral evidence, one can hardly conceive of a more expeditious route to incarceration. It bears a marked similarity to the parole revocation process.[305] The onus of proof has been reduced to a balance of probabilities, and the proof of the

---

300   *Ibid.*, s. 742.6(10).
301   *Ibid.*
302   *Ibid.*, s. 742.6(4).
303   *Ibid.*, s. 742.6(5).
304   *Ibid.*, s. 742.6(8).
305   Of course, one assumes that courts will permit counsel to act in their traditional capacity, not as "assistants" with a limited function as the National Parole Board continues to insist: see the *Corrections and Conditional Release Act*, above note 293, ss. 140(7), (8). See also *MacInnis v. Canada (A.G.)* (1996), [1997] 1 F.C. 115 at 123.

existence of a reasonable excuse lies on the offender. Before one jumps to the conclusion that these two aspects clearly violate the presumption of innocence and the "golden thread" which requires the Crown to prove guilt beyond a reasonble doubt, as guaranteed by section 11(d) of the *Charter*, the issue has been addressed by two appellate courts who have rejected the argument.

### b) R. v. Casey

In *R. v. Casey*,[306] a man who had stolen eighteen bathing suits was given a conditional sentence. One of the conditions was that he attend a Salvation Army program which he failed to do, resulting in an allegation of a breach. After the breach hearing, the judge found a breach and ordered that he serve twelve of the unexpired twenty-one months in custody. He appealed to the Ontario Court of Appeal arguing that the breach process violated sections 11(d), 11(h), and 7 of the *Charter*. The court held that a breach proceeding is not a new charge but part of the sentencing process. Accordingly, relying on *R. v. Lyons*,[307] it concluded that section 11 of the *Charter* does not apply to breach proceedings: relying on *Cunningham v. Canada*,[308] a case dealing with denial of release on mandatory supervision as a result of the new detention provisions, the court held that there was no breach of section 7 arising from the use of the balance of probabilities standard and the reverse onus. The court treated the breach proceedings very much like a parole hearing and did not consider the principle against self-incrimination embedded in section 7 as a basis to read down the reverse onus into an evidentiary onus.

### c) R. v. Whitty

*Casey* involved a breach of condition that is not a new criminal offence. Perhaps a court would be more sympathetic to the arguments about violating the offender's right to be presumed innocent when the alleged breach is also the subject of a new charge which will not come to trial until after the breach allegation. This was the situation in *R. v. Whitty*[309] where the offender had been given a nine-month conditional sentence after a conviction for theft and use of a forged document. Only the compulsory conditions were included in the order. A few months later he was charged with two counts of assault and uttering threats. Before

---

306   (2000), 30 C.R. (5th) 126 (Ont. C.A.).
307   [1987] 2 S.C.R. 309. See the discussion in Chapter 11, below, at 11(D)(3).
308   [1993] 2 S.C.R. 143, McLachlin J. [*Cunningham*].
309   (1999), 135 C.C.C. (3d) 77 (Nfld. C.A.) [*Whitty*].

the trial, the Crown applied under section 742.6(9)(b) to have the conditions varied since Whitty had breached the original order by committing new offences, thereby failing to keep the peace and be of good behaviour. At the breach hearing, the judge dismissed the application, holding that section 742.6(9) violated section 7 of the *Charter* by not requiring the Crown to prove the allegation. This conclusion was reversed on appeal. For the majority, Gushue J.A. held that a conditional sentence is a term of imprisonment that is being served in the community and the breach procedure is "aimed only at determining whether changed circumstances should lead to a variation of the manner in which that imprisonment should be served."[310] In his view, the trial judge's approach would wrongly have the effect of turning it into a de facto criminal trial. Treating the conditional sentence as a continuous process subject to monitoring and revision, Gushue J.A. essentially accepted the parole analogy and relied on *Cunningham*[311] to find that there was no section 7 breach. Similarly, section 11 was not applicable since the issue of guilt or innocence had already been determined.

In dissent, O'Neill J.A. looked at the breach process from the perspective of consequences and concluded that section 11 did apply given the magnitude of options available under section 742.6(9). These were not merely a change in the method of serving the sentence but "true penal consequences" in the language of *R. v. Wigglesworth*.[312] With respect to section 7, O'Neill J.A. applied the *Gardiner* principle[313] and held that

> . . . the same principles which governed the trial judge in considering the appropriate disposition of the matter following trial, should equally apply if any change is to be made in how the sentence is to be served. The alleged breach giving rise to the application by the Crown, whether that breach, in itself, would constitute a criminal offence, should be proved beyond a reasonable doubt as in any sentencing hearing such as this, in reality, is, albeit an extended one, but nevertheless contemplated by the legislation.[314]

Viewing the potential breach process as a continuation of the sentencing would, according to *Gardiner*, require the Crown to prove aggra-

---

310  *Ibid.* at 96.
311  *Cunningham*, above note 308 at 151–52.
312  [1987] 2 S.C.R. 541 at 559, Wilson J.
313  See the discussion in Chapter 8, above.
314  *Whitty*, above note 309 at 160.

vating factors beyond a reasonable doubt, and an alleged breach must be considered an aggravating factor.

### d)  Issues Arising from *Casey* and *Whitty*

If the *Charter* analysis in *Casey* and the majority judgment in *Whitty* are correct, they pose a practical difficulty. Rather than expecting offenders to respond quickly to an alleged breach, which will be determined according to a civil standard if is also the subject of a new criminal charge fairness may require an adjournment until after disposition of the criminal charge. An acquittal on the criminal charge should result in a dismissal of the breach allegation[315] since the obligation to keep the peace and be of good behaviour applies only to breaches of law.[316] Now, a conditional sentence is suspended once the breach procedure is commenced.[317] Accordingly, the hearing can be adjourned until after the criminal trial without prejudice to the state's right to compel compliance with the conditions. This option, however, detracts from the idea that breaches can be dealt with quickly. In other words, the rejection of the *Charter* claims, ostensibly to preserve the conditional sentence as a vehicle which can be easily monitored, may result in delayed breach hearings which will undermine an important feature of the breach mechanism: its expeditious character.

Moreover, long adjournments will make the question of detention or release pending the trial and hearing a pertinent concern and may produce an unexpected section 12 issue. If the breach allegation is subsequently dismissed or withdrawn, the offender who is not detained will get credit towards the sentence for any period during which the running of that sentence was suspended.[318] If the offender is detained under section 515(6), the conditional sentence starts running again and every day served will count towards the expiration of the conditional sentence unless there is a new intervening sentence of imprisonment that triggers section 742.7, which suspends the conditional sentence again.[319] Moreover, if the breach allegation is subsequently dismissed or withdrawn, the detained offender will receive an added credit of one-half the time in custody.[320] This additional credit is likely

---

315  An acquittal must be respected in subsequent proceedings: see *Grdic*, above note 42.
316  See the ruling of the Newfoundland Court of Appeal in *R.(D.)*, above note 92. Discussed in the context of a probation order at 9(D)(4)(a), above.
317  See *Criminal Code*, s. 742.6(10).
318  *Ibid.*, s. 742.6(15)(a).
319  *Ibid.*, s. 742.6(12).
320  *Ibid.*, s. 742.6(15)(b).

a form of compensation for remission which does not accrue during the detention period. Of course, if the breach is proven, the detained offender will still get credit for days in detention[321] but the released offender will not get any credit since the sentence has been suspended. This situation will prove to be a problem since, if the offender is out of custody for a long period, the conditions in the conditional release order continue to apply and the offender can be breached even though the sentence is suspended.[322] This means that the state's grasp over a person subject to a conditional sentence can exceed the two-year threshold set by section 742.1.

While section 742.6(16) gives the court a discretionary power to give credit for time on suspension after a breach finding, this is not mandatory and does not change the fact that the offender will be subject to punitive conditions for a period longer than that authorized by the statute. Arguably, this extension of the punitive period makes the total sentence disproportionate. Depending on the facts, this could present a section 12 challenge to the effect of section 742.6(11). This could be rectified if judges interpreted section 742.6(16) and the "interests of justice" qualification as arising whenever there was no new breach during the suspension period. Alternatively, recognition that section 742.6 violates section 7 by reducing the Crown's burden of proof, as held by O'Neill J.A. in dissent in *Whitty*, would avoid all these difficulties since breach hearings would proceed quickly.

### e)  Options After Finding a Breach

After a finding of a breach, section 742.6(9) provides the judge with a wide range of options. In *Proulx*, Lamer C.J.C. suggested that the presumptive response to a breach of a conditional sentence should be serving the remainder of the sentence in custody.[323] He said that the "constant threat of incarceration will help to ensure that the offender complies with the conditions imposed."[324] However, there are a number of options in section 742.6(9) starting with taking "no action." This implies that there may be breaches of a technical or minor nature which will not require incarceration. Moreover, the individualization

---

321   *Ibid.*, s. 742.6(12).
322   *Ibid.*, s. 742.6(11). By "breached," I mean that the process of adjudicating a breach is commenced.
323   *Proulx*, above note 107 at 89–90.
324   *Ibid.* at 89.

of the process and fundamental fairness require that the judge hearing the breach allegation consider the full factual context before choosing a remedy under section 742.6(9).

Depending on the amount of time left on the conditional sentence and the nature of the breach, a change in conditions may be more appropriate than incarceration. In *R. v. S.(B.J.)*,[325] the offender was given a twenty-month conditional sentence for a number of serious offences committed against his wife[326] in the presence of their children. One of the conditions was that he visit his wife only in connection with access to the children. After being served with divorce papers, he immediately breached this condition and broke down the door to his wife's residence, verbally assaulting and frightening her. At the breach hearing, the judge changed the condition to be an absolute "no contact order" but did not incarcerate the offender. The Crown appealed arguing that the offender should serve the remainder of the conditional sentence in custody.

McEachern C.J.B.C. stated that ordinarily incarceration for the balance of the sentence would be the appropriate response to the seriousness of the situation. Here, however, an experienced local judge was satisfied that there would be no repetition of violence. Furthermore, the economic survival of the family depended on the man maintaining his current employment at a saw mill. This recently obtained job, described by the offender, who only had a Grade eight education, as the best job he ever had, was an important factor. Given that there was no record of offences before the ones that gave rise to the conditional sentence, McEachern C.J.B.C., with Donald J.A. concurring, deferred to the local judge who "believed that the best opportunity for restorative justice was to keep the accused employed for his own rehabilitation and for the benefit of his family."

Southin J.A. would have terminated the conditional sentence. In her view, courts have to take a "stern view" of offenders who breach conditions, although it is not every breach that will warrant termination. Here, the threatening and violent nature of the offender's conduct persuaded her that it was a repetition of the kind of behaviour that produced the original conviction. She therefore concluded that deterrence and denunciation required incarceration for the balance of the sentence. Obviously, this was a difficult case given concerns about the potentially volatile and escalating nature of domestic violence. The

---

325   [2000] B.C.J. No. 321 (C.A.) (QL).
326   They included sexual assault, forcible confinement, uttering a threat, and careless use of a firearm.

result was an example of deference. Regardless of whether one agrees with the majority or the dissent, it is important to note that section 742.6(9)(c) permits a judge to incarcerate for a portion of the unexpired sentence and then order the resumption of the conditional sentence. Depending on the nature of the breach, this permits a more nuanced and individualized response than simply choosing between the extremes of release and termination.

## FURTHER READINGS

BARNETT, JUDGE C.C., "Probation Orders Under the Criminal Code" (1977) 38 C.R.N.S. 165

CANADIAN SENTENCING COMMISSION, *Sentencing Reform: A Canadian Approach* (Ottawa: Supply and Services Canada, 1987)

DOOB, A., & V. MARINOS, "Reconceptualizing Punishment: Understanding the Limitations on the Use of Intermediate Sanctions" (1995) 2 Univ. of Chicago Roundtable 413

EDGAR, A., "Sentencing Options in Canada" in J. Roberts & D. Cole, eds., *Making Sense of Sentencing* (Toronto: University of Toronto Press, 1999)

GREEN, R.G., *Justice in Aboriginal Communities: Sentencing Alternatives* (Saskatoon: Purich Publishing, 1998)

HAMAI, K., R. VILLE, & R. HARRIS, eds., *Probation Round the World: A Comparative Study* (London: Routledge, 1995)

KAISER, A., "*R. v. Bunn*: A Disconcerting Judicial Response to the Dishonest Lawyer" (2000) 30 C.R. (5th) 102

LAW REFORM COMMISSION OF CANADA, *Report: Dispositions and Sentences in the Criminal Process* (Ottawa: Information Canada, 1976)

MAIR, G., "Community Penalties and Probation" in M. Maguire, R. Morgan, & R. Reiner, eds., *The Oxford Handbook of Criminology*, 2nd ed. (Oxford: Clarendon Press, 1997)

MANSON, A., "Conditional Sentences and House Arrest" (1999) 19 C.R. (5th) 353

MANSON, A., "Conditional Sentences: Courts of Appeal Debate the Principles" (1998) 15 C.R. (5th) 176

REPORT OF THE CANADIAN COMMITTEE ON CORRECTIONS, *Toward Unity: Criminal Justice and Corrections* (Ottawa: Queen's Printer, 1969)

ROBERTS, J., & A. VON HIRSCH, "Conditional Sentences of Imprisonment and the Fundamental Principle of Proportionality in Sentencing" (1998) 10 C.R. (5th ) 222

TANOVICH, D., "A Breath of Fresh Air on the Incarceration Addiction in Drug Cases" (1999) 23 C.R. (5th) 242

# CHAPTER 10

# MURDER AND MANSLAUGHTER

## A. MURDER

As in many jurisdictions, the history of sentencing for murder in Canada has been the history of the capital punishment debate. No less than fifteen sections in the *Criminal Code, 1892*, dealt with the process of declaring, implementing, and completing a sentence of death.[1] The last hangings in Canada were the executions of Turpin and Lucas at the Don Jail in Toronto on the evening of December 11, 1962. By that time, murder had already been divided into two categories: capital and non-capital.[2] Between 1962 and 1976, when the death penalty was finally abolished, all sentences of death were considered on an individual basis by the federal Cabinet and all were commuted to life imprisonment.

The 1976 reforms prescribed life imprisonment as the mandatory penalty for murder, which was divided into two categories: first- and second-degree. The practical difference between first- and second-degree is the period of parole ineligibility that applies to the life sentence. A person convicted of first-degree murder is not eligible for parole until twenty-five years of the sentence have been served in con-

---

1    *Criminal Code, 1892* (Can.), 55-56 Vict., c. 29, ss. 935–49.
2    Effected in 1961 by *An Act to amend the Criminal Code (Capital Murder)*, S.C. 1960–61, c. 44, s. 1.

finement, subject to the possibility of a review after fifteen years.[3] For second-degree murder, the parole ineligibility period can be anywhere between ten and twenty-five years as determined by the trial judge. Murder requires a high level of subjective fault, comprising either an intention to kill[4] or at least an intention to cause bodily harm that the offender knows is likely to cause death and is reckless as to whether death ensues or not.[5] Historically, the *Criminal Code* has included forms of constructive liability but these have, for the most part, been declared unconstitutional.[6] First-degree murder now consists of planned and deliberate killings,[7] the killing of a police officer, prison guard or related official,[8] or a killing in the course of certain stipulated offences.[9] All other murders are second-degree. The Supreme Court has concluded that, for sentencing purposes, the first-degree distinctions are intended to classify offences into more or less blameworthy categories as determined by Parliament.[10]

## 1) First-degree Murder

At the time of the 1975–76 capital punishment debate, the impassioned controversy was polarized between the retention and abolitionist camps. The government was committed to abolition and its position was crafted and shepherded under the authority of the Solicitor General Warren Allmand. The issue was not simply one of opposing the death penalty, but also of offering an alternative sanction which would satisfy those who were not committed to retention but were concerned about apparent leniency for murderers. Clearly, the proposed sanction

---

3   The "fifteen year review" established by s. 745.6 of the *Criminal Code*, R.S.C. 1985, c. C-46, is discussed, below, at 10(A)(5).

4   *Ibid.*, s. 229(a)(i).

5   *Ibid.*, s. 229(a)(ii).

6   See *R. v. Vaillancourt* [1987] 2 S.C.R. 636 re: s. 230(d) *R. v. Martineau*, [1980] 2 S.C.R. 633, re: s. 230(a); *R. v. Sit*, [1991] 3 S.C.R. 124, re. s 230(c). The remaining constructive provisions are also deficient in meeting the standard of subjective foresight of death.

7   See *Criminal Code*, s. 231(2).

8   *Ibid.*, s. 231(4).

9   *Ibid.*, s. 231(5). The specific offences are s. 76 (hijacking), s. 271 (sexual assault), s. 272 (sexual assault with a weapon, with bodily harm or threat of bodily harm), s. 273 (aggravated sexual assault), s. 279 (kidnapping and forcible confinement), and s. 279.1 (hostage-taking). The common theme which determines the temporal scope of their applicability is the unlawful domination of another person: see *R. v. Paré*, [1987] 2 S.C.R. 618.

10   See *R. v. Farrant*, [1983] 1 S.C.R. 124.

was going to be life imprisonment. The real issue was the minimum custodial period before someone could apply for parole.

Research suggested a minimum duration in the ten- to fifteen-year zone.[11] First, Canada's own experience with parole and murderers demonstrated that those convicted of non-capital murder and capital murder commuted to life imprisonment had served, on average, about seven years and twelve years respectively.[12] Secondly, international comparisons with places which had abolished the death penalty showed that most jurisdictions chose a minimum custodial period between ten and fifteen years.[13] However, the Canadian Association of Police Chiefs, which opposed abolition, had taken the public position that if the death penalty was to be abolished, the only acceptable alternative would be a minimum of twenty-five years in custody. With this benchmark in mind, the government's ultimate proposal was a compromise. The sentence for first-degree murder would be life imprisonment with no parole for twenty-five years but the prisoner could, after serving fifteen years, apply to a panel of three superior court judges to have the period of parole ineligibility reduced. In committee, just a few weeks before the final vote, it was suggested that the proper reviewing body should be a jury selected in the province where the offence occurred. This was the sentence for first-degree murder that was passed and proclaimed into effect as of July 27, 1976.[14]

With the enactment of the *Charter* in 1982, it was inevitable that Canada's gravest punishment would be scrutinized for constitutionality. This question reached the Supreme Court of Canada in *R. v. Luxton*,[15] a case involving first-degree murder pursuant to what is now section 231(5)(e)[16] of the *Criminal Code*, murder while committing unlawful confinement. The appellant argued that the life sentence with no parole eligibility for twenty-five years violated sections 7, 9, and 12 of the *Charter*. The Court unanimously rejected all these arguments. The Court accepted that, as a principle of fundamental justice, a sentencing scheme must include a proportionate "gradation of punishments according to the malignity of the offences."[17] However, the

---

11  See A. Manson, "The Easy Acceptance of Long Term Confinement in Canada" (1990), 79 C.R. (3d) 265.
12  *Ibid.* at 267.
13  *Ibid.*
14  See *Criminal Law Amendment Act (No. 2), 1976*, S.C. 1974-75-76, c. 105, s. 21.
15  [1990] 2 S.C.R. 711 [*Luxton*].
16  Formerly s. 214(5)(e) of the *Criminal Code*.
17  *Luxton*, above note 15 at 721.

scheme must also respond to the objectives of prevention, deterrence, and rehabilitation. The Court concluded that the sentence conformed with the section 7 standard because it isolated a group of offenders who had murdered while committing an offence involving the illegal domination of the victim, which "markedly enhances the blameworthiness" of the offender. The possibility of a review after fifteen years showed a sensitivity to individual circumstances consistent with individualization being the fundamental lens of sentencing. The arbitrary detention argument under section 9 was rejected on similar grounds because Parliament had narrowly defined a particular class of murder involving the illegal domination of another. This kind of exploitation demands a high degree of societal denunciation. The section 12 "cruel and unusual" argument was the most challenging and potentially the most significant since it could apply to all first-degree sentences. Without any factual record describing the rigours and effects of long-term confinement, the Court dismissed the section 12 claim concluding

> These sections provide for punishment of the most serious crime in our criminal law, that of first degree murder. This is a crime that carries with it the most serious level of moral blameworthiness, namely, subjective foresight of death. The penalty is severe and deservedly so. The minimum 25 years to be served before eligibility for parole reflects society's condemnation of a person who has exploited a position of power and dominance to the gravest extent possible by murdering the person that he or she is forcibly confining. The punishment is not excessive and clearly does not outrage our standards of decency.[18]

Immediately after this passage, the Court made reference to the various extraordinary ways in which individual circumstances could still be raised such as the royal prerogative of mercy, early parole after a fifteen-year review, and temporary absence passes for humanitarian purposes.[19] These illustrations suggest that the existence of these avenues played a role in the constitutionalization of the minimum twenty-five year term. This is important since, in subsequent years, these opportunities to make individual claims for leniency, mercy, or special consideration,

---

18  *Ibid.* at 724.
19  In fact, except for the three years prior to parole eligibility, temporary absence passes can only be granted for medical purposes: see s. 746.1(2)(c) of the *Criminal Code*.

have been diminished both by statute[20] and practice. Perhaps these changes will persuade the Supreme Court to reconsider *Luxton*, especially from the perspective of the effects of long-term confinement on mental and physical health, and potential re-integration. This kind of qualitative assessment was not included in the *Luxton* arguments.[21]

## 2) Second-degree Murder and Parole Ineligibility

After a conviction for second-degree murder, and unless the accused has been convicted of murder before,[22] the jury is asked to make a recommendation about the period of parole ineligibility.[23] Then, after hearing submissions from the parties, the trial judge sets the period at a point between ten and twenty-five years. Section 745.4 indicates that the considerations which the trial judge must take into account are the "character of the offender, the nature of the offence and the circumstances surrounding its commission," and the jury's recommendation, if any. For many years, appellate courts debated whether ten years should be the ordinary period of parole ineligibility in the absence of unusual circumstances. This was predicated on the argument that all murders are inherently violent and grave. Accordingly, the minimum period ought to apply absent excessive brutality, murder in the commission of certain offences, multiple victims, vulnerable victims, multiple perpetrators, and other factors that would enhance gravity.[24] However, the unusual circumstance test no longer applies.

---

20   See the 1997 amendments to the fifteen-year review process discussed below and enacted by *An Act to amend the Criminal Code (judicial review of parole ineligibility) and another Act*, S.C. 1996, c. 34, s. 2(2), which restricted its scope markedly. See also s. 746.1 of the *Criminal Code*, which restricts the availability of temporary passes to medical situations except for the three years before parole eligibility.

21   See Manson, above note 11 at 270–72.

22   In which case s. 745(b) of the *Criminal Code* prescribes the sentence as life imprisonment with no parole eligibility for twenty-five years. Initially, the category of second-time murderers were convicted of first-degree murder, but this was changed probably to facilitate charging the jury when a variety of verdicts are possible and there are party issues on the table.

23   *Ibid.*, s. 745.2. The recommendation does not need to be unanimous: see *R. v. Okkuatsiak* (1993), 80 C.C.C. (3d) 251 (Nfld. C.A.). Moreover, the jury need not make a recommendation at all: see *R. v. Jordan* (1983), 7 C.C.C. (3d) 143 (B.C.C.A.). Whatever the jurors do after being addressed pursuant to s. 745.2 is a factor for the sentencing judge to consider, and no more.

24   See *R. v. Ly* (1992), 72 C.C.C. (3d) 57 (Man. C.A.) and the appendix to it for a discussion of the kinds of situations in which extended periods of parole ineligibility had been imposed.

In *R. v. Shropshire*, the accused pleaded guilty to second-degree murder after admittedly shooting the victim during a marijuana trans-action.[25] The trial judge was concerned that no explanation was offered for the killing. Even though the accused had only a modest record[26] and both counsel had submitted that ten years was the appropriate period of parole ineligibility, the judge set it at twelve years. In the Brit-ish Columbia Court of Appeal, the majority reduced the parole ineligi-bility to ten years. Lambert J.A. ruled that an increase could only be justified in unusual circumstances and the offender's failure to explain the motive did not qualify. Moreover, he was concerned that an extra two years would not produce extra deterrence to warrant the expendi-ture of public funds. The Supreme Court unanimously reversed and restored the twelve-year period of parole ineligibility. Iacobucci J. for the Court concluded that the "unusual circumstances" standard was too high and made it too difficult for judges to properly exercise their sentencing discretion. After examining the statute, he explained Parlia-ment's intention:

> . . . as a general rule, the period of parole ineligibility shall be for 10 years, but this can be ousted by a determination of the trial judge that, according to the criteria enumerated in s. 744 [now s. 745.4], the offender should wait a longer period before having his suitability to be released into the general public assessed. To this end, an exten-sion of the period of parole ineligibility would not be "unusual," although it may well be that, in the median number of cases, a period of 10 years might still be awarded.[27]

This paragraph has, perhaps unwittingly, encouraged trial judges to go beyond the ten years minimum frequently and without ample justifica-tion. Iacobucci J. was concerned that judges be able to delineate "both a range of seriousness and varying degrees of moral culpability" with respect to second-degree murder. However, this should mean respond-ing to appropriate aggravating factors for second-degree murder and increasing parole ineligibility when they are present — it should not mean using the whole range of ten to twenty-five years as a continuum that moves from an offence of little gravity to one of utmost gravity, since, by definition, all second-degree murders are grave.

---

25   [1995] 4 S.C.R. 227.
26   The record consisted of two youth court convictions for robbery, and impaired driving and two narcotics offences as an adult: *ibid.* at 231.
27   *Ibid.* at 242.

In restoring the twelve-year period of parole ineligibility in *Shropshire*, Iacobucci J. noted three aggravating factors, two of which related to the commission of the offence.[28] The third was the absence of an explanation. Viewing the absence of an explanation as an aggravating factor is troubling since it puts a burden on the accused which contradicts the central principle articulated by the Supreme Court in *Gardiner*, that the Crown is responsible for proving aggravation.[29] As well, while murders in the course of robbery or break and enter have been viewed as aggravated, the reason is the need to denounce actions that are, and appear to be, dangerous to innocent people. The same is not true of a killing that has some relation to a marijuana transaction. Still, the Supreme Court restored the twelve-year period. It is important to note that the ten-year parole ineligibility period reflects a minimum period of incarceration which can be commensurate with the inherently grave and violent nature of the crime of second-degree murder. As Iacobucci J. made clear, it would not be surprising if a "median number of cases" resulted in ten-year parole ineligibility periods. This suggests that a large portion, perhaps half or more, will warrant the minimum. Therefore, an increase should only be warranted when circumstances show enhanced culpability.

Recently, in R. v. *Mafi*[30] the British Columbia Court of Appeal dealt with a second-degree murder case where an employee had been caught either during or after a theft and proceeded to kill his employer and a co-worker. The trial judge followed the jury's recommendation and set the parole ineligibility period at twenty years. The majority of McEachern C.J.B.C. and Lambert J.A.[31] in separate decisions reduced the period to fifteen years. Lambert J.A. recognized that the limited scope for appellate review was determined by the relation that the trial sentence bears to the "acceptable range" and, accordingly, tried to narrow that concept. For him, the "acceptable range" means the "range for similar murders committed by similar offenders in similar circumstances."[32] This produced only a few examples of multiple murders which were relevant. Moreover, a "marked departure" must be measured from the centre of the range to ensure that there is proper room both for the trial judge's discretion and the appellate court's reviewing role:

---

28   The third was Shropshire's record: *ibid.* at 246.
29   See the discussion of *R. v. Gardiner*, [1982] 2 S.C.R. 368, in Chapter 8, above, at 8(c).
30   (2000), 142 C.C.C. (3d) 449 (B.C.C.A.) [*Mafi*].
31   Braidwood J.A. dissenting.
32   *Mafi*, above note 30 at 456–57.

So the width of the range must be such that it retains a sufficient width, both above and below the centre point, to allow a full measure of discretion to the sentencing judge, and also to encompass the concept that within the range a variation of the sentence would be a tinkering with the sentence. However, Courts of Appeal must still retain an appropriate measure of sentencing consistency by keeping the range within limits set by identifying the characteristics of the offender and the offence that are significant for sentencing purposes.[33]

He found the acceptable range to be twelve to fifteen years. McEachern C.J.B.C. was more blatantly critical of the *Shropshire* approach of deference and said that it "unduly limits the proper exercise of this right of appeal and often operates in such a way that an unfair and sometimes unjust sentence cannot always be adjusted on appeal because of the expectations of deference."[34] He also observed that most of the objectives of sentencing set out in section 718 have no bearing on the issue of parole ineligibility and those that might, like denunciation and deterrence, are probably satisfied in the circumstances of second-degree murder by the mandatory life sentence. He agreed with Lambert J.A. that prisoners may be unjustly deprived of their liberty because they are detained "too long after there is no further need for their detention."[35] He pointed out that the jury receives no instructions on the law of sentencing before giving its recommendation under section 745.2. He concluded that deference to the twenty-year ineligibility period would entrench an "excessive sentence and amount to a denial of the accused's right of appeal."[36] The decision in *Mafi* illustrates the importance of the need for a careful appellate review and how too much deference to an increased parole eligibility date can produce real unfairness and disparity, especially when each one of those years must be served in full.

## 3) R. v. *Latimer*, the Minimum Penalty and Constitutional Exemptions

When the Sentencing Commission examined mandatory minimum penalties in its 1987 Report and concluded that they should be removed because they came into conflict with the principles of proportionality,

---

33  *Ibid.* at 458.
34  *Ibid.* at 464.
35  *Ibid.* at 468.
36  *Ibid.* at 474.

equity, and restraint, it excluded murder from this recommendation.[37] Parliament, when it dealt with sentencing reform in 1996, did not agree with these well-argued general recommendations about minimum sentences. However, it is important to note that the Sentencing Commission, for good reasons, expressly decided not to consider the mandatory life imprisonment penalty as part of the minimum sentence debate.[38] While no one has placed the mandatory penalty issue on the legislative agenda,[39] the case of R. v. *Latimer* has placed it on the judicial docket.

Latimer was charged with first-degree murder of his severely physically disabled twelve-year-old daughter, who was found dead from asphyxiation. The family was obviously concerned about her pain and the prospect of further surgery which had been recommended. Latimer gave a lengthy statement to the investigators explaining how, to end her misery, he killed her when the rest of the family was away. At his second trial,[40] he was convicted of second-degree murder, but Noble J. accepted the argument that the mandatory penalty of life imprisonment with no parole for at least ten years was a violation of section 12 of the *Charter* since it was grossly disproportionate to the culpability of the offender.[41] Although a similar argument had been rejected by the Saskatchewan Court of Appeal after the first trial,[42] Noble J. distinguished the first prosecution on factual grounds including a change in the prosecution's theory and the recommendation of leniency from the second jury with respect to parole ineligibility. He considered that a constitutional exemption was available as a section 24(1) remedy and sentenced Latimer to one year imprisonment to be followed by one year of probation with a house arrest condition. The Saskatchewan Court of Appeal unanimously reversed the sentencing decision and imposed the mandatory penalty of life imprisonment with no parole for ten years.[43] Subsequently, the Supreme Court granted leave to appeal.[44]

---

37 See Canadian Sentencing Commission, *Sentencing Reform: A Canadian Approach* (Ottawa: Supply and Services Canada, 1987) at 188–90.

38 *Ibid.* at 178.

39 Proposals being discussed about the future of the provocation defence include, as one alternative, turning the penalty for murder into a more discretionary one.

40 The first trial resulted in a conviction for second-degree murder but a new trial was ordered by the Supreme Court as a result of the Crown's misconduct in selecting the jury: see R. v. *Latimer*, [1997] 1 S.C.R. 217.

41 See R. v. *Latimer* (1997), 121 C.C.C. (3d) 326 (Sask. Q.B.).

42 See R. v. *Latimer* (1995), 99 C.C.C. (3d) 481, Bayda C.J.S. dissenting (Sask. C.A.).

43 See R. v. *Latimer* (1998), 131 C.C.C. (3d) 191 (Sask. C.A.).

44 For an analysis of the judgment see below at 377.

This case raises a number of difficult competing issues. How does one who is not in the parent's difficult position assess that person's motives? Can parents make life and death decisions about disabled children without devaluing the lives of those children in comparison with physically healthy children? From a sentencing perspective, however, the issue is more focused: does the mandatory penalty deprive a court in an unconstitutional way of the ability to impose a sentence commensurate with blameworthiness? In many related situations, prosecutors do not choose murder as the charge to pursue and the issue of the mandatory penalty does not arise. This, in my view, is the key because it demonstrates both the variety of views that reasonable people can hold and the potential unfairness that can flow from the fortuity of who exercises prosecutorial discretion.

Although the Supreme Court of Canada has not ruled definitively on the propriety of a constitutional exemption,[45] this avenue seems to be the proper answer to the mandatory penalty issue. As demonstrated by the mandatory firearms prohibition cases,[46] what may seem to be a vehicle of sensible and sound penal policy in the vast majority of cases may, because of individual circumstances, produce a grossly disproportionate effect. In these cases, the most dramatic example of the need for a constitutional exemption was the situation of an aboriginal person who needed a rifle to continue a subsistence way of life in which hunting was an integral facet. In this situation, where a family is unwittingly denied their source of livelihood, it can be argued that the penal effect is disproportionate both to culpability and to the effect on other offenders. Since the prohibition is generally beneficial and not disproportionate in the vast majority of cases, the fair and just response is an individual constitutional exemption. This is not a situation of a "reasonable hypothetical" which can result in a declaration of invalidity[47] but a rare circumstance, insufficiently common to support invalidation but still demanding of relief. In the firearms context, Parliament has now crafted a statutory exemption which forecloses the need for a constitutional

45  See *R. v. Sawyer*, [1992] 3 S.C.R. 809. The acceptance in *Corbière v. Canada (Minister of Indian and Northern Affairs)*, [1999] 2 S.C.R. 203 of an exemption that applies during a suspension of a declaration of invalidity does not answer the *Latimer* point. Also, see the concurring decision of Arbour J. in *R. v. Morrisey*, [2000] S.C.J. No. 39, which supports the utility of case-by-case exemptions.
46  See particularly *R. v. Chief* (1989), 51 C.C.C. (3d) 265 (Y.C.A.).
47  See *R. v. Goltz*, [1991] 3 S.C.R. 485. In *Morrissey*, above note 45, Arbour J. questioned the continued utility of the "reasonable hypothetical" approach as applied by the majority.

exemption.[48] Pending a legislative response, it is the court's function to interpret and apply the *Charter*, and in so doing, ensure that unconstitutional legislative effects do not go without a remedy.

In the case of second-degree murder, the issue is whether a killing represents a degree of moral culpability which, by reason of motive, is less than the normative quality ordinarily associated with murder. Our community values the lives and inherent dignity of all its members and must ensure that everyone within its reach is protected. However, part of this mutual respect and obligation to protect is the duty to exercise compassion. This includes the recognition that we cannot appreciate each other's pain and anguish. When a neighbour kills an intruder we can accept the legitimacy of self-defence to completely exonerate the intentional killing. Even if it is a doubtful situation, the doubt will be resolved in favour of the accused. Similarly, provocation reduces an intentional killing to manslaughter and doubt is resolved in the accused's favour. If we accept these ameliorating situations, and also that prosecutorial discretion can produce a charge of administering a noxious substance in one county and murder in the county next door, we must accept that our judicial system can address the hard questions of sincerity and diminished culpability. If satisfied that a killing was generated by compassion, surely the penalty should, by way of constitutional exemption, be commensurate with that conclusion. Then, the sentence can be determined by blameworthiness, as indicated by the facts of the case. The threshold needs to be high, and the use of the exemption will be rare, but it is an essential tool to ensure both respect for the criminal law and a guarantee of equity in its application.

## 4) The Fifteen-year Parole Eligibility Review

The compromise to setting the minimum custodial period for first-degree murder at twenty-five years was the fifteen-year review. The object of the review structured by section 745.6 is to have a jury consider whether the long period of parole ineligibility should be reduced. This is the only time when a jury plays a decision-making role in

---

48   See s. 113 of the *Criminal Code* which enables the court, when satisfied that the person needs the firearm to hunt or trap for sustenance, or that the prohibition will be a "virtual prohibition against employment in the only vocation open to the person," to authorize a chief firearms officer to issue a license or authorization that permits the person to use a firearm "for sustenance or employment purposes."

respect of sentencing.[49] Section 745.6 has been tagged with the label "faint hope clause" and statistics plainly show that this characterization has had an impact on the number of applications. Only slightly more than one-quarter of eligible prisoners have applied and completed a section 745.6 hearing. As of June 18, 2000, 488 prisoners were eligible to apply for a fifteen-year review but only 104 had made and completed applications for a reduction in parole ineligibility.[50] While a high percentage of those who have seen the process through to completion have received relief,[51] immediate eligibility is rare. The variety of reductions have produced ineligibility periods all the way up to twenty-three years.[52] It must be remembered that the relief sought is a reduction in the parole ineligibility period. It can only enable a prisoner to make application to the National Parole Board, who have turned down some people even though they had received favourable responses at their fifteen-year review.[53] Moreover, even if the Board is favourable, it will require the prisoner to go through a sequenced process of conditional release starting with escorted and unescorted temporary absence passes, followed by day parole and ultimately full parole. This can take a number of years from the point of parole eligibility.[54]

A fifteen-year review was initially available to anyone convicted of first-degree murder, or second-degree if the accompanying parole ineligibility period was set at more than fifteen years. In the original

---

49  The function in s. 745.2, *ibid.*, is only a recommending one. A dangerous offender or long-term offender application must be heard without a jury: see s. 754(2).

50  National Parole Board, *Performance Monitoring Report, 1999–2000* (N.P.B., Ottawa: 2000) at 106.

51  Of the 104 prisoners who had hearings up to June 18, 2000, 85 had received some relief. This represents 81 percent of the hearings but only 17 percent of the eligible prisoners.

52  Of the sixty-three hearings completed between 1987 and the end of 1995, fourteen applicants were denied relief, nineteen had their ineligibility reduced to fifteen years, and the remainder obtained reductions from sixteen to twenty-three years: Department of Justice, *Fact Sheet: s. 745 of the Criminal Code* (Ottawa: Department of Justice, 1996). To completely appreciate the extent of relief actually obtained, it would be necessary to know at what point in a sentence the prisoner applied, since some wait beyond the fifteen-year mark to commence a s. 745.6 application.

53  As of the end of 1995, six successful s. 745.6 applicants had been denied any form of parole: *ibid.* at 2.

54  By 2000, of the eighty-five prisoners who had obtained a reduction at their 745.6 hearings, 30 percent remained in custody while 62 percent were on day or full parole: above, note 50 at 106.

scheme, this would have included second-time murderers who received a mandatory parole ineligibility of twenty-five years.[55] However, the Minister of Justice responded to a demand for the repeal of fifteen-year reviews by limiting access to them and diminishing the prospect of success. There were three major changes. First, anyone who is convicted after January 9, 1997, the date of proclamation in force, of a multiple murder or a murder after having already been convicted of a murder, is entirely disentitled from applying.[56] Secondly, there is no longer an absolute right to a hearing. Upon application, the Chief Justice of the province in which the offence occurred must consider the application and other written material to determine whether, on a balance of probabilities, the application has a reasonable prospect of success.[57] Only if the Chief Justice is satisfied that there is a reasonable prospect of success will a jury be empaneled to hear the application. The third change, which may ultimately have the greatest impact, is the imposition of a jury unanimity requirement.[58] Until 1997, only eight of twelve jurors needed to agree to reduce the period of ineligibility. Now, the prisoner must persuade all twelve jurors that he or she is entitled to a reduction in the period of parole ineligibility. A transitional provision makes this change, as well as the one dealing with the judicial vetting by the Chief Justice, applicable to all applications commenced after January 9, 1997.[59]

The stated intent behind the amendments was to preclude some prisoners from applying and to reduce the prospects of success for those who do apply. This was a political response to vocal criticism of a process that seemed to be working well. Juries were able to discriminate between good cases and undeserving ones, and the National Parole Board scrutinized subsequent applications with serious regard to the issue of risk. The application rate experienced to date has been low, reflecting a pessimistic view by individual prisoners of their chances. Whether they are right depends on one's ability to assess how a jury will respond to the particular case. Certainly, the nature of the killing and the victim are important factors. Cases involving children or police

---

55  See *Criminal Code*, s. 745(b).

56  *Ibid.*, s. 745.6(2), enacted by *An Act to amend the Criminal Code (judicial review of parole ineligibility) and another Act*, above note 20, s. 2, which was proclaimed in force on January 9, 1997.

57  See *Criminal Code*, s. 745.61.

58  *Ibid.*, s. 745.63(3).

59  See *An Act to amend the Criminal Code (judicial review of parole ineligibility) and another Act*, above note 20, s. 7.

officers as victims will only rarely produce a favourable response from a jury. The extent to which the prisoner can show rehabilitative progress is significant. Certainly, it is too soon to assess the impact of the amendments since there have only been a few cases to which they applied.[60] However, it takes little imagination to predict that the imposition of the jury unanimity requirement will have a significant effect.

## 5) Retrospectivity and Jury Unanimity

In the case of R. v. Chaudhary,[61] the applicant argued unsuccessfully that the jury unanimity requirement should not apply to her on the ground that it represented a retrospective change in her sentence in violation of section 7 of the Charter. This was not a question of whether the amendment was procedural or substantive, which often determines retrospective application, since Parliament had included a transitional provision which used the date of application as the determinative date. Accordingly, the unanimity challenge was about the effect of the transitional provision. In this respect, the case was similar to R. v. Gamble.[62] After the 1976 murder amendments, the old law of non-capital murder should have been applied to Ms. Gamble, instead of the new law of first-degree murder which produced a life sentence with no parole eligibility for twenty-five years. The Alberta Court of Appeal noted the error in 1978, but a transitional provision required that a new trial would have to be conducted under the new law, making any relief illusory. After the enactment of the Charter, Ms. Gamble applied for habeas corpus on Charter grounds challenging the extended period of parole ineligibility. The Supreme Court held that the parole ineligibility period is an integral part of the sentence, and that section 7 ensures that it must be determined by the law extant at the time of the offence.[63] Accordingly, the transitional provision could not deprive her of a remedy. She was entitled to be immediately eligible for parole. In Ms. Chaudhary's case, her life sentence was subject to a fifteen-year review where she had only to persuade eight jurors, and now unanimity is the rule. Lesage C.J.S.C. rejected this argument

---

60 Recent data shows that there were twenty-seven hearings between 1997 and 1999. Of this group, twenty-three applicants received some reduction. Some of these would have been conducted under the prior rules. Accordingly, one cannot read much into the rate of success, which remains on a par with what has prevailed so far.
61 (1999), 139 C.C.C. (3d) 547, Lesage C.J.S.C. (Ont. Sup. Ct.).
62 [1988] 2 S.C.R. 595.
63 Ibid. at 646–48.

concluding that the amendment was procedural and did not significantly change the process or the applicable criteria.

To understand the impact of the unanimity requirements, one has
to appreciate the role of the jury, the nature of the question it is being
asked, and the factors it must consider. Section 745.63(1) sets out the
relevant "criteria" to be considered in determining whether the period
of parole ineligibility should be reduced:

(a) the character of the applicant;
(b) the applicant's conduct while serving the sentence;
(c) the nature of the offence for which the applicant was convicted;
(d) any information provided by a victim at the time of the imposition of the sentence or at the time of the hearing under this section; and
(e) any other matters that the judge considers relevant in the circumstances.

It is difficult to understand how these can be described as criteria. They
are, in essence, descriptions of information which the jury must entertain but they do not indicate real criteria or a functional test for the
jury's decision. At the end of the day, the question will be: taking these
factors into account, does the applicant deserve a reduction?

In *R. v. Swietlinski*,[64] the Supreme Court granted leave and considered various issues which arose during the course of a fifteen-year
review. Lamer C.J.C. explained the nature of the decision:

The discretionary nature of the decision also compels the jury to
adopt a different analytical approach from that used in a trial. At a
trial the jury must decide whether it has been proven beyond all reasonable doubt that the accused committed the crime with which he
or she is charged. In such a proceeding the offence is generally
defined by a number of elements which must all be proven for the
accused to be convicted. Each element of the offence is thus a necessary condition for a conviction. At a s. 745 hearing, on the other
hand, the jury does not determine whether the applicant is guilty:
another jury (or, in some cases, a judge) has already performed that
task. Its duty rather is to make a discretionary decision as to the minimum length of the sentence that the applicant must serve. The concept of an element of an offence cannot be transposed onto a discretionary decision. When a person makes such a decision he or she

---

64   [1994] 3 S.C.R. 481 [*Swietlinski*].

does not apply rigid logic, requiring for example that if conditions A, B and C are met, then decision X must be the result.[65]

Ordinarily, juries are required to find facts and apply the law in order to determine criminal responsibility. There is always an opportunity for a judge to examine the evidence, compare it to the issues on the table, and enforce some measure of sufficiency before giving the case to the jury. Where a reasonable jury properly instructed could not convict, the case should be taken from the jury.[66] On appeal, if the factual underpinning is insufficient to support the verdict or the verdict is unreasonable, the appeal should be allowed.[67] With a section 745.6 hearing, however, the issue is amorphous, calling on attitudes and experience. It compels each juror to ask what degree of denunciation a particular offence and offender require. This is not a question that can permit the same kind of judicial review that applies to an ordinary verdict, where the charge can be assessed and the evidence weighed: the object of a section 745.6 hearing is to find out what the jury thinks. This process is not amenable to a review on the usual appellate lines. Moreover, there is no appeal to an appellate court other than the extraordinary route of going directly, with leave, to the Supreme Court of Canada.[68] It is this process which has been changed from requiring the support of eight jurors to compelling unanamity as a pre-condition of a reduction in parole ineligibility.

Changing the rules so that the prisoner must persuade each and every juror is a monumental change. Many people disagree on the basic issue: how much denunciation through imprisonment does an offence require? So long as one juror is unfavourable, or unreasonable, there will be no reduction. By dramatically lessening the chances of success, the amendment changes the sentence from life imprisonment with some prospect of parole after fifteen years to a life sentence with a diminished prospect of parole. The size of that prospect does not matter; it has been substantially diminished. This represents a substantive

---

65   *Ibid.* at 493–94.

66   See *R. v. Charemski*, [1998] 1 S.C.R. 679, especially McLachlin J. in dissent at 692–99.

67   See the explanation of the unreasonable verdict test in *R. v. Biniaris* (2000), 143 C.C.C. (3d) 1 at 20–25 (S.C.C.), where she emphasizes the distinction between, on the one hand, applying "knowledge of the law and the expertise of the courts" and, on the other hand, simply using personal experience and insight to review a verdict. This distinction highlights the legal nature of the verdict in the ordinary case. This can be compared to a s. 745.6 verdict which is comprised intentionally of the personal attitudes of the jurors.

68   See *Swietlinski*, above note 64 at 491. See also *R. v. Vaillancourt* (1989), 49 C.C.C. (3d) 544 (Ont. C.A.).

change to the sentence as determined by the date of the offence and, as determined in *Gamble*, violates section 7 of the *Charter*. Unfortunately, an application for leave to appeal to the Supreme Court in the *Chaudhary* case was denied.[69] As a result, it remains the only decision on this point. However, absent a clear analysis from the Supreme Court, other judges presiding at section 745.6 hearings, especially outside of Ontario, of can consider the issue and may not feel compelled to follow the *Chaudhary* ruling.

# B. MANSLAUGHTER

For sentencing purposes, the offence of manslaughter can encompass an infinite number of situations, but they all share one characteristic: a death has been caused by culpable homicide.[70] Because the taking of a life is a central feature of manslaughter sentencing, courts will emphasize the roles of denunciation and deterrence. However, rehabilitation and re-integration are relevant especially in the examples of "situational" killings where the offender presents little or no risk of future danger. Manslaughter sentencing is completely variable and dependent on the circumstances leading to the death, which permits the court to distinguish between degrees of culpability. The offender's background and the existence of mitigating or aggravating factors round out the sentencing matrix, and produce a variety of sentences that run from the non-custodial to life imprisonment.[71] There are some examples of suspended sentences[72] for manslaughter but these are rare. With the introduction of the conditional sentence, however, it is more common to have a court give serious consideration to a community sentence for manslaughter. Conditional sentences have been granted in some

---

69  [1999] S.C.C.A. No. 613 (QL).

70  See *Criminal Code*, ss. 222(5), 234.

71  See, for example, *R. v. Bezeau* (1958), 122 C.C.C. 35 (Ont. C.A.), upholding a life sentence for a brutal assault on the five-year-old son of the offender's wife. In *R. v. J.(J.T.)* (1991), 73 Man. R. (2d) 103 (C.A.), the court raised a twenty-two-year sentence to life but did so knowing that it would be an advantage since the offender had spent years in custody awaiting the three trials and appeals that ensued. The offender was seventeen at the time of the offence and with a life sentence his time toward parole eligibility would start counting from the date of arrest.

72  See, for example, *R. v. Drake*, [1995] O.J. No. 4375 (Gen. Div.) (QL) [*Drake*], where the offender was a battered woman who killed her spouse. See also *R. v. Millar* (1994), 31 C.R. (4th) 315 (Ont. Gen. Div.) [*Millar*]. Both are discussed below.

cases.[73] The biggest aid to understanding sentencing in manslaughter cases is to search recent similar cases in the jurisdiction. The potential factors are so diverse, the range so broad, and the principles so imprecise, that this is the only safe method to prepare for a case. One can discriminate between categories of manslaughter offences and then proceed to make an assessment of comparative gravity within an individual category. For sentencing purposes, there are four basic categories: murder reduced by provocation; manslaughter by reason of intoxication or mental disorder short of a section 16 defence; unlawful act; and criminal negligence.

## 1) Manslaughter by Reason of Provocation

Section 232 provides the circumstances where murder can be reduced to manslaughter by reason of provocation. This is a serious category of culpable homicide because it arises only when there has been a conclusion that the offender intended to kill, or was reckless in the ways described in section 229. Accordingly the range of sentences, while broad, is quite high. The verdict of guilty to manslaughter does not come with an explanation of the basis for the conclusion. If alternative bases are available in the evidence, a sentencing judge should be clear about whether the case is one of provocation.[74] While the fact of provocation must be considered as part of the manslaughter sentencing,[75] the important factors are the circumstances of the killing, the relationship with the victim, and the nature of the provocation. Excessive violence and brutality are always aggravating factors. The fact of killing one's spouse is usually aggravating with the exception of the situation, discussed below, where the deceased has been the perpetrator of a pattern of abuse. Because an element of provocation is the "on the sudden"

---

73 See, for example, R. v. Oster, [1997] B.C.J. No. 3099 (Prov. Ct.) (QL); R. v. Ferguson, [1997] O.J. No. 2488 (Gen. Div.) (QL) [Ferguson], where a woman who suffered from alcohol abuse and battered woman's syndrome shot her common law spouse; R. v. Turcotte, [1999] O.J. No. 592 (Gen. Div.) (QL), where the offender after a drinking binge with his mother strangled her (aff'd on appeal at (2000), 144 C.C.C. (3d) 139 (Ont. C.A.)); R. v. Mananghaya (1997), 118 Man. R. (2d) 30 (C.A.) (QL), where a woman killed her niece who had been having an affair with her husband; and R. v. Hariczuk, [1999] O.J. No. 3110 (Prov. Div.) (QL), where the offender's six-year-old son consumed some of the offender's methadone and died.

74 This is the judge's obligation under s. 724(2) of the Criminal Code. See also the discussion in R. v. Stone, [1999] 2 S.C.R. 290 [Stone], about the need for clarity.

75 See the discussion of this issue and Stone, above note 74, and Chapter 7, at 7(B)(11).

requirement,[76] it is implicit in the verdict that the killing was a spontaneous response. However, the circumstances may have involved a planned confrontation which would have an aggravating effect on sentencing as compared to an accidental meeting.[77]

Cases will arise where the offender has been the victim of longstanding abuse at the hands of the deceased. Since *R. v. Lavallee*,[78] it is clear that the fear of harm need not be imminent to constitute self-defence and women who have been battered by their spouses have a greater opportunity to be acquitted. This does not answer all situations since self-defence requires an apprehension of death or grievous bodily harm. If there is a manslaughter conviction, the history of abuse will be a very important factor for sentencing, especially if it is clear that the offender presents no future danger. A good example is *R. v. Drake*,[79] where a twenty-six-year old woman with four children was convicted of manslaughter after stabbing her husband. The judge found that she suffered from battered woman's syndrome and represented no risk of future violent actions.[80] He suspended the passing of sentence and placed her on probation for three years. Subsequently, the conditional sentence alternative has been used in similar cases.[81]

Another tragic example is the case of *R. v. Millar*,[82] where a jury convicted the offender of manslaughter based on provocation where he killed his father in a "frenzied state of blind rage." The offender, a man in his early thirties, had been abused both physically and sexually by his father. On top of watching the abuse of his mother and sister, he was subjected to a life of beating, whipping, and domination from the age of seven. On the night of the offence, he had been menaced and castigated in a "cruel and inhuman fashion." Moldaver J. described the killing as the result of pent-up hostility after twenty-five years of "hor-

---

76   *Criminal Code*, s. 232(2). A provoked killing is, for the purposes of s. 232, an intentional killing, that is, a murder, but the mental element must represent an "on the sudden" response to the provocation, in the sense of before passions cool.

77   See, for example, *R. v. Thibert*, [1996] 1 S.C.R. 37, where the accused went to his estranged wife's place of business and brought a rifle with him. Later, he confronted her and her boyfriend and shot the man.

78   [1990] 1 S.C.R. 852.

79   Above note 72.

80   In *R. v. Tran*, [1991] O.J. No. 2052 (Gen. Div.), Watt J. heard from two psychiatrists that the offender suffered from battered woman's syndrome and that recidivism was "extremely remote." He sentenced her to twelve months followed by three years probation.

81   See, for example, *Ferguson*, above note 73.

82   Above note 72.

rendous domination" and called the case "one of the most tragic" he had ever encountered. He suspended the passing of sentence and placed the offender on probation for three years.

## 2) "Unlawful Act" and "Criminal Negligence" Manslaughter

In these two categories, myriad factual premises can underlie the offence or conduct. For sentencing purposes, an appropriate range can only be discerned by looking for cases which arise from a similar premise. Obviously, the nature of the violence will be significant as will be the offender's background and prior record, if any, for violence. However, there is an important common element to both these categories which provides a useful key for sentencing. "Unlawful act" manslaughter requires as a minimum an underlying offence which is inherently dangerous in the sense of representing an objective risk of bodily harm.[83] "Criminal negligence" manslaughter involves risky conduct which represents at least a marked departure from the standard of care expected from a reasonable person in the circumstances.[84] In each case, there will be some underlying act or conduct that involves some degree of inherent risk that leads to a death. Accordingly, the degree of culpability, which is central to the sentencing function, is the amount of risk inherent in the underlying act or conduct. In other words, a single punch must be distinguished from a series of punches or a single blow with a bat. Using a shotgun is different from throwing a stone. For criminal negligence, the risk is central but culpability is also amplified by the nature of the duty in question and the degree of disregard.[85] If a baby has died, it is important to distinguish between a parent who ignores repeated beatings inflicted by another adult and one who, out of ignorance or incompetence, fails to obtain medical assistance for a sick child as soon as necessary. Cases must be distinguished by assessing the degree of culpability.

---

83  See *R. v. Creighton*, [1993] 3 S.C.R. 3.
84  There may be a residual question whether "reckless disregard" in addition to a marked departure is a requirement of criminal negligence: see *R. v. Fortier* (1998), 127 C.C.C. (3d) 217 at 223, LeBel J.A. (Que. C.A.).
85  In *R. v. Browne* (1997), 116 C.C.C. (3d) 183 (Ont. C.A.), a criminal negligence causing death conviction was overturned because no "undertaking of a binding nature" was breached when the accused failed to take the deceased to the hospital. The case highlights the link between the nature of the duty and the imposition of criminal sanctions.

## 3) Manslaughter by Reason of Intoxication or Mental Disorder

Cases arise where a brutal killing has taken place but the resulting conviction is for manslaughter because of evidence of intoxication or mental disorder short of a section 16 defence.[86] In other words, the mental element for murder was not proven because of one of these factors. In intoxication cases, a major issue is whether the offender is a long-term alcohol abuser and whether there is a record of crimes of violence. One often sees sentences in the six- to eight-year range, but this is usually where there is no record for violence.[87]

In cases where there is a psychiatric background, courts need to be careful that the sentence remains proportionate. If there are good indications of treatability or at least a potential for monitoring, there is no reason to expand the sentencing range for protective reasons.[88] Fears about mental illness, particularly when experts can provide no guarantees about treatment prospects, can produce inordinately long sentences. While it is certainly true that the degree of apparent danger can be so great as to warrant a life sentence, this would be a rare circumstance.[89] It is important to note that a person released from a prison or penitentiary who suffers from mental disorder and poses an imminent risk to others can be involuntarily committed under provincial mental health legislation.[90] While the fact of mental illness should not be

---

86   Section 16 ensures that a person is not found criminally responsible if, by reason of mental disorder, the person is incapable of appreciating the nature and quality of her act, or knowing that it is wrong.

87   See, for example, *R. v. Crockford*, [1995] O.J. No. 3264 (Gen. Div.) (QL). The offender received a seven-year sentence for stabbing a stranger with whom he had been drinking. See also *R. v. Nahwegahbow*, [1993] O.J. No. 3205 (Gen. Div.) (QL), where a substance abuser killed a co-resident of a rooming house after drinking and was sentenced to six years.

88   See, for example, *R. v. Gray*, [1995] O.J. No. 236 (Gen. Div.) (QL), where an intoxicated offender kicked his girlfriend in the head. Although he suffered from paranoid schizophrenia, the illness could be monitored and medication suppressed his delusions. A six-year sentence was imposed.

89   In *R. v. Standring*, [1993] O.J. No. 4233 (Gen. Div.) (QL), the partner of one accused was brutally beaten while all participants were on a cocaine binge. The accused was described as having a personality disorder with anti-social, narcissistic, and histrionic features. However, the judge concluded that he did not represent a sufficiently serious danger to warrant a life sentence. A co-accused who played a peripheral role was given a reformatory sentence.

90   This has even been applied, with great controversy, to a paedophile: see *Starnaman v. Penetanguishene Mental Health Centre* (1995), 100 C.C.C. (3d) 190 (Ont. C.A.).

ignored, it should not be overstated. From a sentencing perspective, these cases are difficult; they require a degree of sensitivity to the offender's disability and its potential for treatment or control. Old diagnoses are of little help but carefully prepared and current assessments can place the issues in their proper context. Caution must be exercised to ensure that a sentence is not aggravated based on an unreasonable fear or stereotypical appreciation of mental illness.

## FURTHER READINGS

GRANT, I., C. BOYLE, & J. CHUNN, *Law of Homicide* (Toronto: Carswell, 1994)

CANADIAN SENTENCING COMMISSION REPORT, *Sentencing Reform: A Canadian Approach* (Ottawa: Supply and Services Canada, 1987)

MANSON, A., "The Easy Acceptance of Long-Term Confinement in Canada" (1990) 79 C.R. (3d) 265

# CHAPTER 11

# PREVENTIVE DETENTION

## A. PREVENTIVE DETENTION

Preventive detention refers to confinement or control which, instead of responding to harm that has already been caused, is based on a perception of risk or fear of future crimes. Because it involves prediction it is always suspect. The well-known American jurist and writer Judge David Bazelon has said that preventive detention always raises "profound moral and legal questions."[1] While some jurisdictions have abandoned any form of preventive detention, others, like our neighbours to the south, have chosen to target recidivists with variations on the "three strikes, you're out" theme. Canada has embraced and expanded its use of preventive detention, which now consists of dangerous offender provisions, long-term offender provisions, and various forms of temporary community restraint effected by annual recognizances.

## B. COMPARISON WITH LIFE SENTENCES

While not explicitly a form of preventive detention, a life sentence is sometimes seen as such because of its indeterminacy. It should be reserved for those cases where it can be justified according to the test

---

1   D.L. Bazelon, *Questioning Authority: Justice and Criminal Law* (New York: Knopf, 1988) at 115. Bazelon was a judge for thirty-five years on the United States Circuit Court of Appeal.

for a maximum sentence: worst offence and worst offender.[2] Although not commonly imposed, one does see life sentences for manslaughter, sexual assault, and attempted murder. For crimes of violence, where a life sentence is available as the maximum sentence, the issue is usually one of brutality and previous record. In *Hill* v. *R.*,[3] Ritchie J. used the phrase "stark horror" to describe the rape with a knife that resulted in a life sentence. In *R.* v. *Horvath*,[4] the accused was convicted of attempted murder. He had bound and stabbed the victim before choking her and cutting her jugular vein. Recognizing that the offender had an anti-social personality disorder, the court accepted that a life sentence should not be used as a substitute for a dangerous offender application but upheld the life sentence. In doing so, Martin J.A. offered two justifications. The first was the quality of brutality or cruelty as applied in *Hill*. The second was a prior record that showed a pattern representing a serious threat to the safety of others. Similarly, in *R.* v. *Mesgun*,[5] a life sentence was upheld for attempted murder on a twenty-five-year old man with no previous record where the prolonged stabbing, slashing, gouging, and strangling demonstrated a degree of brutality that met the "stark horror" standard. By contrast, a life sentence for robbery and sexual assault was reduced to twenty years in *R.* v. *Armbruster*[6] notwithstanding a record of "enduring criminality." The offender was a "disadvantaged recidivist" from an aboriginal background. The gravity of the offences, while serious, was not proportionate to a life sentence.

Controversy remains as to whether a life sentence can be justified by a claim of continuing danger alone, or whether the proper response is to commence a dangerous offender application. In *R.* v. *Robinson*,[7] while reducing a life sentence for manslaughter to a sentence of two years imprisonment followed by three years probation, the British Columbia Court of Appeal held that in some cases a life sentence can be maintained. It concluded:

> But there will be cases where the prior criminal record, considered along with the facts of the offence for which the sentence is being imposed, will be enough to support a conclusion that a life sentence is called for in order to protect society.[8]

---

2    See the discussion of maximum sentences in Chapter 6, above, at 6(D).
3    (1975), [1977] 1 S.C.R. 827 at 859.
4    (1982), 2 C.C.C. (3d) 196 (Ont. C.A.).
5    (1997), 121 C.C.C. (3d) 439 (Ont. C.A.).
6    (1999), 138 C.C.C.(3d) 64 (B.C.C.A.).
7    (1997), 121 C.C.C. (3d) 240 (B.C.C.A.).
8    *Ibid.* at 253–54.

This is just another way of saying that the quality of the act, compounded by a record for previous offences, can justify a life sentence but only where there is a compelling need for public protection.[9] This is consistent with the view of the Newfoundland Court of Appeal in *R. v. Cooper*.[10] It concluded that continuing danger is an important factor but that a life sentence can only be justified by the offence and the record of the offender. The current view seems to be that a life sentence can be justified by a qualitative evaluation of the brutality of an offence, viewed in light of prior occurrences, if it compels a conclusion that public safety is the overwhelming sentencing consideration. Conversely, when the argument is that psychiatric evidence of continuing dangerousness compels a preventive response, a life sentence should not be imposed if the nature of the offence, viewed either in isolation or in the light of prior offences, does not justify it. This does not mean that any case with an indicia of dangerousness based on psychiatric opinion must result in a dangerous offender proceeding. The answer may be a lengthy fixed term that can be justifed by the offence and the prior record. A dangerous offender application is intended for the very small group of intensely dangerous people from whom the public needs to be protected.[11]

Prior concerns that substituting a life sentence for a dangerous offender application would[12] bypass the safeguards (and parole review) built into that process have lessened now that it is clear that a dangerous offender label means long periods in custody before release regardless of parole eligibility.[13]

# C. HISTORY OF PREVENTIVE DETENTION IN CANADA

Canada entered the preventive detention field in 1947 with Habitual Criminal provisions[14] and has been expanding the use of this basis for

---

9   See *R. v. Hastings* (1985), 19 C.C.C. (3d) 86 at 90–91 (Alta. C.A.).

10   (1997), 117 C.C.C. (3d) 249 (Nfld. C.A.).

11   See the remarks of Fraser C.J.A. in *R. v. Neve* (1999), 137 C.C.C. (3d) 97 at 194 (Alta. C.A.) [*Neve*], where she posed the central question as whether "relatively speaking compared to all other offenders in Canada — male and female, young and old, advantaged and disadvantaged — Neve falls into that small group of offenders clustered at or near the extreme end of offenders in this country."

12   See, for example, *R. v. Pontello* (1977), 38 C.C.C. (2d) 267 (Ont. C.A.).

13   See 11(D)(2) below.

14   *An Act to amend the Criminal Code*, S.C. 1947, c. 55, s. 18.

confinement ever since. Initially, a "habitual criminal" was defined simply as someone who had been convicted at least three times previously of an indictable offence punishable by more than five years imprisonment. The following year, "criminal sexual psychopath" provisions were added to the *Criminal Code*.[15] The definition of "criminal sexual psychopath" was anyone who "by a course of misconduct in sexual matters has evidenced a lack of power to control his sexual impulses and who as a result is likely to attack or otherwise inflict injury, loss, pain or other evil on any person." By the time of the Ouimet Committee report in 1969, that term had been abandoned in favour of "dangerous sexual offender;" namely, "a person who, by his conduct in any sexual matter, has shown a failure to control his sexual impulses, and who is likely to cause injury, pain or other evil to any person, through failure in the future to control his sexual impulses or is likely to commit a further sexual offence."[16]

The Ouimet Committee, impressed by the failure of preventive detention in England,[17] examined the cases of the eighty habitual offenders detained as of 1968. The legislated standard required that the person had been convicted at least three times since the age of eighteen for an indictable offence punishable by five years or more. There was no personal injury requirement. It concluded that almost 40 percent did not represent a serious threat to the safety of the public. As well, for a substantial number, there was insufficient evidence to conclude that they posed a serious threat to personal safety. Analysed geographically, thirty-nine individuals, almost one half, had been declared habitual offenders in the City of Vancouver. It concluded that "indeterminate detention which may be for life can only be justified in the case of dangerous offenders."[18] Fifty-seven persons were detained at the time as dangerous sexual offenders. While the largest number, eight, came from Vancouver, the cases were more evenly distributed across the country. Observing that psychiatric opinion questioned the degree of accuracy of the predictions of future dangerousness, it also noted that the dangerous sexual offender legislation only encompassed one category of person who could be considered dangerous.

---

15  *An Act to amend the Criminal Code*, S.C. 1948, c. 39, s. 43.
16  See *An Act to amend the Criminal Code*, S.C. 1960-61, c. 43, s. 32.
17  Report of the Canadian Committee on Corrections, *Toward Unity: Criminal Justice and Corrections* (Ottawa: Queen's Printer, 1969) [Ouimet Report] at 244–45.
18  *Ibid.* at 244 (emphasis omitted).

Ultimately, the Committee recommended that the habitual and dangerous sexual offender provisions be repealed and replaced with a new preventive detention regime focused on specified offences. After a diagnostic assessment, a hearing would assess the offender's criminal record and background to determine if the offender was "likely to continue to commit violent crimes."[19] Given the severity of indeterminate detention, the Committee stressed the need for an effective review mechansim. On top of an annual review by the Parole Board, it recommended the opportunity to have the case reviewed every three years by a superior court judge, at a hearing where the prisoner had the right to counsel and the right to call and cross-examine witnesses.

In 1975, the Supreme Court agreed with Ouimet's conclusion that the habitual offender legislation had been wrongly used to incarcerate indefinitely many individuals who were no more than persistent petty nuisances. It held that there must be a demonstrated "propensity for crimes of violence against the person" and a "real and present danger to life or limb."[20] Soon after, Parliament enacted the current "dangerous offender" regime, which followed some but not all of the Ouimet recommendations.[21]

The immediate aftermath of the enactment of the new regime arose from the statutory continuation of all earlier designations. A study by Professor Michael Jackson revealed that many prisoners who could not be considered dangerous were still detained as habitual criminals because they were poor parole candidates.[22] This led to an inquiry conducted by His Honour Judge Leggatt in which all cases were individually considered at a hearing to determine whether each prisoner represented a danger. The resulting report[23] recommended that all but a handful should be immediately released, and this was effected through the exercise of the royal prerogative of mercy. Despite this governmental recognition of how easy it is for a preventive detention regime to run off the rails, more recent cases have demonstrated that

---

19   *Ibid.* at 260.
20   *R. v. Hatchwell* (1975), [1976] 1 S.C.R. 39 at 43.
21   *Criminal Law Amendment Act, 1977*, S.C. 1976-77, c. 53, s. 14.
22   M. Jackson, *Sentences That Never End: The Report on the Habitual Criminal Study* (Vancouver: University of British Columbia, Faculty of Law, 1982).
23   Hon. S.M. Leggatt, *Report of the Inquiry into Habitual Criminals in Canada* (Ottawa: Government of Canada, 1984).

individuals may still be forgotten within a parole process that can fail to distinguish between danger and inadequacy.[24]

The provisions were revised by Bill C-55 in 1997[25] after a public lobby directed the Minister of Justice's concern to the group described as "high risk offenders."[26] Much of this attention was generated by a small number of cases involving a category of violent offenders described as sexual predators.[27] The Minister established the Federal/Provincial/Territorial Task Force on High-Risk Violent Offenders, with the mandate to examine the adequacy of the dangerous offender provisions and provincial mental health legislation as tools for responding to this particular group, and their report[28] provided the framework for Bill C-55. Because of these changes, it is important in any particular case to note the date of the triggering offence. Since a dangerous offender application is part of the sentencing process, an individual is entitled to be sentenced in accordance with the sentencing regime extant at the time of the offence[29] unless a subsequent enactment ameliorates the penalty.[30]

---

24  See, for example, *Steele* v. *Mountain Institution*, [1990] 2 S.C.R. 1385 [*Steele*], in which an offender originally categorized as a criminal sexual psychopath was released by way of habeas corpus after serving thirty-seven years. Similarly, in *Gallichon* v. *Commissioner of Corrections* (1995), 101 C.C.C. (3d) 414 (Ont. C.A.), habeas corpus resulted in the release of a prisoner who had been declared an habitual offender in 1967 where the Court of Appeal was satisfied that he did not meet the criteria of a persistent dangerous offender. His parole failures were characterized as minor.

25  *An Act to amend the Criminal Code (high risk offenders), the Corrections and Conditional Release Act, the Criminal Records Act, the Prisons and Reformatories Act and the Department of the Solicitor General Act*, S.C. 1997, c. 17, ss. 4–8 [*Criminal Code Amendment Act (High Risk Offenders)*].

26  For a discussion of this political process, see I. Grant, "Legislating Public Safety: The Business of Risk" (1998) 3 Can. Crim. L.R. 177; and M. Jackson, "The Sentencing of Dangerous and Habitual Offenders in Canada" (1997) 9 F.S.R. 256.

27  One of the most significant was the tragic killing of Christopher Stephenson by a recently released prisoner. Notwithstanding a record for sexual offences against children, Fredericks had been serving a determinate sentence and was released on mandatory supervision without use of the detention provisions. The subsequent inquest and the jury's recommendations focused considerable public attention on American models for sexual predator legislation: Verdict of Coroner's Jury into the Death of Christopher Stephenson, Brampton, Ontario, January 22, 1993.

28  Federal/Provincial/Territorial Task Force on High-Risk Violent Offenders, *Strategies for Managing High-Risk Offenders* (Victoria: The Task Force, 1995) [*Strategies for Managing High-Risk Offenders*].

29  See *R.* v. *Gamble*, [1988] 2 S.C.R. 595.

30  See *Canadian Charter of Rights and Freedoms*, Part I of the *Constitution Act, 1982*, being Schedule B to the *Canada Act 1982* (U.K.), 1982, c. 11, s. 11(i).

# D. THE DANGEROUS OFFENDER PROVISIONS

## 1) Basic Elements

A dangerous offender hearing, which may lead to indeterminate confinement, occurs after conviction in the place of an ordinary sentencing hearing.[31] There are a number of key elements to the current regime, both in terms of process and the substantive standard for a finding. Central to the dangerous offender designation is a conviction for an antecedent offence which is described as a "serious personal injury offence." Section 752 of the *Criminal Code* defines this category as

> (a) an indictable offence, other than high treason, treason, first degree murder or second degree murder, involving
>> (i)  the use or attempted use of violence against another person, or
>> (ii) conduct endangering or likely to endanger the life or safety of another person or inflicting or likely to inflict severe psychological damage upon another person,
>
> and for which the offender may be sentenced to imprisonment for ten years or more, or
>
> (b) an offence or attempt to commit an offence mentioned in section 271 (sexual assault), 272 (sexual assault with a weapon, threats to a third party or causing bodily harm) or 273 (aggravated sexual assault).

Briefly put, the antecedent offence must either be a sexual assault, regardless of the category, or an indictable offence punishable by more than ten years imprisonment that involved violence, actual or threatened, or represented a danger to the life, safety, or psychological well-being of another person. Some offences which are no longer in the *Criminal Code*, like gross indecency and rape, were part of earlier definitions of "serious personal injury offence." The Supreme Court has held that the deletion of these offences from the definition does not invalidate a prior designation as a dangerous offender.[32]

The 1997 amendments made a small number of very significant changes to the preventive detention regime, including the introduction

---

31   Subject to the limited opportunity to begin a dangerous offender hearing within six months of the imposition of sentence, as provided by s. 753(2) of the *Criminal Code*, discussed below.

32   *Milne* v. *Canada (A.G.)*, [1987] 2 S.C.R. 512, dealing specifically with gross indecency.

of a new designation, the long-term offender,[33] to supplement the dangerous offender provisions. There is a significant degree of procedural integration between the two designations. For both categories, no finding can be made without an assessment report prepared pursuant to section 752.1. Accordingly, the first step for either process is an application by the prosecutor for a remand for up to sixty days to have the assessment completed. The pre-requisites for a demand are as follows:

- the person has been convicted, but not yet sentenced of a personal injury offence[34] or an offence under section 753.1(2)(a),[35] and
- there are reasonable grounds to believe that the offender might be found to be a dangerous or long-term offender.

The resulting assessment will be filed with the court and used in evidence if there is a subsequent dangerous or long-term offender application. This single overarching assessment replaces the previous requirement that each party retain their own psychiatrist to give evidence at the dangerous offender hearing. This change obviously comes from the recommendation of the Task Force on High-Risk Violent Offenders, which resulted from its observations of a multi-disciplinary neutral assessment team in the Netherlands.[36] However, transplanting the mechanism of a single overarching multi-disciplinary assessment into Canadian processes ignores two factors. First, it cannot be said that there is a comparable multi-disciplinary clinic in every Canadian jurisdiction. Secondly, it seems that, in general, Dutch penal attitudes in the post-World War II era have been particularly tolerant and very concerned about deprivations of liberty.[37] One can assume that professionals working in the kind of clinic visited by the Task Force would be imbued with similar

---

33   This is discussed below in detail: see c. 11, (E). The long-term offender designation can result either from an independent application for that status or as a result of a dangerous offender application where the judge was not satisfied that the applicable standard was met but concluded that the evidence satisfied the lower long-term offender test.

34   See *Criminal Code*, s. 752, discussed above.

35   These are the potential antecedents for a long-term offender designation and consist of sexual interference (s. 151), invitation to sexual touching (s. 152), sexual exploitation (s. 153), exposure (s. 173(2)), and sexual assault (ss. 271, 272, & 273). It remains to be determined if the set is larger due to the additional phrase in s. 753.1(2)(a), "or has engaged in serious conduct of a sexual nature in the commission of another offence of which the offender has been convicted."

36   See *Strategies for Managing High-Risk Offenders*, above note 28 at 16.

37   See D.M. Downes, *Contrasts in Tolerance: Post-War Penal Policy in the Netherlands and England and Wales* (Oxford: Clarendon Press, 1988).

attitudes which favour restraint when considering deprivations of liberty. While the Task Force trusted the Dutch to be fair, impartial, and respectful of liberty, Canadian psychiatrists and psychologists with institutional positions often exhibit guarded and conservative responses. Especially given the frequent difficulty that provincial mental health facilities have in hiring staff, can we be sure that professionals working in them should be given the enormous authority that the Task Force recommended? Yet this authority, flowing from the abandonment of the previous requirement of two assessments for dangerous offender applications, was confirmed by section 752.1.

Aside from filing a section 752.1 report, there are a number of procedural requirements before a dangerous offender application can proceed. The attorney general of the province in which the trial took place must consent to the application before the hearing commences.[38] Also, the prosecutor must give at least seven days notice to the offender including "outlining the basis" for the application.[39] There is no requirement that the notice be given prior to the plea.[40] The hearing is always conducted by a judge without a jury.[41]

## a)   The Dangerous Offender Test — #1
The test for determining whether the offender is a dangerous offender is set out in section 753(1) and has two possible branches.

The first branch follows a conviction for a serious personal injury offence described in section 752(a), a violent indictable offence punishable by imprisonment for ten years or more. It requires a finding that the offender "constitutes a threat to the life, safety or physical or mental well-being of other persons." This must be based on evidence that establishes

1. A pattern of behaviour showing "a failure to restrain his or her behaviour and likelihood of causing death or injury to other persons, or inflicting severe psychological damage on other persons, through failure in the future to restrain his or her behaviour,"[42] or

---

38   *Criminal Code*, s. 754(1)(a). The consent need not given before the application is commenced but must be given prior to the hearing.
39   *Ibid.*, s. 754(1)(b).
40   See *R. v. Lyons*, [1987] 2 S.C.R. 309, where the Supreme Court rejected the argument that giving notice after plea violated the principles of fundamental justice. Wilson J. dissented on this point. Lamer J., as he then was, suggested that it might be a defect that could lead to setting aside a guilty plea for the antecedent conviction for the "serious personal injury offence" but it did not otherwise bear on the dangerous offender proceedings.
41   *Criminal Code*, s. 754(2).
42   *Ibid.*, s. 753(1)(a)(i).

2. A pattern of persistent aggressive behaviour "showing a substantial degree of indifference ... respecting the reasonably foreseeable consequences to other persons of his or her behaviour,"[43] or
3. Any behaviour associated with the offence that is "of such a brutal nature as to compel the conclusion that the offender's behaviour in the future is unlikely to be inhibited by normal standards of behavioural restraint."[44]

Recently, the British Columbia Court of Appeal examined the section 753(1)(a)(ii) ground of "pattern of persistent aggressive behaviour" in *R. v. George*.[45] The triggering offence was manslaughter after a seventy-nine-year-old man died from being beaten with a rock. The offender was an aboriginal person abandoned at birth who likely suffered from fetal alcohol syndrome. He was eighteen years old at the time of the offence but had a lengthy young offenders record consisting of property and administration of justice offences.[46] He was found to be a dangerous offender and sentenced to indeterminate detention. The court set aside the dangerous offender designation and ordered a sentencing hearing. It concluded that the trial judge erred in finding a pattern of aggressive behaviour. She combined too many unrelated things and found a pattern by creating a "relationship between unlike elements."[47] Also, she did not assess the quality of much of the youth crime to distinguish what was a function of a disadvantaged background and what indicated dangerousness. The court observed:

> The dangerous offender provisions may fall more heavily on the poor and disadvantaged members of our society if their childhood misconduct is counted against them. This appellant had to face school as an aboriginal foster child living in a non-aboriginal culture with an I.Q. at or near the retarded level, without having ever acquired a sense of discipline or self-control. It is understandable that any child with this background would get into a lot of trouble by lashing out aggressively when challenged by his or her environment.[48]

The court also concluded that the trial judge applied too narow a test of "indifference" by focusing only on the time of the offence and not taking

---

43 *Ibid.*, s. 753(1)(a)(ii).
44 *Ibid.*, s. 753(1)(a)(iii).
45 (1998), 126 C.C.C. (3d) 384 (B.C.C.A.) [*George*].
46 These were theft, break and enter, fail to comply with disposition, and fail to comply with recognizance.
47 *George*, above note 45 at 394.
48 *Ibid.* at 391–92.

into account evidence of genuine remorse. The decision is a refreshing effort to narrow the use of the dangerous offender provisions to ensure that they are used for those who are truly dangerous and not just anyone who seems to meet the letter or the criteria. A similar attitude was demonstrated by the Alberta Court of Appeal in R. v. Neve.[49]

### b)  The Dangerous Offender Test — #2

The second branch follows a conviction for the other set of serious personal injury offences, the categories of sexual assault.[50] This branch requires a finding that

1. the offender's conduct in any sexual matter shows a "failure to control his or her sexual impulses," and
2. there is a likelihood of his or her "causing injury, pain or other evil to other persons through failure in the future to control his or her sexual impulses."[51]

If the judge is satisfied that the standard under either of these branches has been established, she "may" find the offender to be a dangerous offender.

In R. v. Currie,[52] the Supreme Court examined the process under the second branch. The offender had been convicted of three counts of sexual assault arising from a series of incidents at a department store when he sexually touched a number of girls. The touching involved grabbing at their buttocks, breasts, and, in one case, trying to place his hand between a girl's legs. The girls became frightened and reported him. While the event itself was not, objectively viewed, especially serious, he had a long record of sexual assaults including at least two vicious rapes. He was found to be a dangerous offender but the Ontario Court of Appeal set aside the indeterminate sentence because the "serious personal injury offences" that triggered the application were not, objectively viewed, serious. The Supreme Court disagreed. Lamer C.J.C. concluded that it was an error to consider the seriousness of the sexual assaults. He held:

> . . . it is crucial to recognize that the conviction for a "serious personal injury offence" merely triggers the s. 753(b) application process. There remains a second stage to s. 753(b), at which point the trial judge must

---

49    Above note 11.
50    See *Criminal Code*, s. 752(b).
51    *Ibid.*, s. 753(1)(b).
52    [1997] 2 S.C.R. 260 [*Currie*].

be satisfied beyond a reasonable doubt of the likelihood of future danger that an offender presents to society before he or she can impose the dangerous offender designation and an indeterminate sentence.

Parliament has thus created a standard of preventive detention that measures an accused's present condition according to past behaviour and patterns of conduct. Under this statutory arrangement, dangerous offenders who have committed "serious personal injury offences" can be properly sentenced without having to wait for them to strike out in a particularly egregious way.[53]

He agreed with counsel that the lack of seriousness in the triggering offences could be a factor bearing on whether there was a future likelihood of harm, but this was its only relevance.

The use of the word "may" in section 753(1) requires some comment. In most contexts, it supports the existence of some residual discretion. However, the Ontario Court of Appeal in R. v. Moore held that if the criteria are met, the judge has no discretion but must declare the offender to be a dangerous offender.[54] This ruling was made when the legislation included a second "may" that provided some residual discretion by permitting a judge to reject an indeterminate sentence in favour of a fixed sentence. This was repealed in 1997 and replaced with a mandatory indeterminate sentence that follows a dangerous offender designation.[55] The better view of the word "may" is that it emphasizes the qualitative nature of the criteria and requires that the evidence be carefully examined to ensure that the high standard embodied in the tests of "threat to the life, safety or physical or mental well-being of other persons" and "likelihood of causing injury, pain or other evil to other persons" have in fact been met.[56] It must be remembered that the burden of proof is proof beyond a reasonable doubt of the likelihood or threat.[57]

There are strong arguments in favour of maintaining some residual discretion. In fact, some cases seem to assume it exists. In R. v. Lyons, as part of the extensive and detailed constitutional examination of the dangerous offender provisions, La Forest J. observed that "the judge at such a hearing does retain a discretion whether or not to impose the

---

53   Ibid. at 275–76.

54   See R. v. Moore (1985), 16 C.C.C. (3d) 328 (Ont. C.A.) [Moore].

55   Section 753(4).

56   See Neve, above note 11 at 176–77, where the Alberta Court of Appeal offered a similar view of the "threat analysis" to accommodate residual discretion.

57   See Lyons, above note 40 at 363–65; R. v. Knight (1975), 27 C.C.C. (2d) 343 (Ont. H.C.); R. v. Dwyer (1977), 34 C.C.C. (2d) 293 (Alta. S.C. (A.D.)); and R. v. Carleton (1981), 69 C.C.C. (2d) 1 (Alta. C.A.) [Carleton], aff'd [1983] 2 S.C.R. 58.

designation or indeterminate sentence, or both."[58] More importantly, however, are the factors which should be considered even if the criteria have been met. In R. v. Neve, the Alberta Court of Appeal, after arguing for a residual discretion, observed that discretion was essential to accommodate concerns about treatment prospects, the relative serious-ness of the offences, and the "extent of the offender's moral blamewor-thiness."[59] Ultimately, that court concluded that the dangerous offender designation was not reasonable:

> There is no doubt that Neve has a history of offending the law; and we cannot say that Neve will not reoffend. That risk exists and it is a real risk. Indeed, it would be naive to think otherwise. However, the question is not whether there is a possibility or even a probability of Neve's reoffending in the future. While this consideration certainly goes on the scale, the central question which must be addressed at this stage is whether, given her past record and the various factors that we have noted and assessed, Neve falls within the intended small group of dangerous offenders in Canada. In our view, she does not.[60]

The Neve decision highlights the importance of discretion. More signif-icantly, it emphasizes the qualitative difference between an indetermi-nate sentence and a fixed sentence and attempts to narrow the scope of the dangerous offender designation to the "small group of offenders clustered at or near the extreme end of offenders in this country."[61]

Before the 1997 removal of the discretion to impose an indetermi-nate or determinate sentence, courts consistently held that the issue of future treatability and the prospects for change were not relevant to the issue of whether the person was a dangerous offender but were rele-vant in deciding whether an indeterminate sentence should be imposed.[62] If there is no residual discretion, there is no place for this significant consideration, or the issues of seriousness of criminal con-duct, context, blameworthiness, and personal background, which played significant roles in Neve. The issue of discretion and the mean-ing of "may" in section 753(1) should be revisited now that an indeter-minate sentence is a mandatory result to ensure that relevant factors, like those considered in Neve, are not excluded from the matrix.

---

58   Lyons, above note 40 at 361–62. See also Neve, above note 11 at 175–77.
59   Neve, ibid. at 176.
60   Ibid. at 193.
61   Ibid. at 194.
62   See Carleton, above note 57 at 19–21, Clement J.A., aff'd [1983] 2 S.C.R. 58. See also R. v. Pollock (1996), 3 C.R. (5th) 249 (Sask. C.A.).

## c) Commencing a Dangerous Offender Application After Sentencing

One of the issues which captured the public's attention prior to the 1997 amendments was the situation of a person who had already been sentenced but in respect of whom new information suggests that a dangerous offender application may have been the more appropriate response. The arguments usually arose in the context of prisoners about to be released who had been given diagnostic labels that conjured up risk of future offences. Clearly, section 11(h) of the *Charter* prohibits an attempt to re-punish someone who has already been found guilty and punished. Accordingly, efforts to emulate American sexual predator legislation[63] were abandoned.

Instead, Parliament enacted section 753(2) which provides a small window to commence a dangerous offender application after a sentence has been imposed. This is permitted if

- the offender was given notice of this possibility prior to sentencing,
- the application is commenced not later than six months after sentencing, and
- it is "shown that relevant evidence that was not reasonably available to the prosecution at the time of the imposition of sentence became available in the interim."[64]

It would be an unusual case where a prosecutor had a sufficiently strong concern to give notice, but not enough evidence to go forward.

## 2) Consequences of a Dangerous Offender Finding

Since 1997, the mandatory result of a dangerous offender finding is an indeterminate sentence. A dangerous offender may appeal that designation.[65] The 1997 amendments increased the parole review date from three years to seven years from the date of arrest;[66] after the first review, the case is reviewed every two years. It is important to note the general attitude of the National Parole Board to dangerous offenders. Between 1980 and 1986, only six had been granted parole, most having

63 Probably the most extreme example was the Washington State legislation which was declared unconstitutional in *Young v. Weston*, 898 F.Supp. 744 (W.D. Wash. 1995).
64 See *Criminal Code*, ss. 753(2)(a), (b).
65 *Ibid.*, s. 759. Now, s. 759(3)(a)(ii) authorizes an appellate court to remove the dangerous offender label and impose a fixed sentence. Prior to 1997, it was only empowered to deal with the indeterminate sentence and could not quash the dangerous offender finding.
66 *Ibid.*, s. 761(1).

served over fifteen years.[67] In 1992, only four out of twelve dangerous offenders on the federal register were on conditional release.[68] The release rate was less than 1 percent — about one individual per year.[69] Between 1987 and 1992, 98.5 percent of applications for full parole by dangerous offenders were denied; 92.2 percent of day parole applications were rejected.[70] This data shows the slim prospects for release once a person is declared a dangerous offender.

## 3) Constitutionality of the Dangerous Offender Legislation

After the entrenchment of the *Charter* it was inevitable that the dangerous offender regime would be challenged. This was resolved, at least for the time being, by the decision in *R. v. Lyons*.[71] (It is important to note that the statutory framework has been changed in a number of substantial ways since the decision in *Lyons* and therefore one cannot now treat it as conclusive.) In *Lyons*, the offender had been charged, one month after his sixteenth birthday, with break and enter of a dwelling-house, using a weapon in committing a sexual assault, and using a firearm while committing an indictable offence. He elected trial by judge alone, waived the preliminary inquiry, and pleaded guilty. The judge requested a pre-sentence report and adjourned the sentencing. Shortly before the sentencing hearing, defence counsel was advised that the Crown might commence a dangerous offender application. Another adjournment was requested by the Crown so it could consider its position. The application was then made, and the consent of the attorney general was obtained. Given the offender's age, the judge warned the Crown that he would have an "uphill fight." At the hearing, there was an agreed-upon statement of facts plus expert psychiatric evidence. The judge concluded that it had been established beyond a reasonable doubt that the offender qualified as a dangerous offender. He considered him to have a "sociopathic personality" with little conscience to govern his actions. The judge rejected arguments that the dangerous offender regime violated sections 7, 9, and 12 of the *Charter* and sentenced the offender to indeterminate detention in a penitentiary. An appeal to the Nova Scotia Court of Appeal was dismissed.

67   *Lyons*, above note 40 at 340.
68   Canadian Bar Association, National Criminal Justice Section, Submission on Bill C-55.
69   See L. Motiuk & S. Seguin, *Dangerous Offenders in Canada* (Ottawa: Corrections Service of Canada, Research and Statistics Branch, 1992) at 3–4.
70   See *C.B.A. Submission*, above note 68.
71   Above note 40.

In the Supreme Court, the issue was whether the finding and inde-terminate sentence pursuant to the provisions in Part XXI [now Part XXIV] of the *Criminal Code* infringed or denied the appellant's rights under sections 7, 9, 11, or 12 of the *Charter*, and if so, whether they could be saved by section 1. The majority judgment was written by LaForest J. with four other judges concurring. While various claims were made under section 7, La Forest J. commenced with whether the general nature of the dangerous offender process violated the princi-ples of fundamental justice. He subsumed this into the question: did Part XXI sentence someone for future crimes not committed or did it sentence them for past crimes which had already been punished? LaForest J. rejected both these characterizations of the process. Looking at the key section, the counterpart of what is now section 753, he described the process as one in which an indeterminate sentence is imposed in lieu of a fixed sentence for a serious personal injury offence. It flows from the commission of the serious personal injury offence and not simply "fears or suspicions about his criminal proclivities."[72] Although partly punitive and partly preventive, it accords with the fundamental pur-pose of the criminal law, the protection of society. Here, La Forest J. made his often-quoted statement about a "rational system of sentenc-ing" in which the importance of "prevention, deterrence, retribution and rehabilitation" vary with the nature of the offence and the circum-stances of the offender.[73] Within this framework, he situated the role of the dangerous offender regime:

> Preventive detention in the context of Part XXI, however, simply rep-resents a judgment that the relative importance of the objectives of rehabilitation, deterrence and retribution are greatly attenuated in the circumstances of the individual case, and that of prevention, corre-spondingly increased.[74]

While this characterization manifests the validity of the idea of preven-tive detention, it also confirms that the real issue is whether a particu-lar regime has been mounted sufficiently carefully to avoid the violation of constitutional rights. La Forest J. concluded that the

---

72   *Ibid.* at 328.
73   *Ibid.* at 329.
74   *Ibid.*

"penological objectives" of Part XXI did not violate the principles of fundamental justice protected by section 7.[75]

## a)   "Cruel and Unusual Punishment"

With respect to section 12 and the guarantee against cruel and unusual punishment, La Forest J. embarked on a gross-disproportionality analysis by asking whether indeterminate detention is unusually severe and serves no penological purpose beyond what a lesser sentence would provide. He examined the elements of the scheme, particularly the requirements of a serious personal injury offence, a pattern of behaviour, the likelihood to cause specified harms, and substantial intractability. The last element that he noted was the court's residual discretion "not to designate the offender as dangerous or to impose an indeterminate sentence, even in circumstances where all of these criteria are met."[76] On these bases, he found that the scheme carefully defined its target group and observed that "it would be difficult to imagine a better tailored set of criteria that could effectively accomplish the purposes sought to be attained."[77]

Inevitably, the issue of indeterminacy is the hardest nut. La Forest J. explained that if the detention was simply indeterminate, the scheme would violate section 12 because it would undoubtedly result in some sentences which were grossly disproportionate in terms of the gravity of the offence and the characteristics of the offender. However, it is saved by the existence of the parole process which "ensures that incarceration is imposed for only as long as the circumstances of the individual case require." To support this conclusion, he cited the general criteria which, according to the legislation in force at the time, the Parole Board had to consider and concluded:

> While the criteria . . . do not purport to replicate the factual findings required to sentence the offender to an indeterminate term of imprisonment, they do afford a measure of tailoring adequate to save the legislation from violating s. 12.[78]

---

75   In the course of reaching this conclusion, he made observations about the 1967 repeal in England of preventive detention and the American attraction to recidivist legislation: *ibid.* at 331–34. These references have been criticized because they would seem to be more appropriate within a s. 1 *Charter* analysis: see M. Manning, "*Lyons*: A One-Stage Approach to the Charter and Undue 'Constitutional Notice'" (1988), 61 C.R. (3d) 72. Since the time of *Lyons*, England has adopted a form of recidivist legislation dealing with crimes of violence and drug offences.

76   *Lyons*, above note 40 at 338.

77   *Ibid.* at 339.

78   *Ibid.* at 342.

The crucial difference between the parole criteria and the original dangerous offender process is the absence of a need to find dangerousness to support continued detention. This did not trouble La Forest J. because he did not characterize the detention, as specifically constructed, as sentencing an offender "to a term of imprisonment until he is no longer a dangerous offender."[79] Instead, the scheme offered a parole review with parole criteria. He recognized that a true dangerous offender review using identical criteria, as contemplated by Ouimet, would do a better job of tailoring, but was content with the parole review since it included the issue of whether release would constitute an undue risk.

The willingness of La Forest J. to accept a parole review rather than a dangerous offender review is the weakest part of the *Lyons* decision. It fails to appreciate that continuing dangerousness is the lynchpin for justifying continuing detention and assumes that the parole process does what La Forest J. suggests it does. He was betting that the parole criteria (or to use his phrase, "the criteria actually used"[80]) provided sufficient congruence with the justifications for preventive detention that they would protect against error and abuse. Is this in fact the case? The empirical data about dangerous offenders and parole explained above indicate the unlikelihood of release. Of course, this does not necessarily show error. What it does show is that dangerous offenders will be required to spend long periods of time in confinement. As the period of confinement increases, links with family and community diminish, and thus the ability to mount and pursue an acceptable release plan also diminishes. The cases of *Steele*[81] and *Gallichon*[82] show how the Board can confuse personal inadequacy with undue risk.

### b)   Arbitary Detention

La Forest J. also dismissed the arguments that the scheme authorized arbitiary detention even if section 9 went beyond the issue of legislative prescription. Regardless of how broad a meaning was given to arbitrariness, and repeating the views expressed earlier with respect to section 12, he concluded that "the legislation narrowly defines a class of offenders with respect to whom it may properly be invoked, and prescribes quite specifically the conditions under which an offender may be designated as dangerous."[83] Little credence was given to the arguments that

---

79   *Ibid.* at 342 (emphasis omitted).
80   *Ibid.* at 343.
81   Above note 24.
82   Above note 24.
83   *Lyons*, above note 40 at 347.

the existence of prosecutorial discretion and evidence of geographical difference in use of the scheme affected the issue of arbitrariness.

### c) Other *Charter* Issues

A number of specific procedural issues were also raised both in relation to section 11(f) and section 7. Section 11(f) of the *Charter* entitles everyone charged with an offence to have the option of trial by jury if the punishment can be five years or more. Dangerous offender proceedings are conducted without a jury. For La Forest J. the answer was simply that a dangerous offender application is not a new charge but part of the sentencing process.[84] Accordingly, none of the section 11 guarantees apply. In deciding whether section 7 encompasses a right to a jury determination, La Forest J. extended his inquiry to consider in general whether the hearing and review procedures meet the required standard of fairness. Correctly, he proceeded on the basis that "the focus must be on the functional nature of the proceeding and on its potential impact on the liberty of the individual."[85] In rejecting the argument that fairness required a jury determination, he reviewed applicable procedural safeguards in support of his conclusion that the process provides "considerable procedural protection to the offender."[86] Here, again, La Forest J. noted the importance of the residual judicial discretion "not to impose the designation or indeterminate sentence, or both."[87]

Looking at the specific problems of the standard of proof and the use of psychiatric opinion to prove future risk, La Forest J. distinguished between infallibility and relevance. The judge's task was to accept relevant psychiatric evidence and assess its worth, taking into account problems of reliability and false positives. The standard of proof does not apply to what will occur in the future but rather to the "'likelihood' of specified future conduct occurring."[88]

Accordingly, the test is whether the judge is satisfied beyond a reasonable doubt that the offender is a threat, not to predict the future. Understood in this way, neither the standard of proof nor the use of psychiatric evidence presented unfairness.

---

84   Lamer J., as he then was, dissented on this point: *ibid.* at 372–79.

85   *Ibid.* at 354.

86   *Ibid.* at 362, where he listed the need for the consent of the attorney general, the seven-day notice requirement, and the offender's right to attend, present evidence, and cross-examine witnesses.

87   *Ibid.* This sentence seems to suggest a double discretion. See the discussion above regarding the use of "may" in s. 753(1).

88   *Ibid.* at 364.

The last section 7 issue under judicial consideration was whether it was unfair to serve notice after the offender had already pleaded. Counsel submitted that the offender may have pleaded not guilty and elected trial by jury had he known of the prosecutor's intention. La Forest J. rejected this argument as speculative at best, given the fact that the offender was represented by counsel and the absence of any assertion of prejudice. If there was evidence that the plea was based on a misunderstanding of the nature of the charges or the consequences of a guilty plea, the remedy would be to set aside the guilty plea, not to invalidate the indeterminate sentence. Wilson J. dissented on this point, holding that it is "a principle of fundamental justice under section 7 of the *Charter* that an accused know the full extent of his jeopardy before he pleads guilty to a criminal offence for which a term of imprisonment may be imposed."[89] She also argued for a flexible approach to *Charter* remedies which would permit a section 24(21) order limiting the sentence to the maximum fixed term which the *Criminal Code* permitted, since this was the jeopardy which the offender appreciated at the time of the plea.

## 4)  Effect of Bill C-55 on Constitutionality

The enactment of amendments to the dangerous offender scheme in 1997 rejuvenated some of the claims which the Supreme Court rejected in *Lyons*. This results from the importance attached by La Forest J. to various elements of the scheme which have now been diminished or repealed. First, there is the issue of residual discretion to impose a determinate sentence. Now, an indeterminate sentence is the mandatory result of a dangerous offender declaration. Before 1997, however, there existed the option of a fixed sentence, which was only rarely used, but suited situations where there were concerns about proportionality[90] or strong evidence of treatability.[91] The importance of this residual discretion was drawn on twice by La Forest J. in *Lyons*. He used it as one of the aspects which produced an assurance that the process carefully defined its target group so as to preclude a finding that section 12 had been violated. Here, indeed, he argued that it was only when the criteria are "read in the context of the scheme as a whole that the legislation can be upheld."[92] Later, when considering whether the

89   *Ibid.* at 379.
90   See *Moore*, above note 54; and *R. v. Sowa* (1991), 72 Man. R. (2d) 15 (Q.B.).
91   This was held to be a basis for refusing to impose an indeterminate sentence in *Carleton*, above note 57, although it was not used. See also *Neve*, above note 11.
92   *Lyons*, above note 40 at 338.

process required a jury finding to be fair, he again asserted the importance of residual discretion.[93] It is significant that the only justification offered by the Task Force on High-Risk Violent Offenders when recommending removal of the residual discretion was the argument that some prosecutors had expressed disappointment over mounting a dangerous offender application, proving that someone met the criteria, but not getting an indeterminate sentence.[94] This is not a persuasive reason to whittle down La Forest J.'s constitutional model.

The importance of residual judicial discretion has arisen in a number of contexts. In *Baron* v. *Canada*[95] a section of the *Income Tax Act* used mandatory language to provide authorization for a search. Relying on the importance of judicial authorization as an element of the minimum section 8 *Charter* standards, the Supreme Court held that the removal of any residual judicial discretion violated the *Charter*. As a remedy, it did not read the word "shall" into a "may" but declared the provision invalid. Similarly, in *R.* v. *Budreo*,[96] the Ontario Court of Appeal found the removal of judicial discretion in section 810.1(2) to violate sections 7 and 9 of the *Charter*. Although for reasons peculiar to that context the provision was read down, Laskin J.A. took care to say that the usual response to the removal of residual judicial discretion is the invalidation of the legislation.[97]

The second relevant change is the increase in the period of parole ineligibility. Clearly, the parole review is central to La Forest J.'s finding of constitutionality with respect to section 12 and the problems of indeterminacy. While empirical data may show that he overestimated the potential legitimating effect of the review, Parliament has now statutorily diminished it by delaying it to seven years and every two years thereafter. At the time of *Lyons*, the first review had to be conducted after three years.

Another important change is the use of the single assessment under section 752.1. At the time of *Lyons*, the scheme required the evidence of two psychiatrists, one retained by the Crown and the other by the offender. La Forest J., in his summary of the process, expressly noted

---

93   *Ibid.* at 361–62.

94   See *Strategies for Managing High-Risk Offenders*, above note 28 at 16.

95   [1993] 1 S.C.R. 416.

96   (2000), 32 C.R. (5th) 127 (Ont. C.A.) [*Budreo (C.A.)*]. See the detailed discussion, below, at 11(E)(2).

97   *Ibid.* at 148.

this "obligatory" requirement after observing that the "nature of the findings that must be made" require expert opinions.[98] The Task Force characterized the use of two psychiatrists as "expensive and even unnecessary in some instances."[99] It is a real question whether every Canadian jurisdiction has the kind of multi-disciplinary neutral expertise that influenced the Task Force to a single overarching assessment. Moreover, with legal aid funds decreasing, will counsel be able to obtain funds to challenge an assessment? This is significant given the different views within the psychiatric and psychological disciplines on such matters as the validity of actuarial prediction,[100] the use of the psychopathy checklist, whether paedophilia is a mental disorder, and other substantive issues. The absence of disciplinary consensus was manifested in the United States when the American Psychiatric Association filed an amicus curiae brief in a capital punishment case deprecating the use of psychiatric clinical predictions of dangerousness in capital sentencing cases.[101] In Canada, a perusal of dangerous offender cases reveals the complex and nuanced debates of opposing views[102] which may now disappear. Given the amount of liberty at stake, must fairness pay so much homage to expedition and economy? These are issues which another *Charter* challenge may raise.

# E.  LONG-TERM OFFENDERS

This new form of preventive sanction enacted in 1997[103] was part of the package of amendments to Part XXIV of the *Criminal Code* which focused primarily on the dangerous offender provisions. These amendments resulted, in large part, from the recommendations of the Federal/Provincial/Territorial Task Force on Violent High-Risk Offenders. As

---

98  See *Lyons*, above note 40 at 325.
99  *Strategies for Managing High-Risk Offenders*, above note 28 at 15.
100  Even the most ardent and well-respected advocates of actuarial prediction qualify their instruments with a caveat that "[n]o one claims that its use will guarantee 'fairness,' 'accuracy,' and 'absence of bias' in each and every case": C.D. Webster et al., *The Violence Prediction Scheme: Assessing Dangerousness in High Risk Men* (Toronto: University of Toronto, Centre of Criminology, 1994) at 65.
101  See *Barefoot v. Estelle*, 463 U.S. 880 (1983).
102  See, for example, *Pollock*, above note 62; and *Neve*, above note 11.
103  *Criminal Code Amendment Act (High Risk Offenders)*, above note 25, s. 4.

well as recommending various changes to the regime,[104] the Task Force argued that some instances do not satisfy the dangerous offender criteria but still warrant a preventive sanction. The result was the new "long-term offender" designation, a middle ground between an indeterminate sentence and an ordinary fixed-term sanction. In a nutshell, if a person is found to be a long-term offender, that person be sentenced to a term of imprisonment of at least two years followed by supervision on conditions for up to ten years with suspension/revocation-like procedures and a new criminal offence for non-compliance.

## 1) The Long-term Offender Procedure

A long-term offender designation can either be the default position of a dangerous offender application or the actual objective of an application. That is, the long-term offender status can be the objective of an independent application, or it can result from a dangerous offender application where the judge was not satisfied that the higher standard had been met. The two processes are, however, virtually identical. The applications are heard by a judge alone after someone has been convicted but before sentencing [see sections 753.1(1) and 754(2)].[105] A finding requires, as a condition precedent, the filing of an assessment report ordered under section 752.1. This provision empowers a judge who has convicted someone of "a serious personal injury offence" or an offence included in section 753.1(2)(a) to remand the offender for assessment if there are "reasonable grounds to believe that the offender might be found to be a dangerous offender under section 753 or a long-term offender under s. 753.1." The provision says nothing about what the assessment should contain except that it will be used as evidence in the subsequent application. Implicit in section 753.1 is

---

104   The Task Force's recommendations included removing judical discretion to determine whether an indeterminate or determinate sentence should be imposed, raising the parole ineligibility threshold to seven years, using a single-over arching psychiatric assessment rather than obtaining one from each party, and creating a window for the Crown to bring applications after a fixed sentence is imposed when new information is obtained. See 11(C) above.

105   Recently, a controversy arose in Hamilton over whether the Crown could commence a long-term offender application seeking extended post-release supervision after the judge had pronounced sentence. The judge correctly ruled that the long-term offender application should have been made in place of an ordinary sentencing and that there was no jurisdiction to begin one after: see S. Clairmont, "Molester Benefits by Crown Mistake; No Monitoring for Sex Offender," *The Hamilton Spectator* (29 October 1999).

the sense that the assessment may involve the expertise of more than one person but no specific issues or disciplines are mentioned. This use of a single assessment report flows from the 1995 Task Force's observations and very positive impression of a multi-disciplinary clinic in the Netherlands.[106]

Section 754(1)(a) provides that "no such [dangerous offender] application shall be heard" unless "the attorney general of the province in which the offender was tried has, either before or after the making of the application, consented to the application." On its face, this provision appears to be jurisdictional. If the consent relates to a dangerous offender application, the matter can proceed but if the judge does not find the offender to be a dangerous offender, the application may be treated as a long-term offender application and the relevant criteria and dispositions become applicable. The converse is not true. If the attorney general's consent relates only to a long-term offender application, then those features apply and a dangerous offender finding cannot result.

In *R. v. McLeod*,[107] Crown counsel sought the attorney general's consent to a long term offender application but, instead, the attorney general delivered a consent to a dangerous offender application. Since guilty pleas had been entered on an understanding that the sentencing would proceed as a long-term offender application, counsel for McLeod objected to the matter going forward as a dangerous offender application. The judge ruled that the Crown was bound by its plea bargain and proceeded with the matter as a long-term offender application. The Court of Appeal reversed the ultimate finding. For the court, Prowse J.A. concluded:

> . . . this issue is jurisdictional in nature and not amenable to the compromise solution fashioned by the sentencing judge. The only application before the sentencing judge was an application for a dangerous offender designation, together with the consent of the attorney general to that application. While it is understandable that the sentencing judge was unwilling to proceed with the dangerous offender application given the previous position taken by the Crown, which had resulted in Mr. McLeod's guilty pleas, I am satisfied that it was not

---

106  See earlier discussion in this chapter at 11(D)(4).
107  (1999), 136 C.C.C. (3d) 492 (B.C.C.A.) [*McLeod*].

open to the court to override the attorney general's election to proceed in this fashion by unilaterally treating the application as one under s. 753.1 of the Code.[108]

The court also confirmed that if the matter had proceeded as a dangerous offender application, the result could have been, pursuant to section 753(5), a long-term offender designation but that this was no argument for legitimizing the jurisdictional defect.

## 2) The Long-term Offender Criteria

Section 753.1(1) sets out three general prerequisites to a long-term offender designation. The court may find an offender to be a long-term offender when

(a) it would be appropriate to impose a sentence of imprisonment of two years or more for the offence for which the offender has been convicted;

(b) there is a substantial risk that the offender will reoffend; and

(c) there is a reasonable possibility of eventual control of the risk in the community.[109]

Clearly, the novel and hard issue is how to interpret "substantial risk that the offender will reoffend." Section 753.1(1) is followed by section 753.1(2), which deals with "substantial risk" to reoffend, but it is not clear whether this sub-section provides an exhaustive definition of "substantial risk" for these purposes. One might argue that, instead of a definition, it is simply a deeming provision that goes no farther than requiring a finding of "substantial risk" when the described circumstances are present. This would leave it open to the judge to find "substantial risk that the offender will reoffend" in other circumstances. The language is significant:

---

108   *Ibid.* at 506. In *R. v. Rae*, [1998] O.J. No. 3973, Main P.C.J. (Prov. Div.) (QL) [*Rae*], it appears that the matter proceeded to a finding without the attorney general's consent being filed. The last two lines of the decision, at paras. 25–26, reveal a brief conversation between the judge and Crown counsel: "That leaves one remaining perhaps housekeeping item . . . , and that is the Attorney-General's consent. Is that still pending?" "It is, Your Honour." Regardless of the exigencies, which in a busy trial court may be manifold, jurisdictional prerequisites need to be followed.

109   Some courts have ignored this pre-condition while others have required some evidence to support the conclusion: see *R. v. P.(H.J.)* (1999), 173 Nfld. & P.E.I.R. 311 at 323–24 (Nfld. S.C.(T.D.)), where treatment refusals were considered. In *R. v. G.(W.D.)* (1999), 174 N.S.R. (2d) 154 at 159 (S.C.), the court considered evidence of amenability to treatment in reaching a long-term offender finding.

(2) The court shall be satisfied that there is a substantial risk that the offender will reoffend if

(a) the offender has been convicted of an offence under section 151 (sexual interference), 152 (invitation to sexual touching) or 153 (sexual exploitation), subsection 173(2) (exposure) or section 271 (sexual assault), 272 (sexual assault with a weapon) or 273 (aggravated sexual assault), or has engaged in serious conduct of a sexual nature in the commission of another offence of which the offender has been convicted; and

(b) the offender

   (i) has shown a pattern of repetitive behaviour, of which the offence for which he or she has been convicted forms a part, that shows a likelihood of the offender's causing death or injury to other persons or inflicting severe psychological damage on other persons, or

   (ii) by conduct in any sexual matter including that involved in the commission of the offence for which the offender has been convicted, has shown a likelihood of causing injury, pain or other evil to other persons in the future through similar offences.

In *McLeod*, above, it was argued that the trigger for a long-term offender designation must be the commission of a sexual offence as enumerated in section 753.1(2)(a). In other words, while the threshold for a dangerous offender finding is the commission of a "serious personal injury offence" as defined in section 752 (which includes some sexual offences), the comparable threshold for the lesser but related disposition of long-term offender status can only be the set of sexual offences set out in section 753.1(2)(a). The British Columbia Court of Appeal rejected this argument. It observed :

> Subsection 753.1(2)(a) simply provides that the court *must* find ("shall be satisfied") that there is a substantial risk the offender will reoffend if the conditions set out in that subsection are met. . . . Thus, if an offender is convicted of one of the sexual offences delineated in s. 753.1(2)(a), the court must find that there is a substantial risk that the offender will reoffend. . . .[110]

If correct, this means that the provision does not restrict the long-term offender designation to persons who have committed an offence from the prescribed set of sexual offences. Using the example of an offender

---

110   *McLeod*, above note 107 at 503.

340 THE LAW OF SENTENCING

who had repeatedly assaulted his or her spouse when intoxicated, the court concluded that Parliament must have intended that the scope of the new disposition would extend beyond sexual offences.

Underlying this conclusion is the assumption that the purpose behind enacting the long-term offender provisions was to increase public protection by ensuring supervision in the community upon release. By refusing to treat section 753.1(2) as a definition of substantial risk to reoffend in this context,[111] the court suggests that protection from other non-sexual forms of violence can also be achieved through the new provisions. However, the only criteria are the three general factors set out in section 753.1(1), none of which make any reference to violence. Could a recidivist burglar who gets a penitentiary sentence be included in the ten-year supervision net? The better answer is to treat section 753.1(2) as defining the risk element of substantial risk to reoffend. This would ensure that the new disposition is used for the kind of sexual crimes the Minister of Justice spoke about when the enacting legislation was introduced, and not extended to a wide range of offences, both violent and non-violent. Moreover, it is consistent with the statutory structure of the whole scheme which requires an assessment report as a pre-condition to making either a dangerous or long-term offender designation.[112] The power to order the relevant assessment report in section 752.1(1) requires that the offender must have been "convicted of a serious personal injury offence or an offence referred to in paragraph 753.1(2)(a)." "Serious personal injury offence" is the trigger and pre-condition for a dangerous offender designation; the offences in section 753.1(2)(a) ought to play the same role for long-term offenders. This is not just a matter of symmetry but also provides coherence across the whole Part XXIV scheme.

Judges should not lose sight of the word "substantial" which qualifies "risk." The consequences of this new sanction, as discussed below, are far-reaching. While it may seem that they provide a semblance of long-term security, they also dramatically expand the punitive element of a sentence of incarceration which, on its own, should be a fit sanction. Judges should be cautious about leaving their sentencing role for the questionable "risk prevention" bandwagon. As with dangerous offenders, the long-term offender provisions were designed to target a small group who are not adequately sanctioned by the ordinary range

---

111 Which seems to be how Ruby views the provision: see C.C. Ruby, *Sentencing*, 5th ed. (Toronto: Butterworths, 1999) at 156.

112 See *Criminal Code*, ss. 753 and 753.1 respectively, both of which contain the phrase "following the filing of an assessment report under subsection 752.1(2)."

of sentences. There is always a need for restraint and vigilance whenever contemplating a measure provided by Part XXIV.

## 3) Consequences of Long-term Offender Designation

Upon being satisfied that the conditions set out in section 753.1(1) have been met, a judge "may" find the offender to be a "long-term offender." With some uncommon exceptions,[113] the disposition upon finding an offender to be a "long-term offender" is mandatory:

> 753.1(3) Subject to subsections (3.1), (4) and (5), if the court finds an offender to be a long-term offender, it shall
> (a) impose a sentence for the offence for which the offender has been convicted, which sentence must be a minimum punishment of imprisonment for a term of two years; and
> (b) order the offender to be supervised in the community, for a period not exceeding ten years, in accordance with section 753.2 and the *Corrections and Conditional Release Act*.

It is difficult to understand why Parliament would use the discretionary "may" in section 753.1(1) but the mandatory "shall" in section 753.1(3). This seems to suggest that a judge can be satisfied that the criteria have been met but not make the section 753.1(1) designation. Curiously, the dangerous offender regime has now removed any discretion.[114] Perhaps a judge can conclude that the criteria have been met but the designation, which would lead to a mandatory range of sanctions, is not warranted. For example, the judge may not be persuaded that extended supervision will be beneficial or necessary. Then, the judge could, if "may" means discretion, refuse to declare the offender a

---

113 These qualifications in ss. 753.1(3.1), (4), & (5), *ibid.*, relate to the following situations: (1) when the designation arose from a dangerous offender application brought during the six-month post-sentencing window provided by s. 753(2); (2) the offender has been sentenced to life (presumably under s. 753.1(3)(a) but there is no reason to restrict this qualification to the instant offence); and (3) if the offender has previously been designated a long-term offender and receives another designation, the total term of supervision cannot exceed ten years.

114 *Ibid.*, s. 753(4). The pre-existing dangerous offender discretion related not to the designation but to the question of imposing an indeterminate or fixed sentence. Prior to the 1997 amendments, the designation remained and could not even be appealed. Only the indeterminate sentence itself could be affected by an appeal: see *Currie*, above note 52. Now, the range of appellate dispositions include removing the designation, whether dangerous or long-term offender: see *Criminal Code*, ss. 759(3)(a)(i) & (ii), and 759(3.1)(a)(i).

long-term offender and impose the appropriate fixed term without any extended supervision.

While section 753.1(3)(b) clearly provides for extended supervision up to ten years, it is important to note that section 753.2(1) places the actual supervision within the *Corrections and Conditional Release Act*.[115] Section 134.1 of that *Act* provides that authority over conditions and compliance during the period of supervision rests with the National Parole Board. Similarly, section 134.2 makes it clear that the actual community supervision will be conducted by a federal parole officer employed by the Corrections Service of Canada. It is clear that part of Parliament's intention was to integrate this new form of supervision with federal parole supervision, which follows penitentiary sentences, and not with probation supervision, which follows provincial sentences.[116] This suggests that the sentence which precedes the period of supervision must be a federal sentence, imprisonment for a minimum of two years.

In *R. v. Rae*,[117] the sentencing judge was looking at three convictions (threatening to cause bodily harm, probation breach, and harassing telephone calls) committed in circumstances where the threats had been escalating and the offender had a record for harassing calls going back to 1991. On a long-term offender application, the Crown satisfied the judge of the section 753.1 criteria. Part of the conclusion was that a two-year sentence was warranted by the threatening offence; producing, with the addition of appropriate sentences for the other offences, a total sentence of twenty-seven months. However, the offender had "wallowed" for seven-and-a-half months in the Barrie jail prior to sentencing. The judge concluded, on the authority of *R. v. McDonald*,[118] that pre-sentence custody can be used to reduce a minimum punishment. It should be noted that the result in *McDonald* was not the result of a *Charter* argument about minimum sentences under section 344(a)[119] but rather a statutory interpretation argument about the

---

115  S.C. 1992, c. 20 (as am. by S.C. 1997, c.17, s. 30).

116  Of course, an ordinary probation order can be attached to the minimum penitentiary term of two years but cannot follow any sentence or aggregate of sentences which exceeds two years: see *Criminal Code*, s. 731(1)(b), and *R. v. Currie* (1982), 65 C.C.C. (2d) 415 (Ont. C.A.); *R. v. Miller* (1987), 36 C.C.C. (3d) 100 (Ont. C.A.); and *R. v. Young* (1980), 27 C.R. (3d) 85 (B.C.C.A.).

117  Above note 108.

118  (1998), 127 C.C.C. (3d) 57 (Ont. C.A.). The argument was accepted subsequently by the Supreme Court in *R. v. Wust* (2000), 143 C.C.C. (3d) 129 (S.C.C.) discussed above in Chapter 6, at 6(E)(5).

119  This section provides for a minimum punishment of four years imprisonment for robbery with a firearm.

interaction of section 719(3) and section 344(a). Surely, the same argument does not apply when Parliament's supervision scheme presupposes federal custody and contemplates at least a minimum penitentiary term. The judge imposed a sentence of fifteen months and supervision under section 753.1(3)(b) for a period of five years. The proper result would have been to impose the fifteen-month sentence supplemented by the maximum probation period of three years.

## 4) Breach of Supervision

The period of supervision commences when all custodial sentences have been served; which means, subject to detention,[120] after two-thirds[121] of any merged[122] terms. All the statutory conditions which apply to a prisoner released on parole or statutory release apply to long-term supervision.[123] As well, section 134.1 of the *Corrections and Conditional Release Act* provides:

> (2) The Board may establish conditions for the long-term supervision of the offender that it considers reasonable and necessary in order to protect society and to facilitate the successful reintegration into society of the offender.
>
> (3) A condition imposed under subsection (2) is valid for the period that the Board specifies.

While on long-term supervision, failure or refusal to comply, without reasonable excuse, with the long-term supervision order constitutes an indictable offence under section 753.3(1) of the *Criminal Code*, punishable by up to ten years imprisonment. Moreover, section 135.1 of the *Corrections and Conditional Release Act* empowers the National Parole Board and its designated officers to suspend long-term supervision, apprehend the offender, and re-commit the offender until the suspension is cancelled, new conditions imposed, or a charge under section 753.3 is laid. The period of custody on suspension cannot exceed ninety days.[124] Given these wide-ranging powers, it is clear that Parlia-

---

120  See *Corrections and Conditonal Release Act*, above note 115, ss. 129–32.

121  This is the usual statutory release point: see s. 127(3), *ibid.*

122  The concept of merger provides that additional sentences are added to pre-existing ones to form one sentence commencing when the earliest begins and ending upon the latest expiration date: see s. 139, *ibid.*

123  *Ibid.*, s. 134.1(1). See also *Corrections and Conditional Release Regulations*, S.O.R./ 92-620, s. 161.

124  See *Corrections and Conditional Release Act*, above note 115, s. 135.1(2).

ment has contemplated an active supervision role which can have important consequences for the offender even short of prosecution under section 753.3(1).

## F. RECOGNIZANCES UNDER SECTIONS 810.1, 810.2, AND 810.01

Constitutionally, once a person has been found guilty and punished for an offence, she cannot be punished a second time for that offence.[125] Once a sentence has expired the state no longer has authority to deprive a person of their liberty, except in cases of mental disorder where there are indicia of imminent risk.[126] Using the idea of the common law peace bond and section 810 as its model, in 1993[127] and 1997[128] Parliament created three preventive vehicles which can apply post-sentence based on evidence of fear that an offence will be committed. Section 810.1 can be triggered when someone "fears on reasonable grounds" that a sexual offence against a child will be committed, while a section 810.2 application involves a fear of a serious personal injury offence. Section 810.01 is triggered by a fear that someone will commit a "criminal organization offence." All three mechanisms require applications to court that may result in a recognizance lasting for up to twelve months and including specific prohibitions. Both sections 810.01 and 810.2 have the added requirement of the consent of the attorney general. A breach of these recognizances is a hybrid offence punishable by up to two years imprisonment.[129]

---

125   See *Charter*, above note 30, s. 11(h).
126   See *Starnaman v. Penetonguishene Mental Health Centre* (1995), 100 C.C.C. (3d) 190 (Ont. C.A.) for a controversial decision upholding the power to commit a convicted paedophile immediately upon release from penilentiary on the grounds of paedophilia and risk.
127   See *An Act to amend the Criminal Code and the Young Offenders Act*, S.C. 1993, c. 45, s.11.
128   For s. 810.2 of the *Criminal Code*, see *Criminal Code Amendment Act (High Risk Offenders)*, above note 25, s. 9; for s. 810.01, see *An Act to amend the Criminal Code (criminal organizations) and to amend other Acts in consequence*, S.C. 1997, c. 23, s. 19.
129   See *Criminal Code*, s. 811.

## 1) The Section 810.1 Recognizance

The central requirements for this kind of recognizance are set out in section 810.1(1):

> Any person who fears on reasonable grounds that another person will commit an offence under section 151, 152, 155 or 159, subsection 160(2) or (3), section 170 or 171, subsection 173(2) or section 271, 272 or 273, in respect of one or more persons who are under the age of fourteen years, may lay an information before a provincial court judge, whether or not the person or persons in respect of whom it is feared that the offence will be committed are named.

Upon receiving the application, the informant and defendant can be required to appear in court[130] and the provisions of sections 507(4) and 515 apply for the purpose of compelling appearance.[131] The informant must satisfy the judge that there are reasonable grounds for the stipulated fear.[132] If the judge is satisfied, she may order the defendant to enter into a recognizance with specified conditions that can last for up to twelve months. The conditions should include a prohibition from

> engaging in any activity that involves contact with persons under the age of fourteen years and prohibiting the defendant from attending a public park or public swimming area where persons under the age of fourteen years are present or can reasonably be expected to be present, or a daycare centre, schoolground, playground or community centre.[133]

If the defendant does not enter into the recognizance, there can be a committal for up to twelve months.[134] The original conditions can be varied upon application by either party.[135] Although the provision is silent on renewal, there does not seem to be any impediment to successive applications so long as the evidence remains current and is not simply a recycled account of old opinions.

---

130   *Ibid.*, s. 810.1(2). In *R. v. Budreo* (1996), 104 C.C.C. (3d) 245 (Ont. Gen. Div.) [*Budreo (Gen. Div.)*], Then J. found that the mandatory language in this subsection violated both ss. 7 and 9 of the *Charter* since it seemed to require the judge to compel attendance regardless of the sufficiency of the information. He read down the word "shall" to be "may": *ibid.* at 303–5. This was confirmed by the Ontario Court of Appeal: see *Budreo (C.A.)*, above note .
131   See *Budreo (C.A.)*, above note 96 at 149–51.
132   See *Criminal Code*, s. 810.1(3).
133   *Ibid.*
134   *Ibid.*, s. 810.1(3.1).
135   *Ibid.*, s. 810.1(4).

## 2) The Constitutionality of Section 810.1

Obviously, the intention behind this provision is to provide a tool with potential punitive repercussions for community supervision of people who, it is claimed, present a risk to children. The case of *R. v. Budreo*[136] involved a man who had just been released from serving a six-year penitentiary sentence for three counts of sexual assault on young boys. The offences occurred in a park where he asked the boys to lay down and then fondled their stomachs and, in two cases, their genitals. He had been detained until his warrant expiry date[137] and, upon release, was the subject of substantial publicity. After his release, he commenced a treatment plan that involved psychiatric counselling and monthly injections of Luperon, an anti-androgen. Within three days of his release the Crown commenced proceedings under section 810.1 with an information sworn by a police officer who said she feared on reasonable grounds that he would commit one of the specified sexual offences against children. Her fear was based on his psychiatric records from 1963 to 1993, his criminal record, various hospital and parole reports, and a conversation with the man's psychiatrist who considered him a high-risk paedophile if he stopped taking Luperon. He was arrested under section 507(4) and then released on bail with conditions similar to those that might flow from a section 810.1 order. He brought a prohibition application on *Charter* grounds seeking to stop a provincial court judge from continuing with the 810.1. The application found section 810.1 constitutionally valid except for the inclusion of "community centre"[138] and the mandatory "shall" in section 810.1(2) dealing with compelling attendance in court.[139] Then J. deleted the former and read down the latter to become a discretionary "may." The defendant appealed to the Court of Appeal.[140] The 810.1 application was adjourned pending resolution of the constitutional issues and he continued to be subject to bail conditions which were varied from time to time.

---

136   *Budreo (Gen. Div.)*, above note 130.
137   Pursuant to the detention provisions in ss. 129–32 of the *Corrections and Conditional Release Act*, above note 115. For the background, see *Budreo v. Canada (National Parole Board)* (1993), 65 F.T.R. 276 (T.D.), rev'd (1993), 167 N.R. 84 (F.C.A.).
138   Then J. found this to be overboard: *Budreo (Gen. Div.)*, above note 130 at 295–96.
139   Then J. read the word "shall" down to be "may" so that the judge would have discretion to compel the appearance of the parties after considering the application.
140   *Budreo (C.A.)*, above note 96.

In the Court of Appeal, counsel argued that section 810.1 violated section 7 of the *Charter* because it restricted liberty, and was not in accord with the principles of fundamental justice because it created a status offence, was overbroad, and was void for vagueness. There was no debate about a liberty interest since it was evident that a section 810.1 order would prevent him from moving freely in the community. For a unanimous court, Laskin J.A. dismissed the claims commencing with the status offence argument. He held that section 810.1 does not create an offence and is not about status. Since the criminal justice system has the dual objectives of punishing wrongdoers and preventing future harm, he characterized section 810.1 as an exercise of the preventive power encompassed by section 91(27) of the *Constitution Act, 1867*. He concluded:

> . . . s. 810.1 does not create an offence. Its purpose is not to punish crime but to prevent crime from happening. Its sanctions are not punitive, nor are they intended to redress a wrong; they are activity and geographic restrictions on a person's liberty intended to protect a vulnerable group in our society from future harm.[141]

Since courts have consistently held that section 810 is a preventive measure which does not create an offence, Laskin J.A. found it difficult to see how section 810.1 could be interpreted differently. With respect to overbreadth, he approached the issue from the perspective of whether the means chosen to achieve the objective are "sufficiently tailored or narrowly targeted." If the scheme invokes means which are broader than what is needed to accomplish the legislative purpose, it becomes "arbitrary and disproportionate," thereby violating the principles of fundamental justice. Given the legitimacy of protecting children from sexual abuse, Laskin J.A. rejected the claims of overbreadth. While the restrictions under section 810.1 may seem extensive, they are not detention and they permit the defendant to lead a "reasonably normal life." Recognizing that section 7 represents interests beyond those of the accused, he found that the restrictions are proportional to the societal interest in protecting children from harm. They constituted a reasonable compromise of competing interests. As well, once "community centre" is deleted, as Then J. had held, all other locations narrowly target places where children can be expected to be present. Regardless of the language of section 810.1(3), no conditions can be imposed which place broader restrictions on a defendant than those which relate to activities, areas, or places where one would expect to find children.

---

141  *Budreo (C.A.)*, *ibid.* at 139.

Another overbreadth argument was based on the fact that section 810.1 does not require a previous conviction to trigger its operation. Accordingly, it was argued that "fear on reasonable grounds" casts too wide a net. Laskin J.A. held that, while a prior record would be relevant, requiring one would undermine the preventive purpose by requiring that a child be victimized before the provision could ever be activated. Certainly, this involves a prediction of future dangerous conduct but other processes like bail and the dangerous offender scheme do too. Reasonable grounds could be based on a threat, a sexual proposition, a diagnosis of mental disorder, past behaviour including a criminal record, or any combination of these and other relevant factors. Laskin J.A. also rejected the argument that the possibility of pre-trial custody created overbreadth, even if a section 810.1 order could not include detention, since this power could be necessary to complete the process. On the issue of procedural safeguards, he found them to be adequate especially since an order could be appealed and the conditions varied, and it would last no more than a year.

Laskin J.A. explained the void for vagueness principle[142] as requiring a law to sufficiently delineate the scope of the risk of unlawful conduct so that a citizen has fair notice, and so the police will have a structure to their law enforcement discretion. It was argued that "fear" can be "irrational or emotional and is invariably subjective" while "belief," which is used elsewhere in the *Criminal Code*, can be measured by objective standards. Laskin J.A. concludes that one cannot read "fear" in isolation from "reasonable grounds" which provides an acceptable objective standard. Moreover, since section 810.1(3) requires "evidence" that the fear alleged has a reasonable basis, the judge must reach her own decision about the likelihood of future crimes. Laskin J.A. acknowledged that the phrase "fears on reasonable grounds" invokes some degree of imprecision; he concluded that it does delineate an area of risk and provide an "adequate basis for a legal debate."

Laskin J.A. agreed with the ruling below that the use of "shall" on section 810.1(2) violated sections 7 and 9 because it authorized an automatic issuance of process without regard to the sufficiency of the information. He also agreed that the remedy applied by Then J., a reading down to provide for discretion, was appropriate. However, he reached that result by a different means. Then J. had relied on *Baron* v. *Canada* for the proposition that "a residual discretion is a constitu-

142   *Ibid.* at 145–46, relying on the decision of Cory J. in *R. v. Lucas*, [1998] 1 S.C.R. 439.

tional requirement"[143] but Laskin J.A. noted that the remedy in that case was to declare the impugned income tax search provision to be of no force and effect, not read the "shall" into a "may." Accordingly, he remarked that "when legislation expressly excludes a judicial discretion, courts have been reluctant to read one in as a constitutional remedy,"[144] leaving the task of developing a response to Parliament. Looking at the subsequently enacted provisions in sections 810.01(2) and 810.2(2), elements of the related processes for criminal organization offences or serious personal injury offences, he noted that Parliament had used "may," signalling a willingness to accept the view of Then J. Accordingly, he was satisfied that reading the "shall" into a "may" in section 810.1(2) was not an intrusion into Parliament's sphere of competence.

## 3) Recognizances Under Section 810.2

Enacted in 1997 by Bill C-55,[145] this sanction expands the scope of preventive detention to encompass a fear that a serious personal injury offence will be committed, whether or not a specific victim can be named. As with section 810.1, there does not need to be a triggering offence or previous record to commence an application. It is based solely on the test of "fears on reasonable grounds." While section 810.2(3) only requires that the judge be satisfied that "the informant has reasonable grounds for the fear," its counterpart in section 810.1(3) has been interpreted as requiring an independent conclusion by the judge about the likelihood that a specified offence will be committed.[146] The conditions that can attach to a section 810.2 recognizance must be reasonable, and accordingly must relate to the fear alleged. They can also include conditions prohibiting the possession of firearms and other weapons[147] and a judge who does not insert a condition dealing with firearms must provide in the record the reasons why such a condition was not imposed.[148] It is important to note that in the original bill, electronic monitoring was included as an available option but this was deleted before final enactment.

---

143  *Budreo (Gen. Div.)*, above note 130 at 300.

144  *Budreo (C.A.)*, above note 96 at 148.

145  *Criminal Code Amendment Act (High Risk Offenders)*, above note 25, s. 9.

146  See *Budreo (C.A.)*, above note 96 at 146–47.

147  *Criminal Code*, ss. 810.2(5), (5.1).

148  *Ibid.*, s. 810.2(5.2).

There have been few occasions for courts to consider the scope and content of section 810.2. In *R. v. Baker*,[149] Cohen J. heard an appeal[150] from a section 810(2) order granted shortly after the defendant's release from penitentiary. He applied the reasoning of Then J. in *Budreo*[151] to reject the constitutional challenge. In doing so, he concluded that the process is "preventative in nature, results in minimal impairment to an individual's liberty, and does not create a criminal offence."[152] In upholding the order based on previous convictions, reports from penitentiary authorities, and three forensic assessments, he held that there was no need to find a "contemporary act," although evidence of this sort would "undoubtedly bolster the Crown's case."[153] There was a different result in *R. v. Obed*[154] in which the application was brought by a police officer in respect of a man just released at warrant expiry date from a penitentiary sentence of five years and ten months for sexual assault, attempted murder, and aggravated assault. The defendant, an Inuit, was part of a group who had been forcibly relocated in the 1950s. The evidence adduced consisted entirely of his record and assessments done while he was in the penitentiary which admittedly may have reflected cultural biases in their application to Inuit persons. While in the penitentiary, the defendant was reluctant to enter sex-offender counselling out of concern for his own safety within that group. The judge concluded that there must be some "triggering behaviour" beyond past acts to come within section 810.2:

> . . . even on a s. 810.2 *Criminal Code* application, and as a matter of principle and procedure, in order to establish objectively the fear that an applicant relies upon, he or she must first point to and establish some present and independent activity of the defendant that would trigger subjectively the perceived fear.[155]

On this basis, he dismissed the application. As well, he dismissed the constitutional challenges but this ruling was predicated on an interpretation of section 810.2 that conformed with the *Charter* guarantees. For example, he interpreted the "person or persons" requirement in

---

149   [1999] B.C.J. No. 681 (S.C.) (QL) [*Baker*].
150   Since s. 810.2 falls within Part XXVII of the *Criminal Code*, the defendant can appeal under s. 813(a)(i).
151   *Budreo* (*Gen. Div.*), above note 130.
152   *Baker*, above note 149 at para. 33.
153   *Ibid.* at para. 32.
154   [2000] N.S.J. No. 18 (Prov. Ct.) (QL).
155   *Ibid.* at para. 31.

section 810.2(1) to mean an identifiable person and not the community at large. The *Obed* decision is respectful of the interests of the defendant and attempts to ensure compliance with *Charter* guarantees in a way that strikes a dissonant chord when compared with both *Baker* and *Budreo*, discussed above. The major disagreement is with respect to a triggering act requirement. Even if *Obed* goes too far in asserting this requirement, it demonstrates the importance of the currency of evidence, which is consistent with Laskin J.A.'s assertion that section 810.1 involves a finding of a "present likelihood of future dangerousness."[156] Whether in regard to section 810.1 or section 810.2, a present likelihood can only be established if the evidence, whether factual or opinion, has currency to it. Here, it is necessary to carefully evaluate expert opinions to ensure that they are current and not simply re-cycled versions of old evaluations.

## 4) Recognizances Under Section 810.01

This provision was enacted to provide a preventive aspect to the recent anti-gang legislative package, the central feature of which was the creation of the new offence of participating in a criminal organization. Section 810.01 permits a person, with the consent of the attorney general, to lay an information before a judge of the person "fears on reasonable grounds that another person will commit a criminal organization offence." The ultimate object is to obtain a recognizance with conditions for up to twelve months. Usual conditions will involve restrictions on, or prohibitions against, association with other members of the group but can also include prohibitions against the possession of weapons, ammunition, and explosives.[157] The recognizance can provide some mechanism for constraining conduct since a breach of the recognizance, like a breach of the other preventive measures in sections 810, 810.1 and 810.2, can be prosecuted as a hybrid offence under section 811. To obtain a recognizance under section 810.01, the judge need only be satisfied that there are reasonable grounds for the fear that the named person will commit a section 467.1 offence. In other words, if the informant has a basis for this conclusion, a recognizance will likely be granted. Accordingly, any consideration of section

---

156  *Budreo (C.A.)*, above note 96 at 143.
157  See s. 810.01(5). If a recognizance is granted but no order is made under this subsection, the judge must include a statement of reasons for not imposing these conditions: see s. 810.01(5.2).

810.01 returns to the controversy over the offence of participating in a criminal organization.

The definition of criminal organization in section 2 is any group or association, formal or informal, of five or more who have "as one of its primary activities the commission of an indictable offence" and any of its members have within five years engaged in a series of indictable offences. A criminal organization offence is defined as an offence under section 467.1 or another indictable offence punishable by more than five years if it was committed "for the benefit of, at the direction of, or in association with a criminal organization." Section 467.1 provides:

Every one who

(a) participates in or substantially contributes to the activities of a criminal organization knowing that any or all of the members of the organization engage in or have, within the preceding five years, engaged in the commission of a series of indictable offences under this or any other Act of Parliament for each of which the maximum punishment is imprisonment for five years or more, and

(b) is a party to the commission of an indictable offence for the benefits of, at the direction of or in association with the criminal organization for which the maximum punishment is imprisonment for five years or more

is guilty of an indictable offence and liable to imprisonment for a team not exceeding fourteen years.

It also provides that any sentences imposed under section 467.1 shall be served consecutively to any other sentences previously imposed or imposed for offences arising out of the same event or series of events.[158] Clearly, these are provisions intended to be used against organized crime. However, in their breadth, they may encompass other offenders who do not warrant this characterization but are nonetheless subject to mandatory consecutive sentences under section 467.1(2) and the preventive grasp of section 810.01. Section 810.01 is significant because it operates in the absence of an offence but can result in an offence simply by a breach of its conditions. If a police officer is concerned about a group of young offenders and their involvement with drugs, so long as the group, loosely defined, can be described as consisting of at least five individuals and one of them has committed an offence like "break and enter" or trafficking, then the officer can prepare an information

---

158   Section 467.1(2).

which will support a recognizance naming of any member of the group. Then, in the absence of an offence, the person is subject to the restraint of the imposed conditions, any breach of which will produce an offence under section 811, still without the commission of any real crime. Given the breadth of the definitions which apply under section 810.01 and the minimal judicial test, the only feature that may prevent abuse is the requirement of the attorney general's consent which should only be granted in clear cases of serious organized crime activity.

## FURTHER READINGS

DOWNES, D., *Contrasts in Tolerance: Post-War Penal Policy in the Netherlands and England and Wales* (Oxford: Clarendon Press, 1988)

GRANT, I., "Legislating Public Safety: The Business of Risk" (1998) 3 Can. Crim. L.R. 177

JACKSON, M., "The Sentencing of Dangerous and Habitual Offenders in Canada" (1997) 9 F.S.R. 256

MONAHAN, J., & H. STEADMAN, "Violence and Mental Disorder: Developments in Risk Assessment" (Chicago: University of Chicago Press, 1994)

REPORT OF THE CANADIAN COMMITTE ON CORRECTIONS, *Toward Unity: Criminal Justice and Corrections* (Ottawa: Queen's Printer, 1969)

REPORT OF THE FEDERAL/PROVINCIAL/TERRITORIAL TASK FORCE ON HIGH-RISK VIOLENT OFFENDERS, *Strategies for Managing High-Risk Offenders*, January 1995

WEBSTER, C.D., *The Violence Prediction Scheme* (Toronto: Centre of Criminology, 1994)

# CHAPTER 12

# THE ROLE OF THE APPELLATE COURTS

## A. THE HISTORY OF APPELLATE REVIEW

Although the *Criminal Code, 1892*, established formal appeals in criminal cases, it did not include the power to appeal a sentence. When the English Court of Appeal was established in 1907, this power was granted, but only to the convicted person. The prosecution had no right of appeal, against either acquittal or against sentence. The English courts endeavoured to insulate trial level decisions by ruling that appellate interference was not warranted "unless it was apparent that the judge at trial had proceeded upon a wrong principle or given undue weight to some of the facts."[1] In *R. v. Wolff*, the Court remarked that it would not alter a sentence simply because it would have imposed a more lenient sentence but only if the "sentence appealed is manifestly wrong."[2] In *R. v. Gumbs*, Lord Hewart explained the Court of Appeal's view of its authority:

> This court never interferes with the discretion of the court below merely on the ground that this court might have passed a somewhat different sentence; for this court to revise a sentence there must be some error in principle.[3]

---

1   *R. v. Sidlow* (1908), 1 Cr. App. R. 28 (C.C.A.).
2   (1914), 10 Cr. App. R. 107 (C.C.A.).
3   (1926), 19 Cr. App. R. 74 (C.C.A.).

These deferential admonitions reflect the general approach of appellate courts to the exercise of judicial discretion. At the time of establishing a right to appeal against sentence, the prospect raised concerns about a flood of frivolous or desperate appeals that resulted in powers in the 1907 *Criminal Appeal Act* intended to discourage sentence appeals.[4] First, there was a presumption that time in custody pending appeal did not count toward the sentence unless the appellate court specifically ordered it. Secondly, the Court of Appeal had the power to increase a sentence. It rarely utilized this power and it was repealed in 1966.[5] The *Criminal Appeal Act 1968* provided that the appellant should not be dealt with "more severely" than the sentence imposed by the Crown Court.[6] The ability of the prosecution to raise concerns about an arguably unduly lenient sentence was resurrected in 1988 by extending the role of an attorney general's reference to include sentence issues.[7]

In Canada, sentence appeals were first authorized by amendments to the *Criminal Code* passed in 1921.[8] Apart from minor modifications in 1923,[9] the powers of the court of appeal in respect of sentence read as follows until the major *Code* revision which took effect in 1955:

> 1015.(1) On an appeal against sentence, unless the sentence is one fixed by law, the court of appeal shall consider the fitness of the sentence appealed against, and may upon such evidence, if any, as it thinks fit to require or to receive,
>   (a) refuse to alter that sentence; or
>   (b) diminish or increase the punishment imposed by that sentence, but always so that the diminution or increase be within the limits of the punishment prescribed by law for the offence of which the offender has been convicted; or
>   (c) otherwise, but within such limits, modify the punishment imposed by that sentence; and

4   See R. Pattenden, *English Criminal Appeals, 1844–1994* (Oxford: Clarendon Press, 1996) at 243.
5   *Ibid.* at 295. Between 1907 and 1926, the power was used only fourteen times. During Lord Parker's tenure as Chief Justice, sentences were increased, on average, three times per year.
6   See *Criminal Appeal Act 1968* (U.K.), 1968, c. 19, s. 11(3), which, subject to this caveat, enables the Court of Appeal to "substitute another sentence or make such order" as it thinks appropriate.
7   See Pattenden, above note 4 at 292–302.
8   *An Act to amend the Criminal Code*, S.C. 1921, c. 25, s. 22.
9   *An Act to amend the Criminal Code*, S.C. 1923, c. 41, s. 9, which changed a few words and added subsection (d).

> (d)  in any other case shall dismiss the appeal.
> (2)  A judgment whereby the court of appeal so diminishes, increases or modifies the punishment of an offender shall have the same force and effect as if it were a sentence passed by the trial court.

Early response by Canadian courts to this new power accepted the similarity to the English provisions and recognized the deferential English approach to appellate intervention.[10] The Saskatchewan Court of Appeal considered English cases and the question of deference in *R. v. Finlay*.[11] It observed that the English Court of Appeal had, in fact, exercised a "wide latitude" and intervened frequently. It was reluctant to express a clear rule on appellate intervention but concluded:

> [Parliament] must have intended that the Court of Appeal should modify such sentence, if, in their opinion, it should be modified. The Court of Appeal can only exercise its best judgment after a careful consideration of all the circumstances, and will always remember that the trial Judge, having seen the accused and heard the witnesses, has an advantage in reaching a conclusion as compared with a Court which has not, a circumstance which cannot be lightly regarded.[12]

In *R. v. Zimmerman*, the British Columbia Court of Appeal, also appreciating the English deferential approach, concluded that a Canadian appellate court should be reluctant to interfere with the sentence unless it is clearly of the opinion that it should do so having regard to all the circumstances of the particular case and bearing in mind the advantage possessed by the judge below of personal observation of the convict and his conduct and condition at the time.[13]

In 1955 the *Criminal Code* was amended[14] to change the form of the appellate power by eliminating the references to altering, diminishing, or increasing punishment and replacing them with the current expression, now found in section 687(1), which empowers the court to "vary the sentence within the limits prescribed by law for the offence of which the accused was convicted." Until recent rulings by the Supreme Court of Canada, discussed below, some appellate courts continued to

---

10  See *R. v. Adams* (1921), 36 C.C.C. 180 (Alta. S.C. (A.D.)).
11  (1924), 43 C.C.C. 62 (Sask. C.A.) [*Finlay*].
12  *Ibid.* at 65. For other examples of a liberal power of review, see *R. v. Fox*, [1925] O.W.N. 154 (C.A.); and *R. v. Brayden* (1926), 46 C.C.C. 336 (N.B. S.C.(A.D.)).
13  (1926), 46 C.C.C. 78 at 80 (B.C.C.A.).
14  See *Criminal Code*, S.C. 1953-54, c. 51, s. 593.

circumscribe their review powers by looking for errors in principle while other courts exercised a more active power of intervention.

In *R. v. Simmons*, an appeal against six-year sentences for rape, the dissenting judge would have dismissed the appeal, arguing for a limited appellate role where an alleged inadequate or excessive sentence would only be varied if it was "so manifestly inadequate or excessive as to be clearly erroneous."[15] The majority reduced the sentences to four years. It recognized the advantageous position which trial judges occupied but, regardless of the absence of an error in principle, the court of appeal should alter a sentence if it considers it inadequate or excessive. This was not an example of minor tinkering. Two years is hardly insignificant. It was a decision which recognized the individual impact of a four-year sentence and rejected the use of a longer disproportionate term solely for a presumed deterrent purpose.

In 1976, Chief Justice Farris of British Columbia addressed a meeting of County Court judges and gave the following account of the role of a court of appeal:

> First, the court does not intervene only in cases where there has been an error in principle. I recognize that you will be able to refer me to many cases where the court has said that as there is no error in principle we will not intervene. That, however, is not the practice today. The fact is that we do "consider the fitness of the sentence" in the particular case and even though there can be no error assigned in principle, the court, if it thinks that the sentence doesn't fit the crime or the surrounding circumstances, will alter it.
>
> Secondly, we do not tinker with sentences. In our view, if there is going to be a variation in the sentence it should be a substantial one. In general, I think you will find that this is our practice today.[16]

These comments express the same approach as that exercised by the Ontario Court of Appeal in *Simmons*.

Insulating a trial judge's discretion is not a self-evident proposition. It was the approach adopted in England shortly after 1907 and was carried into Canada by the early cases. These cases focused on the similarities between the appellate powers, without appreciating the substantial differences given that only the offender could appeal against sentence in England. While insulating discretion may seem necessary from a practical perspective in most examples of judicial

---

15   (1973), 13 C.C.C. (2d) 65 at 67, Schroeder J.A. (Ont. C.A.).
16   J. Farris, "Sentencing" (1976) 18 Crim. L.Q. 421 at 422.

discretion, these are almost always dealing with binary choices. One must question whether the identical approach should apply to issues which are as nuanced, detailed, and diverse as crafting a sentence or imposing a prison term within broadly set limits. Certainly, an appellate court does not want its docket filled with frivolous sentence appeals. This is why courts of appeal do not tinker in the sense of making minor adjustments to a sentence. Moreover, it is recognized that the sentencing judge often has the advantage of hearing the evidence of the offence, if there was a trial, or at least seeing the offender personally if there was a guilty plea. This is why substantial deference must be paid to a trial judge's acceptance of a prospect of rehabilitation which leads to a non-custodial sentence when custody would be the usual response. A useful example of this form of deference is *R. v. Preston* in which a recidivist heroin addict received a suspended sentence with a structured probation order for three counts of possession of heroin.[17] The British Columbia Court of Appeal affirmed the sentence, notwithstanding numerous previous convictions, holding that another short term of incarceration would be futile. The court supported the trial judge's view that a reasonable chance of rehabilitation provided a greater benefit to both society and the offender. This case indicates how deference may be relevant given the trial judge's advantage in having assessed the sincerity and rehabilitative potential of the offender. But this advantage is not always present.

## B. THE SUPREME COURT AND DEFERENCE

In the mid-1990s, the Supreme Court of Canada became interested in the standard of appellate review of sentences. *R. v. Shropshire*[18] involved the issue of the fit parole ineligibility period following a second-degree murder conviction. The British Columbia Court of Appeal disagreed with a twelve-year period of ineligibility finding no unusual circumstances to justify it. After the period was reduced to the minimum of ten years, the Crown appealed to the Supreme Court of Canada. In finding that the Court of Appeal had erred in interfering with the trial judge's discretion, Iacobucci J. for a unanimous court articulated the principle of deference which characterizes the relationship between the appellate and trial levels for sentencing purposes. In his

---

17   (1990), 79 C.R. (3d) 61 (B.C.C.A.) [*Preston*].
18   [1995] 4 S.C.R. 227 [*Shropshire*]. See discussion in Chapter 10, at 10(A)(2).

view, appellate intervention is only justified when there is an error in principle or a "clearly unreasonable" sentence. In the subsequent case of *R. v. M.(C.A.)*,[19] Lamer C.J.C. explained the "functional justifications" for deference. Again, for a unanimous court, he held that deference was warranted given the trial judge's advantage — her ability to hear the witnesses and assess the sentencing submissions within the local context taking into account "the needs and current conditions of and in the community." To some extent, as discussed later, the sentencing judge's advantage may be overstated given the large number of cases which proceed by way of guilty plea with the facts adduced by submission only.

By 1999, Lamer C.J.C. was referring to the review threshold as premised on the "longstanding principle that sentencing judges are owed tremendous deference due to the delicate nature of the sentencing process."[20] Earlier, he had described the scope of appellate intervention in the following terms:

> Put simply, absent an error in principle, failure to consider a relevant factor, or an overemphasis of the appropriate factors, a court of appeal should only intervene to vary a sentence imposed at trial if the sentence is demonstrably unfit.[21]

Now, it is clear that there are two avenues of review. The first is unfitness, which has been described variously in terms of "clearly excessive or inadequate,"[22] "outside the acceptable range,"[23] "clearly unreasonable,"[24] "a marked departure from the sentences customarily imposed,"[25] and "demonstrably unfit."[26] The second avenue, error in principle, would include wrongly interpreting or applying a legal requirement, failing to consider a relevant factor, and "overemphasis" or underemphasis[27] of a relevant consideration.[28]

---

19   [1996] 1 S.C.R. 500 [*M.(C.A.)*].

20   *R. v. W.(G.)*, [1999] 3 S.C.R. 597 at 609.

21   *M.(C.A.)*, above note 19 at 565.

22   *Shropshire*, above note 18 at 250, citing *R. v. Muise* (1994), 94 C.C.C. (3d) 119 at 123–24 (N.S. S.C.(A.D.)).

23   *Ibid.*

24   *Ibid.* at 249.

25   *M.(C.A.)*, above note 19 at 567.

26   *Ibid.* at 565.

27   See the dissent of McLachlin J. in *R. v. McDonnell*, [1997] 1 S.C.R. 948 at 1010 [*McDonnell*].

28   While Lamer C.J.C. spoke only of overemphasis in *M.(C.A.)*, above note 19, the correlative concept of underemphasis must also apply. This was the view of McLachlin J., as she then was, in her dissent in *McDonnell, ibid.* at 1010.

It is too soon to evaluate the impact of imposing deference as the guiding principle of appellate review. It has been the subject of criticism, however, from various sources that express concern about its ability to limit both the scope and the creativity of appellate review. In the context of second-degree murder and parole ineligibility, the British Columbia Court of Appeal has commented that deference may lead to excessive imprisonment and to a diminution of the right to appeal.[29] Lambert J.A. was concerned about how the notion of an acceptable range, if broadly defined, would insulate increases in ineligibility from parole review even though the prisoner has to serve every day of every year without a justification that satisfies the appellate court. McEachern C.J.B.C. observed that most of the objectives of sentencing were unaffected by parole ineligibility given the mandatory life sentence. Accordingly increases could produce unjustified detention which might be beyond the scope of appellate review. He said that

> . . . the present jurisprudence unduly limits the proper exercise of this right of appeal and often operates in such a way that an unfair and sometimes unjust sentence cannot always be adjusted on appeal because of the expectations of deference.[30]

The problem with deference is not that it is wrong but that it is not universally right. There are situations where it ought to be the guiding principle but the attempt to make it universal ignores the fact that some of its justifications are absent in many cases. And the absence is often material.

In the recent package of conditional sentence cases, the Supreme Court again emphasized deference. In his unanimous judgment in *R. v. Proulx*,[31] Lamer C.J.C. repeated his admonition that appellate courts should not "second-guess" sentencing judges and explained the justifications for deference by quoting from his earlier decision in *M.(C.A.)*:

> This deferential standard of review has profound functional justifications. As Iacobucci J. explained in *Shropshire*, . . . where the sentencing judge has had the benefit of presiding over the trial of the offender, he or she will have had the comparative advantage of having seen and heard the witnesses to the crime. But in the absence of a full trial, where the offender has pleaded guilty to an offence and the sentencing judge

---

29  See *R. v. Mafi* (2000), 142 C.C.C. (3d) 449 (B.C.C.A.) [*Mafi*], discussed in Chapter 10, at 10(A)(2).

30  *Ibid.* at 464.

31  [2000] 1 S.C.R. 61, discussed in detail in Chapter 9, at 9(J)(1).

has only enjoyed the benefit of oral and written sentencing submissions (as was the case in both *Shropshire* and this instance), the argument in favour of deference remains compelling. A sentencing judge still enjoys a position of advantage over an appellate judge in being able to directly assess the sentencing submissions of both the Crown and the offender. A sentencing judge also possesses the unique qualifications of experience and judgment from having served on the front lines of our criminal justice system. Perhaps most importantly, the sentencing judge will normally preside near or within the community which has suffered the consequences of the offender's crime. As such, the sentencing judge will have a strong sense of the particular blend of sentencing goals that will be "just and appropriate" for the protection of that community. The determination of a just and appropriate sentence is a delicate art which attempts to balance carefully the societal goals of sentencing against the moral blameworthiness of the offender and the circumstances of the offence, while at all times taking into account the needs and current conditions of and in the community. The discretion of a sentencing judge should thus not be interfered with lightly.[32]

He finished the summary of justifications by pointing out how, especially for conditional sentences, knowledge of both the "needs and resources of the community" are integral to crafting an appropriate sentence.

## 1) Problems with the Universal Application of Deference

If one looks carefully at these justifications of deference, one would agree that, if present, most of them support a claim for deference. However, they are not universally present; in many situations, they will commonly be absent. When, in the most common situation, a sentencing is preceded by a guilty plea, what the judge knows about the offender she learns from counsel. *Viva voce* evidence on a sentencing hearing is exceptional. Of course she can see the offender, but it's questionable how much that reveals: age, physical appearance, manner of dress, and demeanour in the courtroom. If there has been a trial, the judge may have a greater opportunity to make some assessment of the accused but this depends on the nature of the evidence and whether the accused gave testimony. In cases where there is a claim about rehabilitative prospects and treatment opportunities, the presiding judge will have some opportunity to assess sincerity.[33] If a novel combination

---

32 *Ibid.* at 125–26 (emphasis omitted).
33 See, for example, *R. v. Preston*, above note 17.

of local resources can produce a sentence that is tailored to the offender, the offence, and the community, then the presiding judge may have the local experience or the opportunity to assess whether the proposed combination is practicable. In summary, there are situations where the sentencing judge may have local experience which, combined with first-hand contact, produces an advantage, but in many cases, the appellate court is in no worse position.

It is true that an experienced trial judge is in the front lines, but this can cut both ways. Sometimes, disappointment over the response to recent sentences either by offenders or the public can produce a disproportionate reaction.[34] Sometimes the emotional impact of seeing and hearing survivors and victims can be so dramatic that it blurs the factors. In other cases, local furor and interest may exacerbate the complexity of a decision. In these situations, the distant scrutiny of an appellate court may be an advantage. Unless the case raises an issue of sincerity or commitment to treatment, punitive decisions and calculations can be made just as easily by an appellate court isolated from local tensions.

It would take a huge empirical exercise to try to assess whether the articulation of the standard of deference in the mid-1990s has had an impact on the extent of appellate review. But it is noteworthy that appellate courts themselves feel that the standard of deference is constraining their reviewing discretion. In *R. v. Mafi*,[35] a case of a double murder where the trial judge imposed a twenty-year parole ineligibility period, McEachern C.J.B.C. said:

> It must, however, be recognized and accepted that a reasonable measure of deference should be given to trial sentences. The Supreme Court of Canada has endorsed this view on a number of occasions, a fact which we must keep very much in mind. As will be seen, however, undue deference carries the risk of depriving an appellant of an effective right of appeal. In my respectful view, the present jurisprudence unduly limits the proper exercise of this right of appeal and often operates in such a way that an unfair and sometimes unjust sentence cannot always be adjusted on appeal because of the expectations of deference.[36]

---

34   See *R. v. Priest* (1996), 110 C.C.C. (3d) 289 (Ont. C.A.).
35   Above note 29.
36   *Ibid.* at 464.

This suggests that the operative concept should be one of "due deference," meaning the degree of deference that a case warrants, which recognizes a more flexible approach to the trial judge's position.

Of course, appellate courts are creatures of statute and the enabling provision for sentence appeals is extremely broad. It authorizes a court of appeal to "consider the fitness of the sentence" after which it "may" vary the sentence "within the limits prescribed by law" or dismiss the appeal.[37] Also in *Mafi*, Lambert J.A. addressed the question of how an appellate court applies a standard such as "marked departure" or "outside the acceptable range" when a survey of similar cases demonstrates a very broad range. Ultimately, he suggested that the departure should be measured from the centre of the range and not from its external limits. Otherwise, a sentence just outside may not be considered a marked departure, and will serve to incrementally expand the range. When combined with the issue of the right to appeal, this analysis shows that an appellant has the right to know that a panel of appellate justices considers the sentence fit. That does not mean within a broad range; it means suitable to the culpability and circumstances which the specific case demonstrates. While over time one might observe a range of three to six years for a given offence, a particular offender is not sentenced to the range but to a specific term. There is a substantial difference between the low end and the high end, more than a thousand days.

It is also interesting to note that a sentence appeal only proceeds with leave.[38] It is now common practice to deal with leave and the appeal at the same hearing. However, the issue of leave was raised recently in a way that also reflects a concern to ensure that appellate courts continue to play a significant role in sentencing. In *R. v. Laliberte*,[39] the Saskatchewan Court of Appeal was faced with a Crown appeal against a conditional sentence for small-scale trafficking by an aboriginal offender. The appeal was dismissed. In her concurring decision, Jackson J.A. considered the issue of when leave should be granted. She said that

> . . . a Court of Appeal has the authority to grant leave not only when there is an arguable case for intervention but also to settle an issue of significance either in practice or law. The onus on counsel seeking leave is to demonstrate a case of sufficient merit and importance to warrant intervention or review.[40]

---

37   See *Criminal Code*, s. 687(1).
38   *Ibid.*, s. 675(1)(b).
39   (2000), 143 C.C.C. (3d) 503 (Sask. C.A.).
40   *Ibid.* at 552–53.

She went on to assess current conditional sentence jurisprudence and conclude that disparity with similar cases should rarely be the basis for an appellate rejection of a conditional sentence. What is significant, though, is her discussion of the leave decision in terms of encouraging appellate courts to play an active role in sentencing issues.

Where deference is warranted, it should be applied; where there is no basis to justify deference, an appellate court should be able to assess fitness and impose a fit sentence. If the case does not reflect any special factors, considerations, or evaluative opportunities that give an advantage to the presiding judge, and if the sentence does not have the appearance of a carefully tailored effort that required personal contact and local experience, the appellate court will not be disadvantaged and should not be hampered by deference. Offenders are entitled to know that an appellate court agrees with a sentence, not just that it is close enough to an amorphous standard to avoid intervention.

## FURTHER READINGS

PATTENDEN, R., *English Criminal Appeals 1844–1994* (Oxford: Clarendon Press, 1996)

TROTTER, G., "*R. v. Shropshire*: Murder, Sentencing and the Supreme Court of Canada" (1995) 43 C.R. (4th) 288

# CHAPTER 13

# THE FUTURE OF SENTENCING

## A. INTRODUCTION

This book has been about the law of sentencing and how it structures and implements sentences. This has been the major focus of my own work as a a lawyer and law teacher. I believe that it is essential for participants and observers to understand the legal framework including its historical sources, current applications, and potential for creativity. However, the legal instrument is only a small part of the landscape of sentencing. Its contours may be affected by the law, but they are really determined by underlying penal policy which is shaped by legislative acts, governmental decisions, judicial attitudes, media interest, and perceptions of public opinion. Note that I have used the phrase "perceptions of public opinion." There are no effective ongoing determinants of public opinion about sentencing and penal issues. Various decision makers claim to be influenced by public opinion but, at most, they are responding to their own perceptions or misperceptions of public opinion. While public opinion can be manipulated, studies confirm that when Canadians are given ample information about crime and sentencing options, they are fair-minded and moderate in their responses.[1]

---

1   See A. Doob & J. Roberts, "Public Punitiveness and Public Knowledge of the Facts: Some Canadian Surveys," in N. Walker & M. Hough, eds., *Public Attitudes to Sentencing: Surveys from Five Countries* (Cambridge, U.K.: Gower, 1988).

Without a crystal ball, it is impossible to make any predictions about the future of sentencing and penal policy in Canada. History shows that these issues are subject to political and economic forces, social conditions, and even philosophical trends, all of which have their own unpredictable engines. Fortuitous events can capture the public imagination, injecting new and unforeseen influences into the evolving process of scrutiny, debate, and change. Yet there are several factors which will inevitably, at least in the short run, play a role in the development of penal policy in Canada: resources, restorative justice, and the politics of victimization.

## B. RESOURCES

We live in a time when public fiscal policy is dominated by deficit reduction and tax cutting. As a result, governments have compelled departments to shrink their operating budgets. This has produced a number of significant implications for penal policy. The first arises from the high cost of imprisonment.[2] Over time, the size of federal, provincial, and territorial spending on incarceration can be reduced. The answer lies in the recognition that Canada has traditionally over-used incarceration in comparison to other developed countries, aside from the United States.[3] This should encourage participants within the system to work towards reducing the size of the prison population. Many people believe that sending fewer people to prison has its own value, but it also produces the concomitant result of requiring less money to fund imprisonment. The 1996 amendments, particularly the inclusion of the principle of restraint and the conditional sentence, reflect Parliament's intention to achieve this objective. However, this cannot be achieved by sentiments alone. More importantly, it cannot be achieved by attempts to rationalize the budgets of prison systems without regard to internal environmental implications.

---

2   In 1998, at the federal level, the budget of the Correctional Service of Canada was $1.13 billion: see Solicitor General, *Towards a Just, Peaceful and Safe Society: The Corrections and Conditional Release Act Five Years Later: Consultation Paper* (Ottawa: Solicitor General, 1998). This represents an average annual cost of $47,500 per prisoner, or $133 per prisoner per day.

3   See the discussion by the Supreme Court of Canada in R. v. *Gladue*, [1999] 1 S.C.R. 688 at 715–19.

While we have a uniform legislative framework in the *Criminal Code*, *Corrections and Conditional Release Act*, and *Prisons and Reformatories Act*, each province and territory runs its own system. Outside of the federal system, disparities across the country are stark. There are no national minimum standards for administering prison systems. In Ontario, money is being invested in large mega-institutions which will house more prisoners than have ever before been confined in a single prison in Canada. With modern technology that focuses on perimeter security and reduced internal movement, costs per prisoner can be dramatically reduced. But what about programming? Whether we like to admit it or not, people in jail come from disadvantaged backgrounds and bring their personal problems with them. Alcohol and substance abuse, educational deficits, illiteracy, lack of job skills, psychological problems, and mental illness are rife in the prison populations across Canada. If we do not address these issues inside our prisons, we are not making any attempt to reduce crime. We are simply postponing its occurrence.

Of course, the genesis of these problems lies in our communities, and the second budgetary issue relates to resources in the community. If the size of the prison population is going to be diminished, we need sufficient community resources to provide effective alternatives to imprisonment and mechanisms to assist in the re-integration of people who have been incarcerated. Again, regional disparity is an important issue. Some of the programs that the *Criminal Code* authorizes, like curative discharges[4] or fine option programs,[5] are not available in every jurisdiction. More importantly, the support for probation services varies dramatically. Especially with conditional sentences and the greater emphasis on the nature of community supervision, inadequate supervision can undermine the most carefully tailored sentence. Similarly, the allocation of resources between budget items can be poorly conceived. When the new government took office in Ontario in 1995, it closed a number of halfway houses but announced that the funds would be transferred to an electronic monitoring program for released prisoners. What this failed to recognize was that the two post-release approaches involved different groups of prisoners. The value of a halfway house is that it permits someone with no family support and no job prospects to have a transitional base and some institutional support while attempting to organize re-integration. Conversely, a candidate for electronic monitoring must, by definition, have a home in the community and

---

4  See s. 255(5) of the *Criminal Code*, which is not in force in Newfoundland, Quebec, Ontario, and British Columbia.

5  *Ibid.*, s. 736.

will likely also have a job or educational opportunity ready and waiting. This means that the budget decision gave funds to a group with a high success rate and made it easier for them to succeed by taking funds from a group with a high failure rate, thereby making it easier for them to fail. This is not good penal policy.

Perhaps the largest consequence of the new public economies is the way that funds have been taken from education, health care, child welfare services, mental health services, and other agencies whose mandate involves them with the day-to-day problems of the burgeoning underclass. While there is no easy answer to the question of what causes crime, it is clear that poverty and family dysfunction provide a crucible which incubates a great deal of it. Moreover, it is clear that the difficulties experienced by many children can be assessed early and can be the subject of constructive intervention.[6] But this requires resources. Accordingly, budget reductions that reduce services to poor families, deprive troubled children of needed assistance, and leave people who are unwell without treatment only replicate the conditions that produce criminality.

## C. THE POLITICS OF VICTIMIZATION

The formal victims' lobby has grown substantially over the past two decades.[7] This lobby consists of a number of groups and organizations, the best known of which are Victims of Violence and CAVEAT, both of which were started by people who had lost children to acts of violence. Since their inception they have received public support from some police associations and some political parties. They have also grown to the point where they employ, or can retain, professional assistance from lawyers and others to help with promoting their agenda. The agenda of the victims' lobby consists partly of issues which deal directly with the needs of victims of crime. However, it also extends to general issues of criminal justice and penal policy. In this area, the vic-

---

6   See R. Tremblay & W. Craig, "Developmental Crime Prevention" (1995) 19 Crime & Just. 151.

7   See the discussion in K. Roach, *Due Process and Victims' Rights: The New Law and Politics of Criminal Justice* (Toronto: University of Toronto Press, 1999) at 278–309. Here, I am referring to the politically-active groups who take a punitive approach to crime. Not all victims or groups that represent victims speak with the same retributive voice. There are examples of others who direct their attention to forgiveness, rehabilitation, and restorative efforts.

tims' lobby is frank in its emphasis on retribution and incapacitation. In Canada, it has succeeded in carving out a real role for victims during the sentencing process.[8] Some of the lobby's other political successes can, from the perspective of sound penal policy, at best be described as questionable.[9] First, there were the 1997 amendments to section 745.6, the fifteen-year review mechanism for first-degree murderers.[10] The victims' lobby, with the help of the Reform Party, used the spectre of Clifford Olson to persuade the Minister of Justice that the existing procedure should be dramatically tightened. There was no evidence that it was not working in a fair and discriminating way. It was also clear that, on constitutional grounds, Olson could not be precluded from applying for a review. Any legislative attempt to quash this right would have been considered a retrospective attempt to vary a sentence since parole eligibility is an integral part of a life sentence.[11] This would have produced the unseemly spectacle of Olson being vindicated in court where he would obtain a ruling that he was entitled to his hearing — a hearing which, as we now know, would not succeed. Still, instead of standing up to the pressure, legislation was introduced which not only precludes multiple murderers from seeking a fifteen-year review but also, amongst other amendments, requires a unanimous jury before the period of parole ineligibility will be reduced below twenty-five years. Notwithstanding how easy it is for reasonable people to disagree about an issue as visceral as punishment for murder, relief now requires unanimous support. Certainly, this will reduce the number of successful applications. But, in so doing, it will inevitably extend the period of incarceration beyond what can be justified by the offence and the circumstances of the offender. This is neither fair nor sound.

Another success, still in the legislative works, is Bill C-251.[12] This piece of legislation, promoted by a Liberal backbencher, will, if passed by the Senate, immediately double our gravest penalty by providing for consecutive parole ineligibility periods for murder. We may see prisoners serving life sentences for murder with no parole eligibility for fifty

---

8   See the discussion of victim impact statements in Chapter 8, at 8(I).
9   In general, see I. Grant, "Legislating Public Safety: The Business of Risk" (1998) 3 Can. Crim. L.R. 177; and Roach, above note 7 at 308–9.
10   See the discussion in Chapter 10, above, at 10(A)(4) and (5).
11   See R. v. Gamble, [1988] 2 S.C.R. 595.
12   See Bill C-247, An Act to amend the Criminal Code and the Corrections and Conditional Release Act (cumulative sentences), 2d Sess., 36th Parl., 1999. Bill C-251 was reinstated as Bill C-247 in the second session of the House of Commons. It was referred to committee by the Senate on May 18, 2000. Discussed above in Chapter 6, at 6(B)(6).

years. Surely, our current regime is harsh enough. In terms of the number of years that first-degree murderers serve before release, it is predicted that the norm will be 28.4 years.[13] A comparison of fourteen western democracies produces an average of 15.9 years.[14] Apparently, for some people, Canada should be striving for the gold medal at the incarceration Olympics. Another aspect of Bill C-251 is mandatory consecutive sentences for multiple sexual assault convictions. The apparent rationale is to ensure that a victim can identify which pocket of time in the sentence can be attributed to that offence. It is extremely doubtful that any victim has ever expressed this desire. Surely it is the total sentence that should matter, and the judiciary continues to treat sexual assaults very seriously. If there is a case where a trial judge has not recognized the gravity of an offence, the appellate court will intervene to ensure that the penalty reflects blameworthiness. Sentences must be fair and just, not vengeful and excessive. Regardless of what some may think, long terms of incarceration in Canadian penitentiaries are harsh, oppressive, and soul-destroying. They should only be imposed when properly justified by relevant sentencing principles.

You may disagree with my characterizations of the section 745.6 amendments and Bill C-251, or, you may ask, what is the harm? Should we really care about murderers and sex offenders? The simple answer is that when people are sentenced and imprisoned it is done by the state in our names. If we believe in the rule of law, we must be vigilant that our laws operate fairly and not excessively or without justification. More importantly, these apparent victories by the formal victims' lobby permit governments to say that they are listening, that they are concerned about crime, and that they are working to make our communities safer. In other words, these illusory successes can be used in the place of real efforts to build safer communities. Going back to the discussion of resources, by pandering to demands for longer sentences and harsher controls, the same governments that cut budgets and deny aid and treatment to people in need can portray themselves as being concerned about crime while entrenching the conditions which produce it.

---

13   Corrections Directorate, *Life Sentences for First Degree Murder (Canada) and International Equivalents* (Ottawa: Solicitor General, 1999).

14   *Ibid.* This document produced an average of 14.3 years by using various ranges for countries which had differential levels of sentencing. I have used the highest sentence to produce the average of 15.9 years. For example, for the United States I used the figure of 29 years representing those states where life without parole is the mandatory sentence.

The politics of sentencing is subsumed by the "law and order" rhetoric which peppers contemporary discourse. While rates of crime in Canada, including violent crime, are diminishing,[15] it is always worth examining the extent of crime and considering ways to reduce it. This, however, does not seem to be the objective of the "law and order" agenda, which is usually expressed in a moralistic and retributive tone. It is difficult to be certain about the attraction of this movement, but it is likely generated by the changes within our communities over the past few decades which tend to inject feelings of instability. Economic influences have led to "downsizing" which not only exacerbates unemployment but has also diminished confidence in one's ability to continue in a job until retirement. Immigration has changed the racial and ethnic character of many of our large cities and suburban areas. The combination of longevity and the "baby boom" effect has skewed the age distribution so that a larger portion of the community is either retired or approaching retirement, looking at the prospects of fixed incomes in an uncertain economic climate. Prices go up unpredictably based on difficult-to-understand events that happen halfway around the world. As a result of these and other factors, political conservatism and religious fundamentalism have prospered. The politics of "law and order" gives the impression of working to preserve traditional values in the battle to protect against the fear of change. Many politicians have adopted this banner. Re-enforcing the legal structure gives the impression of shoring up the social structure. *Criminal Code* amendments are demanded and sometimes legislated in an attempt to appear responsive to public concerns. It is likely true that many individuals and groups are concerned about security but this is a function of a complex matrix of social factors within which crime plays, at most, a small role. It is an easy target, but it is not the real source of feelings of instability.

# D. RESTORATIVE JUSTICE

The past two decades have witnessed a substantial international embrace of "restorative justice." In very general terms, this encompasses the various responses to crime which are directed towards reparation, and the restoration of equilibrium. Unlike a retributive response, which

---

15   See S. Tremblay, "Crime Statistics in Canada, 1998" *Juristat* 19:9 (July 1999), which reported a 4.1 percent decrease in the overall crime rate (the lowest since 1979) and a 1.5 percent reduction in the rate of violent crime. This represented the seventh year in a row in which the rate of violent crime diminished.

aims to punish, a restorative sanction is intended to reconcile and repair the harm caused by an offence. Its beneficiaries include the offender, the victim, and the community at large. Around the world, a number of very successful programs and approaches are premised on restorative principles: family group counselling, re-integrative shaming, victim-offender reconciliation.

In Canada, we have seen the coincidence of support for restorative justice models from the law, from First Nations, and from church-sponsored and other community organizations. The Supreme Court of Canada has interpreted some of the recently entrenched objectives and principles of sentencing as encouraging sanctions premised on restorative principles. In *R. v. Gladue*, it described its understanding of restorative justice principles:

> The concept and principles of a restorative approach will necessarily have to be developed over time in the jurisprudence, as different issues and different conceptions of sentencing are addressed in their appropriate context. In general terms, restorative justice may be described as an approach to remedying crime in which it is understood that all things are interrelated and that crime disrupts the harmony which existed prior to its occurrence, or at least which it is felt should exist. The appropriateness of a particular sanction is largely determined by the needs of the victims, and the community, as well as the offender. The focus is on the human beings closely affected by the crime.[16]

Subsequently, the Supreme Court endorsed the conditional sentence as a useful vehicle for promoting the objectives of restorative justice.[17]

First Nations have been adapting restorative justice concepts for some time. In some communities, the recognition of the limitations of the traditional justice system has led to the development of specific responses to deeply entrenched local problems. Probably the best example is Hollow Water in Manitoba where the community concluded that incarceration was not successful in stopping sexual abuse of children. It developed the Community Holistic Circle Healing Program which seeks to involve the victim, the offender, and their families, along with the assessment team, in moving through a series of steps that ends in a cleansing ceremony.[18] Other communities, particu-

---

16   Above note 3 at 726.

17   See *R. v. Proulx*, [2000] 1 S.C.R. 61 at 114–15; and *R. v. Wells*, [2000] 1 S.C.R. 207 at 223–24, discussed in Chapter 9, at 9(J)(1).

18   See the description in R.G. Green, *Justice in Aboriginal Communities: Sentencing Alternatives* (Saskatoon: Purich, 1998) at 81–95.

larly in the Yukon and Saskatchewan, use sentencing circles to provide community input into the crafting of an appropriate sentence.[19] These processes not only ensure greater information about the offender but also encourage community participation in the implementation of a community-based sentence which increases the resources beyond what the justice system could ordinarily provide. The models vary from community to community, and have evolved over time to address local needs. Sentencing circles have been welcomed by community members and local justice professionals. They have demonstrated the potential value of a restorative justice approach both in producing beneficial results in individual cases and, perhaps more importantly, generating community empowerment. This does not mean that all cases have been successful[20] or that there are no serious questions to ask.[21] One criticism has been the treatment of victims within the circle.[22] More recently, one observes serious efforts on the part of communities to encourage victim participation and provide support for victims within the circle process. Of course, there are the larger questions of whether the sentencing circle can be expanded to urban communities[23] or even non-aboriginal communities. While these questions cannot be minimized, the success of the Aboriginal Legal Services diversion project in Toronto[24] is an example of how, with commitment and support, a cultural approach can be translated into an urban context. Another helpful example of transcending the usual model is the Nova Scotia

---

19 See the processes explained in R. v. *Moses* (1992), 71 C.C.C. (3d) 347, Stuart J. (Y. Terr. Ct.); R. v. *Joseyounen*, [1995] 6 W.W.R. 438, Fafard J. (Sask. Prov. Ct.); and R. v. *Gingell* (1996), 50 C.R. (4th) 326, Lilles J. (Y. Terr. Ct.). Note the commonality and the differences.

20 Even the often-cited *Moses* case, above note 19, presented problems. The offender was subsequently incarcerated for fifteen months for aggravated assault. This is not indicative of an inherent deficiency in the process. However, the decision to start with a difficult case before the community had experience with, and its own infrastructure for, sentencing circles resulted in discouraging community participation for some time after.

21 See the discussion in Green, above note 18 at 148–61.

22 See M. Crnkovich, *Report on the Sentencing Circle in Kangiqsujuaq: Inuit Women and Justice* (Progress Report #21).

23 See the issues raised in R. v. *Morin* (1995), 101 C.C.C. (3d) 124 (Sask. C.A.), particularly the question of how to define community.

24 See J. Rudin, "Sentencing Alternatives" in J.V. Roberts & D.P. Cole, eds., *Making Sense of Sentencing* (Toronto: University of Toronto Press, 1999) 295 at 304–7.

Restorative Justice Program that provides a "continuum" of options at different points along the criminal justice process.[25] With proper scrutiny, time will tell what we can learn from these imaginative efforts.

Other organizations, especially church-related groups, have been attempting to encourage the use of restorative justice principles in sentencing.[26] A number of projects have already been the subject of evaluations,[27] and these early evaluations show ample reasons for optimism. However, it must be noted that the projects involved were relatively small and the cases carefully screened. Screening does not necessarily mean that hard cases are excluded: although a restorative project in Winnipeg ruled out sex offenders, gang-related offences, domestic violence, and drug offences,[28] the Langley victim-offender mediation project (VOMP), on the other hand, has accepted sex offenders, armed robbers and even murderers.[29]

One of the virtues of restorative justice is also a point of potential vulnerability. Programs require community support and community involvement. Accordingly, many of the participants are volunteers. They need to be trained and prepared to ensure that they act responsibly and also that they do not become discouraged by a lack or slowness of positive results. The volunteer element, of course, represents cost-saving. When an idea represents saving, one must be cautious about government encouragement. Is it real or just an attempt to latch on to a cheap alternative? Restorative justice programs need appropriate infrastructures if they are to evolve, weather both successes and failures, and continue as effective community-based vehicles. They will not survive without support.

---

25   See B.P. Archibald, "A Comprehensive Canadian Approach to Restorative Justice: The Prospects for Structuring Fair Alternative Measures in Response to Crime" in D. Stuart, R.J. Delisle, & A. Manson, eds., *Towards a Clear and Just Criminal Law: A Criminal Reports Forum* (Toronto: Carswell, 1999) at 520.

26   See Church Council on Justice and Corrections, *Satisfying Justice: Safe Community Options That Attempt to Repair Harm from Crime or Reduce the Length of Imprisonment* (Ottawa: Church Council on Justice and Corrections, 1996).

27   See J. Bonta, S. Wallace-Capretta, & J. Rooney, *Restorative Justice: An Evaluation of the Restorative Resolutions Project* (Ottawa: Solicitor General Canada, 1998) [*Restorative Resolutions Project*]; and T. Roberts, *Evaluation of the Victim-Offender Mediation Project: Final Report for the Solicitor General* (Langley, B.C.: Focus Consultants, 1995) [unpublished].

28   See *Restorative Resolutions Project*, *ibid.* at 6.

29   See Roberts, above note 27 at iv.

# E. CONCLUSION

The future of sentencing will be determined by the interaction of a number of variables, including those discussed above. Especially in a country where authority over the major participants is split between federal, provincial, and territorial jurisdictions, Ottawa must play a decisive role in setting national policy. Given the number of empirical and conceptual questions that warrant attention, perhaps we need a permanent sentencing commission to provide objective data and new insights. Internationally, there are a number of examples of innovative approaches including day fines, day reporting, intensive supervision, and drug treatment courts. These all need to be evaluated for the Canadian context.

As far as the law of sentencing is concerned, the path from Ouimet to the end of the century has taken many turns. It has passed through the capital punishment debates, new community sentencing options, the introduction of a role for victims, the recognition of the plight of aboriginal persons, efforts through litigation and legislation to ameliorate discrimination against women, and the statutory inclusion of principles and objectives. In retrospect, Hogarth[30] was right when he pointed out the importance of judges' personal experience, and how this plays a major role in their day-to-day sentencing. The biggest change since Ouimet, and perhaps the most telling indicator for the future, is a diverse, well-trained judiciary which accurately reflects the gender, race, and ethnic distinctions of the country. This may be the best way to rid the sentencing process of the discriminatory remnants of the past. While class distinctions cannot be remedied in the same way, judges will need to find other vehicles to ensure that no one suffers unfair or stereotypical treatment.

Sentencing is the instrumental tool of the criminal law, and the criminal law is not value-neutral. It reflects the values which a community considers central to its security and well-being. Those responsible for the law of sentencing must strive to ensure that it responds to the demands of fairness and equality, is sensitive to the rigours of incarceration, and operates constructively within its ambit to encourage just sanctions. We cannot, and should not, expect the law of sentencing to resolve the problems of crime and criminality. But we can expect it to provide a framework that empowers courts with the necessary tools to do their job. Each case must be viewed with a careful and creative eye, and appropriate measures of firmness and compassion.

---

30   J. Hogarth, *Sentencing as a Human Process* (Toronto: University of Toronto Press, 1971).

## FURTHER READINGS

ARCHIBALD, B., "A Comprehensive Canadian Approach to Restorative Justice: The Prospects for Structuring Fair Alternative Measures in Response to Crime" in D. Stuart, R. Delisle, & A. Manson, eds., *Towards a Clear and Just Criminal Law* (Toronto: Carswell, 1999)

CHURCH COUNCIL ON JUSTICE AND CORRECTIONS, *Satisfying Justice: Safe Community Options That Attempt to Repair Harm from Crime or Reduce the Length of Imprisonment* (Ottawa: Church Council on Justice and Corrections, 1996)

GRANT, I., "Legislating Public Safety: The Business of Risk" (1998) 3 Can. Crim. L.R. 177

GREEN, R.G., *Justice in Aboriginal Communities: Sentencing Alternatives* (Saskatoon: Purich Publishing, 1998)

HOGARTH, J., *Sentencing as a Human Process* (Toronto: University of Toronto Press, 1971)

ROACH, K., *Due Process and Victims' Rights: The New Law and Politics of Criminal Justice* (Toronto: University of Toronto Press, 1999)

TREMBLAY, R., & W. CRAIG, "Developmental Crime Prevention" (1995) 19 Crime and Justice 151

# THE SUPREME COURT OF CANADA DECISIONS IN *R. v. LATIMER* AND *R. v. KNOBLAUCH*

After I completed this book, the Supreme Court of Canada delivered two decisions that bear directly and intimately on issues discussed within the text. I am speaking, of course, about *R. v. Latimer*,[1] which has recently occupied the media, and also about *R. v. Knoblauch*,[2] the conditional sentence case released late last year. My publisher has been indulgent and has permitted me to add some explanation and commentary.

## A. THE *LATIMER* DECISION

In the *Latimer* case, a unanimous Court dismissed the appeal against conviction that was based on issues principally related to the defence of necessity.[3] Perhaps more importantly, the Court also rejected the

---

1   [2001] S.C.J. No.1 (QL), released January 14, 2001.

2   (2000), 149 C.C.C.(3d) 1 (S.C.C.)

3   Most of the judgment is directed to the conclusions that the trial judge was correct in ruling that the defence of necessity was not available on the facts, and also that there was no error affecting trial fairness in waiting until after counsel's address to announce this ruling. Another interesting challenge, also rejected, involved the issue of jury nullification. It was argued that the trial judge's assurance to the members of the jury that they would be able to make a recommendation in relation to the eventual sentence diminished the prospect that they would refuse to convict.

appeal against the life sentence mandated by the *Criminal Code*. On this second point, the thrust of the appellant's argument was directed to whether the particular circumstances of the case warranted a *Charter*-based exemption from the mandatory minimum penalty. The trial judge had used this exemption to avoid imposing a mandatory life sentence with a ten-year parole ineligibility, after being satisfied that Mr. Latimer's act was motivated by compassion and that his culpability was at the "low end" of the intentional killing scale.[4] He concluded that the mandatory sentence would be grossly disproportionate and would violate section 12 of the *Charter*, the guarantee against cruel and unusual punishment.

The Supreme Court unanimously disagreed. While the impact of the decision for Mr. Latimer is clear, it is harder to discern the Court's message beyond the immediate situation, especially with respect to the larger issue of the relation among homicide, culpability, and compassion.

Generally, motive can provide either a mitigating or aggravating influence on a sentencing decision, depending on whether it diminishes or increases the gravity of the offence. This case, however, involved a mandatory minimum sentence. Mr. Latimer's claim for an exemption was based on the argument that the mandatory minimum sentence of life imprisonment with no parole eligibility for ten years produced a grossly disproportionate penalty in relation to his blameworthiness. He argued that the offence, viewed through the lens of his own particular circumstances, was substantially different from what is commonly encompassed by second-degree murder. In other words, the offence was still murder but it manifested a lower degree of blameworthiness because of his motivation. Certainly, this conclusion was reached by the trial judge and by the jury who actually heard the evidence. The trial judge had found that "Mr. Latimer was motivated solely by his love and compassion for Tracy and the need — at least in his mind — that she should not suffer any more pain."[5] The jury must have agreed since it recommended that Mr. Latimer be eligible for parole after serving only one year.[6]

However, the Supreme Court concluded that motive does not matter — or, more accurately, not to this extent. It focussed on intention as the major determinant of culpability and described the offence as one where "the gravest possible consequences resulted from an act of the

---

4    See the reasons of the trial judge at (1997), 12 C.R.(5th) 112 (Sask.Q.B.) at 127.

5    *Ibid.* at 126.

6    One juror has recently indicated that he would not have supported a conviction if he had known that the result would be a life sentence with no parole for at least ten years. See *Globe and Mail*, January 20, 2001, at A-4.

most serious and morally blameworthy intentionality."[7] Later, when listing the potential mitigating circumstances of the case, it included the appellant's "tortured anxiety about Tracy's well-being, and his laudable perseverance as a caring and involved parent" but concluded:

> Considered together we cannot find that the personal characteristics and particular circumstances of this case displace the serious gravity of the offence.[8]

Clearly, the Supreme Court was not persuaded that there was a sufficiently different level of blameworthiness as a result of the appellant's motivation to support a claim of gross disproportionality. The Court was not prepared, at least in the circumstances of this case, to embark on the project of developing any category of murder encompassing compassionate killing that would produce a punishment other than the legislated response of life imprisonment with a minimum of ten years incarceration.

One can appreciate the arguments, both substantive and institutional, against the Supreme Court's moving in this direction, but it is a troubling conclusion nonetheless. There is no doubt that Mr. Latimer's actions, as admitted by him, satisfied the definition of murder. In fact, they described the elements of a planned and deliberate murder with a vulnerable person as the victim. Ordinarily, this would result in a conviction for murder and a mandatory life sentence with extended parole ineligibility. The Supreme Court was correct in applying the view that, in general, intention is not congruent with desire or ultimate purpose but this is a principle of responsibility, not sentencing. Some things about the Canadian law of homicide and intentional killing are worth noting. Not all intentional killings are treated as representing the same degree of gravity and blameworthiness. Some people who kill intentionally but suddenly and out of anger may see their offence mitigated to manslaughter, leaving the sentence up to the discretion of the trial judge.[9] Moreover, some people kill intentionally and advance claims of self-defence that can produce complete exoneration even in unclear circumstances. This defence need only raise a doubt and can even be based on a mistaken apprehension so long as it meets the statutory requirements.[10] Accordingly, provocation and self-defence are two examples where, in law, motive matters.

---

7   Above, note 1 at ¶ 84.
8   *Ibid.* at ¶ 85.
9   See *Criminal Code*, section 232.
10   See *Criminal Code*, sections 34(1) and (2).

We can also look at how the law is applied. At the prosecutorial stage, some prosecutors do not proceed with a murder charge when faced with a killing for compassionate reasons.[11] Lesser offences are charged, which free the trial judge to impose a sentence that matches the gravity of the offence and the culpability of the offender. These choices are within the allowable scope of prosecutorial discretion. Hence, they are essentially unreviewable and are subject to no universally accepted or publicly debated guidelines.

What is clear is that the law, both in its substance and its application, sometimes distinguishes between intentional killings based on the question of motivation. More to the point, for sentencing purposes, culpability transcends the issue of intention. Accordingly, there are arguments that support moving beyond the issue of intention and examining motivation when reviewing a mandated sentence. Because the Supreme Court was not persuaded that Mr. Latimer's motive diminished his culpability sufficiently to produce gross disproportionality that would trigger a section 12 violation, there could be no departure from the legislated penalty. This highlights the fundamental unfairness of mandatory minimum sentences: they are insulated from the ordinary sentencing process that requires a sentence to be commensurate with the circumstances of a case and the characteristics of an offender.

The *Latimer* decision also highlights the political nature of the debate over the relation between compassion and killing. Early in its reasoning on the sentencing issue, the Supreme Court states that it must "defer to the valid legislative objectives underlying the criminal law responsibilities of Parliament."[12] Later, the Court expressed concern about deterrence and denunciation. Yet, the ability of the law to deter and denounce is surely found in the authority to prosecute for murder and to seek a life sentence. Is there any diminution in the deterrent or denunciatory effect by leaving other sentencing options available to a judge, after a trial where a jury returns a verdict of guilty to second-degree murder?

Perhaps it was wrong to permit the *Latimer* case to be perceived as a choice between a one-year sentence and life imprisonment, when it can be argued that the appropriate penalty lies somewhere in-between. The essential question is whether a minimum of ten years confinement is always required in every case of murder, regardless of the situation,

---

11   Examples were given by Noble, J., above, note 4, at 127-128. See also the authorities discussed by Bayda, C.J.S. in dissent in the first appeal at (1995), 41 C.R. (4th), 1 (S.C.C.) at 60-68.

12   Above, note 1, at ¶ 76.

the precursors, and the motivation. Since the Court rejected the claim that the case presented a situation of diminished blameworthiness sufficient to constitute a section 12 violation, it did not need to pursue the hard questions about the kind of motive, requisite circumstances, or degree of proof that would apply if some amelioration of penalty were legally possible. The Court's comments about deterrence and denunciation, consistent with a concern to preserve the expressive and cultural function of sentencing, do not necessarily support the need for a universal minimum penalty. This question, unanswered by the Court, has now been placed within the crucible of political debate.

The *Latimer* judgment ends with a reminder that Mr. Latimer can apply for the exercise of the Royal Prerogative of Mercy, an ancient mode of relief against a sentence,[13] granted by the Governor-in-Council in its discretion. It has been used only rarely. The Supreme Court pointed out the relevance of the pressure of two trials, numerous appeals, the glare of public attention, and the "consequential agony" for Mr. Latimer and his family. In addition to motivation, these are important factors when assessing a claim for clemency. However, for the Cabinet, the political question will be whether granting some form of relief for Mr. Latimer would signal any danger to, or disrespect for, the disabled. This is a significant question, which has been cast in terms of devaluing the lives of the disabled. Would clemency at some point necessarily send such a message? I think not, but it may be impossible to ensure that it would not be perceived by some in that way. The issue of executive clemency should respond to the question of what is a fair punishment for Mr. Latimer. When does continuing penitentiary confinement represent an excessive sanction for his act, taking into account how others are treated by the criminal justice system? Viewed in this way, clemency would simply say that, at some point, Mr. Latimer had suffered enough pain for his criminal responsibility.

The *Latimer* decision illustrates the complex nature of a multidimensional and controversial ethical issue. We have no societal consensus on mercy killing or assisted suicide. There is no agreement about when it may be justifiable, excusable, or less culpable to end the life of another for compassionate motives. Although we are starting to see legislated initiatives in other countries, this difficult debate is still evolving in Canada. The unanimous decision of the Supreme Court is part of that evolution. In *Latimer*, it was obviously significant to the

---

13  It can take a number of forms: pardon, conditional pardon, or remission of sentence.

Court that the victim was a 12-year old who could not express her own views on her painful situation and who, while struggling with a severely debilitating condition, was not in the final stages of life. To accept the father's claim of reduced culpability would have been the first step in crafting the contours of a new category of homicide. The fact that the Court would not take this step does not make the general issue less compelling.

The decision in *Latimer*, while clear on its facts, does not provide a comprehensive legal answer to the general question of mercy killing. It gave no indication that an act of compassion in other circumstances might produce a different result, but does not foreclose a claim based on different facts. The decision does not respond to the legal situation of assisted suicide, where an adult agrees to the informed and reasoned request of another adult to end a pain-ridden or time-limited existence. It does not resolve the dilemma of the potential disparity that depends on where an offence occurs and the specific views of the relevant prosecutorial and police authorities. These questions are still begging for attention within a context where, throughout Canada, there is pervasive and accepted use of DNR (do not resuscitate) memoranda in hospitals. This is a multi-layered ethical problem that raises hard questions, which tear at deeply-held values — questions that cannot be ignored indefinitely. There is a degree of societal hypocrisy inherent in a continued attempt to ignore them, leaving a trail of pain, tragedy, and litigation in the wake of our inaction. However, it may be illusory to expect societal consensus.

The *Latimer* decision also demonstrates the inadequacy of the current section 12 methodology. Although the Supreme Court had not previously ruled on the availability of what has become known as a constitutional exemption,[14] implicit in the *Latimer* analysis is the acceptance of this potentially ameliorative vehicle. There is no point where the Court expressly accepted the availability of constitutional exemptions. However, a unanimous Court recognized that this was the focus of the appellant's position and then devoted ten paragraphs to discussing it. When the Court concluded that, in the absence of a section 12 violation, "there is no basis for granting a constitutional exemption,"[15] it could only have meant that, in theory, a case can be made for an exemption on constitutional grounds from an otherwise constitutionally-valid provision. Some might argue this does not mean acceptance. By anal-

---

14   See the discussion in Chapter 10.
15   Above, note 1, at ¶ 87.

ogy, atheists and agnostics can still discuss God, but one would hope that they would declare their disbelief and uncertainty. The unanimous Supreme Court expressed no dissent, disquiet, or doubt about the existence of a constitutional exemption. Unfortunately, given the dismissal of Mr. Latimer's claim for an exemption, we have not had the benefit of a Supreme Court discussion of its potential role or dimensions.

The major obstacle to constitutional exemptions on section 12 grounds has been the use of "reasonable hypotheticals" in the applicable methodology. This has produced the argument that a court that finds that an individual case results in gross disproportionality must invalidate the provision and not exempt the offender from its application.[16] Yet, there is no reason why a provision cannot be valid in its common and general application but still permit relief when an unusual or rare individual circumstance arises. The *Latimer* decision, and the earlier decision in R. v. *Morrissey*,[17] demonstrate that the current state of section 12 jurisprudence is lacking both in substance and methodology. It has not evolved beyond its inception and makes it difficult for courts to respond to new situations.[18] The analysis offered in R. v. *Goltz*,[19] especially in relation to reasonable hypotheticals, has not provided courts with the right tools to respond to section 12 claims. When dealing with mandatory minimum sentences, the set of which is regrettably increasing, a section 12 claim needs to be based on gross disproportionality, which can arise either between blameworthiness and the sentence, or as a result of the personal impact of the mandated sentence on the offender in light of relevant characteristics that distinguish her from others. The circumstances in which offences are committed and the personal characteristics of offenders can produce infinite permutations. Even accepting gross disproportionality as the test, the standard of what is cruel and unusual punishment cannot be static to the extent that an historical finding of validity precludes future claims based on their particular facts. The constitutional methodology ought to permit a dynamic analysis of cases and not a sterile one that hides important distinctions behind a conservative formulation of legal tests. Section 12 is the constitutional protection against excessive punishment. In a democracy that generates diverse views, it is essential that the essence of section 12 be protected by a vibrant jurisprudence that strug-

---

16   See R. v. *Kelly* (1990), 59 C.C.C.(3d) 497 (Ont.C.A.); R. v. *McDonald* (1998), 17 C.R.(5th) 1 (Ont.C.A.) at 31-32.
17   (2000), 36 C.R.(5th) 85 (S.C.C.)
18   See the comments of Arbour, J. in R. v. *Morrissey*, *ibid.*, at 118-119.
19   [1991] 3 S.C.R. 485.

gles to appreciate the effects of legislated punishments, especially those that are implemented behind the walls of total institutions over long periods of time. In the context of section 15 of the *Charter*, the Supreme Court has risen to the challenge of developing an effective and flexible framework for protecting constitutional equality guarantees. It must approach section 12 with similar vigour and creativity. In any society, the true meaning of liberty is determined not by how it is exercised by the privileged but by how it is protected and nurtured by the powerful.

Perhaps the most telling implication of the *Latimer* decision is what it says about mandatory minimum penalties. For the most part, Canadian sentencing policy and jurisprudence employ an individualized focus. That is, a judge should find the sanction that most fairly fits the culpability of the offender, and that responds to the circumstances of the case, including its gravity, the potential for reparation, and the future risk and rehabilitative prospects of the offender. Mandatory minimum penalties provide an aberrant and unrealistic "one-size-fits-all" approach, which is antithetical to the Canadian approach to sentencing. Necessarily, by submerging individual characteristics and the infinite circumstances in which offences can be committed into a uniform mould, the mandated sentence will produce unfair and individually harsh responses. Since the section 12 test is based on gross disproportionality, there is no room for judicial intervention in the face of disproportionality that cannot be described as gross. Surely, a community that makes the claim that it seeks "fair and just sanctions" ought not to resort to mandatory sentences that produce long terms of penal confinement. Sentencing discretion is amply able to identify those cases that justify harsh sentences. Parliament should direct its attention to enabling sentencing discretion through a range of properly resourced options, not to rendering it ineffectual with mandated sentences.

## B. THE *KNOBLAUCH* DECISION

In this case, a five-to-four majority adopted a pragmatic approach to the scope of conditional sentences and the needs of mentally-ill offenders. The appellant had pleaded guilty to possession of explosives while prohibited and possession of a weapon dangerous to the public peace. He had a long history of mental illness, described as "an unusual case of longstanding deeply-ingrained personality difficulties with features of obsessive-compulsiveness and depression." He had become preoccupied with explosives in response to his feelings of being "overwhelmed, rejected and belittled." The instant offences related to his possession of various explosive material and devices but, in particular, a car that contained a bomb which, if exploded, could destroy people and buildings within a 75-metre radius. Clearly, Mr. Knoblauch represented a danger to the public. However, at the time of the original sentencing, the appellant had been residing with his consent at a psychiatric hospital, the Alberta Hospital Edmonton, for five months. Evidence was adduced that the best context for treatment that would enhance his future ability to re-integrate with the community was in a hospital setting, where he could be medicated and involved in long-term psychotherapy.

The trial judge imposed a conditional sentence of two years less a day to be followed by three years probation, both of which required that he reside at the Alberta Hospital in a locked secure unit until a "consensus of psychiatric professionals" decided that he could be transferred from that unit. A few months later, the Alberta Court of Appeal allowed a Crown appeal and substituted a sentence of incarceration for two years less a day. Mr. Knoblauch was transferred to a provincial correctional institution. He successfully sought leave to appeal to the Supreme Court. After spending seven months in prison, he was granted parole by the National Parole Board on the condition that he reside at the Alberta Hospital where he resumed his treatment.

The majority allowed the appeal and restored the original conditional sentence followed by three years probation. This decision may have expanded the potential scope of conditional sentences. The reasoning of the majority decision by Arbour, J. commenced with the recognition that the case was at least notionally within the conditional sentence regime, since the Court of Appeal imposed a custodial sentence of less than two years. Accordingly, the major issue was whether the "would not endanger the safety of the community" prerequisite in section 742.1 of the *Criminal Code* could be satisfied. Arbour, J. was not naive about the facts of the case and noted that "the gravity of the damage in the case of re-offence could be extreme."[20] In addressing the issue of endangerment, she applied the earlier decision in R. v. *Proulx*[21] and, in particular, the statement of Lamer, C.J.C. that the issue had to be "assessed in light of the conditions attached to the sentence." It was clear from *Proulx* that the statutory provision was not a zero-tolerance standard, rather it permitted a sentencing judge to accommodate some

---

20   Above, note 2, at 16.
21   [2000] 1 S.C.R. 61.

degree of risk, especially if conditions were directed to the amelioration of that risk. She concluded that:

> . . . if the conditions contemplated by the trial judge are taken into
> account in evaluating the risk that the appellant would re-offend
> while serving his conditional sentence, that risk is reduced to a point
> that it is no greater than the risk that the appellant would re-offend
> while incarcerated in a penal institution. The sentence fashioned by
> the trial judge provided that the appellant would be in a locked,
> secure psychiatric facility, in the care and custody of forensic psychi-
> atrists who were well aware of his history, and who by no means min-
> imized his dangerousness.[22]

Recognizing that any future dangerousness is a product of both Mr.
Knoblauch's mental illness and the accessibility of explosives, she concluded that imprisonment might preclude the latter but would do little
or nothing for the former concern.

While the ruling in relation to endangerment might be seen as an
extension of the scope of conditional sentences, the major expansion
arose from the use of the new sanction to produce what is essentially
confinement, albeit in a psychiatric facility rather than in a prison or
penitentiary. In defining the central characteristic of a conditional sentence, Arbour, J. placed it in direct distinction to imprisonment in a
correctional facility, which is characterized by involuntary constraint
within a controlled environment that is principally custodial and not
therapeutic. Some might argue that both environments diminish and
constrain liberty. Certainly, that is true. However, it is important to
note that Mr. Knoblauch had consented to treatment with confinement
in a psychiatric facility. The majority decision would not, in my view,
apply if there was no real consent, notwithstanding the power to order
treatment under section 742.3(2)(e). More importantly, even with consent, any judge contemplating following this approach would need to
be satisfied not only about the need for psychiatric confinement but
also of the commitment of the mental-health professionals to provide
consistent therapeutic resources over the course of the sentence. There
is no room to re-negotiate the basic bargain. The optional conditions of
a conditional sentence can be varied[23] but the offender cannot be incarcerated in a prison if the psychiatric facility changes its mind. After the
initial decision to permit service in the community under section

---

22   Above, note 2, at 16-17.
23   On application of the supervisor after notice to the offender, prosecutor, and
     court. See section 742.4.

742.1, the sentence can only result in incarceration if a court finds that the offender has breached a condition without reasonable excuse.[24] There is no mechanism to convert a conditional sentence into a prison sentence in the absence of a proven breach.

In the *Knoblauch* case, the principal minority decision by Bastarache, J.[25] disagreed with the finding on the endangerment prerequisite but also concluded that a conditional sentence was not intended by Parliament to produce psychiatric confinement. Here, the minority was persuaded that conditional sentences were contemplated as "non-institutional in nature," as a form of community-based sanction. Certainly, looking at the history of the conditional sentence, it was always considered to be a community-based alternative to imprisonment. However, it is unlikely that anyone put his or her mind to the problem that confronted the courts in the *Knoblauch* case. Bastarache, J. was influenced by the decision not to proclaim in force the hospital order provisions in sections 747 to 747.8. As passed by Parliament, they were never intended to duplicate the kind of hospital orders that one sees in other countries. They were short-term responses to offenders in states of crisis and not intended to provide long-term psychiatric treatment for convicted persons who suffer from mental illness. While his decision notes that the *Corrections and Conditional Release Act*[26] permits federal-provincial agreements that can result in a transfer from a penitentiary to a provincial psychiatric facility for treatment, this can only be done with the consent of the provincial institution. Provincial facilities are stretched for resources and do not readily accept penitentiary prisoners. Bastarache, J. made the important observation that "intergovernmental financial disputes" have deprived both the general public and mentally-ill offenders of necessary treatment resources. In addition, he said:

> There is no doubt that an appropriate scheme to provide for the treatment of mentally ill offenders should be in force which takes into account the reality of offenders who suffer from mental disorders.[27]

---

24  See section 742.6(9).

25  Concurred with by Justices L'Heureux-Dube and Gonthier. Iacobucci, J. concurred with his view that a conditional sentence was not available because of the dangerousness issue but agreed with Arbour, J.'s reasoning on whether a conditional sentence could, in an appropriate case, result in psychiatric confinement.

26  S.C. 1992, c.20, s.16.

27  Above, note 2, at 56.

As noted by Bastarache, J., there are limited psychiatric resources within the various correctional regimes in Canada. While there are Regional Treatment Centres in each penitentiary region, they have limited beds and constantly suffer from limited resources, both in terms of mental health professionals and security staff needed to ensure the delivery of regular treatment programs. A fair and humane prison system cannot ignore the problem of inadequate resources for mentally-ill prisoners.

In general, the situation of mentally-ill offenders is a serious issue in Canada. It has been over a decade since the important *Criminal Code* reforms[28] that revised the available responses to individuals found unfit or not criminally responsible, but there has been no serious evaluation of these new dispositions. Moreover, in prisons and penitentiaries the number of prisoners with mental-health problems seems to represent a large and growing proportion of the populations. The comments of Bastarache, J. about the need for resources may help in the campaign to improve the treatment situation in general.

However, leaving Mr. Knoblauch in a correctional institution would not assist him or promote public safety. The majority decision was a pragmatic one that applied a liberal interpretation to the conditional sentence regime in an effort to provide a therapeutic response, albeit with no guarantees. At the same time, it recognized that there are limits to how the criminal process can use sentences to achieve particular results. Early in her judgment, Arbour, J. said:

> There is no mechanism in criminal law to remove dangerous people from society merely in anticipation of the harm that they may cause. The limit of the reach of the criminal sanction is to address what offenders have done. At that stage, dangerousness is but one factor to be considered in the assessment of the appropriate sentence. Even extreme dangerousness cannot, in and of itself, justify imposing the maximum punishment in order to elevate the protection of society above all other considerations.[29]

This represents an approach to sentencing consistent with merged theories that pursue traditional objectives but are limited in extent by a sense of proportionality, which flows from the offence and the harm actually caused. In a different world, other options might be available. In Canada, the plight of the mentally-ill who come in conflict with the law always produces a hard question for the sentencing judge. She is

---

28   See *Criminal Code*, Part XX.1, sections 672.1-672.95.
29   *Ibid.* at 13.

equipped with few resources and caught within the triangle of stereo-typical fears, legitimate concerns about public safety, and the need to be fair in responding to the individual offender. The majority decision in *Knoblauch*, while not free of difficulty, should be applauded for rec-ognizing that sometimes it is neither fair nor constructive to make the offender pay the price for our failure to provide sufficient resources to the sentencing system.

# TABLE OF CASES